DOCTOR SYNTAX

(overleaf)
1. Silhouette of William Combe
British Museum

DOCTOR SYNTAX

A Silhouette of William Combe, Esq.

(1742–1823)

BY

HARLAN W. HAMILTON

THE KENT STATE
UNIVERSITY PRESS

1969

TO MY WIFE

INTRODUCTION

William Combe was determined to be known as a gentleman; he looked and acted the part, he cultivated aristocratic acquaintances, and he expected his name always to be followed by Esq.—as it usually was, even in debtors' prison. When he came into his inheritance he lived—briefly—like a lord, supplied himself with carriages and a retinue of servants, and frequented the fashionable watering-places. Even after the collapse of his fortune he managed to preserve his aloof posture. Although he gained his livelihood from hackwriting, he never wished it known that he was working for money. He refused to sign his publications, and when their authorship was recognized he blandly passed them off as written for his own entertainment and that of his friends: publication had been far from his mind.

When he was a very old man he let it be understood that he was preparing an account of his life and times, a work which would post-humously reveal the secret of his past. No such manuscript was found among his papers, however, and it is most unlikely that he had written a word of it. By that time he had concealed the embarrassing circumstances of his early life for over sixty years, and they seemed safely buried in the past. The modern reader finds them far from disgraceful, but they were inconsistent with Combe's social preten-tions. He had been born of a Cheapside family, his father an iron-monger. He was middle class.

Combe made such a mystery of his background and put his family origins so firmly out of mind that they virtually ceased to exist. Finally the mask and the man become indistinguishable to his bio-grapher; they certainly puzzled his contemporaries. The friends who survived him, all many years younger than he, had listened half credulously to his stories of the past, almost always autobiographical and never quite believable. They liked and admired "Old Combe", as they called him, found his conversation entertaining, and were content to let his stories go unchallenged. He was visibly a man of talent and social polish, a delightful dinner companion, in many ways an admirable person. It was no secret that he was uncomplainingly spending his declining years under the jurisdiction of the King's Bench Prison, for a number of those years actually confined within its walls. But he was turning out book after book, always with competence, sometimes with surprising originality. He had been doing so as long as anyone could remember.

Among themselves, Combe's acquaintances often talked about him in mixed terms of curiosity, amusement, and admiration, but the mystery of his life remained unfathomed. When he died in 1823 all the leading journals published memorials, several of them by writers who had known him for fifteen or twenty years. Men on *The Times* had known him longer than that: his association with the paper extended over thirty-seven years, and from 1803 to 1808 he had been its editor. Yet the leading article published by *The Times* the day after his death, a fine tribute to an old and respected friend, is not more notably detailed than the other obituaries. There can be no doubt that he was highly regarded, both as a man and as a writer, but no one could write his biography. Combe had successfully covered his tracks.

His reputation persisted in these vague terms throughout the nineteenth century, though just who he was and what he had written remained generally unknown. Two writers published short accounts of Combe, really little more than collections of anecdotes and conjectures. John Camden Hotten wrote one as an introduction to his edition of the *Tours of Doctor Syntax* (1868); H. R. Tedder wrote the other for the *Dictionary of National Biography* (1887). As biographies both fall wide of the mark, but they at least make a start on a bibliography, basing their information on an important article published in the *Gentleman's Magazine* (May 1852) by Robert Cole. Antiquarians occasionally repeated the anecdotes, usually with embellishments, but except for occasional communications published in *Notes & Queries* nothing more appeared in print until students of Laurence Sterne began raising questions about him early in the present century.

The neglect of Combe for so many years, though injurious to his reputation, has at least not blurred the record. It has forced me to rely almost entirely on primary sources. They have not always been easy to discover, but I have found it a great advantage to study the eighteenth century and the Regency without the intervention of subsequent critics and historians. Unable to see Combe through the eyes of Victorian or Edwardian commentators, I have been compelled to see him as best I could through the eyes of his contemporaries. It has been an illuminating experience which I hope will be reflected in the pages of this book. Perhaps the contemporary engravings which accompany the text will strengthen the image.

I have sought out such facts of Combe's life as I could discover in the public records or in private letters and journals—his own and those of his associates. The results, if somewhat fragmentary, are neither fantasy nor rumour; they provide a factual basis for this account of his career. My larger task, however, has been to discover and read Combe's many separate publications, then to relate them to their background in the age itself. I have reported these findings rather more completely than would ordinarily be necessary, for the books and pamphlets are far to seek even in the great libraries, and the background material can only be discovered after extensive reading of eighteenth-century newspapers, volumes of letters and journals, and collections of unpublished manuscripts. I have found this a rewarding search, but since I can scarcely expect others to engage in it along these lines, I give as full account of the facts and circumstances as the reader is likely to wish.

Those facts and circumstances often relate to matters of less than earth-shaking importance: fads and fashions, talk of the town, forgotten gossip about forgotten people—the very stuff of daily life in London during the tense half-century extending from the American War of Independence through the French Revolution and the Napoleonic conflict to the post-Waterloo years. The momentous events of that period fill the pages of history, but they did not necessarily fill the minds of contemporaries. No doubt Londoners worried about the stirring events which were taking place across the Atlantic or across the Channel, but life continued to go on, even while Cornwallis was surrendering at Yorktown and the Paris mob was storming the Bastille. Taxes were becoming unbearable and the cost of living was mounting, yet people continued to live their private lives as best they could. The public masquerades did not want for patrons, and the Drury Lane and Covent Garden theatres were crowded every evening. Men and women of social standing or of none were getting themselves married or murdered or talked about very much as usual, and hackwriters, observing all this with an eye to business, were turning out a running commentary on whatever caught public fancy, whether it be the scandal of Sunday card-parties at Lambeth Palace or the edifying spectacle of justice triumphing on Tyburn Hill.

The historian and the biographer of great men may deal with larger issues and events, but the chronicler of a hackwriter's career, like the hackwriter himself, must concern himself with ordinary life. William Combe could do so without difficulty; although he cultivated a superior attitude toward the commonality, he was not in actual fact so far removed from his ordinary readers as to lack an instinctive sympathy with their ever-changing attitudes and interests. His writings provide a reliable index to the popular mind of his period, not because of his vaunted superiority to that mind but because he was actually more closely identified with it than he realized—certainly more closely than he could ever admit. Had his social and intellectual pretensions been entirely justified, he could never have reflected so faithfully the ordinary Englishman of his time. But had there not been some justification for them, had he not had talent and a superior posture, he could never have written so effectively. Aloofness itself gave him detachment.

Combe was a professional who wrote for a living; he was a businessman of letters, a hackwriter. For many years of his life he made the business pay very well by producing what his readers wanted or what his employers required and by writing as well as time, space, and subject permitted. He met deadlines, and whatever his private vanity he displayed no pride of authorship. He never permitted his name to appear on a title-page, though he often quietly inserted it, William Combe, Esq., in the lists of illustrious subscribers to his books. He was a journeyman writer and a good one, but he prudently chose not to advertise the fact. His talents were well known to the London booksellers, however, and for nearly half a century he was perhaps the most productive and best-paid hackwriter in the trade.

The word *hackwriter* carried strong overtones of contempt for the working literary man; to some extent it still does so, though the implied snobbery is inconsistent with modern attitudes. In Combe's time a man like Samuel Johnson, secure in his professional position, could be undaunted by the contempt; a hackwriter, he said, was one who accepted literary assignments much as drivers of hackney coaches accepted fares. Johnson himself often did just this, and some of his best works, notably the *Lives of the Poets*, were written to order. He was extremely impatient, in fact, with the convention of literary amateurism; "No man but a blockhead," he stoutly asserted, "ever wrote, except for money." Lesser men might applaud the sentiment, but until the profession of letters was more firmly established they had good reason to remain anonymous. Many of them, then as now, had an even better reason for they were bad writers, time-servers, even blackmailers. But many, too, were men of integrity, education, and literary ability. They were hard-working, productive, and often well rewarded. The term *hackwriter* does such professionals little justice, and they have long since found other words to describe their calling: free-lance writer, journalist, columnist, editor, publicist, or ghost-writer. Combe was all of these things before the words were invented.

A book about a successful hackwriter inevitably deals with the business side of his life, with changing literary markets, costs and charges, promotional schemes, advertising, and other non-literary matters. Combe had a very shrewd knowledge of these practical concerns, and much can be learned about the business of letters in the eighteenth century by reviewing his career. But Combe must not be written off merely as a hack; he had genuine talent, literary as well as commercial. He was an able though minor prose writer, a witty and vigorous satirist, an effective polemicist, a competent editor of books and newspapers, an imitator of Sterne at a time when such imitators were widely admired, and finally a genial comic poet, creator of the popular Doctor Syntax. Had he not been too vain to acknowledge his writings, he would have attained his well-earned place in literary history.

I have, moreover, found the man himself interesting, likeable, on occasion exasperating, but finally admirable. Even his lifelong aristocratic pose, which must have been extremely difficult to maintain under the circumstances, no longer seems entirely spurious to me. In a sense, he *was* a gentleman, an extraordinarily hard-pressed gentleman who never to my knowledge stepped out of his role. And I find myself hoping that my book does justice to Old Combe himself.

HARLAN W. HAMILTON

Case Western Reserve University
Cleveland, Ohio
August 15, 1968

ACKNOWLEDGEMENTS

Professor Ernest Hunter Wright of Columbia University was the first to suggest that I write on William Combe; the late Professor Leslie N. Broughton of Cornell University encouraged me to continue, and under his direction I completed my dissertation on Combe in 1934. There the matter stood until after the war, when visits to the British Museum again became feasible. I had long since become involved in other concerns, however, and did not return to this subject until ten years ago. Encouraged by my friend and colleague, Professor William Powell Jones, I then spent a sabbatical year in London reviewing the material and realizing new dimensions of the problem. The search for William Combe has occupied every succeeding summer and I have inevitably accumulated many obligations.

I must acknowledge first my indebtedness to Franz Montgomery, now Professor of English at the University of Minnesota. As a graduate student there, and unaware of my work at Cornell, he began writing a dissertation on Combe just as I was finishing mine. Our two studies, written independently and at approximately the same time, inevitably covered much the same ground; each of us made a few mistakes (sometimes the same ones), and each of us found material unknown to the other. It was Montgomery, however, who first discovered the facts of Combe's birth, which he subsequently published in an article entitled "The Birth and Parentage of William Combe" (*Notes & Queries*, April 12, 1941). This important discovery greatly facilitated my research from the start. I have also made use of certain other information first stated in his dissertation, acknowledging my indebtedness in footnotes. Finally, I have collated my bibliography with his, noting the results by the use of initials after each entry. I very much appreciate Professor Montgomery's contribution to this book.

My indebtedness to individuals, both in England and in America, is very great indeed. Edward Hutchinson, Esq., O.B.E., and Mrs Enid Hutchinson have helped me in countless ways; in particular, their knowledge of English education and social history has been a constant source of help. Two Etonians have provided useful suggestions, both about Eton in the eighteenth century and about various aspects of English cultural history: Sir Charles Tennyson and the Reverend Ronald G. Lunt. The late Stanley Morison, Esq., historian of *The Times*, generously shared with me his knowledge of Combe's long connection with that newspaper. L. M. Payne, Esq., the Librarian of the Royal College of Physicians, personally undertook research in eighteenth-century manuscript records to find such information as survives concerning Stephen Casey's madhouse where Combe's first wife was confined. W. W. S. Breem, Esq., Librarian of the Inner Temple, and Miss Elizabeth Ralph, Bristol City Archivist, have supplied highly useful information. And John C. T. Oates, Esq., of the Cambridge University Library, has generously given me assistance with the bibliography.

Among American scholars, my chief indebtedness is to Professor Lewis Perry Curtis of Yale University. As editor of Laurence Sterne's *Letters*, he was compelled to make a close study of Combe's imitations of Sterne. It is understandable that he should not be an admirer of William Combe, but he has been a friend to the present work and has generously placed his knowledge of both the man and the age at my disposal. Finally he read and criticized the entire manuscript. I am grateful for his long-continued encouragement and invaluable assistance. Professor Arthur Cash of the State University College, New Paltz, N.Y., another Sterne scholar, has also been of great assistance in dealing with the knotty points concerning the Sterne-Combe relationship. He, too, read and criticized the final version of the entire manuscript, as did also Professor Benjamin Boyce of Duke University. I have no doubt that these scholars helped me eliminate some of the faults which lurked in my manuscript. Any which remain, I regret to say, are my own responsibility.

Friends and colleagues have given me counsel when my subject touched on their fields. Professor Donald Grove Barnes, a distinguished authority on the younger Pitt, gave me invaluable assistance with my discussion of Combe's political pamphlets; Professor Conrad Rawski criticized the bibliography and gave helpful suggestions; Dean John S. Diekhoff read various sections and made useful com-

ACKNOWLEDGEMENTS

ments on the management of my material; Mr Clark Livensparger, an editor of *Webster's New World Dictionary*, read and criticized an early version of the manuscript; Mr Ben D. Zevin gave encouragement and support to the project, particularly during one visit to the New York libraries; Mr John F. Fleming generously permitted me to study his Combe manuscripts; and each of the following read and criticized as least one chapter: Professors William Powell Jones, William McCollom, Henry Pettit, and Lyon Richardson. My friend Professor Morton Bloomfield has also helped me on several occasions. I much appreciate the support of these friends.

My obligations to the libraries and public repositories in England will be evident on every page; my specific obligations to them, especially for permission to quote from their manuscripts, is acknowledged in footnotes to the relevant passages. I cannot omit expressing my great and continuing appreciation, however, of the resources and the very helpful staff of the British Museum. It would have been impossible to write this book without the vast collections there, including many Combe items not available elsewhere and the incomparable Burney Collection of newspapers. I am grateful for the privilege of spending so many weeks and months under the great dome of the Reading Room or in the quiet seclusion of the North Library.

I am indebted also to the Royal Library at Windsor Castle (for making the manuscript of Joseph Farington's diary available to scholars and placing an indexed typescript in the Print Room of the British Museum), Dr Williams's Library (for permitting access to the manuscripts of Henry Crabb Robinson's diary and reminiscences, also largely available in typescript), the Guildhall Library (for its great collection, largely in manuscript, of City records), the Public Record Office (for documents relating to Combe's trials and imprisonment for debt), the Probate Registry, Somerset House (for making readily available the wills of various persons connected with Combe), the Bodleian and the Cambridge University Libraries (for important books and manuscripts), and the Bristol Central Library (for newspapers and other materials bearing upon Combe's visit to that city).

I have also levied upon many American libraries, notably the Library of Congress, the Pierpont Morgan Library, the Henry E. Huntington Library and Art Museum, the New York Public Library (especially the Berg Collection), the Harvard College Library (the

Harry Elkins Widner collection), the Newberry Library, and the libraries of Princeton University and the University of Chicago. The Freiberger Library, Western Reserve University, has given me much aid by obtaining through purchase or inter-library loan many books bearing upon my subject. To all these libraries I express my thanks.

I am indebted to the Marquess of Hertford, to Sir John Summerson, to the National Portrait Gallery, and to the British Museum for permission to reproduce paintings and engravings in their collections.

Two expert typists have given Trojan service well beyond the call of duty: Mrs Antoinette Uffner and Mrs Carol Prael. I feel a special indebtedness to them and also to my research assistant, Mrs Susan Hollenberg, who helped me find the contemporary reviews of Combe's publications.

I am grateful to the American Philosophical Society, which generously supported this project by two travel grants enabling me to spend the summers of 1961 and 1962 in England. And I wish particularly to thank President John S. Millis and Western Reserve University for granting me two sabbatical leaves and for research grants.

My wife has been an active partner in this project from the first, supplying as seemed appropriate encouragement, criticism, patience, and impatience. She is a good critic, and she has a sense of style. The book is better for her steadfast support.

H. W. H.

CONTENTS

LIST OF ILLUSTRATIONS

CHAPTER I

TRADESMAN'S SON

═══════════

I sought gay Fashion's motley throng,
On Pleasure's tide I sail'd along;
Till, by rude storms and tempests toss'd,
My shatter'd bark at length was lost,
While I stood naked on the shore,
My treasure gone, my pleasure o'er.
                    —Doctor Syntax

WHEN Henry Crabb Robinson joined the staff of *The Times* in 1807 he found "a remarkably fine old gentleman" in the office, a tall man with "stately figure and handsome face" who assisted the proprietor in managing the paper. Members of the staff privately called him "Old Combe", but they treated him with deference and regarded him as something of a mystery. Even his first name was a mystery to Robinson, or at any rate it was so little used that he could never remember it, although the two men were business associates and occasional dinner companions for more than a decade.

On first acquaintance Combe seemed anything but mysterious. He was an entertaining raconteur, never lacking stories to tell of his past and of the famous men and women he had known. Robinson listened eagerly until he learned that these anecdotes, so far as they concerned Combe himself, were largely fabrications, "lies of ostentation and vanity". They often contained a grain of truth, but Combe could never resist making himself a party to every important action, mixing truth with fiction in a manner at once amusing and exasperating. No one could long be deceived by the absurd habit, and his friends simply accepted it as his "comic infirmity"—evidently relishing the Combe-comic pun. Robinson's ultimate discovery of the infirmity came as a rude shock, for he had intended to collect for posterity many "valuable facts of Sterne, Johnson, Garrick, Mrs. Siddons, and other worthies of the last generation". It was a disappointment, of course, but he continued to enjoy the old man's company and thought him "more worth writing about" than anyone else in the *Times* set. "Indeed," he wrote, "I have known few to compare with him."[1]

Others who encountered Combe in his later years were similarly impressed. Horace Smith thought that "a faithful biography of this singular character might justly be entitled a Romance of Real Life", and Sir Egerton Brydges was certain that Combe's life "would furnish a series of the most extraordinary and romantic incidents". These remarks suggest that both men had listened overcredulously to Combe's anecdotes, but Samuel Rogers, who had known Combe much longer and who was aware of his "infirmity", also thought him a remarkable person and took pains to tell Alexander Dyce all he knew about him. The most vivid and intimate portrait of Old Combe, however, is that recorded by Dr (later Sir) George Lefevre, who met him in May 1820, a few weeks after Combe's seventy-eighth birthday. Lefevre, then only twenty-two, had just returned from an extended stay on the Continent and had taken quarters with a family in Thavies Inn, Holborn, while he looked about for a suitable place to establish his medical practice. Combe, for the moment, was staying at the same place, and the two met one afternoon in the back parlour.

The old man, just waking up from a nap, started talking immediately, "You must write a book," he said. The suggestion came automatically from one who in forty-six years had written, edited, or "produced" nearly a hundred works and was now writing yet another one. "I want to see you write a book."

He yawned, took a pinch of snuff, then abruptly inquired, "Where are the young ladies?"

Getting no answer to this question, he reverted to his favourite topic. "A young physician must publish himself into practice," he said, warming to the subject. "I have helped more than one in this way. Nay, John Hunter was the worst writer that ever took pen in hand. I wrote his essay on the teeth for him, and it was a hard job; for not only could I not understand him, but he evidently did not comprehend his own meaning. It was an Herculean labour to him to compose a sentence, and a week's work to make it intelligible, and yet he was a most extraordinary man, and the most laborious one I ever knew."

The two men talked at some length of the great Dr Hunter's

scientific and metaphysical theories before they were interrupted by the arrival of the young ladies, who "as usual" greeted the old man with affectionate hugs. He responded in a grandfatherly way, then posed the question which had been lurking in his mind ever since his nap: "Is there any of the gooseberry pie remaining, my dears? Pray let me have some of it."

The girls promptly brought him what was left of the pie and custards, and then to the astonishment of the young doctor this strange character proceeded to eat "with a peculiar gusto" eleven custards and as much of the pie as they would cover. Meanwhile, to divert attention from his rapacious appetite, he regaled his audience with an anecdote concerning a Lord Mayor's banquet at which there had been a disastrous shortage of gooseberry tarts.

At this point Lefevre's narrative dramatically breaks off with the question, "Who was this old man, so fond of metaphysics and gooseberry pie? Who this patriarch with hoary head and furrowed cheek, who, not bent down by the infirmities of old age, proved that man can physically and morally laugh at four-score?" Postponing for a moment the answer to his question, the author summarizes his impressions of the old gentleman: "Replete with anecdote and polished in his manners, he won the affections of all who knew him; and notwithstanding the mystery attached to his history, you forgot all . . . in the fund of entertainment which his conversation afforded."

Then comes the long-delayed revelation of the old man's identity. "It was the author of *Dr. Syntax*, who visited in the family where I resided." Neither here nor elsewhere in the book does Lefevre mention Combe's name. Very possibly he did not even know it.[2]

Anonymity had been a lifelong passion with Combe, and to an amazing degree he was to maintain it even after his death. During a half-century of industrious writing, he never signed his name to a single work. In the late 1770s he was known to the public only as the author of the *Diaboliad*. Twenty years later he was the author of the *Letter from A Country Gentleman*. When young Lefevre encountered him he could be identified quite adequately as the author of *Dr Syntax*, or even simply as Dr Syntax. Of all the many nineteenth-century editions of the *Tours of Doctor Syntax*, only those edited by Alfred Crowquill (1838) and J. C. Hotten (1868) mention Combe's name. As late as 1903 another edition was published in both London and New York—anonymously.

Yet Dr Syntax was no other than William Combe, Esq. He invariably insisted on the Esq., for he wished to identify himself as a gentleman rather than as a professional who wrote for sordid cash considerations. That is why, though he never attached his name to a title-page, he was not above printing it in the subscription lists of his own books. Even those who knew his full name might well know little else about him. So much seemed to have happened in his life so very long ago—before the Napoleonic wars, before the Revolution in France, even before the American War of Independence. That remote past often figured in his conversation, to be sure, but who could distinguish fact from fiction in his endless flow of anecdotes? What is more, his behaviour must on occasion have been as devious as his tales. Laurence Sterne had observed this characteristic as early as 1767, when he had written to Combe, then in Paris, that "there were some little mysterious turns and windings in the manner of your leaving England, which mark'd the steps of an entangled man'.[3] Given his concealments, his anonymity, his "comic infirmity", there is little wonder that posterity has seen fit to remember Dr Syntax and never discover William Combe, Esq.

The obituaries published at the time of his death testify to the affection and tolerant admiration of his friends; with one exception they also show how completely he had imposed his view of himself as a man of mystery. Of all who wrote of him then, only "one of his contemporaries" quoted in the Bristol *Observer* (July 16, 1823) seems to have been untouched by Old Combe's myth-making. "Since the year 1768", he declares, "I have not seen him, or known anything of him except by his publications." Although offered as a modest disclaimer, the statement does, in fact, give the writer unique authority; Combe has had no chance to embroider the legend: "It was said that he was the son of a tradesman in London, who left him a very handsome fortune, but which it is supposed he soon dissipated, and then commenced author." This, we now know, is the simple truth of the matter.

* * *

Readers of the *Gentleman's Magazine* for December 1740 must have found little to enthrall them in the body of that highly respectable journal. It opened with the usual parliamentary report, thinly disguised under the title of "Proceedings and Debates in the Senate of Lilliput". This was followed by an impressive "Essay on Epitaphs" —scarcely an enticing topic, one would think—and instalments of two biographies, the fourth of the "Life of Sir Francis Drake" and the first of the "Life of John Philip Barretier". We know today that all these and possibly other things in the issue were produced by a single hard-working writer, young Samuel Johnson, but contemporary readers knew nothing of the kind. They may have thought the better of themselves for having such impressive reading matter in their hands, but they probably turned the pages rapidly, if deferentially, until they came to those eye-catching announcements of important births, deaths, and marriages at the back of the magazine. One item in that section must have prompted more comment at the time than any of the more weighty materials in the issue; a marriage had taken place, it seems, between Mr Robert Combes of Wood Street and a "Miss Hill" who brought her husband a dowry of £10,000! The amount seems substantial today, but in 1740 its buying power would have been much greater, perhaps ten times greater. Even if the *Gentleman's Magazine* was not exaggerating, as it may have been, the dowry would not seem unduly large to readers living within the sound of Bow Bells, for in that prosperous quarter of London the two families were well known, and the financial implications of this alliance would seem more impressive than the marriage portion itself. The *London Magazine* (December 1740) evidently sensed something of the kind, for its announcement omitted all mention of the dowry and simply identified the bride and groom: "Mr. Coombes, a whole-sale Ironmonger in Wood-street, to Miss Hill, Daughter of the late Mr. Humphry Hill, a West-India Merchant." Neither magazine gave the date; from another source we know that the marriage took place on December 8, 1740.[4]

Robert Combes* was a rising young businessman of Wood Street, a vestryman and benefactor of St Alban's Church, a man of substance in his own right. He had been set up in business some ten years before his marriage by his father, also named Robert Combes, a wealthy brewer of Harmondsworth at the western edge of Middlesex. The Wood Street business had evidently prospered, for the son was now taking an active role in the community. The Minute Book of the

* So spelled by the father and grandfather; after middle life the son habitually wrote the name *Combe*. Other spellings frequently occur.

St Alban's vestry, of which he was a member, testifies to his standing in the parish throughout the 1730s, and on February 20, 1738, it makes special mention of his generosity: "At this vestry a vote of thanks was given to Mr. Robert Combes for his noble present of the brass pillars and curtain rods to the organ loft."[5] He was a decidedly eligible bachelor, not undeserving a richly dowered young wife.

And just such a wife was Susanna Hill, who was well able to bring her husband a large wedding portion. Her father, Humphrey Hill, a wealthy Quaker merchant, had died "of a stoppage" on March 24, 1740, aged sixty.[6] Early in life he had engaged in business requiring capital, probably supplied by his father, a prosperous brewer of Hackney. He began his career as an importer of silks and lived in Whitechapel just east of the Tower of London. His first wife, Mary Brain, brought him a good dowry which he invested in a farm near Finchingfield, Essex. Mary died in childbed a year later, and in 1711 Humphrey married a second wife, Elizabeth Thompson. He invested £1,000 of her dowry in the South Sea Company which was then being formed for trade with Spanish America. When he wrote his will twenty-eight years later, long after the disastrous South Sea Bubble, he was still in possession of £1,140 of South Sea securities; evidently he had not been drawn into the frenzy of speculation in 1720 and had emerged with substantial profits—for at the height of the madness these securities had paid dividends of 100 per cent. He early gave up the silk business and became engaged in the West India trade, importing sugar, rum, and perhaps mahogany. What his ships carried on their return voyage is never stated. There is no mention of Africa, but trade with the Caribbean usually involved a stop on the west coast of the Dark Continent. However that may be, his business was highly profitable, and he was able to move into a fine house in Friday Street. There, and also at his country place in Putney, he must have lived in unQuakerish luxury. His will specifies, for example, that his wife shall have "all her wearing apparel, gold chain, diamond buckle, and all my diamonds and jewels whatsoever, with all my gold buckles, gold rings, gold buttons, gold toothpick, and all my wrought gold whatsoever, except the gold watch and chain and equipage" which Susanna wears and may keep. The will shows Humphrey still in possession of the farm at Finchingfield and the South Seas securities, as well as other substantial holdings: a freehold messuage in Wine Street, a valuable leasehold in the parish of St Catharine's near the

Tower (presumably his former residence), a copyhold estate in Brook Green, Hammersmith, 600 acres near "Philadelphia in Pensilvania", navigation rights, smelting stock—manifestly he was a wealthy man. On his death in May 1740 the bulk of this property was divided between his son, Joseph, and his widow, but Susanna was not forgotten. In particular, the properties near the Tower and in Hammersmith were ultimately to go to her on the death or remarriage of her mother.[7] Although the estate would not be settled by December, when the marriage took place, Susanna's dowry would be forthcoming.

Such are the families of the two principals to the marriage announced by the *Gentleman's Magazine*. In this instance, however, a third party must be mentioned, the mutual friend and intermediary, the neighbour of Humphrey Hill, the business associate of Robert Combes, witness to the marriage contract, godfather and ultimately guardian and benefactor of Robert and Susanna's son, the man who was to say he "should have been" that young man's father—William Alexander. He figures prominently, albeit somewhat mysteriously, in the story of this marriage which he helped to arrange.

William Alexander was the very man to promote the interests of his friend and partner, even while taking care of his own. As a boy he had been apprenticed to a tallow chandler,[8] and in 1716, having served out his seven-year term and reached the age of twenty-one, he had been duly admitted into the freedom of the Tallow Chandlers Company.[9] Tallow, oils, and soap did not long hold his interest, however, and he became an iron-founder. By 1738 he was established in Wood Street as William Alexander and Company, the "Company" being Robert Combes; some ten years later they took the name Alexander & Combes.[10] Since there was no longer any necessary relationship between a man's trade and the livery company to which he belonged, Alexander remained a member of the Tallow Chandlers as long as he lived. In 1747 and again in 1750 he was elected Master of the Company.[11] Toward the end of his life he became active in City politics, serving as Sheriff for a year, then after 1753 as Alderman for Cordwainers Ward.[12] He was expected to succeed Alderman Beckford as Lord Mayor of London, but died in 1762 just as Beckford began his year in office.[13] Clearly he was a man to get things done for himself and his friends. Having no legitimate children of his own (though he acknowledged paternity of a daughter born to one Mary Gibbons in 1749 and baptized Sarah),[14] he willed his property to

[7]

nephews and to the son of Robert and Susanna Combes. Inevitably, it had been William Alexander who stood as godfather[15] to that son, born on March 25, 1742, baptized in St Alban's Church, Wood Street (Plate 2), on April 16, and christened—how could it be otherwise?—William.[16]

* * *

Historians of mid-eighteenth-century London society have told us substantially more about the dissipation of fortunes in St James's Street and the miserable poverty of Gin Lane than about the sober, middle-class life of Cheapside. It was middle-class Cheapside, however, both the street and the state of mind, which produced William Combe. His family lived in the very heart of the district, the Hills in Friday Street (now no more) just off Cheapside to the south, the Combes in Wood Street almost opposite and to the north. William Alexander lived in the one and had his foundry in the other. Cheapside itself, in a sense the Regent Street of the eighteenth century, was lined with attractive and fashionable shops, chiefly of mercers and drapers (Plate 3). Before the Great Fire of 1666 it had been one of the most important thoroughfares in London, famous for its monuments, its spectacles, its pleasure haunts. The Mermaid Tavern stood between Friday and Wood Streets, and there, too, stood an ancient Eleanor Cross. After the Fire had destroyed the old Tudor structures and the public monuments, a new Cheapside had come into existence under the spire of Wren's rebuilt church of St Mary-le-Bow, and by the 1730s the area had become a striking manifestation of the new bourgeois prosperity. Recently installed street lamps gave a new brightness to the area, but until late at night these were supplemented by light from the shop windows, for long hours and hard work were characteristic of the district, which respected them as evidence of industry and, indeed, virtue.

Cheapside tradesmen and merchants were sober citizens, often dissenters holding religious views by no means inconsistent with good business. They lived prudent, industrious lives, married wisely after giving careful attention to the contracted marriage portion, often amassed fortunes and achieved a degree of luxury comparable to that of West End families. As a rule, each tradesman lived with his wife and children in quarters over the shop, but often he maintained a

2. St Alban's, Wood Street, c. 1747. British Museum

second home in the country. Humphrey Hill had such a place in Putney; Robert Combes had one near his parents in Harmondsworth. These men and their families accepted the rigorous conditions of life imposed by Cheapside and reaped the solid rewards available on those conditions. Their unsensational lives followed the conservative, middle-class pattern of industry, prudent management, and steadily increasing wealth.

By all rights William Combe should have remained in Wood Street, married a tradesman's daughter with a good dowry, taken over his father's business, and accumulated in time a vast fortune of his own. He refused to do anything of the kind. "I bless heaven that I am not a man of merchandise," he exclaimed in his first book. He made every effort to obliterate the mark which Cheapside left on his character, but he only partially succeeded. He rejected the middle-class virtues which surrounded his childhood; he declined the restraints of thrift, industry, and prudence until every penny of his inheritance was gone, and even then he could never practise thrift. He did perforce become industrious, but he scrupulously concealed his industry to pose as a man of leisure, a dilettante. Not one of his autobiographical anecdotes ever mentioned the ironmonger, the founder, or the West India merchant.

Harmondsworth fared no better. Some part of Combe's childhood, quite possibly a large part, was spent at his father's country home in that quiet village fifteen miles west of the City. Even in the twentieth century Harmondsworth retains the aspect of a peaceful hamlet offering rural seclusion within easy reach of London. Many of its eighteenth-century features survive. A row of picturesque Tudor cottages was demolished some years ago, but the ancient parish church, the great fourteenth-century tithe barn, the Sun Inn (a Tudor structure now a private dwelling), "The Grange" dated 1675, and Harmondsworth Hall (new in Combe's time) all still impose their character on the modern village.[17] The appearance of quiet security must always have been somewhat deceptive, however, for the village lies just north of the old Roman road to Bath, once a stagecoach route, today a main arterial highway. Across this road now lies London Airport; when Combe was a boy, it was Hounslow Heath, the haunt of highwaymen and other desperate characters. No doubt many generations of small boys in Harmondsworth have been warned by their grandmothers to stay away from the Bath Road. But northward

A View of the Church of St. Mary le Bow in Cheapside London. ········ Vüe de l'Eglise de St. Marie le Bow dans Cheapside à Londres.

Printed for .... Bowles & Son, at the Black Horse in Cornhill London.

3. *Cheapside, c. 1755. British Museum*

from the village lies pleasant country through which a boy might ramble in relative safety. Indeed, the neighbourhood should have provided Combe with many happy memories—his grandfather's big house, his uncles and aunts and cousins, the annual Harvest Home celebrated by the whole village in the tithe barn. But these, too, were memories which Combe firmly suppressed. Only once does any mention of the place occur in his writings. His topographical description of the Thames valley, published when he was fifty-two, mentions Harmondsworth cryptically as a place where "there is still a barn of a very uncommon size and construction, whose foundations were not laid for the purpose to which they are now employed".[18] Neither the original nor the present purpose is explained.

His rejection of his earliest years was complete. The Harmondsworth parish register notes the burial on March 8, 1748, of "Mrs. Susanna Combes, wife of Mr. Robert Combes, Citizen of London". This was two weeks before the boy's sixth birthday. Combe never alludes to it. Was the infant James Combes who had been buried a few months earlier a brother or a cousin? Who cared for William after his mother's death? Was it Grandmother Combes in Harmondsworth? Or Grandmother Hill in Putney or in Friday Street? Or was it possibly Mrs Elizabeth Anderson, the trusted housekeeper for whom Combe's father made generous provision in his will? Answers to these questions are not forthcoming. Combe kept his secret well. Once, when he was thirty-three, he wrote, "For my part, I love the Quakers!———they are certainly an harmless, and, I think, a conscientious set of people, who act in a manner more conformable to their own particular principles than any religious sect I know of."[19] Was this an oblique reference to his mother's family, the Hills? He says he writes these words about the Quakers "from real experience and intimate knowledge of many among them whom I know". Perhaps for a moment he was thinking of his childhood, but he quickly brushed the thought aside and buried the memory under a pious generalization.

One experience of his boyhood, however, was *not* suppressed; in fact, Combe never ceased mentioning it. Some time after October 13, 1752, within a few weeks or months of his eleventh birthday, he was entered as a student at Eton College,[20] and his experience there was a source of gratification as long as he lived. His father could easily have found a good school for him in the City; most of the livery companies (though not the Tallow Chandlers) had their own schools, and some like that of the Merchant Tailors were excellent. But Combe may not have lived in his father's Wood Street house after the death of his mother, and Eton is only eight miles of west Harmondsworth. The great school could have been selected merely because it happened to be at hand. In any event, Combe spent the next four years at Eton and was never the same again.

Admitted as an oppidan, a student not on the foundation, he lodged in town rather than in college. With a half-dozen other boys he was assigned to a "dame", Mrs Prior, and lived in her boarding-house at the corner of Woodward's (now Keate's) Lane just across the High Street from the chapel. He read the Latin poets, more or less, and struggled through Lily's *Short Introduction of Grammar*, the classic textbook of the time. In later years he sometimes assumed a scholarly pose, but his Latin tags are unconvincing evidence of learning. When he was eighty years old, however, he named a comic character of ambiguous parentage Quae Genus after a famous section of William Lily's grammar. His study of the Greek *New Testament* must have been more superficial than his Latin, though a manuscript dating from his last years does contain a few Greek quotations in his own hand.[21] His gentlemanly taste for English authors, especially those in vogue during the mid-eighteenth century, presumably dated from his Eton years. The range of literary allusion in his published works is not great, but he often quotes Pope, Addison, Shenstone, Gray, and Young. His frequent quotations from Milton usually come from *Paradise Lost*, but he also quotes from *Comus*. On one occasion he published a poem in Spenserian stanzas, but the text scarcely justifies his claim that he was imitating Spenser. In a word, he shared the conventional literary tastes of his time and enjoyed a reputation, not entirely undeserved, of being something of a scholar.

Whatever the depth of his learning, however, Combe was tireless in praise of his old school, always speaking of it with filial pride. He had been there in the days of the great Dr Edward Barnard, whom he once called "the most able schoolmaster that ever grasped the birch".[22] In 1794 he voiced "the emotions of a grateful mind" in praising Dr Barnard as the man "whose skill in the police, if it may be so called, of school government, has remained unrivalled to the present hour; and who raised Eton College to a pre-eminence, which it never enjoyed before, or has attained since".[23] In 1816, sixty years after he had left Eton, Combe was still writing about Dr

Barnard, his memory of the birch by that time somewhat dimmed. The great schoolmaster "had that power of impressing his dictates and opinions on his scholars, which lessened the necessity of practising corporal correction". Students "trembled at his rebuke" who would have been unresponsive to birching. It was by his great personality as a teacher that Dr Barnard "illuminated classical instruction, and instilled the principles of a gentleman". The passage runs to some length and is a fine tribute to a great man, written, so Combe assures his reader, "by one who knew him well".[24]

Although Combe put gentlemanly principles and classical learning side by side in this passage, there can be little doubt which of the two mattered more, both to the schoolboy and to the mature man. Throughout his life it was of first importance to Combe that he maintain the posture of a gentleman, whatever his middle-class origins and however in actual fact he was earning his living. Always skilful in adapting to his environment, Combe must quickly have picked up a veneer of sophistication once he found himself at Eton. His schoolmates included sons of men prominent in social or political life, many of them from noble families, some of them already lords in their own right. His contemporaries included Henry Conway (son of the first Earl of Hertford), Viscount Beauchamp (later the second Earl of Hertford), Stephen Fox (eldest son of the first Lord Holland), Lord Gainsborough, Lord Greville, Peniston Lamb (later Lord Melbourne), Constantine John Phipps (later second Baron Mulgrave), James Wright (later the second Baronet). Others who were at Eton with Combe, though not of the nobility, were destined to achieve prominence in Combe's lifetime and were then inevitably claimed as old classmates: George Steevens (later the Shakespearean scholar), Joseph Banks (later Sir Joseph and President of the Royal Society), Topham Beauclerk (Samuel Johnson's friend-to-be), Charles Cornwallis (later General), and Arthur Lee (the American patriot). With many of these, though probably not so many as he later claimed, Combe remained to some degree intimate for many years. With others he quarrelled, and his satires perpetuate their memory with initials, asterisks, and dashes. Either way, his habit of identifying himself with the great world which they represented developed at Eton and grew upon him in later life.

Even while he was adapting himself to this new social environment, his family ties began to disappear. His mother had died, as we have

seen, in 1748. The Harmondsworth parish register notes the burial
of his grandmother on November 7, 1753, his grandfather on September 22, 1755, and his uncle, Richard Combes, on May 26, 1756. And
then, on October 29, 1756, his father, the ironmonger of Wood
Street, was interred "in the family burying platt" as requested in
his will. Before his fifteenth birthday William Combe had lost both
parents, three grandparents, and several other close relatives. Only
his godfather and (possibly) his maternal grandmother were left.

The exact date of his father's death is not recorded, but the court
records show that his will was probated on October 26 "by the
oath of William Alexander, Esquire, the surviving executor . . . to
whom administration was granted of all and singular the goods,
chattels, and credits of the deceased". Originally Robert Combes had
named his father, the Harmondsworth brewer, as co-executor with
Alexander, and had provided for his son's maintenance and education
"which I leave entirely to the discretion of my said executors".[25]
The boy's grandfather having died, this discretion was left to Alexander alone. And Combe's education at Eton was forthwith terminated;
his name is missing from the school list of 1757.

*　　*　　*

Almost nothing can be discovered concerning Combe's life during the
three years following Eton. Some hints may be found in his father's
will, but other positive evidence is totally lacking. We know that the
boy's needs were to be provided for—but at the discretion of his
surviving guardian. Prudent management was clearly indicated.
Robert Combes's estate was not so large as one would expect; his will
is generous, but it is not that of a very wealthy man. It makes perfunctory acknowledgement of the marriage contract, but gives no
such accounting of funds as one would expect had the dowry actually
been £10,000 as stated in the Gentleman's Magazine. After gifts
totalling about £1,150 had been set aside for relatives, servants, and
"the poor of Harmondsworth", William was made residuary heir.
A generous estimate of the amount he would finally receive can
scarcely exceed £2,500. The estate was chargeable with the cost of
the boy's maintenance and education until he should reach the age of
twenty-one, but the normal income from this property should have
met his needs, even had he continued at Eton. Board and tuition at

the college cost no more than £50 a year, though it is true that extracurricular luxuries might cost several times as much. It was a time when many of the boys were living most extravagantly, and Combe's income would scarcely justify school life on the grand scale. Dr Barnard was soon taking steps to curb this extravagance, but by that time Combe had left the college.

It is possible that Alderman Alexander doubted the suitability of an Eton education for a career in Cheapside and that he undertook to direct the boy toward something more immediately practical. Nearly fifty years later Combe told his friend Joseph Farington that as a boy he had "learnt accounts at a school in Windmill Street".[26] That would be in Finsbury, not far from the family home in Wood Street. The remark may have been another of his impromptu fabrications, but since it displays no "ostentation and vanity" it may be the simple truth. Except for this hint, no information concerning Combe's life between the ages of fifteen and eighteen has come to light.

One common assumption about Combe must be rejected: he did not attend Oxford, either now or later. Without exception the friends of his old age believed he had done so, and Combe evidently did not discourage the belief. But his name does not appear in the university records. Nor does Combe in his writings ever explicitly lay claim to an Oxford education. His topographical descriptions of the colleges are formal and impersonal; they never once display "the emotions of a grateful mind" as in the references to Eton. Doctor Syntax visits the town, to be sure, and stays all night at the Mitre; perhaps since Combe remembered that goodly inn he had stayed there himself at one time or another. But there is not the slightest evidence of his having been in residence elsewhere in Oxford.

Just a month before Combe's eighteenth birthday, however, he and his guardian took a step consistent both with the Alderman's practical turn of mind and with the youth's social aspirations. On February 22, 1760, the Benchers of the Inner Temple (the governing body of senior members) admitted to membership in the Society "Combes, William, son and heir apparent of Robt. C. late of London, Gent." To insure payment of such bills as might be incurred, a bond for £30 was duly posted on that same day, signed by "William Combes of the Inner Temple, Gent, and William Alexander of the City of London, Esquire, and Alderman of the said City." Combe began keeping terms by dining at the Inner Temple without delay. A year later, on April

24, 1761, the Benchers sold him a chamber described as "two pairs of stairs on the left hand in the third staircase in the King's Bench Buildings"—still readily identifiable in a structure which fortunately escaped the disastrous bombing of the Temple in World War II. It would seem an enviable address for a young man making his entry into the world, but Combe cherished, as he thought, higher ambitions. Although the chamber was assigned to him for life (and strong pressure must have been exerted to obtain it for him), he occupied it for little more than two years. The opportune death of his guardian on September 23, 1762, freed him from the last restraining hand, and the arrival of his twenty-first birthday the following March gave him full control of the long-promised legacy from his father. He would not receive anything from his guardian's estate for another three years; William Alexander, the foresighted businessman, had left Combe £2,000 but had prudently stipulated that he should not receive it until reaching the age of twenty-four.[27] Even so, Combe must have felt that he was a wealthy man, and he vacated his chamber forthwith. It was sold to someone else on February 7, 1764.[28] By that time Combe was in France.

Whatever else his residence at the Inner Temple may have meant to Combe, his education in the law had necessarily been most casual. At that period the Inns of Court had virtually given up even the pretense of training students. The performance of exercises, the fulfilment of residence requirements, and the keeping of terms had become little more than forms; students were readily excused from them. Only a small proportion of the members were ever called to the Bar, and those who were had necessarily prepared themselves elsewhere, usually in offices of practising attorneys. The mid-eighteenth century was educationally a low point in the history of the Inns of Court, just as it was in that of the two universities. For the rest of his life, Combe had a ready store of legal anecdotes and could summon legal jargon to his aid when it seemed appropriate, but his actual knowledge of the law was meagre. He was certainly never called to the Bar; he would not have been eligible until he had been a member of the Inner Temple for five years—that is, until 1765. By that time he was busily spending his fortune as a fashionable young man about town. He had been to France and was already back in England, reputed to have "resided abroad for many years". Evidently he always had the knack of creating legends about himself: he had probably been abroad for less than a year, perhaps for only six months, and had travelled no farther than Paris. But for the moment that was long enough and far enough.

*   *   *

Combe was not the only young man to go abroad in 1763, for the lifting of travel restrictions after the Seven Years War permitted a host of others to begin their Grand Tour at once, many of them somewhat belatedly, with a visit to Paris. Even before the signing of the peace treaty some adventurous souls had made the crossing. Laurence Sterne had managed it in January 1762 and, though technically an enemy alien, had been hospitably received. But the coming of peace opened the flood-gates. Always loath to leave their own country, Frenchmen viewed this impulse of their neighbours with complaisant astonishment, calling it the *maladie du pays*. For the travellers, however, the grand tour had become a vital part of the social ritual, a recognized feature of a gentleman's education.

Although many youths set out on this expedition with formidable itineraries and private tutors, or "bear leaders", others quite frankly went in search of unsupervised adventure, often with the tacit approval of their parents. Combe followed neither of these courses. He might pretend to have intellectual interests, and to some extent he did have them, but he was not given to dissolute behaviour, whether at home or abroad. Throughout his life he displayed an almost priggish distaste for even the milder dissipations. Until he was sixty-five he never so much as tasted a glass of wine—or at least he said so and his friends believed him. He wasted his money in ostentatious ways, but he never gambled. One learns with surprise that he took snuff. He was fond of female companionship and had a long succession of very proper sentimental encounters, but there is not the slightest evidence of passion—least of all in his two marriages. In his books and in his personal life he shunned even the suggestion of indelicacy; his conversation might sometimes be boring, but it was never indecorous. In an age much given to gross talk, Combe avoided the sly *double entendre* as scrupulously as the frankly salacious. These oddities of behaviour would have seemed middle-class prudishness in a less flamboyant youth, but in Combe they were put down to a not unattractive eccentricity. They made him an object of curious interest in the fashionable world and contributed a special flavour to the mystery which surrounded him.

For William Combe a year's residence in France was neither a great intellectual experience nor an opportunity to sow wild oats. His purpose was social, and Paris during the winter of 1763–4 offered him a matchless opportunity to cultivate the graces. The visitor most popular with the Parisians that winter was the Scottish philosopher, David Hume, then secretary to the English ambassador. There is no evidence that Combe ever met him or sought to do so. A more likely acquaintance was the ambassador himself, the enormously wealthy and hospitable Earl of Hertford. He made himself readily available to travelling Englishmen, and Combe had a perfect approach through his old Eton contemporary, Viscount Beauchamp, the ambassador's son. To be sure, Combe later turned bitterly upon the Hertfords, but at this time he and Beauchamp must have been acquaintances, probably friends. Other Eton contemporaries were also in France that winter, and Combe would find ways of meeting them as they passed through Paris. Stephen Fox was there in January, and both Constantine John Phipps and Arthur Lee may have been there later. Combe would undertake to ingratiate himself with such men, and they in turn would introduce him to their friends. For he was undeniably a most attractive, socially acceptable youth. He had, or he quickly acquired, impeccable manners and a dignified bearing which set him apart from others of his age and certainly of his background. "His courtly dress, his handsome liveries, and, it may be added, his tall stature and fine appearance, procured him the appellation of Duke Combe", according to Thomas Campbell.[29] There is, in fact, every reason to believe that he was freely admitted to circles of wealth and refinement, and that it was in the salons of pre-revolutionary France that he gained the social polish for which he was long to be famous. Some remnant of that polish was still discernable in his manner sixty years later in post-Napoleonic London—a faded anachronism by then, but still oddly attractive in that alien world of the Regency.

*   *   *

By January 1764 Laurence Sterne was preparing to end his two-year stay in France and return to England. He intended to hurry straight to Calais and reach London by the middle of February, but the attractions of Paris, "this city of seductions", understandably delayed his progress. When he had passed through the city in January 1762 he had been lionized by the French, to whom "Tristram was almost as much known as in London", but because of the war few Englishmen had been there at that time. How different now! Lord Hertford had taken a sumptuous mansion for the newly opened embassy and entertained Sterne, as indeed he did other travelling Englishmen of distinction. Sterne preached at the ambassador's chapel, dined with his son, Viscount Beauchamp, and engaged in witty controversy with his secretary, David Hume. What with another flirtation, "the tenderest passion that ever tender wight underwent", he had a very gay spring and made "a most jolly nonsensical life of it".[30] Circumstances point to these three or four months as the time of Combe's first meeting with the man who was to exert such lasting influence on his life. He would not fail to seek out such a fashionable celebrity, he may very well have been entertained at embassy functions himself, and he had acquaintances in Sterne's circle. The circumstances of their meeting cannot now be known, but meet they did, and rather more probably in the spring of 1764 than at any other time.

The course of their friendship and some few of Combe's movements during the ensuing four years may be traced faintly in the *Original Letters of the Late Reverend Mr Laurence Sterne* (1788), three of which are believed to be authentic, others fabricated by Combe but evidently based on authentic originals. The fabrications, a major source of vexation to Sterne scholars, will be discussed in a subsequent chapter; for the moment it will suffice to say that these letters consist largely of sentimental moralizing interspersed with phrases and images quoted from Sterne's writings and with passages culled from authentic letters in Combe's possession. The imitative element almost never contains an assertion subject to verification; whenever any particularization occurs, it seems to be based on personal knowledge of the facts or on information drawn from an authentic letter. Some elements of biographical information may, with caution, be inferred even from the forgeries.[31]

Sterne, we know, managed to pull himself away from Paris and return to London at the end of May 1764, arriving in York on June 23[32] and in Coxwold by the end of the month. Combe then has him addressing a letter to "W. C., Esq." on July 1, inviting that young man to visit him in Coxwold. The letter begins in Sterne's manner, "I am safe arrived at my bower—and I trust that you have no longer any doubt about coming to embower it with me. Having, for six months together, been running at the ring of pleasure, you will find that repose here which, all young as you are, you ought to want. We will be witty, or classical, or sentimental, as it shall please you best."[33] This is the first of a series of letters supposed to be addressed to Combe as he proceeds northward in leisurely fashion. Although overlaid with imitative flourishes, these letters contain a number of obscure details which have been fully verified from independent sources. One is finally forced to believe that the journey actually took place, that Combe accepted Sterne's invitation and started north at once, that he lingered five days in Cambridge with Thomas Scrope before going on to Lincolnshire with him, that he sprained his ankle by a fall out of a chaise, that by the second week of August he had reached William Hewett's at Stretton, Rutlandshire, and that by the following week he reached York. The sixth and last of this series of letters, addressed from Coxwold on a Monday morning, promises to meet Combe in York on the following day; the races began on Tuesday, August 21, and we know from other sources that Sterne attended them. Here the letters break off, and one is led to assume that the visit is taking place.

Three months later, on November 13, 1764, Sterne wrote a letter (this one not a Combe fabrication) to his friend John Hall-Stevenson saying that he has heard from "C——". The identification with Combe is not certain, but no one has seriously doubted it. C——, it seems, has been ill and is coming to Coxwold for a visit of a week or ten days. "Now I know that he is ambitious of being better acquainted with you; and longs from his soul for a sight of you in your own castle. ——I cannot do otherwise, than bring him with me——nor can I gallop away and leave him an empty house to pay a visit to from London, as he comes half express to see me."[34] Whether C—— actually arrived and was taken to Skelton Castle remains unconfirmed. There is nothing in the letter inconsistent with his having visited Sterne in August; he wishes to be *better* acquainted with Hall-Stevenson—the expression suggests a recent brief meeting. And there is a slightly apologetic tone in Sterne's letter, as though the writer were somewhat embarrassed by the young man's persistence.

The relationship between Sterne and Combe during the following year, 1765, rests on no such tenuous evidence, though the details of when and where are lacking. By March, Sterne was soliciting subscriptions to Volumes III and IV of his *Sermons*. He boasted to Garrick that this new publication would go into the world "with a prancing list . . . *de toute la noblesse*",[35] and it certainly did so. A splendid list of 693 subscribers takes up twenty-four pages of the printed work, and there with the others appears the name of "Wm. Combes, Esq." The two men had communicated with each other, either by letter or in person.

The subscription list is visible evidence, also, of the company which Combe was keeping or desired to keep. From various contemporary sources we learn of his social triumphs at this period. As one commentator subsequently remarked, "Combe . . . burst on the world as a wonderfully well-dressed *beau*, and was received with *éclat* for the sake of his wealth, talents, grace, and personal beauty."[36] Such was indeed the figure he cut in the fashionable world as long as any part of his inheritance remained, and in 1766 his resources were substantially replenished. On his twenty-fourth birthday he became eligible to claim his godfather's legacy of £2,000. We hear that "his horses, his equipage, and his establishment in general, were allowed to surpass in beauty and elegance those of the most dashing leaders of fashion".[37] He maintained a West End residence which one writer places in Bury Street, just east of St James's.[38] This address was across Piccadilly from 37 Hill Street, where, so he tells us, he often visited his two friends of contrasting character, George (the "Good") Lord Lyttelton and Thomas, his scapegrace son, later the second ("Wicked") Lord. It was the latter who called him "the immovable, the fascinating, the polished Combe".[39] Such, at any rate, was Combe's story a half-century later. It may be true.

In July 1766 he evidently paid another visit to Coxwold, for on the fifteenth Sterne wrote that "B——— has left me his post chaise". A manuscript in Sterne's hand at the Morgan Library shows that before writing "B——" Sterne had written and then crossed out "Combes".[40] In a letter dated August 19 (one of Combe's fabrications, but consistent with the letter about the post chaise and with the equally authentic letters which follow), Sterne is made to say that "the spirit of modern romance" has led Combe from Coxwold to Bristol "for no other earthly purpose, but to let a Phthysical maiden lean upon thine arm, and receive the healing waters from thine hand".[41] On August

30, Sterne is enquiring about Combe in a fully authentic letter address-ed to Thomas Becket in London. "Is Mr. Combes in Town? If you see him, tell him to write to me."[42] But Combe was just then in-volving himself in some scrape, whether with his "Phthysical maiden" or another, and soon he was off in some haste to France. Sterne heard from him on January 6 and immediately replied as follows:

London Bond street
    I arrived here but yesterday, where, (after a terrible journey in most inhospitable weather) I was met agreeably with your Letter from Paris—I first sympathize for the unkind greeting upon french-ground which you met with by your over throw—may it be the last shock you receive in this world!—this reflection, costs me a deep Sigh—& alas! my friend! I dread it will let you go off no cheaper—I fear some thing has gone wrong with you; if so; why would not you make me a partner? I am a dab at giving advice,—& I esteemd and loved you—& you knew it.
    If I am wrong; my friendship has only been too quick sighted and perhaps too easily alarm'd by false appearances; only there were some little mysteri-ous turns & windings in the manner of your leaving England, which mark'd the steps of an entangled man. is it some nasty scrape of gallantry?—or a more cleanly one of simple Love? If it is the latter, I'll put off my Cassoc & turn Knight Errant for you, & say the kindest things of you to Dulcinea that Dulcinea ever heard—if she has a Champion—and words will not atchieve it—I'll enter the Lists with him and break a spear in your behalf; tho by the by, mine is half rusty, and should be hung up in the old family hall amongst Pistols without Cocks, and Helmets which have lost their Vizards—
    I miscarried of my tenth Volume by the violence of a fever, I have just got thro'—I have however gone on to my reckoning with the ninth, of w[ch] I am all this week in Labour pains; & if to Day's Advertiser is to be depended upon shall be safely deliver'd by tuesday.
    adieu. I heartily wish your happiness—seek it where you will, my dear Sir, You will find it no where, but in Company with Virtue and Honour.
I am &c———
L. S.[43]

It has been conjectured from this letter that Combe finally ex-hausted his resources toward the end of 1766 and that the "over-throw" which Sterne mentions was in sober reality financial collapse. At first glance the conjecture seems plausible, but it must be rejected. Although he was living extravagantly, he could scarcely have ex-hausted by December the £2,000 he had inherited in March. And there is evidence that he had returned to England and resumed his flamboyant style of living before the end of 1767.
Sterne's letter suggests that it was an amorous entanglement

which had sent Combe off to France, and though the suggestion is perhaps a convention of the game of sentiment, there is really nothing implausible in it. Combe was not yet twenty-five, he was a handsome, free-spending young man of fashion. Under the circumstances it would be a miracle if he did not find himself involved with the ladies. His own imitations of Sterne's letters contain hints of such affairs. In a letter dated August 29, 1765, for example, he has Sterne say, "B—— is here, and tells me that he left you continually driving between London and Richmond—what beauty of the Hill has enchanted you there? Or what swan of the silver Thames are you dying for?" Another visitor has even hinted of a marriage, "to which I replied, God forbid! . . . with your dispositions, and in your situation, I hardly think there is a woman in the kingdom who would be an happy match for you."[44] Combe does not permit Sterne to explain the remark; possibly the whole story was fiction—Combe's fiction, be it noted, the image of himself at twenty-three which he suggests in letters half real, half fabricated, and published many years later.

We are not likely to discover what sent Combe in haste to France in December 1766. That he returned the following year, however, is indicated by the survival in good condition of a set of nine volumes of *Tristram Shandy*, all first editions, bearing in Combe's unmistakable hand the following note: "Given to me by the Revd Mr Sterne in the year 1767. —— Wm Combe." That he carefully preserved the books through long years of hardship is indicated by a second notation in the first volume: "Given to me by my dear friend Wm Combe in the year 1818. A. T. Ryves."[45] Anthony Ryves was the son of Combe's landlady and, until they quarrelled, virtually an adopted son to Combe. It is most unlikely that these volumes would have been sent to Combe while he was abroad, nor could they have been given to him before his departure. The ninth volume of *Tristram Shandy* did not appear until January 29, 1767,[46] and Sterne died March 18, 1768. Sometime between those dates Combe was in England.

Two of the stories which Combe told in his later years place him in the company of Augustus John Hervey, probably at Bath, during 1768. The tales as usual are absurdly exaggerated, but they further support the belief that Combe was back from the Continent by that time.[47] Moreover, the authority quoted by the Bristol *Observer* in 1823, an old man already mentioned as remarkably accurate in his memory of young Combe, vividly recalled his presence at the Bristol

Hotwells a half-century earlier; he thought it was "about the year 1768". And he repeated the usual words in praise of Combe's general appearance at that time: "He was tall and handsome in person, an elegant scholar, and highly accomplished in manners and behaviour". This writer also confirms the legend of Combe's lavish household: "He lived in a most princely style, and, though a bachelor, kept two carriages, several horses, and a large retinue of servants. . . . He was generally recognized by the appellation of 'Count Coombe'."

The most sensational incident in Combe's social career and the one most gossiped about at the time occurred in the late summer or early autumn of 1769. Combe was then still appearing in fashionable circles, for though the stories which survive disagree on details, they all give the episode an aristocratic setting. Possibly, as Horace Walpole believed, that setting was a supper in Almack's assembly rooms in King Street.[48] Possibly, as Thomas Campbell heard, it was in Albemarle Street at the Coterie, a new and very exclusive club founded by a group of ladies in 1769. Samuel Rogers had it taking place at a fashionable watering-place.[49] All agree that the three principal actors were Lady Archer, a beautiful woman who attained great notoriety through the excessive use of rouge, Thomas Lyttelton, later the "Wicked" Lord, and finally "Duke" Combe, drinking water and poised as always. Lady Archer was seated conversing with Combe when young Lyttelton staggered into the room and approached them. With a drink held rather shakily in one hand, he came to a halt in front of Lady Archer and stood leering at her. After an embarrassing pause, he addressed her with insults which are variously reported, but which always involve a comparison between her rouged cheeks and the colours of "a drunken peacock". When Lady Archer understandably protested, he threw the glass of wine in her face. In the general confusion which followed only the water-drinker remained cool. According to Walpole, he immediately said to Lyttelton, "My Lord, I take the insult as intended at me, for you could not be brutal enough to aim it at a woman". With that, he challenged Lyttleton, or indicated that his seconds would shortly wait upon him, or—as Samuel Rogers had it—"kicked Lyttelton downstairs".

Whatever the literal truth of this story, Lyttelton is known to have left London almost immediately for France. He had adopted this expedient twice before when his affairs had become tangled at home, and according to his biographer this third abrupt departure took place in the autumn of 1769.[50] For a brief period Combe was once more a celebrated figure, now as protector of outraged womanhood. The affair made this his most notorious season in London society, but it was his last appearance as man-about-town. Not a single account of Combe's adventures, even among those he himself reported, suggests that his social triumphs survived the winter of 1769–70. No precise date can be assigned to his downfall. Such awkward turns of furtune do not ordinarily occur in a moment. But somehow, as bills accumulated and tradesmen became more insistent, he slipped out of sight without anyone's noticing. And presently he had disappeared without a trace. For the next few years his friends had no knowledge whatever of his whereabouts.

A View of Bristol Hot Well-House and St Vincents Rocks.
Taken near Rownham Ferry.

4. *Bristol Hot Wells in the Eighteenth Century* (*see pages 33 ff.*)

CHAPTER II

SENTIMENTAL PHILOSOPHER

Commerce, I envy not thy gains,
Thy hard-earn'd wealth, thy golden pains,
(For that's hard-earn'd, though gain'd with ease,
Where Honour's sacred functions cease).
—Doctor Syntax

FROM THE winter of 1769–70 to the summer of 1773, Combe avoided his friends and scrambled for a bare living, partly in France, partly in the West Midlands and Wales. The full story of his life during this period is far to seek, despite—or possibly because of—the abundance of surviving anecdotes. Combe evidently concealed the harsh realities of his experience by throwing dust in the eyes of the curious—hinting at an impossible variety of picaresque adventures and creating a legend as one who could meet adversity with jaunty insouciance. Such is the image suggested, for example, by Thomas Campbell's story concerning the recognition of Combe in the red-coat uniform of a private as he walked along Wolverhampton High Street.

"Is it possible, Combe, that you can bear this condition?"

"Fiddlesticks!" replied the ex-duke, taking a pinch of snuff. "A philosopher can bear anything."[1]

Combe wanted to be thought a man of imperturbable poise, whether philosopher or man of mystery. Another of Campbell's stories concerns a benefit night which Roger Kemble is supposed to have given Combe at the theatre. It was rumoured that at the end of the evening the mystery of his identity would be explained, and a full house waited attentively as Combe mounted the stage to speak. We are told that "expectation was all agog" as he concluded his remarks by saying, "Now, ladies and gentlemen, I shall tell you what I am. I am, ladies and gentlemen, your most obedient and humble servant". Whereupon

he bowed and left the stage. The whole absurd tale sounds like fiction
—which it very probably is. But it perpetuates the legend which
Combe cherished.

At least three and a half years elapsed between Combe's disappear-
ance from fashionable circles and his reappearance as a man of letters
and self-confessed philosopher. His movements during this time are
vaguely discernible, though in sober fact most of the romantic legend
must be dismissed. There is good reason to believe that his first
expedient was to get himself over to France, but no one is obliged to
accept the report that he joined the French Army. Several stories
place him at Douai, and indeed he may have found shelter for a time
at the seminary maintained there by English Catholics. Douai is in
northern France about sixty-five miles from Calais, more accessible
than Paris, and less likely to prove embarrassing. Richard Fitzpatrick
remembered seeing him there during the winter of 1771–2.[2] That
must have been near the end of Combe's stay in France, however, for
his English adventures would occupy the time remaining before he
got back on his feet. The numerous references to his service in the
English Army cannot easily be explained away. Horace Walpole
called him "Captain Coombes",[3] but others more plausibly thought he
was a private. Several anecdotes have him discovered in his uniform
reading Latin (or even, according to Horace Smith, Greek),[4] thus
revealing that he was a gentleman with a proper education who should
be released from the army without delay. Thomas Campbell places
the episode in a public house in Wolverhampton:

"What, my friend, can you read that book in the original?"

"If I cannot, a great deal of money has been thrown away on my
education!"

The story is a stock situation in novels of the time, and Campbell
adds the usual narrative embellishment: "His landlord soon found the
literary red-coat an attractive ornament to his tap-room, which was
filled every night with the wondering auditors of the learned soldier.
They . . . clubbed their money to procure his discharge." Sir Egerton
Brydges tells much the same story, placing it thirty-five miles away
at Derby—an insignificant difference as these anecdotes go. His
version is without the conventional embroidery and seems rather
more credible: "At length he was discovered in the ranks of a regiment of the line in an inn, at Derby, by George Steevens, an old crony,
to whom he long denied himself, but who persevered in rescuing him

from his degraded situation."[5] It is not difficult to believe that Steevens did, in fact, aid Combe at this time; their friendship, or at least association, extended over many years from their boyhood at Eton to their employment as co-workers by John and Josiah Boydell at the end of the century. For every reason, the story of Combe's rescue sounds less fictional as Sir Egerton tells it.

However much Campbell may have elaborated the narrative, he was evidently right in saying that Roger Kemble befriended Combe at this time. During the 1770s Kemble's company of actors was regularly performing in the West Midlands, where many stories also place Combe. Campbell's statement that at Wolverhampton Combe "narrowly missed the honour of being Mrs. Siddons's reading master" may be regarded with scepticism, though it is reported as literal truth. The story goes that Sarah's father, Roger Kemble, actually engaged Combe to teach her elocution, but that her mother promptly "interposed her veto". Nothing in Combe's character suggests that he would be reluctant to tutor the dark-eyed seventeen-year-old girl, and the story has been repeated by every biographer of Sarah Kemble Siddons. From various sources we know that Combe was indeed acquainted with the famous actress in later years. It was probably in the 1790s that he told Samuel Rogers about seeing her, "when a very young woman, standing by the side of her father's stage, and knocking a pair of snuffers against a candlestick, to imitate the sound of a windmill, during the representation of some Harlequin-piece".[6] The particularity of the anecdote lends it a certain support. It could very well refer to an actual incident which Combe remembered from the winter of 1772–3, shortly before Sarah left the company.[7] That would be a year after Combe had been seen at Douai, where he could have made the acquaintance of Sarah's brother, John Philip Kemble. The boy and his father were Catholics, and at that time the future great actor was being educated for the priesthood. He did not return to England until 1775, but if Combe had known him in France he could easily use the acquaintance as an excuse for presenting himself to the parents. The evidence is tenuous, but not altogether improbable.

Throughout the later years of his life, and indeed until long after his death, men who had ever known Combe were wont to talk about his strange history. One such conversation which bears upon Combe's years of vagabondage was recorded by Joseph Farington in his diary for November 8, 1796. John Nichols, the printer and author, began by remarking that Combe was not a superior scholar. Vanity, he thought, was his ruling passion. Boyestone, a merchant friend of Farington's, added the information that "he had been a soldier in Spain [!] and in England". Then the Reverend Richard Pennick, Keeper of the British Museum Reading Room, said that "Mr. Kennet a friend of his saw Coombe at Swansea in Glamorganshire, as a waiter at an Inn".[8] Coming from a clearly identified source, this unadorned story can probably be accepted at face value. Thomas Campbell had also heard it, though he could not have seen this entry in Farington's diary. It is possible that Combe had worked elsewhere as a waiter, too; legend associates him with the kitchens at Douai.[9] But whether as a waiter, a private in the army, or a menial in some other capacity, he undoubtedly had a good many experiences during these years which he never subsequently described to his friends. Whatever his pretended nonchalance, he must often have suffered humiliation and physical hardship before re-establishing himself as a gentleman. But the worst of his ordeal was ended in the summer of 1773 when he was given his first editorial assignment—and that not twenty-five miles from Wolverhampton.

The man who gave Combe this work was Robert Berkeley of Spetchley Park, an estate some three miles south-east of Worcester. He was a Catholic who in 1771 had invited the Reverend Thomas Falkner, an aged Jesuit missionary, to live with him as chaplain and write an account of his experiences in South America. Father Falkner had lived in Argentina and Paraguay for thirty-eight years, much of the time living and working with the Indians. Thomas Pennant, who visited him at Spetchley Park, found him something of an original, a man of about seventy who had "lost all European guile" and "acquired all the simplicity and honest impetuosity of the people he [had] been so long conversant with".[10] The manuscript which Falkner produced was evidently a reflection of his personality, for Berkeley felt that it required careful revision. Perhaps "honest impetuosity" was not to Berkeley's taste. At any rate, he soon began casting about for someone to revise the work and see it through the press.

How Berkeley heard about Combe and was persuaded to employ him for the task can only be conjectured, but it is interesting to note that Roger Kemble's company of actors was performing in Worcester during April and May;[11] it seems at least possible that the two co-religionists should have met and that Kemble should have suggested the man for the job. Combe was also in the neighbourhood, living just then at Evesham, eight miles from Spetchley Park. And some time in the summer he suddenly and without notice disappeared from his rented quarters, leaving his possessions and his unpaid bills behind him.[12] Since new duties called him elsewhere, he simply took his departure. It was one more humiliation, but perhaps he told himself that he would return later to take care of the formalities.

*　　*　　*

The editorial work on Father Falkner's manuscript was carried out as Berkeley wished and under his immediate supervision. Readers have sometimes regretted that in the process all trace of the author's colourful personality was removed, and Father Falkner himself is said to have been dissatisfied with the result. But Combe, whatever his own view of the matter, did not question the hackwriter's obligation to carry out instructions and produce a work according to specifications. Berkeley had certain political and religious ends in view, and he was paying the bill. Why, then, should the book be expected to reflect the personality of the author or the taste of the editor? By the standards of the time, more businesslike than romantic, the manuscript was properly and professionally edited.

Combe dealt with the practical problems of seeing the book through the press in the Hereford printing office of Charles Pugh and under the eye of the proprietor himself or that of Rathbone, his editor. It was a large and well-equipped shop, capable of handling a substantial printing contract while at the same time producing a weekly newspaper, the *British Chronicle, or Pugh's Hereford Journal*. Pugh ran a prosperous and diversified printing business with bookseller connections throughout the West Midlands and in London.[13] His establishment was evidently a good place for Combe to learn the elements of his craft. The man-of-all-work for the printers and booksellers had to know something of typography in order to prepare manuscript for the compositor, and he had to understand the discipline of reading proof. Combe must have learned his lesson well in Pugh's establishment, for he was quickly to achieve a solid reputation in the London book trade, and over the years he was to have responsibility for numerous works of typographical distinction, not least of which was this very first volume.

Pugh's newspaper announced the publication of the book in Hereford on January 27, 1774, six or seven months after Combe began work on the manuscript. The title-page gives as much information about its contents as the reader today or the prospective buyer of the past would require: *A Description of Patagonia, and the Adjoining Parts of South America: Containing an Account of the Soil, Produce, Animals, Vales, Mountains, Rivers, Lakes, &c. of Those Countries; the Religion, Government, Policy, Customs, Dress, Arms, and Language of the Indian Inhabitants; and Some Particulars Relating to Falkland's Islands. By Thomas Falkner, Who Resided Near Forty Years in Those Parts. Illustrated with a New Map of the Southern Parts of America, Engraved by Mr. Kitchen, Hydrographer to His Majesty. Hereford: Printed by C. Pugh; and Sold by T. Lewis, Russell-Street, Covent-Garden, London. M.DCC.LXXIV.* The work was a notable production, and it still retains some significance to students of South American history and ethnology. It was carried on scientific expeditions by both Sir Joseph Banks and Charles Darwin. It was translated into German (1775), French (1787), and Spanish (1835 and 1911), and a new English edition appeared in Chicago as recently as 1935. Neither Falkner nor Combe could ask for better recognition.

In more ways than one this initiation into the mysteries of editing was a fortunate one. Combe seems at once to have discovered an aptitude for the work. The duties were consistent with his gentlemanly pretensions, and though the pay was low it was doubtless better than that yielded by his other recent employments. Perhaps at first he thought he was only adopting another temporary expedient, but he had, in fact, begun a career which he was to follow almost without interruption for half a century.

He seems to have lingered in the neighbourhood of Worcester and Hereford for some months, conceivably trying his hand at miscellaneous tasks for Pugh. Since this is the only time he seems to have been in that part of England, it must have been in 1774 that he visited Foxley, the celebrated country estate of Uvedale Price, a few miles north of Hereford. Unfortunately, while Combe was there some banknotes were stolen from another guest—or, as Horace Walpole has it, the host himself missed some silverware.[14] Price mentioned the loss to Combe, adding the insulting suggestion that perhaps he should take his leave. Combe never forgot the incident, but he did manage to give Samuel Rogers a version of the story in keeping with his famous nonchalance.

"Perhaps it would be as well if you cut your visit short here," said Price.

"Oh, certainly," replied Combe with the greatest coolness. "And allow me to ask whether we are to be friends or acquaintances?"

"Acquaintances, if you please," said Price.

That Combe had actually stolen the missing property will seem most unlikely to anyone familiar with his character. He might borrow and neglect to return, and he certainly had a gentlemanly disregard of debt, but he was not light-fingered. When pressed by circumstances, as he must have been at this juncture, he might be inclined to overstay his welcome and, in a word, to sponge. But he was justified in resenting the accusation of theft. And resent it he did; years afterwards he saw Price walking in Leicester Square with Samuel Rogers, and thereafter he was even cool to Rogers![15]

*　*　*

On February 18, 1775, *Felix Farley's Bristol Journal* reported the arrival in neighbouring Bath of a "Mr. Coombs", and on April 8 the arrival of the same gentleman at the Bristol Hotwells. In all probability this was no other than William Combe, Esq., returning to the scenes of his former celebrity. That he did return at about this time is fully evident from the book which he published in Bristol on June 12. Although he intimates in that book that he had been in the city as early as the previous November to witness the celebration of Burke's election, his account of that event gives no evidence of first-hand information. Nor does his mention of the Pen Park tragedy in March contain any details which were not common knowledge. Suffice to say that Combe was in Bristol by the first week in April and probably no earlier.

He arrived in that city, moreover, with his finances substantially replenished from a source which only becomes apparent nine years later when his creditor undertook legal action to collect the debt. In 1784, as we shall see, Combe formally acknowledged a debt of £100 to John Palmer, who in 1775 had been manager of the Bath theatre. The amount of the original loan is never stated; the sum mentioned in the court records may have been merely the unpaid balance or it may have included both the principal and accumulated interest. In either event, the loan was substantial in terms of the buying power of money at the time. It lasted Combe only a year, but it sufficed to launch him on his literary career.

There is no explanation of how Palmer came to lend him this money, but one possibility presents itself. One of the half-dozen boys who had lived with Combe at Mrs Prior's boarding-house in Eton was a Palmer whose first name is unrecorded.[16] This may well have been John Palmer, who was the same age as Combe and whose father was a prosperous brewer in Bath. A schoolboy association dating from 1753 might explain the loan made in 1775, especially in view of Combe's habit of exploiting his Eton connections. But the records, alas, are silent. Palmer was never repaid, but as we shall see he eventually felt amply compensated. And whatever the details of the original transaction, Combe was able to spend five productive months in Bristol, publishing three small books at his own expense and acquiring a modish reputation as a man of taste, sensibility, and literary talent.

Bristol had much to offer a young writer in 1775.[17] With some 50,000 inhabitants, it was the second largest city in England, proud of its traditions as a great shipping and trading centre. The River Avon, winding through its spectacular gorge, brought ships from all parts of the world to quays in the very heart of the city. Many of these ships, financed by Bristol merchants, were active in the famous (or infamous) triangular trade, taking manufactured goods to be exchanged on the coast of Africa for slaves which in turn were exchanged in the West Indies for sugar and rum to be brought to England and distributed throughout the country by Bristol traders. The city's prosperity was thus vitally threatened when colonial troubles began to interfere with American trade. It was inevitable that Burke's conciliatory views should make him a popular candidate for Parliament in Bristol, and that his election in 1774 should prompt a demonstration famous in the annals of the city.

Great changes were taking place in Bristol during these years. As trade had grown the quays had become increasingly busy and the nearby streets impossibly congested. The city centre was still medieval in aspect, with narrow passages and overhanging half-timbered buildings—picturesque, doubtless, but ill adapted to commercial activity and no longer desirable for human habitation. Some effort was being made to improve conditions by demolishing old structures and opening new squares in the Georgian manner. The greatest improvements were those rising on the heights above the city, where wealthy merchants and retired sea captains were building their mansions near the open downs and creating the attractive settlement of Clifton. In the Avon gorge itself, at the foot of St Vincent's Rock and some three hundred feet below Clifton, warm mineral springs had made possible the development of an attractive spa at the edge of the river (Plate 4, p. 26). Hotwell House provided the expected amenities of a watering-place, and the springs were discovered to have various curative properties, especially for leprosy, scurvy, and phthisis. (Only the upper classes suffered from phthisis; others simply had consumption.) This newly fashionable spa brought a variety of men and women to the city, some pathetically in quest of health, others simply looking for the usual watering-place recreations: cards, music, dancing, strolling on the Parade, picnics on the near-by downs, frivolous tittle-tattle, and other polite relaxations. Combe had experienced these diverse pleasures when he could still afford the role of Man of Fashion; now that he was an onlooker he could take a more detached view of them.[18] And he would presently discover with cultivated distaste the crass materialism, the vulgar money-grubbing behind the scenes which made possible all this visible luxury. The discovery was not strikingly new, but it sufficed to provide a theme for his first original work.

That work was announced in the Bristol papers on Saturday, June 10: "On Monday next will be published, price 2s. 6d., *The Philosopher in Bristol*. . . . Printed by G. Routh in the Maiden-Tavern". This little volume was the first of three which appeared in less than seven weeks, the other two being *Clifton, a Poem* (July 3) and *The Philosopher in Bristol, Part the Second* (July 26). All three were printed by George Routh at the expense of the anonymous author. The original bill, preserved in the Berg Collection of the New York Public Library, reads as follows:

Bristol

William Coombe, Esq.

D^r to Geo. Routh.

1775. June 10—Printing 7 sheets "Philosopher in Bristol"

@ 17/- per sheet	5.19.—
Paper for ditto—8 Reams—@ 8/- ..	3. 4.—
Folding & Stitching in blue paper—	
@ 7/6 per 100	2.12. 6

July 29—Printing 10 sheets—Second part of d⁰
    @ 17/-   ..   ..   8.10.—
    Paper for ditto—11 Ream—@ 8/-   ..   4. 8.—
    Folding, &c   ..   ..   3.15.—
July 8—Printing 3 sheets & ½—"Clifton—a
    Poem" @ 21/- per sheet 3.13. 6
    Paper for ditto—4 Ream—@ 12/- pr Ream   2. 8.—
    Folding, &c   ..   ..   −.17. 6
    Duty on "Clifton"   ..   ..   ..   −. 7.—
    Adv. "Philosopher" in Cocking's Paper @ 4/   −. 8.—
    ———Ditto———in Bonner's ..   ..   1.—.—
    ———Ditto———in Pine's   ..   ..   1.—.—
    ———Ditto———in S. Farley's   ..   1. 8.—
    ———Ditto—in 4 London papers—@ 3/6   1. 8.—

                               £40.18. 6
Cʳ By two £10 Bills   ..   ..   20.—.—

                               £20.18. 6[19]

    This itemized statement is vivid evidence of the buying power of the pound in 1775. The two volumes of the *Philosopher in Bristol* were printed, it seems, in editions of 700 each at a total cost of only £28. 8*s*. 6*d*. If all 1,400 copies were sold at 2*s*. 6*d*. each, the advertised price, receipts would total £175, some of which would go to the booksellers. Did John Palmer, then, finance this project as a business venture? *Clifton* was more expensively printed on better paper and in a smaller edition; evidently a topographical poem was expected to enhance the author's reputation rather than to bring him profits. In all three books, however, Combe employs local materials and current topics; even in these first original publications he reveals the hackwriter's instinct for marketable wares. His motives were mixed; he desperately needed to find a source of income, but he also craved recognition as a writer, a man of letters. Both desires are evident in these Bristol publications, and the evidence suggests that Combe must have been pleased with the success of this venture.

* * *

It is easy to see why the *Philosopher in Bristol* pleased its first readers. Even today it retains a certain charm, partly as a period piece in the sentimental mode, partly as a portrait of the hackwriter as a young man. It is written, of course, in a style long since gone out of fashion, but it made its appearance when men of feeling and sentimental journeys were at the height of their popularity. Although commonly listed as a novel, the work is totally without narrative thread to unify its various scenes, episodes, and meditations. Only the observer himself, the Philosopher who writes in the first person, remains continuously in the foreground. To be sure, Combe begins with the usual disclaimer concerning resemblance to persons living or dead: "As in this little book a certain character is personated, no offence should be taken at any sentiments contained in it" (page 8). And certainly the book is not literal autobiography, but the "personated" Philosopher can only be an idealized self-image. Combe was never one to keep himself out of the foreground. Besides, he was now paying the bills himself and producing a book of his own—not written to order, not a revision of someone else's manuscript, but a work, however imitative in style and content, in which he might speak for himself. And inevitably, since he was a young man writing in the 1770s, he would assume the conventional posture; he would be the Man of Sensibility, the unworldly observer of the world, the Man of Feeling.

"What have I done, that I should not, during my stay in this great and flourishing city, take up the trade of Philosopher, and observe upon everything around me!—My eye has not been idle, nor, I trust, impertinent; but has attentively viewed the promiscuous objects which presented themselves before it, from the Phaetonic Honours of a triumphant Representative,—to the poor Blind-boy who sells tawdry pictures, for a penny a piece, at the Blind Stairs" (pages 10–11). With these words Combe reveals at once his knack of writing about topics currently in the news. For Bristol was still talking of the exciting polls of the previous October which had culminated in the election of Edmund Burke and his being accorded "Phaetonic Honours"—i.e. his being chaired through the streets of the city on November 3, "amidst an incredible number of people", one newspaper reported, "whose acclamations were beyond every thing of the kind that was ever seen or heard in this city". The Blind Stairs were also being talked about at the moment, for this old passageway between St Nicholas and Baldwin Streets was being repaired, and buildings were being torn down to widen the formerly dark and treacherous steps.

Topical references like these, always gratifying to a local audience, continue throughout the book. Inevitably the writer takes his "philosophical dish of tea" at Lamp-Lighter's Hall, a fashionable rendezvous much frequented by the very people most likely to read the book. The place derived its odd name from a former owner who had the contract for lighting street lamps in several city parishes. The quays, the Hotwells, Clifton, the new ferry across the Avon, Durdham Down, King's Weston, and other near-by sights are all visited and enjoyed by the Philosopher, making the work a kind of Sentimental Journey through Bristol. In a sense the city and its environs constitute the unifying principle of the book. "I love and admire the place", said the author, "which I mean to celebrate, with a real enthusiasm!" This sentiment would not harm the sale of the book locally, and for the moment there was little expectation that it would sell elsewhere, though Combe had paid to have it advertised in London.

Combe does not fail to mention the event which had profoundly shocked the city that spring, and which after two centuries is still remembered there, the accident at Pen Park Hole. The Reverend Thomas Newnham (or Newnam), a minor canon of the cathedral and son of a locally prominent banker, had gone out on March 17 with three other young people to inspect the "Hole", a cave extending perpendicularly into the earth some two hundred feet. The clergyman slipped and fell into the pit, and his body was not recovered until April 25. He was buried two days later on what would have been his twenty-fifth birthday.[20]

> ————Some weeks have flown away since, in a morning's ride, upon this part of the Down I met a young party, which consisted of two ladies and as many gentlemen;—one of whom, by his dress, appeared to be a clergyman.————A boy followed them, at some small distance, carrying a basket.————I passed them at a place, which being marshy, the ladies found a difficulty in getting over.————This trifling circumstance occasioned some lively sallies of imagination which engaged my attention.————When they had surmounted this little obstruction,—they all laughed so heartily and seemed to be in such good humour, that I quite longed to be of the party. But not knowing them,—I was obliged to content myself with wishing them happy on their little expedition, whatever it might be,—and a safe return.————But in the evening I heard, alas, that my wishes had been ineffectual.————A sad tale of misfortune was told me respecting this little groupe of social beings!————
>
> —But it has been on every tongue!—Nay, I hope, in every heart!—

I am sure it is, at this moment, in mine,—and I cannot dwell upon
it,———

(Pages 64–65)

Given the melodramatic possibilities of the incident, Combe seems
to have handled it with some restraint, possibly because the topic had
by this time almost exhausted itself, possibly because he really knew
little about the affair. But restraint was not a virtue much practised
or esteemed by sentimental writers, and Combe finds a good many
occasions in this book to portray pathetic characters or situations.
Eventually these sentimental passages are seen to form a kind of
logical structure supporting Combe's interpretation of human happiness. For throughout the book the Philosopher is taking stock of his
anomalous situation: though relatively poor in this prosperous city,
he finds himself the happiest of men. He gratefully notices, for example, that he is capable of sympathies which are denied businessmen.
He modestly tries not to flaunt his superiority, for "men of merchandize are useful, very useful beings in all communities;—and the
absolute support of many:—But if the love of gain so entirely en-
vellopes all traits of feeling and delicacy of sentiment, . . . I bless
heaven that I am not a man of merchandize" (page 27).

He observes a happy-go-lucky sailor sharing his pennies with a
blind ballad-singer and rewards him with four shillings. "God bless
your noble honour", the sailor exclaims. "But we will divide the
prize-money fairly". With that, he bestows two of the shillings on the
blind man. The episode gives the Philosopher pause. "Would the man
of trade have observed the blind songster?——Or if he had, would
he not have thought of a Beadle and a Work-house?——Would his
eyes have been open or his senses awake to the noble act of the honest
seaman?—or if they had,—would he not have sheltered himself in the
old observation,——that sailors get their money like horses and
spend it like asses?—If this be so;———I thank my propitious stars
that I am not a man of trade!" (pages 30–31).

The newspapers have informed the Philosopher that a friend is
newly arrived at the Hotwells, and he goes to pay a call.[21] Together
they look out the window at the people passing by. "There was youth
already grown old;——and beauty withered e'er it had bloomed:
———I beheld the middle-aged striving to secure old-age,——and
the old as anxious after life as if it was a new thing" (page 35). Then,
after various types of people stroll past,

a tall gentleman with a ghastly but smiling countenance came into the room.——I am really, said he, so much better and in such good spirits that I flatter myself I shall be able to dine with you.——Do so, said my friend, at half past three I shall expect you.——You may depend upon seeing me, added the gentleman, unless something very particular happens;——and accordingly he took his leave.——At half past three a message was sent to inform him that dinner was ready; but he could not come;—something very particular indeed had happened;—he was under an engagement he could not break:——for the servant returned and informed us——that he was dead.

(Pages 38–39)

After several more pathetic characters are described, the Philosopher exclaims, "And what would the Man of Gain say to all this?" These scenes, he feels, would only make the businessman congratulate himself on his exemption from such ills. The Philosopher's friend is deeply moved, and he forcefully replies, "If this be so;—'though I could be possessed of all the riches which the muddy stream before us bears on its tide,—I would not be a man of gain" (page 50).

An interlude prompted by the accident at Pen Park Hole occurs here as the Philosopher broods on the sorrows of life and records his somewhat lugubrious night-thoughts.

I look at the taper which burns dimly before me,—and it preaches with most pathetic eloquence.——I open the window-shutter, and not a star is visible!——It is all darkness;—and the darkness preaches also.

——The day is past,—and life hastes away!—It is now the hour of night,—and I look forwards to the tomb!——The sun which this evening blazed on the distant mountain,—e'er it sets again, may glimmer upon my grave!——O Amanda!—thou art fair as the lilly!—the rose is in the blush of thy cheek;—and thy heart is the temple of virtue!——I saw thee on thy evening walk,—and my eye followed thee till thou wert lost.——That eye, Amanda, may see thee no more!—and e'er a few hasty days are passed away, the worm may riot on thy cheek, —and thy heart become a clod of the valley.

May heaven have mercy upon us both!——I return again to my taper, and I behold it almost exhausted;—the flame begins to dance in the socket,—and will scarce light me to my chamber.——

——But I must have done!——

(Pages 68–69)

This style of writing has mercifully passed into history, though by comparison with other midnight-taper meditations of the time this one seems moderately controlled. Combe's Bristol readers would find it sensitive and touching, particularly because of the reference to

Amanda. For Combe was imitating Sterne in more than prose style, and Amanda was the name he was giving to the current object of his sentimental attention, Clara Stonhouse, daughter of Dr James Stonhouse.[22] Amanda is mentioned only twice in this book, but other and more personal references occur in the continuation published six weeks later—ample time for the relationship to assume more substance in Combe's imagination.

Before concluding his survey of the distribution of happiness, the Philosopher pauses to remark upon the orderly behaviour of the lower classes in Bristol. When he has had occasion to walk the streets at night he has been struck by the absence of noise and riot. "The Bacchanalian revels of midnight hours, which are so common in all other places, seem to be unknown in this peaceful city" (page 81). Such "civil and proper demeanor" is a credit to the lower classes and is evidence of "the attentive and correct conduct of the clergy,—the vigilance of the magistracy,—the grave deportment of the eminent and the wealthy,—and the industry of all.—For wherever idleness prevails,—there rudeness and riot and crimes will predominate" (page 83). It is a conventional passage which would scarcely have seemed alien to Cheapside itself.

The book concludes with a section showing the essential justice in the distribution of happiness among mankind. The Philosopher understands that men are differentiated by the extent to which they are dominated by mind and spirit rather than by body and sensual appetites. He takes a comprehensive view of society from labourer, to mechanic, to tradesman, to merchant, and on up through the learned professions till he reaches at the top "the man who is engaged in the practice of true philosophy". These varieties of life form links in "the great chain of social happiness" (page 97). Ignorance and sordid desire prevail at the lower end, intellectual and spiritual perfection at the upper. Every link in the chain has its function, and all ranks of society are useful and necessary. "But learning and the endowments of the mind alone, are now, have ever been, and will for ever be the objects of universal honour and admiration" (page 100). The book is then brought to conclusion by a description in elevated style of the philosopher himself. "If the most reasonable happiness springs from a tender and moderate tranquillity of the mind,——— undisturbed by the intrusions of sense or the turbulence of passion,— the philosopher may be said to approach nearer to the attainment of it, than any other character in life" (pages 105–6). Not unnaturally Combe can only conclude with the words, "I bless heaven———That I am a philosopher".

*   *   *

The Philosopher's complacency did not long go unchallenged. The opening pages of *Part the Second*, which appeared six weeks after the first volume, show him visibly suffering from various objections which readers have voiced. Although he protests that he cares only for the criticism of the virtuous (specifying Honorius, Engenius, and—"ah Heavens!"—Amanda), he undertakes to placate those critics who have found him "very hard upon the trading professions". He insists that he has been misunderstood. "When I mentioned the Man of Trade, the Man of Gain, and the Man of Merchandize, I wished to expose the sordid narrow soul,—not as belonging to any person, place, or station, but in whomsoever or wheresoever it might be found, or to whatever station it might be associated" (pages 44–45). He now trims his sails sufficiently to eulogize the businessman in terms altogether different from anything in the earlier work. "The . . . merchant is one of the most respectable characters of the British community.—The man, whose gain is the reward of his honest and laborious industry, is truly worthy of respect and estimation:—and the fair retail dealer, tho' inferior in station, is no less useful and necessary to the welfare and convenience of society. . . . I know many who are engaged in the trading and gainful professions, who would do honour to any situation in life,—and on whom nature has written gentleman in such legible characters, that they who run may read" (pages 49–50). Perhaps the Philosopher has not actually retracted anything, but he has managed to put his argument much more tactfully.

He tells an anecdote intended to win approval from contemporary Bristol readers, though certain to have a very different effect upon readers today. Having recently found himself in a gathering where the slave trade was being discussed, he had expressed himself strongly: it was an inhuman traffic, and no Christian could possibly engage in it. Then "a gentleman of a very pleasing appearance, informed me in a very genteel manner, that he had been and was, at that time, much concerned in that species of traffic.—But, Sir, he was pleased to add, I give you this information that I may have an oppor-

[42]

tunity of assuring you how much I approve your observations upon it". He freely acknowledged that the trade in slaves could not be justified on moral grounds, but said that as long as the colonies continued to use slave labour, the trade would continue. He would rejoice if substitutes could be found, "and would willingly forego a commerce which is so dishonourable to the human species". But until that time should come "there cannot be any good reason why I may not receive those profits which, if I were to relinquish them, would be eagerly pursued and gladly obtained by another". He makes it a matter of conscience to see that his employees treat the slaves "with the utmost humanity". He hopes that while the trade itself is condemned, "they, who follow it upon the most liberal and humane principles of which it is capable, may not be involved in the general censure" (pages 51–53).

A great many traders in Bristol and elsewhere undoubtedly justified their participation in the slave trade very much in these terms. They found themselves involved in something which they had not started and which they could not, as individuals, stop. Unwilling to give up their profits to other traders, they made themselves believe that they might operate on "humane principles". Combe's portrayal of this mild-mannered gentleman is a telling piece of historical evidence, the more convincing in that it is written without the slightest sense of the trader's bland rationalization. "I was delighted," the Philosopher exclaims, "and could, with real pleasure, have taken him to my bosom". This sentiment, which Combe expected his readers to echo, tells much of the social attitude which acquiesced in the slave traffic, and which was perhaps as culpable as the self-deception of the trader himself.

There is a curious epilogue to this story, and it also strikes the reader today in ways not anticipated by the author. The trader is just concluding his pious remarks when another man in the group suddenly quits the room, slamming the door behind him. Then, just as suddenly, he returns and angrily shouts, "You may say what you please of the Guinea-Trade,—that it is contrary to religion and humanity and all that;—but this I know," he adds, holding forth his hat, "that I have got this full of money by it." And with that he stalks out, slamming the door a second time. Here at any rate was no hypocrite, but the Philosopher merely says, "This is the sordid character whom I have marked for disgust" (pages 53–54).

The rest of *Part the Second* illustrates in various ways the pleasures which are available to the sensitive human being who is capable of enjoying them. The Philosopher attends a concert and writes an ode on "The Powers of Harmony". He indulges in nocturnal meditation and composes a sonnet to Philomel ("thy melting song . . . my pensive musings . . . the mournful strain . . . my ravish'd ear . . . And Fancy, to compleat my soul's delight, Displays the lov'd Amanda to my sight"). He recounts a "tender tale of distress" and moralizes on the vanity of human wishes. He composes a Shandian fragment on widows, ending it with three lines of *&c*'s and one of asterisks. Finally, he describes at length his parting with a clerical friend who is going to assume a valuable living in Ireland. He thinks of the pain arising from attachments which must be broken, and as he approaches the last page of the book he thinks of the last page of his life and envisions his own death-bed, thus providing by anticipation the death scene which always seemed to Combe the proper way to end a sentimental narrative:

> Amanda stealing into my chamber, shall gently open the curtains and present her dear form before me!—and when, with a pale face and streaming eyes, with an air of desolation and a look of inexpressive tenderness and anguish, she shall strive to speak, but strive in vain;— How shall I be able to wave my hand, as a signal to bid her depart,—— and not arrest my thoughts in their passage to Heaven!
>
> Or if it is decreed by the Great Arbiter of human allotments, that I should survive thee;——how, Amanda, shall I support those fearful moments, when I draw nigh to take my last look of thee as thou layest in thy coffin; and, having put the flowers into thy cold hands, I bend down to kiss thy pale, senseless lips, and bid thee an eternal adieu!
>
> All-gracious power?——that canst make firm the feeble knees, and give strength to the drooping spirits;—if I am doomed to meet this trying hour,——Oh strengthen me!—sustain me!——
>
> ——Have mercy upon me!——

FINIS.

The modern reader may need to be reminded that to Combe's contemporaries this passage came as the climax of the Philosopher's argument. A capacity for melancholy feelings accompanied literally by tears was to readers of sentimental prose the mark of moral superiority. The labouring man and the man of gain alike suffered from dulled sensibility and so were deprived of vital human sympathies. Only men with superior powers of feeling could possess the ultimate human capacity for appreciating sorrow. Perfectly to feel and to sympathize constituted both the highest obligation and the greatest reward of man at the very top of the great chain of social happiness.

* * *

On July 3, just three weeks after the first appearance of the *Philosopher in Bristol* and while the continuation of that work was being hastily written, Combe issued his poem, *Clifton*. In this work the writer, always sensitive to current tastes, managed to combine two popular genres, the Spenserian imitation and the topographical poem. To be sure, Spenserians were becoming a little passé by this time ("One more, then, and be satisfied!" exclaimed the *Monthly Review*, August 1776), but interest in topographical poems, particularly those describing hills, towns, and spas, was at its height. *Clifton* describes all three and makes a strong appeal to local loyalties by mentioning neighbouring towns and praising the whole city of Bristol. In his Preface Combe apologizes for using Spenser's quaint and obsolete expressions, but actually such expressions almost never appear in the poem. One may reasonably doubt that Combe knew much more of Spenser than could be found in Shenstone. His title-page bears a quotation from the latter and one from Virgil, but for the Latin Combe need not have gone farther than to Shenstone's *Elegies*, where it appears as an epigraph. But he is well aware of the topographical tradition and cites at once the then classical precedents of Pope, Dyer, and Pye:

> Times yet to come shall dwell upon his name;
> To him immortal praises do belong,
> Who gave to *Windsor's* woods eternal fame,
> And made the Thames to murmur in his song!
> Nor would I do his gentle spirit wrong
> Who hail'd on *Grongar* Hill the rising sun,
> And tun'd his reed the Cambrian Vales among.
> He too, of late, the Muses' wreath has won
> Who sung, in pleasing strains, the *Hill of Farringdon*.
>
> (Stanza II)

Combe, in emulation of these poets, will write of Clifton. But first he must praise Bristol itself and, in particular, the city's daughters. Sprowle appears and the muses prepare a garland for her. Then there is Stonhouse (the Muse is enraptured); he might praise her till sun-down, but the other dryads would complain of neglect. This is en-chanted ground; "unnumbered beauties meet my ravished eyes". He praises great men who live here or who are associated with the place: Goldney, Chatham, and Draper ("thou honor to the human race"). 'Tis noon, and the poet climbs to the hilltop, where he looks out over "Avon's winding wave". His eye seeks the place where "Southwell's fair domain rises, in awful beauty, from the vale". He would like to visit Henbury and King's Weston, neighbouring villages, but the Muse is fatigued. He speaks of health and illness, themes suggested by the spa at the foot of the hill. The last ten stanzas revert to melancholy themes. Even Flirtilla must prepare to die. How deceptive are life's gay delights! In vain he appeals for Laura's life to be spared. She dies, hapless fate. Oh lead me where the gloomy cypress grows; there shall I tell my grievous tale of woe. There will I tell that Laura is no more. But I must sing no more. "Ah, then, farewell my Lyre!—Thy strains are o'er: Farewell! for I shall strike thy sounding strings no more".

Clifton survives today only in bibliographies as an example of the topographical poem. Combe was incapable of writing serious poetry, a fact which he himself often acknowledged—though expecting, perhaps, to be contradicted. He was incapable, however, of resisting the impulse to write, and a great many of his efforts survive. *Clifton* is by all odds the most interesting poem of serious intent that he ever published, and his first readers found it compelling evidence of the author's talent and sensitivity. The view of the larger audience, to whom Combe was unknown, was tersely expressed by the *Town and Country Magazine* (October 1776): "a pretty descriptive poem".

*   *   *

While Combe was busy writing and publishing these books in Bristol, a small volume appeared in London which, though apparently not of his planning, consisted largely of things from his pen. This was *Sterne's Letters to His Friends on Various Occasions*, printed for George Kearsly and Joseph Johnson and published on June 28. Of the twelve letters in this volume, Combe subsequently acknowledged authorship of Letters IV to X, inclusive. They had "made their first appearance in a provincial newspaper", he said, implying that they had been reprinted in various magazines and finally in this book without his knowledge or permission.[23] Scholars have searched for the letters in many newspapers without result, but Letter V has been discovered in the *London Magazine* for March 1774, more than a year before the book was published.

Of the seven letters which Combe called his own, one (Letter IX) has been found to survive in Sterne's handwriting; the other six are believed to be indeed Combe's. Two of the remaining letters (XI and XII) are unaccounted for and have been ascribed unconvincingly to Combe. He has also been held responsible for the book itself, but it is difficult to see how he could have assembled and edited the volume while publishing books in Bristol on June 12, July 3, and July 26. The Introduction is written somewhat in Combe's manner, but its authorship remains very much in question. Combe makes no mention of this publication in the lists of his works which he so carefully prepared before his death. His other imitations are mentioned, but not this one.

For the next twenty-eight years Combe was to publish from time to time more "Sterne" letters which he had himself contrived. No one has paid higher or more reluctant tribute to Combe's skill in creating these letters than the scholars who have attempted to winnow the true from the false in the Sterne canon. Their problem has been rendered more difficult by the knowledge that Combe did, in fact, have genuine Sterne letters in his possession—how many, no one can say. He sometimes printed them more or less accurately, but often he seems to have made a single letter provide the basic material of two or more of his own manufacture. Nothing could be more exasperating to modern scholarship, but it must be said that eighteenth-century readers accepted the practice without the indignation we now feel. *Sterne's Letters to His Friends* was recognized on publication as another of the many imitative works which had been cluttering the bookstalls for fifteen years. Readers took up the volume with mildly sceptical interest, not looking for an accurate or even a semi-authentic text, but rather hoping to find new ingenuity and wit applied to themes made popular by Laurence Sterne. Of this particular publication, the *Monthly Review* (September 1775) simply remarked, "Some of these [letters] have formerly appeared in the newspapers, and these carry with them a strong internal evidence of authenticity: of a few others, in this little collection, we have some doubts; but in a case of this nature it is impossible to speak with certainty".

Combe was proud of his skill in putting together such letters, and he had reason to be. No one would be more surprised than he to know that readers of another century have been outraged by his "supposititious" writings. "As to their imitative merits", he wrote, "I shall say little;—tho' I believe there will be few who, on reading them, will not be sometimes put in mind of the style and manner of the late Mr. Sterne's writings. . . . But mere imitations of style and manner are of little value, unless they heighten those sentiments, and enforce those instructions, which soften and improve the heart".[24] Combe honestly believed that these letters were "well calculated to produce such beneficial effects".

*　　*　　*

Throughout the summer Samuel Reddish's company of actors had been performing at the theatre in King Street, Bristol, with a repertory ranging from *The Beggar's Opera*, *The Conscious Lovers*, *She Stoops to Conquer*, *Othello*, *A New Way to Pay Old Debts*, and *Much Ado about Nothing*, to such long-forgotten pieces as *Braganza*, *Lionel and Clarissa*, and *The Choleric Man*. Near the end of the season the company performed a series of benefit nights honouring and rewarding each of twelve popular actors, the last such night being reserved for the most popular of all, John Henderson, soon to become a leading actor on the London stage. He was to play Falstaff in *The Merry Wives of Windsor*, eventually his most famous role.

The event was announced for September 11 by a playbill distributed the previous week (Plate 5) and by advertisements in the Bristol newspapers, one of which added a note calling particular attention to the afterpiece: "We are informed that the piece called *The Flattering Milliner*, or *Modern Half-Hour*, now in rehearsal at the Theatre in King-Street, to be performed on Monday next, for the benefit of Mr. Henderson, is written by the ingenious Author of the *Philosopher in Bristol*".[25]

Our knowledge of this play is limited to the cast of characters printed on the playbill; it was never published, and even the manuscript has now disappeared. Ordinarily these afterpieces were trivial farces offering (as evidently in this instance) an opportunity for the singers and dancers in the company to perform. But even if *The Flattering Milliner* was a trifle, Combe understandably cherished the

The last BENEFIT *this Season.*
(Not acted Here these Seven Years.)
For the Benefit of Mr. HENDERSON.
AT the THEATRE, in KING-STREET, on
MONDAY next, the 11th of *September*, will be
perform'd a COMEDY call'd,

The Merry Wives of Windsor.

Ford by Mr. Reddish, Sir Hugh Evans, by Mr. Parsons,
Slender by Mr. Cautherley, Doctor Caius by Mr. Quick,
Mr. Page by Mr. Davies, Justice Shallow by Mr. Wrighten,
Host of the Garter by Mr. Booth, Fenton by Mr. Garland,
Antient Pistol by Mr. Carpenter, Simple by Mr. Floor, Bar-
dolph by Mr. Fox, Nym by Mr. Edkins, and Sir John Fal-
staff, by Mr. Henderson.——Mrs. Page by Mrs. Davies, Ann
Page by Miss Wheeler, Mrs. Quickly by Mrs. Booth, and
Mrs. Ford by Miss Barsanti.

After the Play will be perform'd A NEW PIECE
of One Act, call'd
The FLATTERING MILLINER;
Or, A MODERN HALF HOUR.
Written expressly on this Occasion by a GENTLEMAN *residing*
near this City.
Mr. Hobbleworth by Mr. Parsons, Sir Flippery Flirtem by
Mr. Davies, Sailor by Mr. Quick, Lady Dorothy Doubtful by
Mrs. Davies, Isabella by Mrs. Brett, Sailor's Wife by Miss
Costallo, and Mrs. Blond by Mrs. Wrighten.
DANCING by Mr. SIMONET, and Signora VIDINI.

To which will be added,
An   O   D   E,
Upon Dedicating a STATUE to SHAKESPEARE, at
Stratford-upon-Avon, written by DAVID GARRICK,
Esq; and spoken by himself at the JUBILEE, there insti-
tuted in Honor of that Poet.
The ODE to be spoken by Mr. HENDERSON.
The Vocal Parts by *Mrs. Wrighten, Mr. Davies, &c. &c.*

TICKETS to be had of Mr. HENDERSON, at Mrs. MOF-
FET's, in Prince's-street, and of Mr. HEATH, at the
Theatre, where Places for the Boxes may be taken.

5. *Playbill for the Theatre in King Street, Bristol, September 11, 1775.*
Bristol Archives Office

[49]

memory of its performance, preserving the manuscript as long as he lived. In 1852 it was in the possession of Robert Cole, who described it in the *Gentleman's Magazine*.[26] Written entirely in Combe's hand, the manuscript bore the following notation: "This little performance was written in one evening and part of the succeeding morning." Believe this who will, the remark is characteristic of Combe's pose of gentlemanly negligence. "These observations", he writes of the *Philosopher in Bristol*, "were written in the evening's solitary hour, when, after the glare of day is past, I sometimes repose from severer studies". And he assures us that the Spenserian stanzas of *Clifton* came into his mind "without the least premeditation". In point of fact, there is good reason to believe that Combe prepared these first literary works and many of those which followed with painstaking care, notwithstanding his dilettante posture.

It will be observed that Henderson did not appear in the farce. After playing Falstaff in the *Merry Wives*, he was now preparing for the final item on the evening's bill, the reading of "An Ode, Upon Dedicating a STATUE to SHAKESPEARE, at Stratford-upon-Avon, written by DAVID GARRICK, Esq., and spoken by himself at the JUBILEE, there instituted in Honour of the Poet". In the six years since the Stratford Jubilee, Henderson had made a specialty of reading this ode. His own friends preferred an informal version reserved for private audiences in which he imitated Garrick's reading of the lines while being frequently interrupted by Dr Johnson, interposing critical remarks.[27] But on the night of his Bristol benefit, Henderson gave his most formal rendition with "Vocal Parts by Mrs. Wrighten, Mr Davies, &c. &c."

In accordance with provincial custom, no review of the performance was published, and no information about it survives from any other source. It was evidently something of a Bristol gala, however, the last benefit of the season and for the best actor in the company. It is inconceivable that Combe should have been absent on the occasion; very probably he held court in a prominent box of the circle surrounding the stalls. The playhouse, which still stands in King Street, is an intimate theatre with a strongly local character even today. All of Combe's friends would certainly be present, as much to see *The Flattering Milliner* as to see Henderson's performance.

The evening may well have climaxed Combe's triumphs in Bristol. It was, however, the last we hear of him in the city. He evidently packed his possessions—this time, so far as we know, paying his bills—and took his departure for London. It was only necessary for him to take a place in the new "Bristol Dilligence, or Flying Post Chaise" to arrive in Fleet Street, 114 miles away, sixteen hours later. He evidently did so without delay, and there is no evidence that Bristol ever saw him again.

To the end of his life, however, he remembered the summer of 1775 with pleasure—as well he might, considering the literary and social recognition he had achieved at that time. For the *Philosopher in Bristol* had no sooner been published than Combe found himself again surrounded by admirers in the city where seven years earlier he had lived like a duke. But now he was admired, not for his extravagance but for his talents—even, probably, for some he did not have. It was a new and gratifying experience.

Although he had been deprived of congenial social life during the years of his hand-to-mouth existence, he had by no means lost his social bearing and personal attractiveness. In Bristol he had an opportunity to display them to advantage, and he found himself enjoying once again the civilized pleasures of friendship with a group of cultivated people who shared his tastes and—apparently more important—his sentiments. Even the names of these friends come through to some extent, though as individuals they remain shadowy. Who, for example, was the Charles Hayward, Esq., whom Combe singles out for special mention in the dedication of the *Philosopher in Bristol*? Was he possibly the Hayward (first name unrecorded) who had been a contemporary of Combe's at Eton? Was he the friend whom Combe, imitating Sterne and Hall-Stevenson, called "Eugenius"? Then there was the Reverend William Speare, a youth just out of Oxford whose acquaintance with Combe is evident from annotations in his copy of the *Philosopher in Bristol*. (He it is who identifies Amanda as Clara Stonhouse.) And there was also the Reverend John Prior Estlin, a young clergyman recently come to Lewin's Mead Unitarian Chapel. From him we learn of an unnamed friend who remembered meeting Combe in Tyndall's Park with Hannah More and another young lady, very possibly Amanda, both in tears over something which the Philosopher was telling them.

"In the name of Heaven, Combe," his acquaintance later demanded, "what had you been saying to those poor girls with whom I met you the other day, to produce such distress?"

"What distress? When?" asked the nonchalant Combe. On being reminded of the occasion, he replied, "Oh! Nothing at all—some melancholy tale of imagination, trumped up to suit their palate and diversify the scene. But of the pearly drops I was not so keen an observer as yourself".[28]

The story is the more credible for having survived without Combe's assistance. Hannah More was three years younger than Combe and was teaching in her sister's boarding-school at 10 Park Street. Amanda's father, Dr James Stonhouse, lived at No. 7 in the same street[29] and advised Hannah on her reading. She, too, was launching her literary career in 1775 and would be well aware of Combe's activities. There is no reason to doubt that she and Combe were acquainted, nor that Combe would be averse to telling two young ladies a pathetic tale.

Nothing whatever is known of "Sprowle" and "B——y", two young ladies mentioned in *Clifton*. Was the second of these possibly a Bristol relative of Robert Berkeley? And did Combe meet his old friend and, on one occasion, his antagonist, Thomas, the Wicked Lord Lyttelton, in Bristol? From a passage in Lyttelton's *Letters* (actually forged by Combe and published a few years later), one may infer that the two met when Lyttelton visited the Hotwells that summer.[30] There was also the actor, John Henderson, with whom Combe must have had some dealings regarding *The Flattering Milliner*. Some basis for acquaintance existed between the two men; both had been born in the Cheapside area, though a few years apart, and both were great admirers of Laurence Sterne; Henderson, in fact, was always called Shandy by his friends.

These questions, though unanswered, inevitably suggest something of the life which Combe led that summer. And if the personalities are somewhat dim, social activities are more detailed: riding out to King's Weston, a fashionable recreation of the upper classes; walking about the quays, watching the loading and unloading of vessels; breakfasting at the Hotwells House and afterwards sauntering along the Hotwells Parade; crossing the ferry "to take my favourite airing on Leigh Down"; strolling across Durdham Down on May Day, watching children gather their flowers; having tea at Lamp-Lighter's Hall and watching the activity on the quay outside; walking home from church with Amanda; spending an evening in conversation with Honorius and Honoria; attending a concert—"The company was not large but very select"; sitting thoughtfully under an oak in a friend's garden; attending the theatre in King Street. Life in Bristol was evidently not without its compensations for a young man just discovering his literary talents and living for the nonce as a Man of Feeling.

Long afterward, remembering this summer with nostalgic pleasure, Combe told his friends about the *Philosopher in Bristol* and reprinted two sections of the book in a London newspaper.[31] He wished for, but could not obtain, a copy of *Clifton*. A touching bit of evidence is to be found in a copy of that book now on the shelves of the Bristol Central Library. On its title-page appears the following inscription: "By Mr Coomb, Author of Dr Syntax. I have searched for this Poem for many years without success for the purpose of presenting it to its author who expressed to me a strong wish to possess a copy. But it has come into my hand too late—my old Friend is no more.— G. F. E. Novemb^r 1823". The identity of G. F. E. is lost beyond recovery, but his words have just the touch of pathos which would have been appreciated by the one-time Sentimental Philosopher.

CHAPTER III

SATIRIST

But now, another act displays
The folly of my former days:
A new scene opens of my life;
For faith, my Lord, I took a wife.
—Doctor Syntax

AFTER AN absence of five years, Combe returned to London in the autumn of 1775 a man in his early thirties with a new posture. He was a Man of Feeling who had discovered his literary talents and was now determined to transfer his provincial success to the capital. Never one to underestimate his abilities, he was taking a longer chance than he knew, but he had good reason to make the move at this time. He was not penniless, and he had—or thought he had—useful connections in both Mayfair and Paternoster Row. He settled accordingly in the parish of St Martin-in-the-Fields, midway between those sections of town, and began his assault on both. Within six months he had made some impression in each direction, though unfortunately not just what he had anticipated.

His literary experience had been of two kinds, editing (including revising, ghost-writing, proofreading, and other routine tasks) and original writing. There were booksellers in London who had already handled both kinds of his work, though very possibly without knowing his name. Thomas Lewis's name had appeared on the title-page of the *Description of Patagonia* which Combe had edited and largely re-written; other assignments of the same kind might reasonably be solicited from that bookseller. And the two men who had published *Sterne's Letters to His Friends* containing six of Combe's imitations had displayed, perhaps unwittingly, an interest in his original writing. Whatever his relationship with them may have been, he would think of them as possible employers, and both did eventually publish more of his work, though not immediately.

Yet Combe met with only moderate success in launching his new career, either as an original writer or as an editor and man-of-all-work for the booksellers. He did procure one editorial assignment in connection with an ill-fated didactic poem, *The Œconomy of Health*, published jointly by John Almon, Thomas Becket, Peter De Hondt, and Francis Newbery. The book was handsomely printed octavo with engraved title-page and seems to have been edited with care, but it was an expensive failure.[1] Perhaps Combe did no more than write the thirteen-page introduction and prepare the copy for the press; it seems most unlikely that he was responsible for any part of the verses, which are very bad and not at all in his style. However that may be, he was never again employed by any of these prominent booksellers.

As for his original writing, he succeeded only in republishing his *Philosopher in Bristol* and *Clifton*, this time with the name of a London bookseller, George Robinson of Paternoster Row, on the title-page, together with that of the Bristol printers, Rouths & Nelson, successors to George Routh. These titles appeared simultaneously on June 1, 1776, and evidently disappeared almost at once. They were scornfully dismissed by the *Monthly Review* (August and September), and Robinson was another bookseller with whom Combe never had further dealings. It was not an encouraging start.

Meanwhile, there were Combe's supposed friends in Mayfair. Of his headway in that more exalted neighbourhood, one damaging bit of evidence survives: by spring 1776 he had again made himself known to the Hertfords. It will be recalled that Lord Hertford had been the English ambassador in Paris at the time of Combe's visit in 1763–4 and that two of his sons, Viscount Beauchamp and Henry Conway, had been at Eton with him. The renewal of this old acquaintanceship must have raised Combe's hopes at a time when his private affairs were going badly. Just how badly they were going, indeed, becomes evident from the upshot of this new encounter with that noble family: under some highly ambiguous arrangement, he agreed to marry Beauchamp's discarded mistress. The circumstances remain in doubt, but the consequences were written large on the pages of the *Morning Post* and were remembered for many years.

* * *

Neither Combe's marriage nor the satires to which it gave rise can be discussed without reference to the temper of those times so very different from our own. Perhaps the year 1775, when Combe arrived in London, was "the best of times and the worst of times", as Dickens says in the memorable first paragraph of *A Tale of Two Cities*, but the novelist's striking review of those times does little justice to them. It is not so much false as distorted and exaggerated. The same criticism applies to much of the social history written during the past hundred and fifty years. It has usually tended to underscore the details which have seemed most striking to the historians rather than those of contemporary significance. In particular, the Victorians were shocked, not unpleasurably, by the amorous escapades of their ancestors, partly because they were carried on with so little concealment. Sex indeed provided delicious scandal in the 1770s, as the newspapers abundantly reveal. Sheridan made comic use of it in *The School for Scandal*, but the central and serious issue of that play concerns inheritance of property. When readers of the *Morning Post* were supplied with innuendoes concerning the irregular sex life of the nobility, they were amused by its absurdity or its comic embarrassments. What scandalized them more than adultery was the madness of wastrels in St James's Street, gambling away their patrimony on the turn of a card. Seduction of young girls, at least if they were members of the upper or middle class, was regarded as vicious, but the casual adulteries of men and women whose marriages were often coldly calculated financial or social arrangements seemed routine and often comic. *The Town and Country Magazine* was taking this point of view in every issue.

There was certainly no lack of sensational material in the newspapers when Combe arrived in the city. They were filled as perhaps never before or since with lurid accounts of street robberies, riots, hangings, and violence of all kinds. These incidents constituted the daily routine and perhaps excited no more uneasiness than today's usual toll of traffic fatalities. On the brighter side, "paragraphers", purveyors of gossip, supplied a running comment on the follies and indiscretions of the nobility, hinting at outrageous behaviour, commonly amorous, and setting forth the financial involvements. This lively commentary provided a much-needed comic relief from the serious news, mainly discouraging communications from America. Occasionally the two subjects were combined: "A gentleman of consequence in the political world", reported the *Morning Post*

(December 31, 1776), "made a bet of 1000 guineas last night at one of the fashionable clubs in St James's-street, that America was at the feet of Great Britain before the 25th of June, 1777." Hundreds of such bets were formally entered in the books of the various clubs and constituted obligations of high priority, certainly to be paid before the tradesmen's bills. Fortunes were won and lost nightly at the faro tables, and the paragraphers shocked their readers with the news, concealing identities under titillating disguises.

Women were not admitted to these clubs, but they had clubs of their own and were by no means exempt from the vice. "A young new married Countess [probably recognizable to contemporaries] lost the other night at *Vingt une* [*sic*], six hundred guineas, which her Lord very readily paid next morning" (*Morning Post*, November 23, 1776). The most dazzling young woman in London, Georgiana, Duchess of Devonshire, lost vast sums at cards and in speculation; lacking courage to confide in her husband, she borrowed to meet her debts and borrowed again to pay exorbitant interest. When her plight became known to the Duke he paid up in full and advised her not to repeat the mistake, but such advice was futile in such times.[2]

Inevitably and ominously, the trade of moneylending flourished. Ordinarily ten or more of the advertisements on the front page of the *Morning Post* offered large loans to those who could provide good security, and the big losers were necessarily those with inherited property or with prospects of inheritance. The moneylenders explicitly addressed these individuals, assuming frankly that they might find themselves suddenly in need of large sums. "Money expedititiously on bond," one Mr. Bonnel repeatedly announces. "Noblemen, Gentlemen, Ladies of Fortune, or immediate heirs to such, having occasion privately to borrow any permanent or temporary sum on bond, or by annuity, or otherways, may positively have from 300 l. to any amount in the space of five hours". One such moneylender advertised loans at five per cent, but in actual fact the interest usually ran much higher, not infrequently as high as the fifty per cent mentioned by Moses in Sheridan's play. It was not only at the faro table that fortunes were lost.

The School for Scandal, which opened on May 8, 1777, makes high comedy of all these upper-class follies, and the modern audience laughs at what it assumes to be fantastic exaggeration. The contemporary audience laughed because it recognized a witty handling of familiar material, fully realistic, outrageous, and amusing. Sheridan stresses, of course, the popular taste for gossip, and indeed many other writers noted that as gambling destroyed fortunes, the passion for scandal destroyed reputations. In a satire published three weeks before the play opened, Combe had dealt with the same subject more specifically. Until a month before the opening, Sheridan was still calling the play *The School for Slander*,[3] but in the interest of accuracy he changed the title. Only that which is untrue can be called slanderous, and much of the sensational gossip of the time was based on undeniable fact.

Four of the most notorious scandals of the century occurred within the first eighteen months after Combe's arrival from Bristol. They were recounted in great detail by the newspapers, which treated them with great seriousness; three of them had overtones of sex, but all of them hinged basically on money. The first of these scandals was the trial of Mrs Margaret Caroline Rudd and the two Perreau brothers for forgery. The two brothers (one of them her paramour) were convicted and hanged, largely on the evidence of Mrs Rudd, their accomplice, whom the jury found "not guilty according to the evidence before us" (*Morning Chronicle*, January 13, 1776). This verdict struck the public as more than slightly ambiguous, and everyone believed that the evidence presented against Mrs Rudd was suspiciously inadequate. Many thought her the most guilty of the three, but she escaped punishment altogether and was for some time afterward a notorious London celebrity.[4] A curious footnote to the case appeared in the *Gazetteer* on January 16, 1776: "The custom of gambling on matters of life and death, was never more shockingly conspicuous than in the case of the Perreaus, immense sums having been *done* (as it is phrased) and large bets having been made at several Coffee-houses on the fate of the unhappy Brothers. Bets of 100 guineas to five were offered and refused at a coffee-house near St James's, that Robert Perreau would receive his Majesty's clemency before twelve o'clock this day." The execution took place the following day.

In April, Elizabeth Chudleigh, Duchess of Kingston, was brought to trial before the Lords on a charge of bigamy. She had been a famous court beauty when, many years earlier, she had secretly married Augustus John Hervey, later the third Earl of Bristol and an acquaintance of Combe's. There was never a legal divorce, but in 1769, after

an ecclesiastical court had annulled the marriage, she became the wife
of the Duke of Kingston. When the Duke died in 1773 his very extensive estate passed into the hands of the Duchess, and the residuary
heirs brought suit for bigamy, hoping to obtain the property for
themselves. By 1775 the story was in the newspapers, and for months
it was bandied about the schools for scandal. Gossip added colour to
the subject by resurrecting anecdotes (there were plenty of them) concerning the youthful follies of the Duchess when she had been Maid
of Honour to the Princess of Wales. Her trial in Westminster Hall
before the Lords in full regalia was the most brilliant spectacle since
the coronation of George III. It lasted for five days and was the
greatest social event for many seasons. Found guilty, the Duchess
became a Countess (for her first husband was now an Earl), was
granted benefit of clergy, and escaped punishment. She left England
for a bizarre life on the Continent, her fortune essentially intact, the
paragraphers in hot pursuit.[5]

Four months later London was supplied with a new topic for
horrified conversation, the suicide of John Damer, eldest son of the
enormously wealthy Earl of Dorchester and contemporary of Combe's
at Eton. He had married Anne Seymour, daughter of Field-Marshal
Henry Seymour Conway and cousin (later heir) of Horace Walpole.
What is more to the point, she was a cousin of Viscount Beauchamp.
By the summer of 1776 Damer had accumulated debts of £70,000,
partly at the gaming-tables, partly in acquiring a fantastically costly
wardrobe. His father refused to pay his debts, and on August 15 he
shot himself at the Bedford Arms, Covent Garden, after having had
supper, said the newspapers, "with a blind fiddler and three women
of the town". This "terrible and shocking event" dominated conversation for weeks, and when Damer's personal effects were auctioned women of wealth and prominence sought to outbid each other
for pieces of his apparel. The sale, which was reported with great
gaiety by the paragraphers, produced in all some £15,000.[6]

The *Morning Post* was still supplying its readers with the latest
information concerning Damer's wardrobe when, on February 10,
1777, it announced an even more sensational event. A fashionable
clergyman, the Reverend Dr Dodd, had been arrested on a charge of
forging Lord Chesterfield's signature to a bond for £4,200 and receiving the money. Over the next five months the story of this "Unfortunate Divine" dominated conversation and filled the newspapers.

Dodd's trial and conviction at the Old Bailey, the unsuccessful efforts
to obtain a pardon, the final scene on Tyburn Hill—the whole sordid
story was made to order for the scandal industry, and scores of hackwriters produced suitable moral pamphlets on the subject.

Here indeed was material for sensational journalism and for satire
more scathing than Sheridan's witty commentary. Combe was fully
aware of it and eventually exploited all of these topics in his writings,
but at first he remained silent; he had not come to London to be a
critic of society. His success in Bristol as a Man of Feeling and literary
dilettante had been notably gratifying, and he had no intention of
changing roles. He would write in a genteel way, perhaps quietly
doing some editorial work—hackwriting, to put it bluntly—but he
must at all costs maintain his amateur standing as a man of letters and
a gentleman. Frankly to accept employment and to busy himself
earning his living, even by his pen, would be to relinquish his social
pretensions altogether. This he was as yet unwilling to do. His
personal vanity and his determination to be a gentleman at all costs—
that is, to live in fashion without visible means of support[7]—urged
him to make one last effort to establish himself with his former
friends in West End society. Then on short notice he found himself
married, and a bomb exploded beneath his feet. It was Beauchamp
(Plate 6) who had lighted the fuse.

* * *

An entry in the Marriage Register of fashionable St George's Church,
Hanover Square, tersely sets forth the facts of Combe's marriage:
"William Combes, of St. Martin's in the Fields, Esq., & Maria
Foster, of this parish. License." Marriage by licence took place without the formality and delay of publishing banns; in other words, the
wedding was a hasty affair. The *Morning Post* (May 22) provided
additional detail and innuendo:

> On Thursday last, the 16th instant, were married Mr.
> William Combes of the parish of St. Martin's in the
> Field, "a Gentleman who is universally known, from
> having distinguished himself in this, and other
> countries, in various shapes and characters," and
> Maria Foster, commonly called Miss Harley, of
> Norfolk-street, near the west end of Oxford-road, at

6. *Viscount Beauchamp, by Reynolds. From the original in Ragley Hall, by permission of Lord Hertford*

St. George's Church, Hanover, by the Rev. Richard
Pitt, in the presence of Mr. R[ichard] C[osway],
Painter, who gave the Lady away, and of Mr. Caleb
Grenville, Clerk of the church. It is said that the Lady
is possessed of an income of about 150 l. per ann. in
annuities, and about 1000 l. in money, partly in
effects, and partly in the funds. The ceremony was
conducted with the greatest privacy, and the married
pair immediately left London, without informing any
body where they were going.

A letter subsequently written by Horace Walpole to William
Mason supplies details which the *Morning Post* had only insinuated.
The author of certain satires "hurled at the heads of the Hertfords",
says Walpole, is "a Captain Coombes" who has derived his right to
be executioner from "having married a common woman, who was
kept by Lord Beauchamp, and dismissed by him for having *made him
a present* that she cannot pardon his not having pardoned, though he
gave her £500 at parting". The "present", Walpole's editors remark, was presumably "a venereal one". Walpole later amended this
story slightly, asserting that Combe "married a common woman,
who had been kept by Francis, Lord Beauchamp . . . and who dismissed her for boundless infidelities, yet settled £300 a year on
her".[8] Walpole was Beauchamp's cousin and correspondent, and this
candid acknowledgement of a cast mistress is doubtless the simple
truth of the matter. Some cash settlement would naturally be forthcoming, though no two accounts of the financial arrangements agree
in detail.

Neither of the two reasons advanced by Walpole for the dismissal
of Maria can have been the compelling one. Beauchamp was on the
point of marrying a second time, and once Maria was safely wedded
to Combe she would not further embarrass him. The arrangements
were evidently concluded with dispatch, for only four days after
Combe's marriage, and also by special licence, "Lord Viscount Beauchamp, eldest son of the Earl of Hertford" was married to "the Hon.
Lady Isabella Ann Ingram Shepheard, Daughter of Lord Viscount
Irwin". His first wife had died four years after their marriage, leaving
no surviving children; his second, Lady Isabella, commonly called
"The Sultana", provided him with a son, Francis Charles, who
became the third Marquis and ultimately the original of Thackeray's
Lord Steyne. Thirty years after her marriage the Sultana succeeded

Lady Jersey as mistress to the Prince of Wales. Romantic love was no more the issue in Beauchamp's marriage than in Combe's. What mattered was money, and before he was thirty-four Beauchamp had married two of the richest heiresses in England.

Combe's willingness to enter into his wretched marriage must be judged partly by the times, partly by his desperate financial straits. Prudent men, of course, whether in Cheapside or in Mayfair, were expected to give thought to the financial promise of marriage. Combe's father had done so thirty-six years earlier, and Lord Beauchamp was doing so now. But Combe had neither fortune nor prospects to justify any claim to a well-dowered wife. If he was to escape a second plunge into the submerged world of tavern waiters, he must accept any expedient which presented itself. His delusions of social superiority debarred him from sordid middle-class employment; he had no intention of becoming a "Man of Gain". Cheapside, he hoped, was irrevocably buried. Then he thought he saw a way out of his difficulties by marrying Maria Foster. Others, including the once fashionable though now disgraced Dr Dodd, had improved their chances by marrying discarded mistresses. But Combe needed the kind of hard-headed advice which his father had received from William Alexander. Without such help, he omitted some necessary precaution and things went wrong. Either he misunderstood the agreement, or Beauchamp defaulted, or both. Thomas Campbell thought that Combe had been promised an annuity which, once the marriage had taken place, was not forthcoming.[9] Whatever happened, Combe quickly came to feel that his aristocratic friends had taken advantage of him. In the phrase of the time, they had simply regarded him as a pigeon to be plucked. It was bitterly disillusioning.

Apart from his immediate disappointment, galling as that was, the episode forced upon Combe the realization that all his hopes of identifying with the life of fashion were dashed. Whatever his personal qualifications, he would always encounter barriers. He had the wrong background, the wrong accent,[10] and insufficient funds. Blazing with indignation, he now saw his former acquaintances in a new light, and what he saw was repugnant. He could no longer be the languid spectator of life, the sentimental philosopher; he could only be an outraged human being. The shattering experience must have been extremely painful for the man, but it made the writer. He exploded with nine separate satires in 1777 and continued the series until 1785, though with diminishing rapidity as his anger waned and he recovered his poise. These satires included some of the best serious writing he was ever to produce.

* * *

Nothing whatever is known of Combe's movements or activities during the eight months which followed his wedding. Perhaps the *Morning Post* was right in saying that "the married pair immediately left London without informing any body where they were going". Some kind of immediate cash settlement had almost certainly been arranged, and with the prospect of more to come the couple might feel justified in taking an expensive holiday, whether or not it was an idyllic honeymoon. By the end of the year, however, they knew that disappointment was in store, and when Combe's attempts—whatever they were—to effect a satisfactory agreement with the Hertfords had failed, he began writing his first satire.

On January 25, 1777, the *Evening Post* carried the following announcement:

> This day was published, in 4to, price 1s. 6d.
> THE DIABOLIAD, A POEM. Dedicated to the worst
> Man in his Majesty's dominions.
> To reign is worth ambition, tho' in hell!—Milton.
> Printed for G. Kearsly, No. 46, Fleet-street.

Combe's enemies evidently had a good idea of what was coming, and indeed a preliminary announcement of the *Diaboliad* had appeared in the newspapers a week earlier. Someone had immediately prepared an advertisement embarrassing to Combe and had been able to place it in the *Evening-Post* within an inch of Kearsly's advertisement:

> WHEREAS Mr. WILLIAM COMBES, left his Lodgings
> at Evesham, in Worcestershire, about three years and
> a half ago, without any previous notice given.—
> This is to inform the said Mr. Combes if he does
> not pay his debt for board and lodging, within the
> space of two months from the date hereof, his effects
> will be sold to discharge the same.
> Evesham, January 17, 1777.

Three and a half years earlier would be in mid-July 1773, just before Combe's employment by Robert Berkeley at Spetchley Park, less than twenty miles from Evesham. It looks very much as though the advertisement was based on factual information, but a more awkward moment for Combe to be publicly reminded of that episode can scarcely be imagined.

Combe's state of mind is made unmistakably clear by the first sentence of his "Dedication to the Worst Man in His Majesty's Dominions":

MY LORD,

I have not the honour of being acquainted with your Lordship; and as I do not wish there should be any attempt to violate my property, to estrange the affections of my wife, to seduce my daughter, or corrupt my son; it is a matter of real satisfaction to me, that I have not formed any connections with you.

The "worst man" is by no means Lord Beauchamp, whom Combe contemptuously passes over as "without one vice that e'er exalts to fame". Contemporary readers were agreed that Combe's dedication was addressed to Simon Luttrell, Baron Irnham, a notorious sinner of the day. It was commonly believed that he had challenged his own son to a duel and had been refused on the grounds of his being only doubtfully a gentleman.[11] As Combe implies in the sentence just quoted, Irnham's speciality in vice was corrupting the innocent. There is no evidence that Combe had any personal grudge against him; apparently the man was merely a convenient peg on which to hang the Hertfords.

The poem follows the familiar satiric scheme of having various candidates for office appear and set forth their claims, which in this instance were to the throne of Hell.[12]

> The Devil, grown old, was anxious to prepare
> A fit Successor for the Infernal Chair.
> At length, he summon'd forth his Chosen Band:
> And thus the Monarch gave his last command:
> "Expand your sable wings, and speed to Earth!
> "To every Knave of Power, and Imp of Birth,
> "Statesmen and Peers, these welcome tidings tell,
> "That I resolve to quit the Throne of HELL:
> "But, ere I cease to reign, 'twill be my care
> "From my dear Children to elect an Heir."
>
> (Pages 1–2)

Satan's envoys take wing and alighting in the Strand they disperse and seek for promising candidates in the places most likely to provide them.

> Some take their fav'rite way
> To those fam'd mansions—where the Sons of Play
> By trick and rapine share a base reward;
> Shake the false dye, and pack the ready card:
> In solemn tone their errand they proclaim,
> Their high commission, and their Sovereign's name.

The news is no sooner announced in St James's Street than

> With joy and wonder struck, the Parties rise!
> "Hell is worth trying for," F[itzpatrick] cries;
> Pigeons are left unpluck'd, the game unplay'd,
> And F[ox] forgets the certain Bett he made;
> E'en S[e]l[wy]n feels Ambition fire his breast,
> And leaves, half-told, the fabricated Jest.

(Page 3)

Richard Fitzpatrick, who remembered seeing Combe in France, was the friend and gambling companion of Charles James Fox. George Selwyn was famous for his wit and his morbid interest in executions; he could never forgo a joke, and he never missed a hanging. He was said to be most witty after losing great sums of money.[13] Satan's agents would readily find all three men in St James's.

Meanwhile, other envoys from Hell were seeking candidates in even more exalted neighbourhoods. They made their way

> To the corrupted Purlieus of the Court;
> To lure the Statesman from his deep-lay'd scheme,
> To wake the Courtier from his golden dream,
> And make the C- -b- -l- -n desire to hold
> Hell's weighty Sceptre, - -for 'tis made of gold.
> Sure He'd resign for such a tempting fee!
> HELL's Sceptre far outweighs the Golden Key!
> But cautious H******* shrinks, when risks are run,
> And leaves such Honours for his ELDEST SON.

(Page 4)

The C- -b- -l- -n is Lord Hertford, Chamberlain of the Household; Beauchamp was his eldest son.

A third group of Satan's agents goes to those disreputable parts of the town "where prostitution rules her needy slaves". Finally, the candidates are gathered together and conveyed to the scene of the ceremony.

Lords of the Chamber,—Ministers of State,
With Sons of Lords, and Hirelings of the Great;
Men whom the Villian only loves, the Worthy hate;
Follow'd by Pimps, Bawds, Parasites and Whores,
In crouds, approach'd Hell's adamantine doors.

(Page 5)

The doors open, and the claimants are ushered into the presence of
Satan. In a setting obviously, but somewhat remotely, suggested by
Paradise Lost, the ceremony begins. Satan announces his intention of
retiring and invites the various candidates to present their claims to
the throne. Fitzpatrick is the first to step forth, but before he can
speak Satan addresses him. He has admirably bad intentions, Satan
says, but he must be disqualified because of those seeds of virtue
which now lie hidden in his nature. It is true, he says, that for the
present "baneful passions do their place supply". These he particular-
izes, but he finally dismisses the candidate as not qualified.

Charles James Fox is the next to appear. Having already exhausted his fortune, by 1777 Fox had also exhausted his credit with
the tradesmen, and his appearance was often unkempt.

In order due, VOLPONE next appear'd;
Loose was his hair, unshaven was his beard:
O'er his whole face was spread a yellow hue,
Borrow'd, perhaps, from some relenting Jew
Not anxious to be paid.—gold he had none;
Th' inverted pocket told that all was gone.
But ere he made his claim to Hell's rewards,
His right hand wav'd aloft the fatal Cards.

(Pages 10–11)

He offers to gamble with Satan for his soul, but Satan waves him
aside.

"Thy soul's already mine,"
SATAN replied:—" and I this day assign
"Thy earthly duty.—Hence, begone, to bait,
"With mastiff zeal,—a Minister of State."

(Page 11)

Whereupon Fox leaves to rejoin the Whig opposition to Lord
North.

The next candidate is Henry Herbert, Earl of Pembroke, an avid
horseman who took credit for having written the *Method of Breaking
Horses*. Combe informs us that this book had been ghost-written by

one "Angeloni"—the pseudonym of John Shebbeare. He then bluntly accuses Pembroke of voyeurism, citing a scandalous manuscript soon to be published, Mrs Godby's *Nocturnals*, as his (rather questionable) authority.

> E'en Saint-like GODBY blasts her eyes, and swears,
> P[embroke]'s the most abandon'd of his Peers.
>
> (Page 12)

Without his ghost-writer, Pembroke is unable to argue his case and is promptly dismissed.

Now Beauchamp approaches the throne and Combe allots him forty-six lines of verse and three long footnotes.

> Without one Virtue that can grace a name;
> Without one Vice that e'er exalts to Fame;
> The despicable B******** next appears,
> His bosom panting with its usual fears:
> He strives in vain,—and fruitless proves the art,
> To hide, with vacant smile, the treacherous heart.
> The faithful HARRY stands not by his side,
> His learned Counsel, and his constant guide;
> Who for an hard-earn'd narrow competence,
> Supplies his tongue with words, his head with sense.
> At length, recovered from his huge affright,
> He, stammering, reads the Speech he did not write:
>   "Curst with hereditary love of pelf,
> "I hate all human beings but myself;
> "Cross and perplex my wife, because she prov'd,
> "Poor girl!—not rich enough to be belov'd."
>
> (Pages 13–14)

"The faithful Harry" is Beauchamp's younger brother, Henry Conway, whom Combe in a footnote calls "a most amiable character". Combe evidently believed that the Sultana had not brought Beauchamp as much wealth as he expected, and there may be some justification for the belief. Viscount Irvine died in 1778, leaving his entire estate to his wife. Beauchamp got no part of the property until the widow died thirty years later.[14]

Beauchamp continues his halting speech by arguing that everyone on earth despises him.

> "Thus, without Friends on earth, I humbly sue
> "To find, my gracious Liege, a Friend in you.
> "*Hated by all*,—I'm fit to be allied
> "To your Imperial State!"—The King replied:

"If vacant smiles and hypocritic air
"Could form pretensions to this sov'reign Chair;
"If my pale Crown by *meanness* could be won,
"Who'd have so fair a claim as H[ertford]'s Son?"

But even devils disdain meanness, and Satan condemns Beauchamp to

"*Find neither Friends on Earth,—nor Friends in Hell.*"
(Pages 15–16)

George Selwyn is next on the list, but when the herald calls his name, George is not to be found. He has been unable to resist looking around at the suffering in Hell!

He was gone to hear the dismal yells
Of tortur'd Ghosts and suffering Criminals. . . .
With GEORGE, all know Ambition must give place,
When there's an Execution in the case.
(Page 17)

A lengthy prose footnote elaborates this sketch, arguing wittily that Selwyn is in reality a humane individual: "I would not be guilty of injustice to any Character. George does not want humanity! nay, he has an uncommon portion of this virtue: it extends even to the *gallows*. . . . And I may venture to assert, that he never saw a man hang'd in his life but, when the *sport was over*, he would have been really happy to have restored him to life" (page 18).

Thomas, second Lord Lyttelton, is the next candidate to present himself. Though still flamboyantly "wicked", he had succeeded to the title in 1773 and was now making a new name for himself in the House of Lords. After eloquently attacking the ministry for its conduct of American affairs, he had been quieted by the gift of a sinecure and had been publicly defended by Lord Sandwich, the profligate First Lord of the Admiralty and inventor of an ingenious means of eating bread and meat without leaving the gaming-table. Sandwich had called one of Lyttelton's speeches the finest he had ever heard in the Lords.[15]

Then in Succession came a Peer of words,
Well known,—and *honour'd* in the *House of Lords*,
Whose Eloquence all Parallel defies!
So SANDWICH says, and SANDWICH never lies.
(Pages 18–19)

Lyttelton is runner-up in this contest, and with his despised cousin
and parasite, Captain George Edward Ayscough, he gets a total of
seventy-four lines. There is a short dialogue between these two in
which Lyttelton asks Ayscough to testify for him. "You've always
lied for me on earth," says Lyttelton; "Now speak the truth in Hell."
Ayscough, the perfect yes-man, is at first shocked by this request, but
he complies as follows:

> "Is there a guilty deed I have not done?
> "What say you, Coz?" The Captain answer'd, "None!"
> "Have I not whor'd myself, and made thee whore?
> "Confirm it with an oath!"—The Captain swore.
> "Have I not acted every Villain's part?
> "Have I not broke a Noble Parent's heart?
> "By deeds of ill have I not seem'd to live?"
> The Captain gave a bold affirmative.
> "Do I not daily boast, how I've betrayed
> "The tender Widow, and the virtuous Maid?
> "Swear, Sir!"—By *Egypt's Queen* the Captain swore!
>
> (Page 22)

"Egypt's Queen" was a geographically inexact reference to Semira-
mis; Ayscough's English version of Voltaire's tragedy by that name
was currently running at the Drury Lane. Combe corrected his error
in the second edition, calling her "Ninus' Queen".

Lyttelton seems on the point of winning the contest when Lord
Irnham suddenly appears and carries the day with one short speech:

> "I boast superior claim
> "To Hell's dark Throne, and ****** is my name.
> "What, shall that stripling Lord contend with me?
> "I have four Sons as old and bad as he!
> "Whate'er he swears, I'll swear—he says, I'll say!
> "And look, All-gracious King, *my hairs are grey!*"
>
> Th' astonished Demons on each other gaz'd,
> And SATAN'S self sat silent and amazed.

At that point Nesbitt's "raving Ghost" appears and

> With piteous look he did a Tale unfold,
> Black with such horrid deeds, that, being told,
> Hell's craggy vaults with Acclamations ring,
> And joyful shouts of———" ****** shall be King!"
>
> (Pages 23–24)

There the work ends without specifying the nature of Nesbitt's tale, but contemporary readers evidently knew it well. Although Nesbitt appears in the satire only as * * * * * * *, now faded annotation in virtually every surviving copy indicates that no mystery was involved. The name is carefully written over the seven asterisks as *Irnham* is over the six. Albert Nesbitt, Esq., had died the previous March. He was possibly the unnamed youth whom Junius describes as having been seduced by Irnham into marrying a prostitute. Combe might reasonably be sensitive on this point. According to the *Town and Country Magazine* (January 1775), Nesbitt's wife "laughed at his folly, ridiculed his weakness, and satyrized his personal defects"— chiefly impediments in speech. Tiring of these amusements, she left him to become mistress to Augustus John Hervey, third Earl of Bristol, who had himself been abandoned by Elizabeth Chudleigh before she became first the mistress and then the bigamous wife of the Duke of Kingston. One recalls Parson Primrose's concern over the "deuterogamy of the age".

The Diaboliad met with immediate success. The first edition was quickly exhausted, and paragraphs began to appear in the papers. On February 7 the *Morning Post* carried the following letter:

To Mr. C——, of the Board of O——.
   Malignant Friend,
Your language and invention are well known—your cloven-foot is traced; and, well may you expect to be sent speedily to that infernal Board of Ordnance below, where you and your patron will reap the just *fruits* of such diabolical practices, and false, cowardly defamation!
                                   Feb. 3, 1777.

It is difficult to avoid suspecting that this communication had been placed in the newspaper by Combe's bookseller: such veiled advertisements could be inserted for a modest price, and few readers would be deceived. At any rate, on the following day the same paper announced a new edition of the *Diaboliad*. Within a month appeared the first of numerous continuations, *The Diabo-Lady*; not by Combe though published by Kearsly, it helped to kindle a fire which burned through a lively series of imitations, replies, counter-replies, and burlesques throughout the spring. Not since Churchill's *Rosciad* in 1761 had the town been so stirred by satires. Nearly fifty years later, Sir Edgerton Brydges could write, "I remember distinctly the great impression these satires made, when I was a boy; and how many of the severest passages were on every one's lips."[16] George III also remembered; when Combe was identified to him in 1794 as the author of the *Diaboliad*, the King replied, "He was a clever man."[17]

* * *

If Combe expected the Hertfords to be crushed by the *Diaboliad* attack, he was disappointed. So far as can now be ascertained, neither Lord Hertford nor Lord Beauchamp took the slightest notice. Their attitude may be inferred from a speech made in the Commons by General Conway, Lord Hertford's brother. Discussing some abuse of himself which had recently appeared in the papers—abuse which Walpole thought Combe had written—he remarked that these things should be ignored. No one was attacked in this fashion more than he, and no one minded it less. If the author could get sixpence by his abuse, he did not grudge it him.[18] Horace Walpole, who tells this story, took a lively interest in the whole episode. He knew very well who had written the *Diaboliad*; "by Mr. Coombe", he wrote on the title-page of his own copy, and on the opposite page he wrote, "In the public Advertiser was a letter, which said, that if any body wished to know the Author of the Diaboliad, 'Oh ho! says the Devil, tis my John a 'Coombe.' "[19] Walpole refers several times to Combe as an "infamous rascal", but he engages in no recrimination. He merely tells why Combe has a grudge against the Hertfords and genteelly praises the verses.[20]

Nor is there any evidence that Lord Irnham felt called upon to protest, though his son, Henry Lawes Luttrell, manifested some sensitivity. In a signed letter to the *Morning Post* (February 22, 1777) a month after the *Diaboliad* came out, he replied to an attack recently made in the newspapers upon himself and incidentally mentioned "the infamous trade of anonymous calumny" which was "but too successfully carried on". No one in February 1777 would fail to see a connection here with the recent satire on his father. There was no great love lost between father and son, to be sure, but anonymous attacks made everyone of any prominence feel vulnerable. Combe was no more guilty than other journalists and pamphleteers, but he had more ability and wrote with greater effect.

The comment of George Selwyn, one of Combe's lesser victims, occurs in a letter written to Lord Carlisle:

The author of a new Grub Street poem, I see, allows me a great share of feeling, at the same time that he relates facts of me, which, if they were true, would, besides making me ridiculous, call very much into question what he asserts with any reasonable man. I do not know if you have received this performance. If I thought you had not, paltry as it is, I should send it to you. The work I mean is called "The Diaboliad." His hero is Lord Ernham [sic]. Lord Hertford and Lord Beauchamp are the chief persons whom he loads with his invectives. Lord Lyttelton [and] his cousin Mr. Ascough are also treated with not much lenity; Lord Pembroke with great familiarity, as well as C. Fox; and Fitzpatrick, although painted in colours bad enough at present, is represented as one whom in time the Devil will lose for his disciple. I am only attacked upon that trite and very foolish opinion concerning le pene e la Dilitté [sic]. acknowledging [it] to proceed from an odd and insatiable curiosity, and not from a *mauvais coeur*. In some places I think there is versification, and a few good lines, and the piece seems to be wrote by one not void of parts, but who, with attention, might write much better.[21]

Although the *Diaboliad* made no perceptible impression on its intended victims, it was a huge success with popular readers. Within a month's time, as we have seen, the first of a large number of imitations appeared, *The Diabo-Lady: or, a Match in Hell. A Poem. Dedicated to the Worst Woman in Her Majesty's Dominions.* This, in turn was followed by the *Anti-Diabo-Lady, Respectfully dedicated to All the Women in Her Majesty's Dominions, in General; and to the Best of Them in Particular, Calculated to Expose the Malevolence of the author of Diabo-Lady.* Neither of these two imitations was by Combe, but his booksellers were involved in their publication and he had been sufficiently busy producing his own *Additions to the Diaboliad* which appeared on March 18 both as a separate pamphlet supplementary to the first and as part of a new edition of the whole poem.

The *Additions* add three more candidates for the throne of Hell. Richard Rigby is carried in drunk, and the shade of the fourth Duke of Bedford steps forward with the request that Rigby be allowed to live on earth and continue his evil influence there. At that, Rigby is carried out again. He is followed by William Douglas, Earl of March, a "batter'd Beau" who "Burns with the proud desire to give the Ton to Hell". The flames, vapours, and winds of Hell disarrange his appearance, however, and "the affrighted Peer" is unable to speak. The third new candidate is Lord Shelburne, who brings as his supporters two friends of America, Isaac Barré and Joseph Priestley. Shelburne argues that these men will be his supporters in Hell just as they have been on earth. With such help he should have a prosperous reign. To this Satan replies that Hell shall not be allowed to suffer "from the soft falsehoods of thy subtle tongue", and that it wants no such sycophants as these. Shelburne's proposals might be more appropriate in America, where Satan has succeeded in subverting people to rebellion. Let him and his friends go to America, then, and stay away from Hell. These new lines added little to the original satire, but they helped maintain public interest. As a separate publication they called for and received new reviews, and they justified the printing of a new edition of the *Diaboliad* "with large additions". Combe's anger did not blind him to the practical steps necessary if a good thing was to be kept alive.

Meanwhile, new publicity was coming from the newspapers and magazines. On March 6, for example, the *Morning Post* published an "Epistle to the Worst Poet in His Majesty's Dominions", comparing the "Laureate of the Shades" unfavourably with four prose writers just then in the public eye: Sir John Hawkins, James Macpherson, "Hermes" Harris, and Dr Richard Price. The anonymous versifier acknowledges that these four have some merit, but he is unable to discover any in the author of *The Diaboliad*.[22] The lines are trifling, but Combe and his booksellers could scarcely object to the free advertising. Three weeks later the March issue of the *London Magazine* appeared "Embellished with a Caricature Engraving of the principal characters in the *Diaboliad*" (Plate 7) and promising a similar engraving of the Diabo-ladies in the next issue. Combe's topic had clearly become the hit of the season.

The reviews appearing in the February issues of the magazines (that is, at the end of that month) were for the most part non-committal notices, but the *Westminster Magazine* took a firmly favourable position:

> [*The Diaboliad*] is by much the best piece of the kind that has appeared since Churchill's death. It has all his spirit and severity in it; and the characters introduced, are each of them extremely well drawn. But whether the pictures are all like their originals, or no, we shall not pretend to determine, as not having the honour to be personally acquainted with any of them. . . .
>
> There is a great deal of well pointed satire in this short Poem; and as the Author has confined his Drama to a few personages, there are many who have good reason to rejoice at not having been exhibited in it.

7. *The Diaboliad, from the London Magazine, March 1777*

We shall leave the Readers to their own knowledge or information, for filling up the blanks of names for themselves.

*   *   *

So many *Diaboliad* items had appeared by this time that Combe, not to push his luck too far, turned for his next satire to an entirely new subject and to some extent a new manner. In writing of masculine vices he had centred his action in Hell; now he concerned himself with follies, chiefly feminine, and used contemporary London as his setting. The result was one of his wittiest and most successful pieces, *The First of April: or, The Triumphs of Folly*. By contrast with the *Diaboliad*, this new work begins in a deceptively mild, urbane style as generalized and topical satire, but after some 300 lines there is a crescendo of indignation as a host of well-known individuals appear and the reader is treated to an inventory of follies and selected vices. It is one of Combe's most vigorous satires, and to the social historian it is his most interesting.

The public masquerade, just then enormously popular in fashionable society, provided Combe with a ready-made scheme for his purpose (Plate 8). This diversion had been revived some years previously when Mrs Teresa Cornelys, a notorious entrepreneur of pleasure, had taken Carlisle House near Soho Square and remodelled it to accommodate subscription concerts, assemblies, and masquerades on a vast scale. So great was her *succès de scandale* that in 1772 she found herself with a rival to contend with, the new Pantheon in Tyburn Road (now Oxford Street). The licensed opera houses and the bench of bishops for their different reasons also gave Mrs Cornelys trouble, and for a time she was forced to close down her establishment. In 1776, however, Carlisle House reopened with a blaze of splendour. Tickets to one of her masquerades cost a guinea and a half, but since the price was the only requirement for admission, the "guests" were a miscellaneous lot, ranging from dukes and duchesses to tradesmen and women of the streets. Under cover of the masks, and stimulated by generous quantities of wine, the crowd's behaviour, to say the least, was uninhibited. By morning the parties tended to become drunken orgies. Fashionable London may have been amused, but the middle classes were suitably scandalized.

Two such masquerades had taken place during the weeks of Combe's

8. *Masquerade, from the Microcosm of London, by Pugin and Rowlandson*

preoccupation with the *Diaboliad*, one at the Pantheon on January 20, the other at Carlisle House on February 10. Combe himself may have attended such affairs on occasion as paragrapher for the newspapers; fourteen years later, at any event, Mrs Damer remembered him at this time as "a sort of fine gentleman about this town, frequenting balls and assemblies, a writer of pamphlets and paragraphs in news-papers".[23] Walpole thought he wrote for the *Daily Advertiser*,[24] but that paper devoted little space indeed to the kind of gossip which a paragrapher usually provided. Both the *Public Advertiser* and the *Morning Post, or Daily Advertiser*, however, carried such material, and even a contemporary might confuse these names. Both of the latter reported in detail the two masquerades just mentioned, and Combe could easily have written either account. Inasmuch as he wrote a satire based on these affairs, he obviously had more than a passing interest in them.

The *Public Advertiser* (January 22) had this to say of the Pantheon ball:

MASQUERADE INTELLIGENCE

On Monday Evening last, at Ten o'Clock, was opened that superb Structure, the Pantheon, with a very magnificent Masked Ball. The Company began to assemble about a Quarter before Eleven, and, on entering the Rotunda, appeared captivated with the surrounding Splendors of that Room. . . .

From the Rotunda the Company repaired to the Supper-tables, where thay had a most plenteous Regale of every Edible and Liquor that the Season or the five Kingdoms could produce. . . .

The Ladies were in very superb Dresses, with elegant Plumes on their Heads, and appeared more like Goddesses than Women: Lady B—— and the two Misses S——, whose beauty no Mask could conceal, seemed to have just dropt from Heaven.

But amiably engaging as some Ladies were, there were others exceedingly disgustful, particularly in their ridiculous Head-dresses. Two Women of the Town (for 'tis impossible they could be otherwise than such) were a Disgrace to the whole Sex.

The two who disgraced their sex were presumably *not* women of the town. Contemporary readers would recognize this as a reference to women of fashion, one of them almost certainly the Duchess of Devonshire, who attended both masquerades. Her feathered head-dress, as we shall see, features in the satire which Combe was presently to write.

As to Fancy Dresses, there were, as usual, Numbers of Fruit and Flower Girls, Shepherds and Shepherdesses, Milkmaids, Haymakers, &c. with several old Men and Women, some of whom supported their characters exceedingly well; Sailors and their Doxies; a Mother Shipton, a most excellent Mask; a French Hair-dresser, very characteristic; an Irish Chairman; some Oxonians; a Courier de France, &c. &c. &c.

The account continues by describing how some of the best costumes were "supported"—for at these masquerades each guest was expected to act out the character suggested by his mask. The result was not always a happy one, and the *Morning Post* on the same day complained that this affair at the Pantheon, "as is ever the case with an English masquerade, was rather dull and uninteresting". The same paper added the following edifying note:

> The company began to withdraw at three, and about five the principal part were retired: leaving a few setts of jolly bacchanals, who in defiance of the musty rules of decency, and decorum, entertained themselves in their usual stile, till nine in the morning, when the rooms were entirely cleared.

Three weeks later (February 12), these papers described in much the same terms the masquerade given by Mrs Cornelys at Carlisle House. About 800 people attended, a "motley assembly of all nations, sects, passions, and languages", causing a three-hour traffic jam in Soho Square, "during which interval the Masks, as usual, were much insulted by the Populace". When all the guests had arrived, they formed a great procession, and "preceded by a number of Janissaries, singing an air . . . , went down to the suite of apartments below to supper". The entire company found seats and a hot supper was served, including "all the rarities in season" and ample supplies of champagne, burgundy, hock, and madeira. "At seven o'clock [a.m.] the rooms were still crowded with company, and many votaries to Bacchus offering full libations to that Diety below stairs, whilst the nimble-footed tribe were amusing themselves with the mazy dance above."

These two masquerades provided Combe with ample material for his new satire which appeared on April 14: *The First of April: or, the Triumphs of Folly: a Poem. Dedicated to a Celebrated Dutchess. By the Author of the Diaboliad* (J. Bew). The poem begins with a description of a festival of folly which would be recognized at once by frequenters of the Pantheon and Carlisle House. Better still, it would be recognized and relished by those even more numerous readers who knew of these goings-on only through reading about them or witnessing the traffic jams which they occasioned. Either way, the satire was bound to find a large audience.

The poem begins with a vision which comes to the poet on the morning of April Fool's Day:

> Methought, a rude impetuous Throng,
> With noise and riot, hurried me along,
> To where a sumptuous Building met my eyes,
> Whose gilded turrets seem'd to dare the skies
> To every Wind it op'd an ample door,
> From every Wind tumultuous thousands pour,
> With these I enter'd a stupendous Hall,
> The scene of some approaching festival.
>
> (Page 2)

The great hall in which he now found himself displayed "every emblem of corrupted taste". The scene is Folly's court, a silken couch taking the place of the throne; the occasion, the official birthday of the Queen of Folly. After seventy lines describing the hall, he seeks "in haste" to leave, but finds his way barred by a great procession, easily recognizable as the usual parade of masks which formed an important part of every masquerade. A band of dancing youths enter, "by friendly Bacchus chear'd". They are followed by "a light and frolic Train of wanton females" announcing the entrance of Fashion. Her costume is constantly changing even as one looks; her hair at one moment is high and at the next hangs low on her neck; her dress now conceals, then reveals. The poet expresses masculine incomprehension: "A form so changeful I had never seen." This "Fickle Princess" is followed by Luxury, wearing a sweeping train "which Dame Cornelys scarcely can sustain", and after her in close succession come a fine lot of personifications: Profusion, Drunkenness, Waste, and Riot. Unseen by all these, but observed by the moral poet, are Ruin, Fever, Disease, Care, Penury, Despair, and Agonizing Death. Finally comes a band of unhappy abstractions, chained and degraded by Folly: Melancholy, Science, Wisdom, Religion, Resignation, and other shadowy favourites. The action pauses for a moment and interest unmistakably palls while the poet wipes away "a silent tear". In more ways than one it is the low moment of the poem.

This sentimental mood passes quickly, however, and presently Queen Folly herself enters and takes her place on the throne.

> And now, in crowds, press'd through the yielding doors,
> High Lords, deep Statesmen, Dutchesses, and Whores;
> All ranks and stations, Publicans and Peers,
> Grooms, Lawyers, Fiddlers, Bawds, and Auctioneers;
> Prudes and Coquettes, the Ugly and the Fair,
> The Pert, the Prim, the Dull, the Debonnair;
> The Weak, the Strong, the Humble and the Proud,
> All help'd to form the motley, mingled Crowd.
>
> (Page 16)

The poet observes "with curious eye" the behaviour of all these
figures, the old trying to act young, the young trying to act wise. He
is particularly shocked by the brazen efforts of mothers to show off
their daughters.

> There I beheld full many a youthful Maid,
> Like colts for sale to public view display'd,
> Shew off their shapes and ply their happiest art,
> While the old Mother acts the Jockey's part;
> Who, well-instructed in the World's great School,
> Knows how to trap the rich and noble Fool.
> Bold Prostitution look'd with downcast eye,
> And veil'd her painted cheeks with modesty;
> While wedded Dames a bold demeanour wear,
> And think their eyes resistless when they stare.
>
> (Page 17)

Up to this point the satire has been general and in a lighter vein
than that of the *Diaboliad*, but now the familiar initials and asterisks
reappear, inviting the reader to play the game of identifications. The
Hertfords are introduced in order that Combe may satirize the efforts
of Lady Hertford to find husbands for her daughters. The disinterested
reader may sympathize somewhat with Lady Hertford; she had to
arrange matches for seven sons and six daughters. Of one of the
latter, Lady Villiers, Combe has an amusing if slightly acid footnote:
"It has been said . . . that she never spoke before her marriage, and
was never silent afterwards. ——This is the true art of managing
Daughters—— To prevent a discovery of their real dispositions 'till
the end of the hypocrisy is answer'd, ——and the *Settlement for Life*
irrevocable" (page 28 n).

The personal satire in *The First of April* is chiefly notable for the
introduction of the Duchess of Devonshire, the "Celebrated Dutchess"
to whom it is dedicated—"too celebrated," remarked the *Gentleman's*

Magazine (July 1777), "not to be as easily known and distinguished as Diana or Calypso among the nymphs". Georgiana, daughter of the first Earl Spencer, had married the phlegmatic William Cavendish, fifth Duke of Devonshire, in 1774. She was seventeen at the time of her marriage to the Duke, who at twenty-five already seemed her senior by twenty years. When she came to London as mistress of Devonshire House, she possessed everything which could excite the envious disapprobation of her less fortunate contemporaries—wealth, social position, vivacity, intelligence, and sensibility—not to mention her fair share of vanity and coquetry. "A lovely girl, natural and full of grace" was Horace Walpole's comment. Posterity remembers her for her sensational role canvassing for Fox in the Westminster elections of 1784, though ten years earlier, when newly arrived in London, she was already stirring society with her youthful follies and her devotion to extremes of fashion. In the spring of 1775 she took up wearing ostrich plumes as head-dress, and on March 10 Mrs Harris wrote to her son, later the first Earl of Malmesbury, "A very fine new cantata . . . last night . . . the very best company in town. The Duchess of Devonshire had two plumes sixteen inches long, besides three small ones: this has so far outdone all other plumes, that Mrs Damer, Lady Harriet Stanhope, &c., looked nothing".[25] Mary Moser wrote in similar vein to her friend Mrs Nichols: "Come to London and admire our plumes, we sweep the sky! a Duchess wears six feathers, a lady four, and every milk-maid one at each corner of her cap!"[26] Georgiana's ostrich plumes and her gowns which indiscreetly revealed her youthful figure, though enthusiastically emulated by ladies of fashion, were naturally deemed an affront to middle-class respectability. Sheridan made a good-natured reference to heads "too high in feather'd state" in the Prologue to his *Trip to Scarborough*, and the quip produced a storm of hilarity at the Drury Lane when the play opened on February 24, 1777, with the Duchess herself in the royal box wearing "gargantuan plumes of pink ostrick feathers".[27]

Obviously, Combe could not deny the Duchess her rightful place of honour in his new satire. When Folly invites the guests to come forward and place their gifts upon the altar, the Duchess is granted precedence:

> When D[evonshire], uprising from her seat,
> With careless gesture to the Altar moves,
> Then *Virtue* shriek'd,—and all the *Laughing Loves*

That play'd around, droop'd instant with dismay
And spread their wings, and, weeping, fled away!

(Page 21)

She proceeds to offer all her best possessions (grace, simplicity, modesty, goodness) on the altar, and Folly promptly claims her as her own.

When, lo!—the sudden Plumes her temples grac'd;
The yielding Stays sink downwards to the waist,
And, strange to tell, her rosy lips dispense
Double-entendres and Impertinence.

Pages (22–23)

The other worshippers now parade before the alter of Folly, each identified by an initial and a veiled description. The ladies make their appropriate sacrifices on the altar, and even as at the masquerades themselves, the masks are semi-transparent. Most of the identifications can still be made by the curious, even without the aid of contemporary annotation: The Countess of Derby, Lady Barrymore, Lady Eglinton, "Painted Archer", Mrs Damer (Beauchamp's cousin), Lady Harrington (Beauchamp's aunt, "the modern Messalina"), and finally Lady Villiers and Lady Lincoln (Beauchamp's sisters).

Now shoals of Damsels to the place repair,
To sacrifice their reputations there;
While others, careful of their own good name,
Give to the gaping crowd a neighbour's fame.

(Page 29)

The gentlemen of the court then present themselves and their offerings: Lord Carlisle, Lord Sandwich, "Reeling Weymouth", and various others. Finally, the inevitable Beauchamp makes his offering of "smiles that ne'er pleas'd . . . words as light as air . . . o'er-weening arts . . . a few fair deeds, whose merit has been lost in selfish ends . . . smiling lies . . . bare hypocrisies", and last, but most pointedly, the curses which had poured forth from him on the failure of his marriage to produce "the expected Dower". This is the topic on which the poem ends. Folly rewards Beauchamp with a scroll telling of the "omitted legacy", the crowd breaks into a roar of laughter, and Beauchamp makes off.

The First of April is a creditable performance, given the circumstances which produced it and the haste with which it was written and published. Contemporary reviewers treated the work with notable respect; "the variety and harmony" of the verse reminded a writer in the *Gentleman's Magazine* (July) of Dryden's *Fables*, while "the keenness of . . . satire" recalled Juvenal and Churchill. The *Westminster Magazine* (April) noted that this poem was milder than the *Diaboliad*: "That lashes the vices of the age; this rather tickles the follies of it". The work was well received, too, by the public, which bought up several editions; except possibly for the *Diaboliad*, none of Combe's other satires is so prevalent today in libraries and bookshops.

It was the prose dedication to the Duchess, however, which introduced the theme Combe was now to exploit in several pamphlets. Written in a tone of mixed servility and condescension, it admonishes the "Celebrated Dutchess" to give up folly and assume the "obligations attendant upon your station of female excellence". These were the very sentiments of those readers for whom the work was really intended—not the Devonshires and their friends, but ordinary Londoners whose patronage determined the success or failure of such productions. Sensing the popularity of the theme, Combe continued his moral admonition by publishing on April 24, ten days after the poem, a prose *Letter to Her Grace the Duchess of Devonshire*. Few readers would recognize in this work the hand of the Laureate of Hell, for the phrase "by the author of the *Diaboliad*" is omitted from the title-page, the booksellers Fielding and Walker have replaced J. Bew, and the letter is written as though the author were a woman. "While I leave to men the department of political examination and the vices of their own sex, I shall avail myself of the privilege which the press affords me, to hold forth the examples of Female Error which are so glaring a disgrace to the times wherein we live" (page 2). There follow sixteen pages of humourless advice, by implication assuring the reader of his own moral superiority to duchesses. A second edition was announced two weeks later. But there was some dissent. Immediately after the first edition of the *Letter*, a set of verses appeared in the *Chronicle* (April 22–24) and the *Public Advertizer* (April 25), significantly entitled "To her Grace the Duchess of Devonshire, in answer to all the absurd and illiberal aspersions cast on the fashionable Feathers by churlish old Women, ridiculous Prudes, and brutish Censors". Combe's answer to this was the publication on May 17 of a rather more severe *Second Letter to Her Grace the Duchess of Devonshire* (Fielding and Walker). Writing as though he were the same woman, he quotes in full the newspaper poem as evidently directed against "the spirited Author of that well-known Satire, *The First of April*, and myself", and asserts that the Duchess must have purchased the poem and paid for the newspaper space it occupied. The publication of these verses may indeed have been inspired, but one is much less inclined to place responsibility upon the Devonshires than upon Combe and his booksellers. The increasing heat of the *Second Letter* led a writer in the *Monthly Review* for May to express the pious hope that "the Author has not been endeavouring to levy contributions on the Duchess!" There is not the slightest evidence to support this insinuation of blackmail; Combe and his bookseller were simply promoting the sale of their wares.

By this time interest in the Duchess and her feathers was fully aroused, and other hackwriters hastily entered the fray. A number of pamphlets appeared in rapid succession, their titles a good deal more picturesque than their contents: *The Duchess of Devonshire's Cow; a Poem* (attributed to Lord Carlisle and published by Bew on May 19); *Heroic Epistle to the Noble Author of the Duchess of Devonshire's Cow* (one of Combe's negligible efforts, published by Bew, June 2); *The Duke of Devonshire's Bull, to the Duchess of Devonshire's Cow, a Poem* (published by Bew, June 3); *A letter to the Duchess of D——, answered cursorily, by Democritus* (published by Baldwin, June 28), *Desultory Thoughts upon Reading an Interesting Letter to the Duchess of Devonshire* (Longman, June). Even Sheridan's *School for Scandal* may be included in this otherwise undistinguished list; it glances at the feathers theme, and in the relationship between Sir Peter and Lady Teazle it portrays a marriage which contemporaries identified with that of the Devonshires.[28] Mrs Montagu missed the opening of this play, but writing to a friend a few days later she reported that everyone was praising its attack on scandal and detraction. "The scribblers", she wrote, "weekly let fly their pop-guns at the Duchess of Devonshire's feathers. Her grace is innocent, good-humoured, and beautiful; but these adders are blind and deaf, and cannot be charmed". She was willing to excuse the scribblers, for they were all hungry, but she thought the circulators of scandal "sad vermin". They had "neither hunger for their excuse, nor wit to give it a seasoning". She was glad that Mr Sheridan had exposed such people.[29]

*   *   *

Two pamphlets in the spring of 1777 illustrate Combe's readiness to keep the bookstalls supplied with commentary on events of current interest. The first of these was announced a week after the opening of the annual exhibition of the Royal Academy and published by Fielding and Walker a few days later, some time in the first week of May: *A Poetical Epistle to Sir Joshua Reynolds, Knt. and President of the Royal Academy*. It develops the idea that Sir Joshua's colours fade rapidly and that his pictures will survive only in engraved reproductions:

> Unhappy Artist, to survive
> The means by which your fame should live!
> And on the *Scraper's* art rely
> For hopes of Immortality.

(Pages 6–7)

The charge was a commonplace of the time, and one of the papers had already reported Sir Joshua's quip that he was happy to come off with flying colours![30]

The second pamphlet which Combe produced at this time is a much more interesting piece on the sensational case of Dr Dodd. From the moment that fashionable clergyman was arrested on February 7 to his execution on June 27 the newspapers and bookstalls were filled with the rhetoric of controversy. It was a serious matter, involving both the sanctity of property and the reputation of the Church. On June 28 the newspapers carried long "eyewitness accounts" of the hanging, and for days thereafter they supplied edifying commentary on Dodd's life, his virtues, and his errors. From beginning to end the episode had been treated with unrelieved bathos. The public preferred it that way. Combe had been too busy during these months to enter the controversy, but two weeks after its melodramatic conclusion he published his comment. To his credit, but not to his profit, he ventured to treat the subject with levity.

On Monday, June 30, the papers announced the death early Saturday morning of a well-known wit and *bon vivant*, Chace (sometimes Chase) Price, Member of Parliament for Radnor, Wales. The *Public Advertiser* account reads as follows:

> On Saturday Morning June 28 early Chace Price, Esq; Member for the County of Radnor, was found in his Bed, at his House in Upper Grosvenor-street; When he went to Bed he desired to be called at a certain Hour, and when the Servant came to call him,

he found him quite dead;—It appeared that he had died without a Struggle. Mr. Price had long laboured under a Complication of Disorders, the chief of which was the Dropsy; but he had flattered himself lately that he had entirely cured himself of that Disease by Means of an old Woman's *Recipe*, Gin and Garlick.

The Loss of Chace Price, says a Correspondent, will make a great Blank in many convivial *Societies*, of which he used to be the Life and Soul. *"Quando ullum invenient parem?"*

The death, less than twenty-four hours apart, of two men so different as Dodd and Price gave Combe an idea for his pamphlet: *Dialogue in the Shades between an Unfortunate Divine, and a Welch* [sic] *Member, lately deceased* (J. Bew, July 11).

Mr. P——. So, my good Doctor, I have overtaken you!—Things turn out strangely with us mortals: when I saw you dangling at Tyburn, I little thought that I should be so soon on your heels.

Dr. D——. Time and chance, Mr. P——, happen unto all men! Life is an uncertain possession, as you, I fear, have experienced; for as you were in a state of health which permitted your attendance on my execution, your death, surely, must have been very sudden and un-expected.

Mr. P——. Almost as sudden as yours, my good friend, but more unexpected, I assure you. However, I had the advantage of your Reverence; I died by Burgundy—you by a halter.

Dr. D——. Excess, then, was the cause of both our deaths; only yours was not made criminal by Act of Parliament, mine was: so you suffered without an executioner, while all the horrid forms of legal death were exercised upon me.

Mr. P——. That you were a most egregious coxcomb throughout your life, is universally known; and I perceive the character sticks by you to the last.—What! compare the death of a Felon at *Tyburn* to a Gentleman's dying in a quiet way in his own house, without giving anyone the least trouble!—For shame, Doctor! for shame! Your logic's intolerable.

(Pages 1–2)

Dr Dodd acknowledges that in the eyes of men his death was the more disgraceful, but having had an opportunity to confess his sins he hopes for acceptance at the last judgement. What, he asks, were Price's preparations for death?

Mr. P——. Why, egad, none at all. I had not the least hint given me of the journey: For this self-same scare-crow of a fellow called *Death*, was as unceremonious with me as he was punctilious with you. But, if you wish to be informed of what preceded it, I'll tell you. A dinner with a jovial party of honest fellows, who know how to enjoy life, to laugh away the sorrows of it, and have recourse to the Body to dissipate the troubles of the mind. . . .

Dr. D——. From this account of yourself, Mr. P——, I do not think that I have done you any dishonour in the comparison of my death with yours. Whatever might have been the case on Friday morning last, I would not change situations with you, believe me, at this hour.—Here you are come *unannointed, unannealed, no reckoning made,* —Oh, Sir! think of that—.

(Pages 2–3)

Dr Dodd then proceeds to lecture the other on his worldly vices and says it would have been far better if he had cast them off long before death. He rebukes him for his present jesting about the matter and says such a light-hearted attitude will be held against him at the last judgement. This discourse reminds Price of "The Convict's Address to His Unhappy Brethern", written by Dr Johnson for Dodd, who delivered it in the chapel of Newgate Prison three weeks before his execution.

Mr. P——. Be so good, my dear Doctor, as to recollect that I am not an unhappy brother-convict; that I want no serious Address from any honest Divine, who has been condemned for forgery, to prepare me to go and be hanged with decency. Such matters are at an end with us; and as I believe your preachment would not at this time do any good, so I am convinced that my mirth cannot be productive of harm. We have both left life behind us somewhat sooner, perhaps, than either of us thought or wished for; and your Reverence in a manner that has given you, I see, a crick in your neck: but as our lives are past, and what is done, whether right or wrong, cannot be undone, it is of little consequence, I should imagine, how we pass our time on the banks of this infernal stream, 'till Charon is ready to take us over. For my part, I shall leave solemnity and a long face for the other side of the water; where, if there should be an absolute necessity, I shall put them on.

(Page 6)

Price reminds the doctor of all the sordid details of his execution, the procession down Tyburn Road in a coach, the transfer to a cart, the "sighing, sobbing, and praying", the removal of his wig, the placing of a cap over his head and face, the pulling away of the cart, and the victim "left swinging for an hour in the full gaze of an unmelted populace". By contrast, Price's own death had been much better managed. "I did not give my friends the least trouble; I took no formal leave, but, with all imaginable politeness, slid, as it were, from among them, without suffering any one to rise from his chair. After passing a very pleasant day with some very pleasant people, I returned home, went to bed, and never awoke 'till Mercury gave me a shake, and told me how matters stood" (page 8). The conversation continues, Dodd rebuking the other for his unseemly jesting, Price declining to accept admonishments from the disgraced cleric. The dialogue ends when Charon arrives to ferry the two across the river.

The pamphlet was too unconventional for Combe's readers. Although the *London Chronicle* published generous selections from the dialogue on its front page for July 10–12, and the *Monthly Review* for August thought the portrait of Price well drawn, the public declined to buy the pamphlet, even at one shilling. The title unfortunately dropped out of sight at once, and so few copies were sold that they are now virtually non-existent.[31] The hackwriter veers from the public mood at his peril.

Combe had been very active during the first five months of 1777. In addition to his work for the newspapers—whatever that may have comprised—he had published at least seven separate pamphlets and has been accused, perhaps unjustly, of having had a hand in producing some of the imitations and replies published by his own booksellers. Within the trade he was gaining recognition for his uncanny skill in throwing together satires at just the right moment to catch public attention. For the most part he had demonstrated that he knew what would take popular fancy—which personalities to accuse of what follies, and what tone to take in satirizing them. He had kept two lines of attack going simultaneously and separately—one featuring the Hertfords and the other the Duchess of Devonshire. While doing so, he had also written these two topical pamphlets on Reynolds and Dodd. After the last of these publications he lapsed into silence for five months.

*   *   *

Advertisements in the Georgian newspapers show that book publication, then as now, slowed down after midsummer to revive again by October. This seasonal decline in the trade was partly responsible for the failure of the Dodd pamphlet and also for Combe's silence through the autumn. When he finally published his next work, on

December 9, the new season was at its height and he again scored a popular success. Meanwhile he had found time to reflect on the career which had suddenly broken around him and to reconsider his role as a writer.

His disastrous marriage had wrecked his fond dream of living as a man of fashion, a genteel dilettante, but it had also impelled him to write his highly successful satires. The anger which gave his verses their caustic power had receded somewhat by this time, though he was to continue sporadically his attacks upon the Hertfords, particularly Lord Beauchamp, until interrupted by the bailiff in 1785. The success of his publications seemed to promise a continuing demand for other satires—general, personal, topical, whatever. Was this, then, to be the literary career he had dreamed of in those innocent Bristol days? If so, a career as satirist must be shown, both publicly and privately, to be worthy of the respect which his vanity required. Both satire and the satirist must be justified.

The immediate consequence of Combe's soul-searching was *The Justification: A Poem*, clearly identified on the title-page as "By the Author of *The Diaboliad.*" Unlike his earlier satires, this pamphlet was not "Printed for J. Bew", but rather "Printed for the Author: and Sold by J. Bew, . . . and H. Gardner". Everyone in the book trade knew that Churchill, a few years earlier, had been offered from three to five guineas for *The Rosciad*, had chosen to publish it himself, and had made £700 in a short time. Combe was now evidently in a position to increase his earnings by the same device, and by late autumn he found enough ready cash to have the fifty-page pamphlet printed as a private venture.

A prose Preface to his new work sets forth the main lines of Combe's justification of satire, following the well-worn arguments without notable originality. Everyone condemns satire, but everyone privately enjoys reading it. Such writing is wrongly condemned, however, for it performs a necessary social function in repressing evil. It serves as a deterrent where neither law nor religion can have effect. Perhaps it cannot inspire evil men to love virtue, but it teaches them prudence and discourages others from imitating them. The author proposes, therefore, to publish "a series of Poems, wherein the Manners and characters of the Present Times will be represented with truth and attention". No doubt his motives will be impugned, but "In such an Age as this, it is well if any motive can induce men possessed of

Satirical Talents to make the Fool ashamed of his folly, and drive the Vermin of the World from their holes and lurking-places" (p. vi).

The poem which follows is not one of Combe's best efforts, though it has a certain candour and manly resolution. It takes the form of a dialogue between the poet and a lord—for Combe was never reluctant to associate himself with the nobility. The poet's friend tries to dissuade him from writing satire and raises the usual objections, while the poet undertakes to justify his course of action by repeating in couplets the arguments of the Preface. His friend replies by asking what reforms have been effected by his satires. Has Ayscough, for example, turned Methodist? The poet acknowledges that sinners do not reform overnight, but he insists that he has made them suffer. The lord then asks whether ridicule might not be more effective than the scourge, but the poet asserts that human deformities require severe measures. The lord protests that everyone defines virtue to suit himself. Is not the poet himself in some measure guilty? Is his own behaviour above reproach? To this the poet replies that imperfection is the lot of man. Are only angels qualified to punish vice? If so, then the poet may indeed be criticized. He strongly asserts that so long as he writes truthfully he is justified in pursuing his course. Perhaps, he continues, he is accused of writing merely for money; to be sure, he gains his lean reward, but are not judges and clergymen paid for their services? Ah, but some have accused the poet of seeking bribes, not honest pay. (The *Monthly Review*, as we have seen, had implied as much.) The poet professes amusement at the thought and asks whether this is the reason he has attacked such *generous* men. Both Hertford and his son would rather lose their reputation than their gold. The lord then cautions the poet against the dangers of his course. The public may turn against him, no matter how well or how truthfully he writes. The poet rejects this warning with justified pride:

> This angry World, in anger's spite,
> Buys up my works and urges me to write:
> And some there are, in these degenerate days,
> Who shed upon my verse the dew of praise.
>
> (Page 36)

He refuses to be moved by possible dangers. He has no reason to seek favour from anyone by writing dishonest, insipid verses. He is no hireling laureate!

Let Whitehead frame for Courts th'Harmonious lie,
And weave his annual wreaths for Flattery:
I would not quit my honourable road
For thrice the profits of a Royal Ode.   (Page 37)

Hackwriter or no, Combe is here expressing the new views of
literary professionalism, asserting the writer's obligation to society,
his freedom to state the truth as he sees it, his right to be paid for his
services like other professionals, and his proper—which is to say,
uncompromising—reliance for support upon the reading public rather
than upon patrons. These ideas were in the air at the time, and Combe
in his usual way was not slow to pick them up and make appropriate
use of them. In a sense he does justify himself in this poem, but rather
in what he says about a writer's professional independence than in
anything he could possibly say about satire. The poem was well
named for the wrong reasons.

Although the reviewers in December found the *Justification* on the
whole a worthy successor to the *Diaboliad*, both the *Monthly* and the
Critical spoke of the author's tendency to produce faulty rhymes, and
a writer in the *Gentleman's Magazine* stoutly asserted, "This may be
sense, but it is no more poetry than Donne's", and quoted a few lines
from Donne's *Satires* to prove the point. The *London Magazine*
(Appendix 1777) raised another objection, remarking that "Some
critics will be apt to think the poet's pen is an instrument of party,
when they read that Savile, Rockingham, Camden, and Chatham are
to call forth his talents for praise, while the scourge is to be exercised
only on their adversaries." The point was well taken; throughout his
career Combe was fairly consistent in criticizing only those who
opposed the ministry. Ultimately he was to become, as we shall see,
a paid propagandist for Pitt's Government. For the moment, however, he had nothing explicit to say on political issues. His concern
was necessarily himself, William Combe, Esq., a man alone against
the world, forced to relinquish his cherished dream of living as a
gentleman in the fashionable world, but now given reason to believe
that he can earn an honourable living by his pen. If it was not quite
the exalted role he had once aspired to, it might yet be justified in one
way or another. And it might not prove totally inconsistent with his
gentlemanly pretensions—provided, of course, he wrote anonymously
and so kept the source of his income private.

* * *

Two days before *The Justification* reached the bookstalls an announcement appeared which required immediate attention from the satirist of the Hertfords. A socially prominent branch of that family had met with reverses (unexplained but not beyond conjecture) and was forced to liquidate its Grafton Street household. The satire which Combe produced in celebration of this event is not one of his most notable pieces, but it is curiously interesting as evidence of the resourceful satirist's methods.

A prominent feature of newspapers at that time was the section devoted to auctions of private property. Many of these were occasioned by the death of wealthy householders and were so announced. But certain other advertisements, rather more ambiguously phrased, announced sales forced by family misfortunes—often, no doubt, traceable to St James's Street. These were usually described as sales of property belonging to "a nobleman retiring to Bath", or a gentleman "on account of his health going to reside abroad". It was notorious, in fact, that a wealthy man who met with disaster at the gaming-table could often arrange a quick auction of his household effects and escape to the Continent before his creditors could levy on him and force him into bankruptcy. Since fashionable London could usually supply the name of the anonymous seller and scandalmongers could always add the sordid details, it is safe to assume that there was no mystery and but little surprise in the West End when on December 4 the *Morning Post* printed the following slightly veiled advertisement:

SALES BY AUCTION

By Mr. Squibb,
At his Great Room, in Saville Row, on Thursday the
11th inst. and following days,
The superb and singularly elegant Household Furniture, magnificent Pier Glasses, rich and beautiful veriegated Damask, Tissues and Sattins in compleat drawing-room suits, of Cabrioles, Confidantes, and Ottomans, statuary inlaid Pier Tables, Commodes and Sheffoniers, cut Glass Lustres and Gerondoles, Seve and Dresden Porcelain, Brussels Carpets, with many other valuable effects
the Property of a NOBLEMAN
Removed from Grafton-street.

N.B. The pier glasses are of most distinguished magnitude, perfectly brilliant, in highly finished frames, and the whole of the furniture in excellent preservation.

To be viewed Tuesday and Wednesday preceding the sale. Catalogues may be then had at Garraway's Coffee-house; at the room, Saville Row. and of Mr. Squibb, Charles-street, Berkley-square.

All pretence of anonymity was dropped the following day when the advertisement was repeated, this time with the owner's name: "The Right Hon. Lord Villiers". Nor was there any concealment of the facts two weeks later when Christie and Ansell advertised the house itself: "The noble, spacious, leasehold mansion, with suitable offices, &c. situate in Grafton Street, the late residence of the Right Hon. Lord Villiers. The premises are sumptuously finished, in a stile singularly elegant, and fit for the reception of a large noble family." The whole episode was perfectly adapted to Combe's needs, for Lord Villiers was Beauchamp's brother-in-law; his wife was Gertrude, third daughter of the Earl of Hertford. The inevitable satire, with preface of suitable admonishment, was published by J. Bew on January 17: *The Auction: A Town Eclogue. By the Honourable Mr. ——*.

Irked by the irony of the phrase "The Right Hon." prefixed to Lord Villiers's name in the advertisement, Combe not only signed himself "The Honourable Mr. ——" but also ostentatiously dedicated the work to "The Right Honourable Lady V-ll-rs" and roundly asserted in his preface that "these Auctions are so many genteel, Honourable, and Right Honourable Bankruptcies". Gossip attributed the distress of Lord Villiers to extravagant living rather than to losses at cards,[32] and Combe devoted his preface entirely to an impersonal discourse on extravagance, a topic on which he could write with authority.

> A late excellent Comedian [Samuel Foote, whe had died on October 21] being asked by a Nobleman who was at his table, how much his side-board of Plate might have cost him, replied, That this circumstance had really escaped his memory; but he believed, in a short time, he should be able to inform his Lordship how much it would fetch to a shilling. This situation seems to be a very common one among our Men of Rank and Figure:—Extravagance is now reduced to System; so that few young men set out upon the career of the Ton, but calculations are made, and frequently supported by considerable Bets, as to the time of its conclusion; and these circumstances are as familiar subjects of conversation among the parties themselves, as if they were matters of the most trifling importance.

(Page i)

The best proof of modern extravagance, he says, is to be found in "the frequent Auctions of the property of *living* persons". It often happens, indeed, that "the domestic apparatus of modern magnificence is almost without an interval of repose between the Warehouse of the Upholsterer and the Repository of the Auctioneer". The only ones visibly to profit from such dissipation are the "Gentlemen of the Wooden Hammer".

The verses which follow portray the distraught Vainetta on the day her household possessions are to be auctioned. She tearfully looks at her Dresden china for the last time and glances about at various items which the advertisement had particularized: her lustre, her crystal mirror, her downy couch, her chair, her "silken sofas, gay in streaky dress of varied colours", wondering what is to become of them all. She recalls in detail the miserly economies practised in the home of her parents, when she had learned "the saintly look, and hypocritic air"; she laments the ill fortune which has strewn her name "with long-continued rage, Upon the Morning's foul and tainted page"; she thinks how "Devon in laughter will my fate bewail", and she wishes she had been more like Brother B[eauchamp], "to every sordid interest meanly true". With that she leaves her house, returns an unwelcome guest to "H[ertford]'s door", and enters reluctantly "to learn new systems of Oeconomy". From first to last there is no evidence in the poem that Combe had the slightest knowledge of the Villiers household beyond what was contained in the auctioneers' advertisements.

The Auction was clearly a minor effort; it runs only to four pages of prose and twelve of verse, and it sold for one shilling (as against two shillings and sixpence for *The Justification*). Combe had again struck a popular note, however, and the pamphlet was reprinted in several editions. Few readers would be interested in knowing the author's name, but the curious would have little trouble relating the work to the *Diaboliad* series. The style, the format, the bookseller, and the continued heckling of the Hertfords were the same, and if the reader was still in doubt he would find a hint in the advertisement appended to the poem: "Lately published . . . a new edition of *The Justification: A Poem.* By the author of *The Diaboliad.*" Professionals would recognize the author without such clues. Early the following year, in fact, while discussing another publication, the *Monthly Review* (March 1778) even mentioned him as "Mr. C——" and identified him as the author of the *Diaboliad*.[33] His remarkable success had not gone unnoticed in Paternoster Row, and Combe was never one to keep the secret of his authorship after his writings had been safely launched.

* * *

Only one more satire in the series requires mention in this chapter, for Combe had no sooner "justified" his career than it took a new turn and he found himself occupied with writing of a very different kind. That the wind of favour was veering away from his *Diaboliad* manner is fully evident from the appearance in March of a stinging reply to *The Justification*. This was an anonymous satire published by James Dodsley and entitled *The Refutation: a Poem. Addressed to the Author of The Justification*. A strongly worded Preface declares that satire is "a proof of a discontented mind" rather than "a work for the good of the human race". It is a "cloak, which, in this present age, we too often see lined with the fashionable fur of scandal". The verses which follow tell Combe in no uncertain terms that he is not really interested in reform at all:

> Far diff'rent thy design; not such thy plan;
> Thy aim's to irritate, not mend the man.
> Should B[eauchamp]'s breast with public virtue glow,
> Should S[andwich] quit th'allurements of the fair,
> And D[erby] leave the town for Surry air;
> Should H[ertford]'s hand distribute lib'ral alms,
> And cousin A[yscough] take to singing psalms,
> No Diaboliads would fill your purse,
> But reformation prove to you a curse.
>
> (Pages 11–12)

The able author of *The Refutation* has not been identified, but readers today will tend to agree with contemporary reviewers that Combe was worsted in the debate. He had learned from his own victims to disregard such attacks, and whatever he may have felt privately his only visible response was the publication in April of *The Diaboliad. A Poem. Part the Second. By the Author of Part the First. Dedicated to the Worst Woman in His Majesty's Dominions* (J. Bew). Although twice as long as the first part and written with much the same vigour, this continuation must be called an anticlimax. The scheme of the poem is original, and many of the lines are witty, but the idea has somehow lost its novelty.

Part the Second takes up the narrative where the earlier part left off. Satan takes formal leave of his throne, boasting for ten pages of the evil he has done in the world, and the new king responds with a speech in which he proclaims his "zeal for Diabolic sway". As the new leader of Heaven's opposition party, he asks for a mate: "I want an Eve an Eden to destroy!" Messengers set off as before in search of likely candidates; these promptly appear and set forth their qualifications. The Duchess of Bedford is first, followed by the Duchess of Kingston, Lady Barrymore, Mrs Cavendish, Lady Grosvenor, Mrs Damer, Lady Harrington, and other favourites of scandal. But before any candidate can be successful, the shades of Hell's female inhabitants rise up in revolt. Why is it necessary to look outside Hell itself for a queen? By doing so the new king has shown himself a traitor and must be replaced by "a potent and self-reigning Queen". Civil war breaks out, and as the poem becomes a kind of burlesque *Paradise Lost* in reverse, the poet withdraws to gather new strength before describing "the well-fought battles and the fate of Hell". At this point the poem breaks off, but instead of writing FINIS Combe suggestively writes END OF THE SECOND PART. The response was anything but encouraging, however, and no *Part the Third* ever appeared.

The *Monthly Review* (April) acknowledged that the author was a "distinguished master of the poetical tomahawk and scalping knife", but it found this continuation of the *Diaboliad* inferior to the first part. The *Gentleman's Magazine* (April), more outspoken, asked to "hear no more of the infernal broils of this poet laureate of hell". Although the public bought up the pamphlet and new editions were printed, there was no duplicating the enthusiasm of the year before. The booksellers, to be sure, made some effort to keep the topic alive. In July, Samuel Bladon published *The Devil's Wedding, a Poem* (involving a search for a chaplain to perform the ceremony and for suitable ladies of the bedchamber and maids of honour), and two years later—the marriage presumably on the rocks by that time—M. Smith issued *The Devil Divorced; or, The Diabo-Whore* (a feeble effort describing a search for an acceptable mistress as successor to the dismissed wife). Neither of these satires can be attributed to Combe, who was too sensitive a hackwriter not to know when he had exhausted his audience. He had already started on a new tack by publishing the first volume of his R[oya]l Register (J. Bew), and although this work is in a sense satire, it is so entirely different from anything Combe had yet written that it must be discussed in another chapter. Over the next seven years he wrote one more letter, possibly two letters, to the Duchess of Devonshire and produced five more verse satires, one of them announced as "By the Author of the *Diaboliad*".[34] In none of these efforts did he return to his earlier manner, however, nor did he even in a small way repeat his first success. His career as a verse satirist, except for these sporadic efforts, had lasted just fourteen months.

* * *

Combe's failure to leave a name for himself as a satirist was essentially of his own choosing. Although he was certainly vain of his literary abilities, part of his vanity lay in denying that he had them. These books and pamphlets of his, he seems to say, are mere trifles which he has tossed off at idle moments for his own amusement and that of his friends. "I was not born to refine and polish my own Compositions", he says in the dedication of his *Diaboliad*. "I know, my Lord, that I am a careless Writer: The inaccuracies of this Address, and the pages which succeed it, will, I fear, fully prove my assertion." Despite his "Justification" of the profession of letters, he always insists upon this pose of the elegant dilettante; one is given to understand that it would be beneath his dignity to toil over his manuscripts and painstakingly revise them. To take such pains with these "trifles" would be to acknowledge that he was seriously interested in pleasing the public, perhaps even trying to make his works profitable.

This pose of deliberate carelessness, of elegant trifling, was his defence against his critics, who sometimes treated him with severity. Thus, in December 1777, after the appearance of *The Justification*, all the reviews deplored his failure to write as well as he seemed able. The *Gentleman's Magazine* called him "very unequal in his verse, sometimes soaring like an eagle, at other times sinking like a lark". The *Monthly Review* advised "this promising and spirited Writer, whom we suppose to be a young man, to be more attentive . . . to correctness of taste, and exactness with respect to rhymes". The *Critical Review* specified nineteen faulty rhymes in the poem (boast-lost, soothe-truth, dare-star, etc.) which "ill become the bard who more than stands candidate for, who trusts himself into, the vacant chair of Churchill". It may be doubted that Combe was, in fact, as casual about these matters as he pretended, but readers of his satires have always had the uneasy feeling that he could have written better if he had taken more pains.

More damaging to his reputation than occasional flaws in his verses are the numerous pamphlets, both in prose and verse, which he undeniably produced and which are entirely without literary merit. His fatuous letters to the Duchess of Devonshire, for example, were simply merchandise; Combe wrote them for profit and disguised the fact that they were written by the author of the *Diaboliad*. Scholarship has perhaps done Combe's reputation no kindness by seeking out these meretricious works for inclusion in his bibliography.

The *Diaboliad* series, however, is another story. It included six separately published works: *The Diaboliad, Additions to the Diaboliad, The First of April, The Justification, The Diaboliad: Part the Second,* and *The World as It Goes,* the last five all identified on their title-pages as by the author of the first. Combe's reputation as a verse satirist must rest on these titles, and together they constitute a body of work by no means so negligible as posterity, without reading them, has assumed. They are certainly superior to any comparable writing by Combe's contemporaries, some of whom have been mentioned above, but mercifully left unquoted. *The Diaboliad* cannot hold a candle to *The Dunciad* and is inferior as a sustained satire to *The Rosciad*, though contemporaries often and with some justice compared Combe and Churchill. Yet *The Diaboliad* possesses qualities of wit and indignation which lift it well above the usual Grub Street level. Combe's weapon was neither the rapier nor the bludgeon, but rather, perhaps, the cane, and with it he chastised his erring contemporaries in a manner which, if it did not reform, at least commanded a certain grudging respect.

Why, then, did he not follow his *Diaboliad* series with other verse satires? The Prefaces to *The Justification* says explicitly that he intends to do so, and an advertisement at the end of that work promises that *Satire the First* will be published in the course of the winter. But no such satire appeared. Instead, the first volume of *The R[oya]l Register* came out the following month (January 1778), and the series continued until the ninth volume was published in 1784. During these seven years every one of Combe's works was "Printed for J. Bew", and nearly all were in a new format, small octavo or duodecimo instead of quarto—books instead of pamphlets, and hence adapted to the needs of circulating libraries. It was a new business arrangement of some kind, and it prompted Combe to begin writing in a new way.

There is little likelihood that the *Diaboliad* satires will ever again be read except by scholars. Unless one is willing to review old scandals and rediscover once-notorious personalities, topical and personal satire has little point. Although London society of the 1770s is not without its curious and even sensational interest, posterity has scandals and sensations of its own. To be sure, Combe's satires require no more minute documentation than Pope's, but they are quite without the poetic genius which compels readers of *The Dunciad* to seek out the footnotes. Combe's lines are often well turned and amusing, but they can also occasionally be tedious, even in his best work. He often seems almost deliberate in making them so. There was undeniably a posture about him which was to some extent responsible for his failure to achieve, except in his imagination, the superior role he wished for himself. But the posture itself is so apparent, so contrived, sometimes so preposterous, that it too seems amusing. One does not read him expecting to find the qualities of a Milton, a Pope, or even a Churchill. One expects and finds those of William Combe, Esq.

CHAPTER IV

IMITATOR

Whate'er he said, whate'er he sung
Deceit ne'er glanced upon his tongue;
For if by chance to please the folk,
And laugh and wonder to provoke,
He blink'd at truth,—it was in joke.
                    —Doctor Syntax

WHEN William Combe published the first volume of his R[oya]l
Register in January 1778, he was beginning an activity which was to
occupy most of his attention for nearly seven years. During that time
he produced six works amounting in all to nineteen small volumes,
every one of which was published as though written by someone else.
The *Register* itself, always guardedly called R——l, never *Royal*, was
supposed to read as though it were the King's private notebook. It
appeared at intervals throughout the period, the ninth and last volume
in 1784. Meanwhile, Combe also turned out two volumes of letters
"supposed to have been written by Yorick and Eliza", two of the letters
solemnly (but unconvincingly) attributed to Lord Lyttelton, and three
epistolary novels totalling six volumes. One of these novels was called
a translation from Rousseau, one was identified as an imitation of
Sterne, and the third professed to be a series of actual letters written
by unnamed persons.

The contemporary reader, accustomed to finding such works in the
bookstalls, was seldom deceived. The reviewers normally recognized
them as imitations and, after giving the author a good-natured tap on
the wrist, proceeded to examine each on its merits. Critics were not
unwilling to note "lively strokes of wit and fancy" or to speak of
"abilities in the writer, whoever he may be". In discussing the letters
attributed to Lyttelton, the *Critical Review* (May 1782) gently chides
the author for his "fraud", then asks whether the characterization is

just and well-sustained, whether the letters are on interesting subjects, whether the style is clear and brilliant, and whether the work contains amusing and well-written passages. Finding affirmative answers to all these questions, the writer recommends the book; though not by Lyttelton, the letters do him no discredit and are in themselves entertaining. Other imitative publications were reviewed with similar urbanity. Thus, speaking of one of Combe's epistolary novels, the same journal (October 1784) remarks, "According to the editor's declaration these Letters are not supposititious. But the style in which they are written is no stranger to us, and gives the lie to the assertion. The Letters, however, on this account, cannot have less intrinsic merit; and in point both of composition and sentiment, they are such as may afford pleasure to a reader of taste."[1] The reviewer is not outraged; he simply classifies the novel as an imitation and pronounces it a good one. These works were recognized, though sometimes with mild objection, as a conventional feature of the literary scene. No one in 1766 believed for a moment that the *Vicar of Wakefield*, though "supposed to have been written by himself", was actually the work of Parson Primrose.

Posterity has been more gullible and less generous. Nineteenth- and twentieth-century scholars have sometimes gone to great lengths in order to argue that certain of these publications are authentic (thus making Combe an impostor when he acknowledged them), or that they were forgeries (thus making him a liar when he set forth conventional assurances of authenticity). Some writers have even sought to have it both ways, arguing that certain portions are authentic ("most exquisite harmony of music and meaning")[2] while others are forgeries ("buffoonish interpolations").[3] The only point of agreement among these diverse critics is their exasperation with William Combe, manifestly a forger, a liar, and "an unscrupulous hack".[4]

Modern scholarship, to be sure, cannot ignore the possibility that these books, or some of them, may contain authentic materials. Sterne scholars must give close attention to *Letters Supposed to Have Been Written by Yorick and Eliza*, even though the word *supposed* in the title disclaims literal authorship by the two putative correspondents. It would be most unwise to overlook the possibility that here, as in Combe's other imitations, some authentic strands have been woven into the fabric of the letters. One writer has even ventured to call the two little volumes Sterne's from first to last. The problem has all the fascination of a puzzle to which there is no entirely satisfactory solution.

It must be observed, however, that those who have concerned themselves with the *Letters Supposed* have without exception done so because of their involvement with the man being imitated. Not since the eighteenth century has anyone read the book with the intention of doing justice to the skill of the imitator. To do so now may not finally resolve the doubts of the Sterne scholars, but it may help us understand the relationship between Combe and his contemporary reader. That reader, incidentally, would be astonished by twentieth-century insistence upon authenticity to the last comma, particularly in texts of this kind. He would reject such scholarship as pedantic enthusiasm. His own attitude would be that expressed by the *Monthly Review* (October 1784): supposititious works such as the *Letters Supposed* "may be read with pleasure, whether they are considered as original or fictitious".

*   *   *

On January 29, 1778, appeared the first volume of *The R[oya]l Register. With Annotations by Another Hand* (Bew). The Introduction cautiously suggests that "a Person in the highest rank"—the King, that is—makes a practice of jotting down memoranda concerning persons in the court. Furthermore, it asserts that manuscripts which bear the mark of just such royal origin have come into the hands of the "editor" in a highly mysterious manner. They were brought to him by a woman "in mean but neat apparel" who offered to sell them on behalf of a gentleman lodger, a clergyman who, when interviewed, only mumbled incoherently and promptly died. An examination of the clergyman's private papers has revealed the circumstances of his life. "They will form a melancholy story, and the World shall one day weep at it. When that appears, the motive to this publication will be known,—and, I think, applauded" (page xiv). At this point the reader begins to anticipate the pathetic ordeals of a sentimental novel, for such mystifications were endemic in that genre. The lugubrious note is dropped at once, however, and does not recur in the work. The Introduction itself concludes with the literary tradesman's advertisement that the present volume is but the first of several which the manuscripts will afford and which will be published in due course.

The *Register* is a collection of observations on well-known individuals

[103]

in court society—fifty-one of them in the first volume alone—
each identified only by initials and dashes: E—— G——, D—— of
D—— —— ——, A—— —— —— of C—— —— —— ——. The
dashes indicating syllables facilitate the identifications: Earl Gower,
Duke of Devonshire, Archbishop of Canterbury. Some of the sketches
run to several pages; others consist only of a cryptic sentence or two.
The "annotations by another hand" are footnotes supplied by the
"editor". Sometimes asterisks appear in the main entries instead of
words, suggesting that royalty had expressed itself with indiscreet
frankness. The asterisks, when they occur, usually seem more suggestive than any printable words could be. (Combe had copied the device
from Sterne, but he was incapable of Yorick's more explicit impro-
prieties.) An amusing feature of the work is the contrast between the
solemn and rather pompous main entries and the ironic additions and
insinuations of the annotator. The latter writes very much like a
Morning Post paragrapher, but the body of the text is written in a
manner intended to pass as the royal style. It may have little resemblance to anything ever written by George III, but Combe was
sufficiently versatile to assume a recognizable (and often amusing)
royal stance. The *Gentleman's Magazine* (March 1778), in fact,
thought it prudent to warn its readers that "the writer is but a
clumsy counterfeit". With rather more sense of humour, the *Monthy
Review* (February 1778) remarked that "there is novelty in the
design, and the execution is neither contemptible in itself, nor (on
the whole) dishonourable to the supposed R...y...l Register-
keeper". A year later, after the appearance of the second and third
volumes, the same journal (May 1779) praised the work highly as
"much superior to the common catch-penny things. The Writer has
acquired information; he possesses ability to make the most of it; and
his remarks are enlivened by the number and variety of characters
and anecdotes with which these little volumes abound."

The volumes do indeed contain stores of information and anecdote,
but an important element in the *Register*'s popular success was its air
of exclusiveness, its pretence that these veiled allusions would only be
understood by readers with inside knowledge of court society. In
reality the disguises and concealments were almost transparent;
initials and dashes made identification of the principals easy for anyone who could spell, and the sly references to court scandal would be
fully appreciated by readers of the *Morning Post*. But the work

flattered its readers by making them feel *au courant* with London society, and few of them were able to resist adding their own marginal annotations. Scarcely a surviving copy of the R[oya]l *Register* lacks its pencilled identifications in a contemporary hand. There is little wonder that the work was one of Combe's most successful projects.

Unfortunately for his reputation, the very qualities which once made the *Register* popular now virtually prevent us from reading it at all. Most of the once-notorious characters are quite unknown today, the ancient scandals long since forgotten. Even specialists, unless they undertake specific investigation of the subject, are unlikely to possess that minimum of information which Combe could assume in readers of 1778. And when the old anecdotes are resurrected and duly set forth with full documentation, they may have the dignity of social history, but they have lost the immediacy which once made them sensational. Two examples will suggest what the *Register* meant to contemporary readers and will also explain why this best-seller of the 1780s has become a dusty item on library shelves.

When a reader in 1778 encountered "E—— of S—— ——" in the first volume of the *Register*, he could unhesitatingly write "Earl of Sandwich" in the margin. The Earl was First Lord of the Admiralty and also one of the more notable sinners of the time. Combe had given him a role in the *Diaboliad*, and inevitably he appears early in this prose satire. The royal comment begins as follows:

> The art of robbing vice of it's [*sic*] disgust, and throwing around it the mantle of convivial pleasure, belongs in a very peculiar manner to this Nobleman. I understand, that from his youth to the present time, he has proceeded in one uniform, unblushing course of debauchery and dissipation. His conversation is chiefly tinctured with unchaste expressions and indecent allusions; and some have assured me, that if these were to be omitted by him, much of his Wit, or, at least, what is called his Wit, would be lost.
>
> (I, 76–77)

This comment was calculated to give much satisfaction to the man in the street, who loved scandal as much as he professed to detest vice. Lord Sandwich was a very important man, one of the King's own ministers, and said to be no better than he should be. What must the King think? Here is a plausible answer, but it is only incidental to the particularization which follows. The entry continues with a scornful reference to Sandwich's speech in the House of Lords attacking "a blasphemous production of Mr. W——". A footnote quotes from Sandwich's hypocritical speech concerning John Wilkes's indecent poem, the "Essay on Woman". Wilkes and Sandwich were, in fact, fellow members of the Hell Fire Club, and no one believed Sandwich capable of being shocked by anything. He was simply using this indiscreet publication as a safe means of attacking one whose political views were anathema to him, though popular with the English public. Many people found Sandwich's assumption of moral superiority more offensive than his well-advertised vices.

His opponents thus had a new weapon to use against him when in November 1763, just a week after the speech, he let it be known that he was candidate for election to the post of High Steward of Cambridge. The announcement initiated a controversy which lasted for a year and a half and became the bitterest in the entire history of the University. The issue was finally taken to the courts, and on May 7, 1765, the decision went against Sandwich. The unsavoury episode was by no means forgotten thirteen years later when Combe merely alluded to it in the *Register*. The "royal" entry in that work vaguely mentions Sandwich's unpopularity with the undergraduates when he was candidate for high office at Cambridge. A footnote then describes a dinner given in his honour at Trinity, when "as soon as Grace was pronounced, all the Scholars, &c. to the number of forty, immediately quitted the Hall.—This dignified mark of contempt made, I believe, the soup of that day, and some succeeding ones, very bitter to his Lordship" (I, 82 n). In point of fact, every undergraduate but one left the hall and noisily demonstrated in the court outside. Dr Robert Smith, the Master of Trinity, was a leading proponent of the Sandwich cause and demanded that the students either apologize or be dismissed. The adamant students were supported by a majority of the Trinity dons, however, and eventually Dr Smith was forced to capitulate.[5] The incident was widely publicized at the time, and again Combe need only allude to it. The whole story was useful to the satirist in 1778, when the American War was going badly and Sandwich was accused, probably unjustly, of incompetence in the Admiralty. Readers acquainted with the political battles of 1763, 1764, and 1765 found the sketch amusingly ironic and timely in 1778. Readers today, lacking that knowledge, find it meaningless.

Similarly, any reader of the *Morning Post* or the *Town and Country Magazine* would enjoy the following entry, here quoted in full:

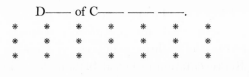

D—— of C—— —— ——.

(1, 66)

No one in 1778 would be surprised to find that the annotator has thought it best to omit the King's comments concerning his brother, the Duke of Cumberland. All London had relished the story of the Duke's awkward predicament when Lord Grosvenor discovered his affair with Lady Grosvenor. Instead of suing for divorce, Lord Grosvenor sued for damages and asked large ones. On July 5, 1770, he brought witnesses and tell-tale letters before Lord Mansfield in the Court of King's Bench. His evidence was detailed and convincing; furthermore, it was reported in all the scandal-sheets of the time. The Duke of Cumberland had to pay damages of £10,000 and, even more humiliating, he had reason to believe that London society, having read his letters to Lady Grosvenor, was more amused by his ungrammatical foolishness than shocked by his adultery.[6] Hence, the asterisks in the *Register* required no annotation by the editor, But one question still remained unanswered. What had the King thought of Lord Grosvenor's conduct in the affair? The very next entry supplies a plausible answer. It is headed "L—— G—— —— ——", and after seven lines of asterisks (the Duke had been granted only three) the sketch concludes with one sentence: "It chagrined me exceedingly, I must own: nevertheless, as an honest man, I firmly believe that in his [Grosvenor's] situation, I should have done the same" (I, 67). The contemporary reader could smile at Combe's trifle, but the reader today is helpless without the background. And unfortunately, trifles do not survive laboured explanations.

The first volume of the R[oya]l Register (1778) caught popular fancy at once, and realizing that they had a good thing, Combe and his bookseller quickly produced a second volume and made plans to extend the series indefinitely. In order to maintain interest, successive volumes introduced new features and promised still others in store. Volume II (1778), for example, begins with a twenty-two-page "character" of Lord Mansfield, who had recently been raised to the peerage, and concludes with a timely twenty-six pages "By the Annotator" on Lord Chatham, who had died while the volume was in preparation. Over half of Volume III (1779) consists of "An

Apology for King Log the Younger"—an extended comparison of George II and George III, also presumably by the annotator. Volume V (1781) devotes forty-three pages to "A Cursory Account of the Diplomatic Representation of Great Britain, &c." This gives Combe an opportunity to mention the Earl of Hertford, "a man of known and established character for niggardly Avarice; and who, during his residence at Paris, practised all the narrow principles of his beggarly Œconomy, to the encrease of his own fortune, but at the expense of his Country's honour" (V, 153). Volume VII (1782) contains "A Brief Account of the Principal Orators of the Present Times" with particular attention to Mansfield, Chatham, Burke, and Dunning.[7]

As the series progressed, the style gradually changed. In the first volumes Combe made a real effort to differentiate between the "royal" style and that of the "annotator", but gradually the two voices were allowed to merge into one. By the ninth volume (1784) the whole convention seems forgotten, and the Introduction frankly states the author's intention concerning future publications in the series. The next volume, he says, will contain observations on "the principal female characters of the present period". Even as Sterne had promised to continue *Tristram Shandy* at the rate of two volumes a year as long as he lived, Combe and Bew seem prepared to keep the *Register* going as long as the public remains interested in this mysterious manuscript—which at one point in the series Combe prudently says is turning out to be much longer and more comprehensive than he had originally thought. By the end of the ninth volume the number of sketches totals exactly three hundred, and the end is not yet in sight. It was to come, however, in the shape of a bailiff before Combe could write the tenth, and a successful publishing venture was unluckily terminated before it could run its course.

*   *   *

The nine volumes of the *Register* do not deserve the total neglect into which thay have fallen. Students of the period may find here a storehouse of anecdote and comment, some of it having unique significance. The observations on public figures are not always very striking, but if read critically they occasionally provide useful sidelights on individuals and their motives. Combe's point of view is pro-ministerial but not violently partisan. By and large the Whig dogs get the worst of it, yet Combe can be fair to Edmund Burke. In a volume published in 1782 he writes, "Mr. Burke's powers of persuasion are scarcely to be equalled, his sources of knowledge are universal and inexhaustible, his memory is comprehensive and faithful, while his mind teems with the most luxuriant imagery, cloathed in the most elegant language, and strengthened by the most fortunate and brilliant expressions." He speaks further of Burke's splendid imagery, "the harmony of his periods", and his amazing command of language even in impromptu speeches. He complains that Burke's flood of images may at times so overwhelm his judgement that he "exerts the same powers on the regulation of a waggon wheel, or some similar subject, as on the most important questions of national honour, or public prosperity. His discourses are sometimes so highly coloured, so profusely embellished, and so thickly sown with brilliant thoughts, that . . . they produce little more than a splendid confusion." Finally, Combe adds the usual criticism of Burke's delivery: "He is wholly inattentive to the common graces of action and delivery: his voice is not harmonious, and he does not seem attentive to remedy the defect, by any artful and judicious management of it." Despite his faults, he is unquestionably "among the most accomplished Orators of his age and country". To all this the annotator ventures only to subjoin his regret that Burke devotes so much attention to "the laborious drudgery of a party, which renders his utility dubious, compresses the powers of his mind, and threatens to obscure his fame" (VII, 161–9).

Combe's personal animosities are held in check in the *Register*; they appear briefly in the first volume, but even there they lack the heat of the verse satires. The Hertfords are not lost sight of, however, and in the final volume of the series Combe inserts the long-promised commentary on his old enemy, Lord Beauchamp. Seven years earlier he had announced in the *Diaboliad* his intention of dealing with Beauchamp "in a separate publication, illustrated and proved by anecdotes of the Character before me when he was at School, the University, in France, Ireland, Warwickshire, and London; as a School-boy, a Collegian, a Traveller, a Secretary, a Militia-commander, a Husband, and so on to the present time,—with collateral relations" (page 17 n). This detailed threat, published early in 1777, is virtually an outline of the piece which he published in 1784. One may even suspect that the sketch as well as the outline was written at the earlier date. Had Combe hoped that his threat, augmented by the continual attacks in subsequent verse satires, might eventually bring his adversary to terms? If so, he was disappointed, and now, his resentment still rankling, he tells the whole story—as much of it, at any rate, as he could repeat without embarrassment to himself or his wife.

The indictment occurs in a long footnote of more than two thousand words. At Eton, Beauchamp had pretended to be a party to an insurrection plotted by the students, but had privately revealed the whole plan to the headmaster. At Oxford he once won a literary competition with an essay which he had paid a professional to write for him. As a young man in Paris (where Combe had probably seen him in 1764), he had been so embarrassed and timid in the presence of women that "mama, with all her piety, was obliged to arrange something of an intrigue for her bashful darling". When he became secretary to his father, then Lord Lieutenant of Ireland, he refused a request made by the Duke of Roxburgh to find a place for "their common friend and school-fellow, Mr. C—— ——, whose unmerited disappointments and amiable qualities rendered him a most deserving object of regard". To this request Beauchamp replied "that he did not consider himself as bound to provide for every necessitous person he might have known at school". (The reference to "Mr. C—— ——" has a suggestive ambiguity, but the dashes require a name of two syllables.) In Ireland, also, he obtained appointment for Dr Gayer at an annual salary of £800, of which sum Beauchamp demanded £600 "for charity". "Every one knows the hereditary principle of the noble Lord,—*That charity begins at home.*" In the provincial militia he exploited his men, obtaining services from them on his own estates without payment. As a public character he is venal and generally distrusted. At this point, in a brief passage of suppressed emotion, Combe finally touches on the real cause of his animosity: "As a lover,—his regards have ever been observed to pass by the lady's charm, to contemplate the dowry that accompanied her.—It is not for his sake, but from a tender appreciation of giving pain to others, who have a right to claim this attention from me, that I omit a detail of circumstances equally curious and contemptible." The concluding three paragraphs of this diatribe (Beauchamp as a brother, as a son, and as a friend) are of a piece with what has gone before and may be passed over now that Combe has arrived at, and skirted, the crucial point (IX, 55–66).

The "circumstances equally curious and contemptible" are never revealed in detail, but the reader will inevitably be reminded of Beauchamp's dismissal of Maria Foster before marrying Lady Isabella in 1776. Combe's reluctance to give these "others" pain suggests an affectionate protectiveness for his wife which is seen, too, in a touching passage from an earlier volume of the *Register*. In that passage Combe has been considering "the rigid severity which is unworthily exercised towards those young women, whom irresistable temptation, impending danger, menacing misfortune, the wiles of the stronger sex, and the artifices of their own, have forced or decoyed from the paths of virtue". He exclaims at the uncharitable attitude of society for such unfortunates:

> With what reason can any woman pretend to be shocked at female vice, or dare to turn her back upon the unchaste, who thinks it a privilege to be admitted to the houses and society of certain Ladies of Rank and Fashion, whose Gallantries, not to say Adulteries, are known to all the world, and are scarcely disavowed by themselves.
>
> There is something, surely, very capricious in the sentiments of modern Honour and modern Charity, or it could never happen, that a woman [who is known to be unfaithful to her husband] . . . is visited and received by the most virtuous of her own sex without even the forms of reluctance; while an unfortunate, deluded female, who is restored to honour by the man who marries her, and whose subsequent conduct justifies his choice, will be regarded with coldness by her own sex, and seldom live long enough to survive the look of contempt, and the circulating whisper of their malevolence, whose whole merit may, perhaps, consist in having been able to conceal a crime which she had too much virtue to disown.————This is the very general conduct of a *charitable* age; a conduct in direct opposition to the commands of the Divine Teacher, and final Rewarder of Christian Charity, who points his anger at the obstinate transgressor, but offers favour, encouragement, and pardon, to the repentant sinner.
>
> (IV, 70–72)

Combe is writing here from personal knowledge, and when the passage is read in the light of his own marriage it provides almost our only glimpse of the man behind the pose which Combe so steadfastly maintained. To lift the mask for a moment, even slightly, is so uncharacteristic of the man that one looks about for a cause. Although Maria is known to have been insane for many years before she died, it is impossible to say just when her husband had to place her where she might receive such meagre care as the age provided for the mentally ill. This sympathetic allusion to the unhappiness of one in

Maria's position occurs in a volume published on March 2, 1780, just at the time when, as we shall presently see, Combe went to the Continent. Since other evidence is altogether lacking, these two circumstances may be noted as at least consistent with Maria's being ill by 1780. So, too, is a chance remark made by a character in a novel which Combe published in 1781: "I should be very low indeed, if I wanted protection from the niece of a man who keeps a mad-house."[8] The remark is entirely gratuitous; nothing in the novel calls for the contemptuous reference.

*   *   *

Early in the summer of 1779 Combe turned from satire to sentiment and produced an imitation of letters exchanged between Sterne and Eliza Draper. Both members of that oddly matched pair were now dead, but there was still a lively market for books exploiting their sentimental relationship. Sterne's letters to Eliza had been published in 1773, but Mrs Draper had taken steps to prevent the publication of her replies and had succeeded in doing so. In 1775 an obliging bookseller had provided the public with a forged set, *Letters from Eliza to Yorick*, and in the same year, the second edition of the *Letters from Yorick to Eliza* had appeared. Combe was beginning his own imitations of Sterne by that time, and these two publications supplied him with some hints, possibly even with the whole idea for his own contribution to the Yorick–Eliza legend. Several of his first supposititious letters had appeared, as we have seen, in June 1775, and there is some reason to suspect that he also began this new project at that time. His plan required the imitation of both Yorick and Eliza in the same work, each pouring out to the other the sentiments occasioned by their separation in April 1767. Combe could confidently undertake to produce Sterne's part of the epistolary dialogue, but could he also supply Mrs Draper's? The question probably never occurred to him. He would be the last person to doubt his ability to improvise letters in the manner of a sentimental woman. His writings, in fact, are filled with such letters. Besides, if we can for the moment suspend our disbelief, he had actually known Eliza. It was one of the boasts of his later years that he had had an affair with her.

The boast cannot be substantiated, though here as in all his fantastic tales one must look for a possible kernel of truth. Combe certainly told Samuel Rogers that "it was with him, not with Sterne, that Eliza was in love", and he embroidered the story with an absurd account of flight from her bedroom without one of his shoes.[9] The scene of this alleged escapade was Brighton, and it is at least theoretically possible that they were both there in 1765 or 1766 before Eliza met Sterne and before Combe exhausted his inheritance. It is also conceivable that the two should have met in Bristol during Combe's affluent years. Eliza is known to have died in or near that city in 1778; she was buried in Bristol Cathedral, apparently at the expense of another literary admirer, the Abbé Raynal. A local tradition, quite unconfirmed, has Eliza spending her last days at the home of Sir William and Lady Draper, relatives of her estranged husband. That would seem an awkward arrangement, however, and in any event she was not in Bristol during Combe's five-month visit in 1775.[10] Some acquaintance with Eliza would undoubtedly be useful to her imitator, but the lack of that advantage would not deter him from providing the public with her "letters". He might hesitate to do so in 1775, when she was still alive, but her death in 1778 would enable him to publish without danger of embarrassment.

Even apart from his friendship with Sterne and his possible acquaintance with Eliza Draper, Combe was well equipped for the imitator's task. He was a clever mimic, and in writing as in conversation he could assume various postures and styles at will. It is almost impossible, in fact, to say which of his various styles is his own. His "man-of-learning" style when writing an introduction to the Œconomy of Health or to John Hunter's Practical Treatise on the Diseases of the Teeth, his complacent moral-counsellor style addressed to the Duchess of Devonshire, his whiplash style in the prose satires, his guide-book style in the History of the Thames, his straight-forward journalistic style in The Times, his man-of-feeling style in the Philosopher in Bristol—all are equally Combe's. But during the first part of his writing career and to some extent throughout his life, his best prose was written in the sentimental manner so popular during the last third of the eighteenth century. Few writers could manage this style with the delicacy of Sterne, but one who sometimes came very close was William Combe.

His contemporaries were fully aware of his imitative skill. When he published his Letters Supposed to Have Been Written by Yorick and Eliza (Bew) in the summer of 1779, the Critical Review (July) commented on the similarity between these letters and Sterne's "genuine productions", remarking somewhat ambiguously that "they might with great appearance of justice be ascribed to that writer". Samuel Badcock discussed the imitation at greater length in the *Monthly Review* (October), defining its merits and limitations in a manner which few readers would amend today:

> We must acknowledge that these little volumes bear a strong resemblance of Mr. Sterne's epistolary style: particularly that which his whim or his weakness led him to adopt when he wrote his amoroso-sentimental letters to Mrs. Draper. His manner in those letters might be easily imitated by a man of very moderate genius with a little fancy and feeling, who would find the superior excellencies of his other writings quite beyond his reach. In vain shall we search these volumes for the enchanting wildness—the original wit and humour—the vivid descriptions—the exquisite pathos, or the acute reflections of *Tristram Shandy* and the *Sentimental Journey*. The spirit is fled:—what is left is mawkish and insipid! The Writer of these Letters hath caught little of Yorick, except the whine and cant of—we know not what to call that species of love with which he addressed Mrs. Draper. It was in truth a sniveling passion;—it was love struck with a palsy: and we never read letters written in this style, but we recall to mind a passage in the Apocrypha concerning "the eunuch who embraceth a virgin—and—sigheth".

By no means the best of Combe's imitations, this little *tour de force* would require no further comment were it not for an effort made some years ago to establish it as an authentic part of the Sterne canon, ranking, indeed, "with the best of his work". Under the title of *Second Journal to Eliza*, it was republished in 1929 and called "the supreme *apologia* of Sterne's genius, the most penetrating and judicious study of his personality that has yet been written, and one that, by its organic connection with his Works, transcends the limits of an imitation".[11] Sterne scholars immediately rejected the heresy, partly on the basis of chronological inconsistencies, partly by citing parallel passages showing how Combe had derived his materials from Sterne's published works,[12] and partly because the style simply does not "come very close to Sterne's or Mrs. Draper's".[13] Anyone who knows Combe's work will reach the same conclusion by a different route. The *Letters* are consistent with everything known about that imitative writer and give every evidence of being his.

The two volumes appeared, of course, with Combe's usual elaborate concealments. "The author" addresses the reader with the familiar statement that these letters "were written for the purpose of private amusement, and as a relaxation from more serious employments". "The editor" also puts in a word of explanation and apology. "I do not aim at imposing on the world", he proclaims; "these are but imitations." He tells of persuading the author to permit publication of these letters in order to avoid their unauthorized appearance in print, possibly with false claims of authenticity like those which had accompanied *Sterne's Letters to His Friends on Various Occasions* (1775), the volume already mentioned as containing several of Combe's imitations. The "editor" tells of bringing that illicit publication to the attention of his friend, who now formally acknowledges a portion of its contents. On discovering that some of his imitations had already been published without his knowledge or consent, the friend "immediately went to his closet, and reaching from the shelf two thin folio paper books in marble covers, 'There,' said he, to me, 'take them;—they are now yours, and consigned to your disposal.'" After unexpected delays, the "editor" has now seen the work through the press without making "the least alteration" in the text (I, [i]–xiii; 1929 ed., [161]–165).

It would be most unwise to accept these editorial explanations as literally true, and no one who understands the conventions of such writing would be tempted to do so. The Preface of the editor does contain some truth, however, and should no more be dismissed than accepted uncritically. Scholars have found, for example, that its enumeration of the author's contributions to the "unauthorized" 1775 volume is faulty in detail but probably true in its general purport. Similarly, the suggestion here that the *Letters Supposed* were already in manuscript when the 1775 volume appeared may be an exaggeration, but internal evidence tends to suggest that at least Yorick's first communication to Eliza may have been written at that time.[14] And throughout these volumes there is much which is reminiscent of the sentimental Bristol philosopher in the summer of 1775.

Whenever either Yorick or Eliza indulges in what is intended as serious reflection, the result is far more like Combe than like Sterne. Thus, Yorick's sermon on Hope (I, 77–99; 1929 ed., 30–39) lacks both the imagination and the intelligence of Sterne's published sermons. The quality of thought which it manifests is regrettably similar to that of the more pretentious passages in the *Philosopher in Bristol* or the fatuous moralizing addressed to the Duchess of

Devonshire. As one scholar has written, "Combe's cloudy trivialities are not the stuff of Sterne's prose".[15]

A hint for the sermon on Hope and for Eliza's supposed reply occurs in one of the *Letters from Yorick to Eliza* (1773) in which Sterne says, "Remember, that Hope shortens all journies, by sweetening them—so sing my little stanza on the subject, with the devotion of an hymn, every morning when thou arisest."[16] In the *Letters Supposed* Eliza is made to reply, "Your little stanza I have sung every morning as you desired me", and she then quotes "a little hymn which I myself have composed to this friendly divinity" (I, 87; 1929 ed., 87–88). It is written in the style of Combe's "Stanzas—to Hope" and "Faith, Hope, and Charity", published many years later in the *Poetical Magazine* (II, 351–52; IV, 115–16).

Eliza's unlucky reference to the *Sentimental Journey*, not yet written when these letters were supposedly composed, and Yorick's mention of plaster casts of his own bust by Nollekens, not available until after Sterne's death, are consistent with authorship in 1775 or later, but not in 1767. Also suggestive of the later date is Eliza's meditation on Happiness (I, 156–68; 1929 ed., 65–71), remarkably similar in thought and expression to a passage on the same theme in the *Philosopher in Bristol* (II, 89–99). But a more telling parallel with the latter work is the striking similarity in phrasing and substance between the two conclusions. It has already been noted that Combe had the habit of closing every sentimental narrative with a death scene, as when the Philosopher, thinking of his own death and of Amanda's, shudders at the thought of possibly surviving her: "All-gracious power!—that canst make firm the feeble knees, and give strength to the drooping spirits;—if I am doomed to meet this trying hour,—Oh strengthen me!—sustain me!—Have mercy upon me!" (II, 159). In the *Letters Supposed*, Yorick also thinks of his death and of Eliza's, and it occurs to him that he might be doomed to survive her. "Gracious Heaven—if, amid the trials that await me, it is decreed that I am to meet this dreadful hour,—support me in thy mercy, give me strength to support myself,—and to be calmly resigned." Yet he may die this very night: "Heaven, have mercy upon me!" He thinks more calmly of other matters for a few pages, then again feels death near. "All-gracious Power!—that canst give strength to the weak,—make firm my feeble knees, which I can scarce bend to ask a blessing of thee! Oh, strengthen me, for I am weak; and my heart is

cold within me!" (II, 144, 146, 167; 1929 ed., 141, 142, 151–52).
Sterne scholars who have been loath to believe that the author of the
Sentimental Journey could possibly have written these things may be
heartened to learn that one who has familiarized himself with the
writings, good and bad, of William Combe is compelled to acknowledge that the author of the *Philosopher in Bristol* very probably wrote
them all.

Combe's habit of quoting from himself also throws some light on
his responsibility for the *Letters Supposed*. Various writers have
pointed out one passage which is quoted with only minor emendations
from the *Philosopher in Bristol*. In fact, lest the reader think it odd that
Sterne, writing supposedly in 1767, should quote from a book written
and published in 1775, the "editor" of the *Letters* explains in a footnote that the "author" had originally composed the story of the sailor
and the blind ballad-singer for this work and had subsequently copied
it for the Bristol volume.[17] However that may be, Combe published
the same story a third time when in 1786 he was regularly contributing such sentimental sketches to the *Daily Universal Register*. In the
issue for October 13, "The Generous Sailor" appeared in that paper—
not as emended for the *Letters* but as first published in 1775.

Various other examples of self-quotation occur in the *Daily Universal Register* during the years when Combe was actively contributing
to that paper. The issue for September 27, 1786, for example, contains "The Nosegay", originally published in the *Letters Supposed*
(II, 130–40; 1929 ed., 135–9). Combe's revisions are only such as
any author might make if given an opportunity after a number of
years quietly to touch up his own style. "There was a certain softness
of expression and gentleness of spirit, which appeared so visible . . ."
becomes more economically "A certain gentleness of spirit appeared
so visible. . . ." A surprising restraint reduces "He thanked me with
a flood of tears" to "He thanked me with a tear". Only a few such
emendations occur, though the beginning and end of the story are
adapted slightly to suit Combe's journalistic purpose, and the punctuation is normalized to newspaper practice. Combe was evidently fond
of "The Nosegay". He printed it yet again, as we shall see, in
1818.

There can be no doubt that Combe sought to make the Yorick
sections of the *Letters Supposed* as Sterne-like as possible, and to the
ultimate confusion of Sterne scholarship he was reasonably successful,

particularly in imitating what the *Monthly Review* called the amoroso-sentimental style. Combe found this style much to his taste and often fell into it even when he was not consciously imitating Sterne. Thus, the reader of these letters will find much in them which resembles Combe's sentimental novels of 1781, when he fancied himself to be writing like Rousseau as well as like Sterne. Indeed, the "editor" of the *Letters* remarks that they strike him as reminiscent of "the tender and fanciful Rousseau". But such exercises, he says, have a higher merit than mere similarity in manner. "Imitations of style and manner are of little value, unless they heighten those sentiments, and enforce those instructions, which soften and improve the heart." He concludes by assuring the reader that "these Letters are well calculated to produce such beneficial effects" (I, vii; 1929 ed., 163).

However convincing to Combe's contemporaries, these pious assurances have long since lost their force. The modern reader wants no part of such writing, whatever its professed ethical purpose. He may go so far as to accept sentimentalism which is authentically Sterne's, embarrassing though it may sometimes be, but imitations of that style, even skilful ones, he rejects as more likely to soften the head than the heart. When first published, however, these supposed letters were read with approval and praised by connoisseurs of "sweet sensibility". It was unnecessary to think them really Sterne's, and apparently no one did so; it was enough that they were in Sterne's manner—his worst manner, perhaps, but at the moment his most popular. Even so, the collection did not survive long; after a new edition in 1780, the title dropped out of sight. But by that time Combe and Bew were launched on a new project of imitation, the most successful of all their collaborations. And again Combe had changed his style.

* * *

The sudden death on November 27, 1779, of Thomas, the "Wicked" Lord Lyttelton (Plate 9), provided the perfect occasion for Combe and John Bew to produce a new imitation. Even under ordinary circumstances, the death of such a prominent sinner would have challenged the booksellers, but certain mysterious occurrences made Lyttelton's death even more sensational than his life. According to a widespread story, generally believed by members of his family, a ghostly figure from the spirit world had announced his approaching

9. *Thomas, second Lord Lyttelton, after Gainsborough. National Portrait Gallery*

death three days before it took place. Lyttelton's uncle, Lord West-cote, signed a formal statement attesting to the truth of the story on February 13, 1780, some ten weeks after the young lord's death. Four years later, Dr Johnson was still talking about it:

JOHNSON. "It is the most extraordinary thing that has happened in my day. I heard it with my own ears, from his uncle, Lord Westcote. I am so glad to have every evidence of the spiritual world, that I am willing to believe it." DR ADAMS. "You have evidence enough; good evidence, which needs not such support." JOHNSON. "I like to have more."[18]

According to Lord Westcote's account, Lyttelton was awakened in the night by a bird which flew into his room, changed suddenly into a woman dressed in white, and told him to prepare for death. Horace Walpole's comment on the story differed somewhat from that of the great moralist. Two weeks after Lyttelton's death he wrote to Mason, "It seems a little odd that an apparition should despair of being able to get access to his Lordship's bed in the shape of a young woman, without being forced to use the disguise of a robin-red-breast."[19]

The revival of interest in Thomas Lord Lyttelton was thus immediate and intense at the time of his death, and neither Combe nor Bew was the man to let occasion slip. Within three months they published the first volume of the *Letters of the Late Lord Lyttelton*. Even so, they were anticipated by Kearsly, who, with remarkable expedition, published on the last day of 1779—just a month and three days after Lyttelton's death—a quarto pamphlet entitled *Poems by a Young Nobleman, of Distinguished Abilities, Lately Deceased*. On February 24, the very day on which Bew published the *Letters*, a fourth edition of the *Poems* appeared, this time with a new and fully explicit title: *Poems by the Late Lord Lyttelton*. This simultaneous use of Lyttelton's name on two separate publications forced the executors to act, and they accordingly placed the following notice in the *Morning Post* on March 8:

> Whereas a Collection of Poems has been published as the Composition of the late Lord Lyttelton, great Part whereof are undoubtedly spurious, and also certain Letters have appeared in Print, with his Name prefixed, which are all falsely ascribed to his Lordship, his Executors think fit to make this Declaration, that the Public may not be imposed upon by these Publications.

Although the statement is rather oddly worded, its meaning is unmistakable: The *Poems* are at least partly spurious, the *Letters*
altogether so.

George Kearsly responded at once. On March 10 both the *Morning
Post* and the *Morning Chronicle* carried an advertisement in which the
publisher offered to prove the poems genuine "by producing the
originals, in a hand writing, which will not admit of dispute". He
asserts that had he not so highly respected "his Lordship's memory
and abilities", he might have printed in full those lines which appear
in the book only as asterisks, lines "which however replete with attic
fire and poetic merit, might not have the approbation of delicate
readers". The advertisement concludes with a note calculated to
challenge an equally candid statement frow Combe and Bew: "N.B.
Mr. Kearsly is not the publisher of the Letters."

Before two weeks had passed Kearsly again advertised the poems
in the *Morning Post* (March 22), adding a significant word to the
title, *Genuine Poems of the Late Lord Lyttelton*. The notice includes a
table of contents, followed by this note: "His Lordship's Executors,
upon examining this Collection, are of opinion that one of the Poems
. . . is not genuine, therefore the publisher has withdrawn it from
the above table of contents." The objections of the executors are thus
at least tacitly withdrawn.

The publisher of the *Letters*, meanwhile, remained silent, and for
the moment even his advertisements made no mention of the disputed
title. Then on March 31, three weeks after the executors' repudiation,
Combe was heard from. The *Morning Post* of that date carries the
following communication:

Lord Lyttelton's Letters

The Editor of Lord Lyttelton's Letters, assures the
Executors of that noble Lord, that as soon as his
private affairs will permit his return to London, he
will give them and the public undoubted proofs of
their authenticity. In the mean time he is free to say,
that many of Lord Lyttelton's intimate friends have
declared, that the Letters possess an internal evidence
by whom they were written, and the demand with
which they have been favoured, proves the opinion
of the public.

Glasgow, March 21, 1780.

The difference between this letter and Kearsly's forthright statement is immediately evident. The "editor" does not offer to show manuscripts. He is away from London and does not say when he will return. He asserts that many of Lord Lyttelton's friends have found the letters to be very like those of the late lord (a fact which has never been disputed), and he notes that the book has been much in demand by the general public. And with this, discussion of the matter in the public prints ended.

The reviewers assumed that the work was spurious, but they nevertheless found it amusing and well written. When a second volume appeared in 1782 they followed the same line. The letters were recognized as imitations, but "if my lord were now alive, he would not wish to disown them".[20] No one asked whether the "editor" had returned to London or demanded to see his "undoubted proofs". The matter was simply dropped. Edition followed edition for forty years; in 1792 Bew issued what he called the eighth edition of Volume I and the fifth of Volume II, and there were subsequent English editions in 1806 and 1816. An edition appeared in Troy, New York, in 1807, and another in Philadelphia as late as 1821. No other work by William Combe except the famous *Tours of Doctor Syntax* ever approached the long-continued popularity of these *Letters*.

Readers today find this popularity hard to understand. There is a certain liveliness of style in many of the letters, to be sure, but the subject-matter now seems remote and most of the personalities are veiled beyond recognition except possibly by scholars. Combe's management of the letters was less than helpful in this respect; mystification—or the pretence of mystification—was part of his plan. Just as in the *R[oya]l Register*, which this work resembles in some ways, names are normally replaced by long dashes, here often without even identifying initials. There is the usual differentiation between the "editor" who writes the Introduction and the "author"—whoever he may be. Apart from the title, which calls these compositions "letters of the late Lord Lyttelton", the work contains no reference whatever to their authorship. The reviewers good-naturedly took this to mean that the letters were to be read *as though* written by Lyttelton and were to be regarded as a kind of portrait of that notorious public character. The editor's Introduction is carefully vague on the point. It suggests that personal letters are of great value to the biographer, that "private communications of friendship may be depended upon as faithful to the mind from whence they arise". It hopefully asserts that "the following letters . . . as proceeding from a nobleman, whose great talents promised no small utility to his country, and whose character has been the subject of such general speculation, will . . . meet with a favourable reception" (I, iii). He does not say, "letters written by . . ." but only "letters *as* proceeding from . . ." The *as* virtually identifies the letters as suppositions. Then there is Combe's usual disclaimer: "That they were not written with the most distant idea of being offered to the world, will be evident to every reader; and, surely, no inconsiderable share of merit will be allowed them from such a circumstance. They may want, perhaps, the correctness and accuracy of prepared compositions; but they possess that easy sincerity, and that open unbosoming of sentiments, which form the charm of epistolary correspondence" (I, iii–iv). As "editor" he avoids saying whether he is dealing with authentic letters or imitations. *Caveat emptor*. Since most of the letters were undated in his originals, he has uniformly omitted all dates. And finally he has thought it prudent to omit the names of all those to whom the letters were addressed, implying that the reader will enjoy playing again the game of identifications. Virtually every sentence in this Introduction, though designed to arouse the interest of the contemporary reader, only exasperates one who innocently comes upon the work today.

Although biographers of Lyttelton have accepted these letters as essentially authentic,[21] they contain nothing which Combe might not have known, they make a few mistakes which Lyttelton himself could not have made,[22] they contain references to Combe's favourite topics, they duplicate subject-matter of the R[oya]l Register and the *Philosopher in Bristol*, and they include a few sentimental anecdotes in Combe's manner. There is nothing in all the fifty-eight letters which Combe might not have written, and readers familiar with his work will be inclined to recognize his hand throughout the collection. This is not to say that there are no authentic Lyttelton letters in the two volumes. Combe would certainly use any such which came into his possession (a few of the letters, notably XVIII and LV, could have been addressed to him), but it would be quite impossible to identify these without manuscript evidence. And no manuscript originals have ever come to light. Nor has a single manuscript of a letter answering or answered by one of these. Even so, biographers of Lyttelton may be excused for making some judicious use of this material; if the letters are not actually Lyttelton's, they are—as contemporary reviewers were the first to say—good imitations by a well-informed if slightly disingenuous contemporary.

Combe knew very well what his public would like to find out about the notoriously "wicked" Lord Lyttelton. The expectant reader is immediately warned not to expect the wickedness: "Some liberties have been taken with the letters", says the editor in his Introduction, "by omitting such as alluded to transactions which the world already too well knows, or which it would be shameful to betray" (I, iv). Several lines of asterisks in Letters XVII and XXIX are his only concession to morbid curiosity. But he supplies lively answers to other questions in the public mind. What, for example, does it feel like suddenly to inherit a title? The answer to this question, whether Lyttelton's or Combe's, was singled out for quotation by contemporary reviewers:

> And I awoke, and behold I was a Lord! It was no unpleasant transition, you will readily believe, from infernal dreams and an uneasy pillow, from insignificance and dereliction, to be a Peer of Great Britain, with all the privileges attendant upon that character, and some little estate into the bargain. My sensations are very different from any I have experienced for some time past. My consequence, both internal and external, is already greatly elevated; and the *empressement* of the people about me is so suddenly encreased as to be ridiculous.
>
> (I, 95–96)

What did Lyttelton really think of his cousin and "parasite", Captain George Ayscough? Letter II is entirely devoted to the subject. "This man is capable of any villany, if money is to be got by it; and I doubt not but he might be bribed to undertake, without hesitation, robbery, seduction, rape, and murder" (I, 15). Combe had said much the same thing of Ayscough in the *Diaboliad*.

What really goes on in the mind of a notorious sinner? The letters dwell on this subject again and again, often taking a whining tone of self-justification which, if by Lyttelton, does him little credit. It would seem most unlikely that his thoughts while alive could coincide so exactly with what his friends were to say of him after his death— that he was really a victim of his family's vanity, that he had been spoiled by his father, that he would discard his bad habits once he came fully into man's estate. "If there were but half a dozen people in the world, who would afford me the kind encouragement I receive

from you, it would, I verily believe, work a reformation in the pro-
digal: but the world has marked me down for so much dissoluteness,
as to doubt, at all times, of the sincerity of my repentance" (I, 9–10).
If written after his death by his friends, this would sound fair enough,
but written by the sinner himself it sounds snivelling. One hopes that
Combe was the author.

Combe certainly claimed authorship. Although he never permitted
his name to appear on this or any other title-page, he was not unwilling to set forth his literary claims in private conversation. The
one work which he seems to have claimed most insistently—for his
friends unfailingly mention it—was the *Letters of the Late Lord
Lyttelton*. In the London book trade, his responsibility for these
letters was apparently recognized at once, though his anonymity was
respected until 1796. In that year Jeremiah Whitaker Newman
publicly identified him in the *Lounger's Common-Place Book* (s.v.
Lyttelton):

> A collection of letters were published soon after his [Lyttelton's]
> death, *supposed* to be written by him, which I read with great pleasure.
> This production of Mr. Combe, the eccentric author of the Diaboliad,
> is said, by good judges, to contain letters, on the score of composition,
> sentiment, and language, exactly such as Lord Lyttelton [*sic*] *would*
> have written; it is a sort of epistolary portrait, a picture of his mind,
> a strange likeness, and the work of an able hand.

In addition to its mention of the author's name, the passage is
significant as a disinterested statement of the contemporary attitude
toward such imitations as those which Combe and others produced.
They were to be read with pleasure, not as authentic letters but as
works of the imagination—in fine, epistolary portraits. Not every
hackwriter could produce such imitations effectively, but William
Combe had "an able hand".

* * *

One evening in the spring of 1818 a member of the Lyttelton family
chanced at the theatre to meet a relative, Major James Pattison
Cockburn, and learned that he had recently talked with Combe about
the origin, thirty-eight years earlier, of the *Letters of the Late Lord
Lyttelton*. Since the Lytteltons were still in some doubt about this
work to which their name was attached, Cockburn agreed to see

Combe again and send the family such particulars as he could glean from the old man. On May 19, he wrote, "I have seen Mr. C. on this subject, and now send you what he said, word for word."[23] It now appears, however, that Cockburn was not reporting a conversation but had copied, with a few omissions, a manuscript which Combe had written out for him. The original manuscript is now in the Henry E. Huntington Library, San Marino, California, and a remarkable document it is. Combe was seventy-six when he wrote it, and he was recalling an episode more than half a lifetime in the past. Looking back over the eventful years to a world not yet disturbed by the fall of the Bastille, he sought to recapture that other era—how different from the post-Waterloo period in which he now found himself! Biographers of Lyttelton have called the whole thing a barefaced lie, and certainly no one familiar with Combe and his "comic infirmity" would be inclined to accept it at face-value. It would have been more than human, indeed, and certainly out of character, had he not embellished the story somewhat. But it is a curiously interesting and by no means negligible account.

At the German Spa about the year 1782—A Mrs. H.—a sort of Literary Lady, & whom I had known for some years, had brought from England Lord L—'s poems then lately published, as I understood by Miles Peter Andrews, a Gunpowder Gentleman whom that Nobleman brought into Parliament for Bewdley.—Mrs. H—who was a Contemporary with me in the great and fashionable world, when I moved in that Sphere, and knew some little circumstances that took place between Lord, when Mr. L— and myself, which made no common noise at the period, as an inducement for me to breakfast with her, she said she would add a plat of Jeux d'Esprit that must very much interest me. I went and beheld the poems, in the form of a Quarto Pamphlet. They were all of them familiar acquaintance of mine that used to occupy a port Folio in the Sanctum Sanctorum, God forgive me, in Curzon Street. Where the Old Lord lived above, and his Son and Heir lived below. And my recollection at this moment would enable me to give a very curious comparative History of those two Apartments, & of the two distinct personages who occupied them; for I was equally well received by both, & I remember, to my no small satisfaction, that difficult as the task might be, I did not play the Hypocrite with either. —O what two Conversations I could repeat, on two successive mornings, between the Noble Father, the Right Reverend Uncle of Carlisle, the Reverend Dr. de Salis & myself. —And on the following day, —between the Noble Son[,] a sneaking, sycophantic, but learned Scotchman, Dr. Baylis a Worcestershire Physician transplanted to London; a Gentleman of Genius, known by the name of Mad Henley, and the self-same expletive, already which L—used to honour with three titles, and at this distance of time they may be mentioned without vanity, the Immoveable, the fascinating & polished C—. And on which three denominations, as you have caused me to touch the spring of a secret Drawer in the Cabinet of my memory, which has not been examined for so many years, I now find sufficient materials to form a volume. —This Episode you will excuse but it is connected most intimately in my mind, with the poems which I left upon Mrs. H—'s breakfast Table at Spa, whither I must beg leave to reconduct You.— I read them aloud; and to my surprise found two of my own trifles among them. —Compliments passed, and it was wished that more from the same mind had been added. —In short the Conversation terminated in my engaging to do something a la Lyttelton, that might be received as his. —I accordingly turned my thoughts to *Dialogues on the Dead*. He I knew had written some to ridicule those of his father and Mrs. Montagu. I remember three of them, and have them somewhere among my immence cargo of papers, the waste of between fifty and sixty years. They were, if I recollect right replete with wit, Spirit and Blasphemy and Patriotism. —The parties were, King David of Israel and Caesar Borgia, —The Saviour of the World and Socrates, —Epaminondas and General Wolfe. —However I changed my Plan for very evident reasons; and began a Series of a Letters, one or more of which were thought to form an amusing article at Mrs. H—'s breakfast Table, till the materials of the first Volume were compleated. She requested the Manuscripts, and I presented them to her. She took them to England, where they became an object of Curiosity in her Circle. On her persuasion I consented to their publication. The public received them with great Avidity; when the Family thought proper to advertise them in the public papers as an imposition, which they certainly were, but as they were not discreditable to his Character, they were rather to blame to consider the writer of them, whom they did not know, in the view in which they thought proper to represent or rather misrepresent him. —I accordingly, by a counter-advertisement dated Edinburgh, but written at Brussels, insisted upon their originality and promised another Volume, which I wrote in the Capital of Brabant. —And here the work closed. Though the Book-seller offered me 200 Guineas which he afterwards advanced to 300 for another Volume. and offered 800, if I would make it two: and I had materials for three or four, with many curious Histories, which I have not yet forgotten: but I had a respect for the family which was fruitful in virtues, and those weaknesses, for there was a little sprinkle of them, were such as are generally associated with worthy Qualities. —It is curious enough that the Old Lady Lyttelton, the widow of the first Lord, a fine, obstinate, clever Woman used to abuse the family to the last hour of her Life, and to that period I knew her, for denying the Authenticity of these Letters; & this she has done to me fifty times. —The last Summer she passed at her Cottage at Ripley in Surrey. At her particular request, I read the Letters through to her. Her observations as you may suppose, which were very frequent, very angry, very severe and not without that wit which she eminently possessed, were very amusing to me and the Spanish Minister,

Del Campo, who passed a couple days there, during this Lecture, and who knew the Author, made the Sofa upon which he lay, shake from his occasional bursts of Laughter; and did not escape frequent sallies of her lively reproach, for breaking the beautiful Compos as she was pleased to call them, of her Son, as she was pleased to call him, though he was not of her Venter,—as she declared that the concentrated Genius of Spain, and all the Doctors of Salamanca and the Archbishop of Toledo at their head, could not produce anything like them.

   —I think I have made out a tolerable Article for you, but don't ask me for another.

   —If I live long enough to correct, I shall leave behind me the history of my own times, —which will be six volumes, at least, in heavy quarto; —and in the part which comprizes the Literature of the period, I shall give by way of an illustrative appendix, a diary of my literary Life; if however I should not live to give it its due polish, and final arrangements, for the materials are compleat to the repeal of the unjustifiable, and groundless suspension of the Habeas Corpus,[24] The whole will be in safe hands, to be consigned emendaturis flammis.[25]

   Though written out at length, this manuscript gives what must be a close approximation of Combe's conversation in the last years of his life. In relaxed after-dinner talk he was famous for his narratives of long-ago events in which, as a matter of course, he had played a leading role. These stories, so his friends believed, always contained some basic element of truth, but Combe would never hesitate to improvise details when memory failed or the story could be improved. Some of his friends believed that they could always separate the truth from the fiction, but Crabb Robinson was not so sure it could be done. Thus, after a dinner party in 1817, he noted in his diary that Combe's conversation had been "very entertaining", but complained, "How much of all this was true I cannot pretend to decide."[26] The complaint is understandable, but with the manuscript before us some discrimination appears possible.

   Three misstatements are immediately apparent. The Lytteltons, father and son, lived at 37 Hill Street, not, as Combe has it, in Curzon Street. Since the two streets are but a short distance apart, their confusion after fifty years is scarcely remarkable. The "counter-advertisement" was dated from Glasgow, not Edinburgh; this mistake also seems trivial, particularly since he now tells us that he wrote the notice in Brussels rather than in either of the Scottish cities. And Miles Peter Andrews could not have been brought into Parliament by Lyttelton, since he did not become a Member until 1796. These pointless errors seem innocent slips of the memory rather than deceptions.

The vagueness about the date may be less accidental. The context would place the episode at Spa in January and February 1780, not as he says, "about the year 1782". That would mean that it occurred during the eight-week interval between the appearance of the *Poems* (December 31) and the *Letters* (February 24). But during that same period Combe was getting two other items through the press, a new volume of the *R[oya]l Register* (published March 2) and a quarto pamphlet, *The Fast Day* (a verse satire published on March 4). It is impossible to believe that Combe was out of London during those busy weeks which culminated in the publication of three titles in nine days. After *The Fast Day*, however, except for the "counter-advertise-ment" which he says was written in Brussels, he published nothing whatever for an entire year. And his publications for several years thereafter were all such as could have been written while absent from London. Legal records presently to be cited prove that Combe was in Brussels on September 21, 1784. Had he also been there, as he says, when he wrote the "counter-advertisement" in March 1780? Was he out of England for four and a half years, or did he make more than one trip? Or is the episode at Spa associated with the second volume of the *Letters* rather than the first, occurring as he says "about the year 1782"? Above all, why does Combe habitually practise these concealments?

The answer to the last question is to be found in the man's lifelong effort to preserve, at least in public, his amateur standing. It would never do to acknowledge that John Bew, a bookseller, a mere trades-man, had proposed the Lyttelton imitations as a business venture. Instead, he must invent a mysterious and unidentifiable "Mrs. H—, a sort of Literary Lady" to compliment him on his "trifles"—poems which he had written in Lyttelton's manner—and to express the wish "that more from the same mind had been added" to the otherwise authentic collection. This bluestocking might also ask him to "do something à la Lyttelton", and he might comply—without, of course, the slightest thought of publication. She must request the manuscripts, must take them to England, and finally must persuade the reluctant author to permit their publication. To serve his purpose, all this must seem to have occurred before the appearance of the first volume. And then, to demonstrate still further his aloofness to monetary considerations, he coolly tells of declining a preposterous offer for additional volumes. Such were the concealments which Combe automatically adopted when speaking of his own literary work; they try the reader's patience, but not his credulity.

What, then, remains of Combe's narrative? Actually, a good deal. There is nothing vague in the mention of Spa and Brussels as associated in some way with the Lyttelton affair. Spa—the original of all the spas—was and is a watering-place not far from Liège. It had been regarded as "without exception, the most agreeable resort of the best company in Europe", very exclusive, and very expensive. The Duchess of Devonshire visited the place in the winter of 1779–80, but it was said by that time to have become a slightly down-at-heels haunt of roués and gamblers.[27] If, as may be suspected, Combe had left England to escape his creditors, "the German Spa" would for the moment serve his purpose. In any event, it seems an odd place for Combe to name had it not actually been related in some way to the episode.

Then there is the vividly recalled memory of Mayfair in the 1760s and of Combe's visiting the two Lytteltons in their town house, of the men he met there, of the portfolio of poems (manuscripts of some of the poems *have* come to light), and of the honorific epithets which had been applied to himself by the younger Lyttelton. If not literally true, all this is at any rate consistent with other sources of information.

Of particular interest is Combe's statement that when prompted to produce a Lyttelton imitation he had first thought of supplying his bookseller with new *Dialogues on* [*sic* for *of*] *the Dead*. For such a work he possessed what he seems usually to have wanted—a few authentic documents, in this instance three dialogues written by young Lyttelton "to ridicule those of his father and Mrs. Montague". (After thirty-eight years he still has them somewhere, he believes, among his "immense cargo of papers".) He might easily supply others in the same manner to fill out a volume, the genuine and the counterfeit virtually indistinguishable. The passage is an acknowledgement of his usual practice in producing imitations. Not improbably there were also a few of his Lordship's letters in that cargo of papers; if so, he might use bits and pieces of them here and there, or he might print them essentially as he found them. To the confusion of modern scholarship, this was Combe's procedure, and it was the source of that verisimilitude which he often achieved, most notably in these Lyttelton

Letters. Even without direct quotation, the information contained in any available manuscripts would be utilized to give the work an air of authenticity. Combe's purpose was to produce a readable book, not a definitive edition.

Finally, there is Combe's amusing account of reading the letters to Lyttelton's stepmother at her cottage in Surrey sometime in 1795, a vividly detailed scene. This, and indeed all these reminiscences, must have some basis in fact; in any event, it is easier to give them cautious credence than to suppose that such a circumstantial account could be made of whole cloth. But the biographer of Combe, seeking information and finding no more than hints and evasions, can only feel secure in offering the narrative—errors, distortions, mystifications, and all— as "a sort of epistolary portrait, a picture of [Combe's] mind, a strong likeness".

* * *

Although Combe published three more of these imitations, two in 1781 and the third in 1784, they may be discussed more briefly because they aroused little interest at the time and also because no one has ever been tempted to argue for their authenticity. They escape being utterly negligible only by illustrating so clearly the hack-writer's methods and his readiness to exploit currently popular topics and manners.

The death of any celebrated person always stimulated the production of imitations, sometimes solemnly put forth with claims of authenticity, sometimes transparently supposititious. We have seen how the deaths of Mrs Draper in 1778 and Lord Lyttelton in 1779 prompted Combe immediately to publish the *Letters Supposed* and the Lyttelton *Letters*. Similarly, the death of Rousseau in July 1778 was duly noted by the "editor" of the *Letters Supposed*, who took occasion in his Preface to suggest the presence in that work of "knots of flowers" planted by the tender French writer. The reader may doubt that he sees much of Rousseau's influence in those letters, but the timely suggestion would not hurt the sale of the work. A year and a half later, however, Combe produced an epistolary novel boldly signed with Rousseau's name: *Letters of an Italian Nun and an English Gentleman. Translated from the French of J. J. Rousseau* (Bew, 1781).

As always when pretending authenticity, Combe felt called upon to provide the reader with an elaborate and mystifying explanation.

According to the Introduction, Rousseau had stayed for a time with an unnamed gentleman near Chambéry in Savoy. While there he had written these letters "without much attention, and, perhaps, as the first sketch of a design which he intended to have rendered more complete and important". He had left the manuscripts behind him, and his host had placed them in the hands of the Marquis de Belle-garde, who had turned them over to an unnamed neighbour, who had translated them and sent them to an equally unnamed English editor, who had seen them through the press and now gave them to the English public. If the reader loses his way here, the explanation has served its intended purpose.

The editor then presents thirty-one letters written by the two principals in a love affair even less conventional than that between Yorick and Eliza, a romance between one Isabella, the Italian nun, and an Englishman, Mr Croli (explained as the French form of Crowley). Eventually Isabella leaves her convent and goes to England, where Croli—for reasons never adequately explained—refuses to marry her, but offers to make her his mistress. Isabella delicately reports all this in a letter to Croli's mother, then returns to take refuge in Italy. Croli also writes to his mother, taking an affecting farewell before committing suicide. Such are the letters which, according to the editor, "contain, though in an inferior degree, the simplicity of story, the delusive improbabilities, the enchanting tenderness, the expressive language, and the romantic virtue, of his [Rousseau's] other works".

The novel received only the briefest mention in the reviews. No one thought it worth serious consideration, but there was the usual disagreement over the authenticity of the work. A writer in the *London Magazine* (June 1781) accepted the novel as Rousseau's and rather surprisingly argued that it was "calculated to promote the Roman catholic religion in this country". Sixteen months later (October 1782) the same magazine published a second notice of the work and called it spurious: "These letters wanted not the fiction of Rousseau's name. They would have supported their own credit, and should have scorned the stale trick of needy impostors." The *Monthly Review* failed to mention the book at all until October 1782, then pronounced it "not Rousseau's, but in many respects worthy of his exquisite pen". The *Critical Review* (June 1781) was more cautious; if these letters "are really the work of that ingenious author, they are greatly inferior to the rest of his performances, being written in an indifferent style, and conveying nothing to the reader very interesting or amusive". The book continued in some demand, however, and in 1784 Bew saw fit to produce a second edition. In 1809 an edition was published in America, and in 1817 a "sixth" edition was published in London.

* * *

Combe's next project was another epistolary novel, this one a good deal more ambitious and, as the title-page indicates, frankly "supposititious": *Letters between Two Lovers and Their Friends. By the Author of Letters Supposed to Have Been Written by Yorick and Eliza* (Bew, 1781). With the circulating library trade in mind, the tradesman-bookseller issued this novel in three small duodecimo volumes— a more profitable format than the one-volume Dublin edition. The author, as always, remains anonymous, but in dedicating the work to Lady Monson ("an eminent and amiable example of conjugal virtue") he assumes his usual posture of the trifling amateur and refers to his book with elegant negligence as "this little offspring of my leisure and retired hours". Under the circumstances there is no need for any mysterious story concerning the manuscript.

The "two lovers" are Jonathan Cosens and Maria Delaunis; "their friends" are Caroline Barker, who lives in Chelsea and corresponds with Maria, and Sir William Singleton of Cavendish Square. Jonathan has been privately educated for twelve years by a moralizing Dr Thomas Lancaster and is now ready to be introduced to the world. Eventually he makes his way to Bath, where, under suitably romantic circumstances, he meets Maria, who is living there with her invalid mother. They forthwith fall in love, but Maria vows that she will never marry as long as her mother lives. Jonathan prepares to retire from the world and nurse his unhappiness. Then, to the surprise of no one, Maria's mother dies. The two lovers marry and take over the estates of Jonathan's uncle; their friends also marry and inherit various estates; several minor characters also are richly and unexpectedly rewarded. Obviously the impecunious Combe was fascinated by the thought of rescue by generous benefaction or timely legacy.

Trivial as this sentimental plot may seem, it serves to tie together a series of diversified letters written by a dozen or more characters in as many different manners. Some of the letters, to be sure, are written in Combe's most affected style: "I am in despair!—my hand trembles as I write; and my heart bleeds with the wounds which you have made.————Cruel perfection!————My happiness is vanished like a dream; and hope, the last comfort of the miserable, fades from before me." There is, however, relatively little of such writing, and what there is resembles *The Man of Feeling* more than the *Sentimental Journey*, though overtones of Yorick and Eliza are inevitably present. ("New Yoricks monthly improve our minds with their sentimental effusions," laconically complained the Honourable John Byng in his diary of 1782.) But other influences are even more apparent. When Bath is described by various characters, each writing from his own point of view, the reader is reminded of *Humphry Clinker*, and the letters of both Maria and Caroline describing the social scene are not unlike those of Smollett's sentimental Lydia. A more recent and more readily recognizable influence is the epistolary *Evelina* (1778), an enormous publishing success which every hackwriter of the time sought to emulate.

A curious feature of the *Letters between Two Lovers* is Combe's use in this work of the same sensational theme found in his *Letters of an Italian Nun*, a love affair involving a nun. In each novel it is finally the man who declines to go through with the ceremony. Mr Williams, in the *Letters between Two Lovers*, unable to obtain his father's consent to the marriage, retires from the world and eventually blows his brains out. The nun, Leonora, is cared for by the Count de Gronstadt and his wife, the latter also an apostate nun! The theme was evidently on the mind of the reading public at the time, for Combe had an unerring sense for the current clichés. Particularly in the *Letters between Two Lovers*, he conscientiously introduces the favourite topics and conventional attitudes of the time: gardens and picturesque beauty, *Tristram Shandy*, love *v.* passion, Ranelagh and Vauxhall, water music on the Thames, Christmas in the country, "the melancholy gloom of enthusiasm", the increase of luxury, the vice of gambling, Garrick's acting, Handel's oratorios, the Italian opera. More, perhaps, than any of his other works, this novel provides an inventory of the stock interests of the time in which it was written.

For every reason, the epistolary form was suited to Combe's purpose. It made detailed planning unnecessary and permitted the writer to shift subject and tone at will. He could at one moment be the moralizing Dr Lancaster, then in the next letter he could assume the bantering tone of Catherine Cosens; he could in rapid succession be the country squire, the sentimental Maria (a favourite role), and the sober William Freeman of Gray's Inn. The successful imitator must have some of the traits of the magpie, and these Combe had in plenty. His improvisations in various styles are, in fact, consistently more readable than his elaborately studied manner, and this novel is consequently far more interesting than his self-consciously formal writings. Despite its flimsy plot and occasional sentimental excesses, it reads surprisingly well. The suitably credulous reader finds himself duly instructed in proper attitudes and decorous behaviour. There are no character problems, no unresolved tensions, no ultimate mysteries. All the fashionable topics are dealt with, and all ends suitably: the ill and sinful die and commit suicide respectively; the worthy young ladies marry worthy and, of course, rich young men; the poor but deserving are more than amply rewarded. That Combe wrote the novel in great haste is evident from the general confusion of names: Benjamin Huddleston is once called George; the father of the mysterious Mr Williams is called Anthony, then Archibald, then Anthony again; Sir William Singleton becomes Sir Charles before the end of the book. But the reader today is on the whole amused by this novel—though not, perhaps, just as Combe intended.

* * *

Combe's careless writing in 1781 cannot be passed over as mere affectation; he was evidently working almost frantically to produce in one year these two novels, two new volumes of the R[oya]l Register, and one more verse satire: The Traitor. A poetical Rhapsody (Bew). In April the Monthly Review called the satire "a furious and feeble invective against Dr. Franklin", and the Critical quoted thirty lines—the only surviving lines of The Traitor, in fact: no copy of the pamphlet has ever come to light. After May of the following year, however, when the second volume of the Lyttelton letters appeared, Combe reverted to a slower pace, entirely consistent with his being in Spa, as he later asserted, "about the year 1782". One date is certain: he was in Brussels by September 1784, his personal affairs hopelessly tangled. That was the month in which Bew published the last of these supposititious works, an epistolary novel entitled Original Love Letters, between a Lady of Quality and a Person of Inferior Station.

In his *Original Love Letters*, Combe is again reminding the reader of Rousseau, for *La Nouvelle Héloïse* (1760) is also an epistolary account of the love of a man of lowly station for a woman of the aristocracy. The title-page of Combe's novel bears as epigraph an apt quotation from his perennial favourite, Addison: "Love, like Death, levels all Distinctions." The thirty-five letters are written by a man "of inferior station" and the daughter of a lord, and once again the story concerns an unsuitable love affair which is not permitted to arrive at marriage. The difference in station is not the only barrier to the lovers' happiness, for the man is ill and goes off to the Bristol Hot Wells to seek renewed health. This enables Combe to utilize familiar material much as he had in Letter XXX of the *Letters of the Late Lord Lyttelton*. While in Bristol he reads a newspaper account of the lady's forthcoming marriage to someone else and dies before he can learn that the story is false. The temerity of a man's falling in love with a woman of much higher rank would seem sensational to Combe's readers, but the situation was not without precedent in the social life of the period. The author, in fact, makes every effort to persuade the reader that these are authentic letters, and that they tell of an unconventional romance between real persons. "If I could have composed them myself, I would not have yielded the reputation of them to supposititious characters" (page vi). And once again he gives the reader a mysterious account of his coming into possession of the manuscripts.

The *Monthly Review* (September 1784) bluntly denies the author's claims to authenticity. "These artifices are become so very common, that they have lost the power of imposition." The letters themselves were nevertheless praised as "elegant, moral, and sentimental". According to the *Critical Review* (October 1784), the letters were not authentic, but they would have intrinsic interest for "a reader of taste". Both of these reviews were perfunctory and conventional. The *European Magazine* (November 1784) introduced a new point in discussing the novel: there was "a strong family-likeness between the Hero of the piece and Harley in the *Man of Feeling*". Henry Mackenzie was not yet ready to acknowledge his authorship of that novel, but he could not remain silent when he saw the sentimental style being debased. In the *Lounger*, Number 20 (June 18, 1785), he printed a thoughtful defence of the novel of feeling. "In the enthusiasm of sentiment," he writes, "there is much the same danger as in the enthusiasm of religion, of substituting certain impulses and feelings of what may be called a visionary kind, in the place of real practical duties, which, in morals, as in theology, we might not improperly denominate good works." He roundly condemns certain publications for their "sickly sort of refinement" and refers contemptuously to "that common herd of novels (the wretched offspring of circulating libraries) which are despised for their insignificance, or proscribed for their immorality". Mackenzie could scarcely have been thinking of Combe's novels when he spoke of immorality, but the *Original Love Letters, between a Lady of Quality and a Person of Inferior Station* was of the "common herd", was published for the circulating library trade, and was in Mackenzie's sense of the word insignificant. The author of the *Man of Feeling* had some reason to deny the existence of any "family-likeness" between Harley and the Person of Inferior Station, but there was a very large and lucrative audience which read both novels with equal "enthusiasm of sentiment". It was not an audience— even the critical reviews did not supply an audience—which was critical of Combe's dilettante posture, his mystifications, his trite sentimentality. Least of all was it critical of his solemn assertion that his own writings were the King's, or Sterne's, or Rousseau's, or an Italian nun's. Like the critic of the *Monthly Review*, Combe's readers were content to find his works "elegant, moral, and sentimental".

*   *   *

Combe's profits from his writings, which at times must have been considerable, were more than absorbed by his improvident habits and by the heavy cost of Maria's maintenance in Stephen Casey's mad-house, which amounted perhaps to as much as £300 a year. That, at any rate, is the figure he mentions in a novel published a few years later.[28] It is not surprising that after mid-1782 his activities seem more than usually devious. In addition to veiling, as he always did, his means of livelihood, he was now trying to conceal his whereabouts. He succeeded temporarily, but one of his creditors caught up with him in Brussels on September 21, 1784. His movements for the next three years are a matter of court record.

Before standing trial for debt, Combe had the usual opportunity of formally acknowledging his obligation by signing a promissory note which gave him a few months to pay. The record shows, in fact, that on that September day in Brussels he signed not one but three separate notes payable at three-monthly intervals on December 29, March 29, and June 29. All were to be paid to the account of his creditor, John Palmer, at the bank office there, payment to be made in "Brabants currency" duly set forth in florins, styvers, and deniers.

Strangely enough, it appears that Combe made almost no effort to write for profit after signing these notes. Earlier in 1784 he had published the ninth volume of the R[oya]l Register and the Original Love Letters between a Lady of Quality and a Person of Inferior Station. The only other work which he produced before he was finally arrested was a satire in an entirely new vein, The Royal Dream; or the P[rince] in a Panic, a moral admonishment addressed to the twenty-two-year-old Prince of Wales. Published for some reason by S. W. Fores rather than by Bew, it was the last of Combe's verse satires. The introduction is dated from Cambridge on April 30, 1785—one more attempt, perhaps, to throw the bailiffs off his trail.

Returning to England, Combe failed to pay the third note on its expiration as he had also failed to pay the first and second. He then met his creditor in Westminster—or more probably John Palmer's solicitor succeeded in finding him there—and the two men "accounted together . . . concerning divers other sums of money before that time due and owing from the said William to the said John and then being in arrear and unpaid". The figure agreed upon was £100, and "he the said William . . . undertook and then and there faithfully promised the said John to pay him the said last mentioned sum of money when he the said William should be thereto afterwards requested".

NEVERTHELESS, [the Plea Roll summary ominously continues] the said William not regarding his said several promises and Undertakings in Manner and form aforesaid made but contriving and fraudulently intending Craftily and subtilly to Deceive and Defraud the said John in this Respect hath not yet paid to the said John the said several Sums of Money or any of them or any part thereof (Although so to do he the said William afterwards . . . hath by the said John been Requested) but to pay the same to the said John or in any manner to satisfy him for the same he the said William hath hitherto altogether Refused and still doth Refuse To the Damage of the said John of one hundred pounds.

Combe was accordingly taken into custody by the Sheriff of Middlesex on October 18, 1785, and a week later he was committed to the King's Bench Prison. His trial did not occur until the following January, for the English practice (which Boswell criticized as less just than the Scottish) permitted a debtor to be imprisoned on the oath of the creditor. When the case was called during Hilary Term of the twenty-sixth regnal year of King George III (January 1786), Combe was brought before Lord Mansfield in the Court of King's Bench, Westminster Hall, to face the charges of John Palmer, represented by his attorney John Isatt. The facts in the case are summarized in intolerable legal jargon on three and a half large vellum pages of the Plea Rolls preserved at the Public Record Office.[29] Final judgement was postponed until a jury could ascertain John Palmer's costs and damages, amounting in all, it was subsequently agreed, to £50. With this figure duly entered into the record, judgement was signed on May 3, 1786. Whereupon "the said William" was once more haled into court and formally committed "to the Custody of the Marshall of the Marshalsea of our said Lord the King in execution for the Damages aforesaid, there to remain until he satisfy the said John".

It was in the new King's Bench Prison, however, rather than the near-by Marshalsea, that Combe was confined, the prisons being under the jurisdiction of the same Marshal. The Commitment Book of the former tersely notes Combe's arrival, and a marginal note adds the date of his formal discharge, May 25, 1787.[30]

CHAPTER V

POLITICAL PAMPHLETEER

I could employ my studious hour
For those who hold the reins of power;
And sure a well-turned pamphlet might
Attention from the court invite;
By which I could, in nervous prose,
Unveil the ministerial foes;
And with no common skill and care,
Praise and support the powers that are.
                    —Doctor Syntax

DEBTOR'S PRISON, when it finally came, can scarcely have taken Combe by surprise. For a long time, and certainly since his unpaid notes had begun to accumulate, he had known that he could not escape it indefinitely. Even so, actual confinement was a shock to his ego—a shock, moreover, which had a salutary effect. For prison fortunately put an end to Combe's posturing as a dilettante and gentlemanly amateur of letters. He had not really deceived others by this affectation, and now he could no longer deceive himself. Unmistakably shorn of his social pretensions, he could only set to work frankly as a professional writer and editor, a businessman-of-letters, and presently a paid pamphleteer for the Ministry. By August 1786 he had his freedom (though not immediately his formal discharge) and was energetically beginning a new career. The ensuing decade was to prove the most prosperous period of his life.

Two men actively aided Combe at this time: John Walter, who now employed him, and John Palmer, who had brought about his incarceration and now released him. Palmer was in a position to take the initiative, for he had known something of Combe's abilities since Bath and Bristol days of 1775, and he was also aware of Walter's urgent need for competent editorial assistance. Unless he could help

Combe get back on his feet, he would never recover his money or any equivalent. But Combe himself, who usually held some expedient in reserve, may also have negotiated the arrangement. Whatever its origin, it immediately proved advantageous to all three men, and within a few months it was to place each of them in a new and highly profitable relationship with the Prime Minister. This turn of events came about through the lucky convergence of three diverse careers at a moment of crisis for each, August 1786.

Combe's new employer was the first of the three John Walters who were successively publishers of *The Times* for a century. He had recently become a printer and bookseller virtually by accident, having purchased as a business venture the patent for logography, a new method of printing from syllables and whole words rather than from individual letters. In order to sell his patent to other printers, he had undertaken to publish a variety of books and pamphlets printed by the new process. On January 1, 1785, he also began publishing a newspaper logographically, the *Daily Universal Register*, renamed *The Times* three years later. But profits from his books never materialized, and he failed to interest other printers in his scheme. Early in 1792 he abandoned logography altogether. It would have been his third bad venture except for *The Times*, which fortunately proved profitable.[1]

In the summer of 1786, however, the paper was not yet prospering, and Walter was having trouble with his other publications. The *Daily Universal Register* for August 10 carried a signed leader in which Walter described difficulties which he had encountered—not, he asserts, from any faults inherent in logography, but from incompetent editing and proofreading. He reassures his readers that these troubles "will now subside, the cause having been removed, and every branch of the business being at present superintended by men, in whose skill, industry, and integrity I can implicitly confide".[2] Someone had evidently been discharged, and someone else, whose identity may with some confidence be conjectured, had taken his place. For the remaining five and a half years of logographic publishing, Walter's most trusted writer, editor, and man-of-all-work was William Combe.

The summer of 1786 also saw the affairs of John Palmer reaching a crisis. Ten years earlier he had been a relatively obscure manager of provincial theatres, but he had now become a public figure actively involved in reforming the postal service. William Pitt, always keenly interested in administrative improvements, encouraged Palmer and in August appointed him Comptroller-General of the Post Office. The would-be reformer was immediately plunged into a bitter controversy with office-holders who had a vested interest in the *status quo*, and he needed as much public support as he could obtain, both to enforce his reforms and to obtain the financial reward which he felt his public service merited. One may reasonably doubt that it was merely Palmer's love of typographical excellence that led him to send a subscription to the Logographic Press, for John Walter was manifestly a publisher who could be useful. In any event, on August 12 Walter published a list of 153 patrons of his Press. Lord Bute, Sir Joseph Banks, Dr Benjamin Franklin, the Duke of Richmond, Sir Joshua Reynolds, Horace Walpole, Lord Mansfield—these and many other distinguished men are listed as having subscribed five guineas each, as is also one man whose first name Walter did not yet know, "Palmer, ———, Esq. General Post-Office." The publisher was not long to remain in ignorance. Within two weeks his newspaper contained a letter to John Palmer, congratulating him on his appointment as Comptroller-General; Palmer's reply was printed in the same issue.[3] The two men had initiated their programme of mutual support.

Unmistakable signs of Combe's hand appear in the *Daily Universal Register* at the end of August, when the paper begins to print many short sentimental effusions vaguely and often explicitly reminiscent of Sterne. Such items were Combe's stock-in-trade, and many of these look very much like his work.[4] Then on September 27 the paper carries a pathetic story entitled "The Nosegay", quoted without acknowledgement from *Letters Supposed to Have Been Written by Yorick and Eliza*. Another unacknowledged quotation, this time from the *Philosopher in Bristol*, appears in the issue for October 3. It is called "Sketch for a Chapter on Widows" and is signed "C". In succeeding weeks seven other sketches carry the same signature. "The Generous Sailor", an unsigned sketch published on October 13, had originally appeared both in the *Philosopher* and in *Letters Supposed*, though neither work is mentioned in the paper. Then on January 11, 1787, appeared the first of thirty-three letters "of the late Reverend Mr. Sterne". After publication at irregular intervals over the ensuing twelve months, the series ends on January 17, 1788, two months before appearing with six additional letters as a volume printed by the Logographic Press, *Original Letters of the Late Reverend Mr. Laurence*

Sterne. All but two of the letters purport to be addressed to the same young man, identified merely as W. C., Esq. Only three, possibly four, of the letters are believed to be substantially as Sterne wrote them; all the others, though evidently based on authentic letters and reliable sources of information, are essentially Combe's handiwork.[5]

The flow of sentimental sketches continues, though somewhat abated, through the first half of 1787. Two which are definitely assignable to Combe appear in the issue for January 31: "Sketch of a Well-Known Man of Fashion", the last of the pieces signed "C", and "Mira of the Dale: a Fragment", later silently reprinted in Combe's *Devil upon Two Sticks in England* (III, 142–8). Others very much in this same manner appear in succeeding issues, "The Blind Man. A Fragment" (February 22), "Rachel and Her Lamb; a Sentimental Fragment" (May 23), and "The Cottage. A sentimental Fragment" (June 1). Combe need not be held responsible for all of these "fragments", but they do strongly suggest the sentimental posture which he could assume at a moment's notice when there was space to be filled. He did not always write in this manner by any means; indeed, after the last of these sketches he turned to something quite different, publishing on June 20 the first of six instalments of his satirical novel, *The Devil upon Two Sticks in England*, published in book form three years later. The sixth instalment appears in the issue for September 8. "Sentimental Fragments" still occasionally occur in the paper throughout 1787, but after the "Sterne" letters have run their course these various voices of William Combe are seldom heard again. Perhaps the new editor of *The Times*, William Finey, had little taste for them; perhaps the news from France which increasingly filled the columns left little space for such trifles; perhaps—and this seems the compelling reason—Combe was so busy preparing books and pamphlets for the Logographic Press that he could no longer contribute to the newspaper.

The files of the *Daily Universal Register*, then, strongly suggest that Combe entered John Walter's newspaper office in mid-August 1786 and spent a good deal of time there for the next year and a half. Yet the records of the King's Bench Prison explicitly state that Combe was not formally released until May 1787. The dates overlap, but they are not necessarily inconsistent. Although Combe could conceivably have sent his contributions to the newspaper from prison, he would be under no compulsion to do so. By paying ten or twelve

guineas, he could obtain the privilege of living "within the rules"—
which is to say outside the walls. "The rules" would theoretically
limit his movements to that section of Southwark immediately
surrounding the prison, but they were notoriously flexible. Certainly
they would not seriously deter Combe from crossing Blackfriars
Bridge to his publisher's office in Printing House Square. If his
presence was desired across the Thames, either Walter or Palmer
could produce the guineas, but who actually produced them and
under just what arrangement remains unexplained. One way or
another, however, each of the three men got what he wanted in
August 1786. Palmer immediately received support in the newspaper and later, as soon as Combe could get the book written,
greater support still from one of Walter's independent publications.
The hard-pressed Walter found a competent editor and man-of-all-
work for his Logographic Press. And Combe, after years of insecurity
and hardship, found honourable employment which gave him a steady
income and gratifying professional recognition. He also got out of
prison.

*   *   *

Combe's contributions to the *Daily Universal Register* were far less
important, either to him or to Walter, than his work for the Logographic Press. No sooner had the two men joined forces than they
began to plan the most ambitious project ever undertaken by the
Press, a new edition of a work published twenty-two years earlier,
*An Historical and Chronological Deduction of the Origin of Commerce,
from the Earliest Accounts to the Present Time,* commonly called Adam
Anderson's *History of Commerce.* On October 12 Walter advertised
his intent to produce "a new and beautiful edition . . . carefully revised, corrected, and continued to the present time. By several
eminent hands." The only hands known to have been engaged in the
work were Combe's. It was, in fact, his first important assignment
under the new arrangement, and he was not formally discharged from
prison until publication was solidly under way. Publication of the
weekly numbers, first announced to begin on January 6, was delayed
until March 3. Three weeks later, on March 27, the newspaper
published a discreet reminder to Palmer of his obligation, pointing to
benefits gained by the public through the exertions of the Comptroller-
General and criticizing "other papers" for their opposition to his

programme. Combe's release was soon forthcoming. On May 25, 1787, the Marshall of the King's Bench was authorized to set him free: "Discharge out of your Custody the Body of the above named Defendant William Combes at the suit of the above named Plaintiff John Palmer he having made him satisfaction."[6] A terse note in the King's Bench Commitment Book confirms his formal discharge on that day.

The weekly numbers of the *History of Commerce* appeared on uninterrupted schedule, and the entire work in four magnificent quarto volumes was ready for distribution to subscribers on June 16, 1789. A notable typographical achievement, the *History* would seem to be a total vindication of Walter's faith in his method of syllabic printing and in his editor. The first three volumes merely reprint Anderson's work essentially as published in 1764; they are competently edited, but the promised revisions and corrections are far to seek. It was the fourth volume which gave the new publication its political significance, for it traced the economic developments of the quarter century which had passed since the appearance of the original work. It had been, as Walter's announcement pointed out, "a period pregnant with new arrangements in the commerce of the world". In particular, Volume IV traced the economic losses during the period of the disastrous American War and contrasted them with the recent gains under the commercial policies of William Pitt. Written entirely by Combe, this volume runs over 700 pages and gives evidence of painstaking research. In his Introduction Combe expressed the hope that the volume would "not disgrace the work it is intended to complete", and a writer in the *Monthly Review* (August 1790) promptly said, "We do not think it will."

Lest any reader miss the political implications, Combe took the precaution of dedicating the *History of Commerce* "by permission" to William Pitt:

Sir,
    It is not in the dedication of this work that you are to look for praise, but in the pages of it that record those commercial arrangements which are the offspring of your administration. . . .
    You were called, Sir, to direct the affairs of Great Britain, at a time when a destructive war had lessened its dominions, exhausted its wealth, and diminished its prosperity. To remedy the evils of that war, whose progress you opposed, you have employed the whole force, and the most uninterrupted exertions of your talents, understanding, and integrity; and the nation at large rejoices on beholding the pleasing prospect of your labours being

crowned with success:—that success, it will be the exulting office of this work to perpetuate. . . .

As the mature wisdom of your illustrious father, by conducting a war, raised Great Britain to a pinnacle of prosperity it had never before attained,— the premature understanding of his son, when that country is involved in distress and embarrassment, by pursuing, extending, and confirming the advantages of peace, promises to restore it to its pristine glory.

This dedication is signed by Pitt's "most faithful, obliged, and devoted humble servant, THE EDITOR". Neither on the title-page nor elsewhere is the editor's name given, but Combe's work on the publication would be known to the trade. Indeed, the Dublin edition explicitly describes itself as "carefully revised, corrected, and continued to the year 1789, by Mr. Coombe". In the *History of Commerce* he began the practice of including his own name in the list of subscribers. In this instance it is a distinguished list, including the names of William Pitt and John Palmer, of course, and also that of "Dr. Franklin, America"—for Franklin, too, was interested in logography and had corresponded with Walter about it. But among the others appears that of "Coombes, Wm. Esq. Harford-street, May-fair". There is no longer a Harford Street in Mayfair; perhaps there never was one. But there is a Harford Road north of Hyde Park in Paddington, and by 1792 Combe certainly lived at an address on Cravin Hill in that neighbourhood. To call Harford Street or Road a Mayfair address stretched the truth no more than half a mile, and the hard-working William Combe, Esq., could not reasonably be denied this small vanity.

The "satisfaction" which Combe had made John Palmer becomes fully apparent only in the Appendix to the fourth volume of the *History of Commerce*, where under the heading "Reform and Improvement of the General Post-Office" Combe publishes a ten-page account of John Palmer's campaign for the adoption of his administrative reforms. He describes the obstacles which were placed in his way by entrenched bureaucracy; he praises the wisdom of Pitt for supporting Palmer, for making him Comptroller-General of the Post Office, and for insisting on the adoption of his plan. "At length", says Combe, "the ability, ingenuity, and indefatigable spirit of the present Comptroller-General, under the protecting wisdom of the present Minister, has brought his undertaking to a very high degree of perfection, and has given an example of public economies which never before existed in this or any other country" (page 712). After several pages of amplification, Combe concludes that "Mr. Palmer, to the very great and acknowledged advantage of the whole kingdom, [has] given accelerated expedition, perfect security, an assured punctuality, and an increased revenue, to the Administration of the General Post Office" (page 718). John Palmer needed such public praise at the moment, for he was claiming a percentage of the increased revenue of the Post Office. He won his case eventually, was granted a pension of £3,000 in 1793, and in 1813 was given an additional £50,000. Combe and others had indeed made him satisfaction.

*   *   *

Although John Palmer may have been instrumental in bringing Combe and Walter together to the advantage of all three, there is no reason to think that the postal reformer ever entered actively into the concerns of the printer and his new editor. He got his support from the *Daily Universal Register*, his "satisfaction" from Combe, and eventually his ten pages in the *History of Commerce*. Apart from those ten pages, however, the great *History* was published to the glory of Pitt and the Logographic Press. In the winter of 1788–9 Pitt himself was in need of support in the newspapers and in a rapidly mounting pamphlet war, and Palmer was in a position to be of service both to the Prime Minister and to the Logographic Press. This was apparently the moment when both Walter and Combe were put on the Treasury payroll. The historian of *The Times* asserts that John Walter's allowance of £300 a year began during the Regency Crisis (November 1788 to February 1789),[7] and certainly his newspaper stoutly supported the Government during and after that perilous time. Combe's allowance of £200 presumably began then, too, for in January he published a vigorously argued pro-Ministry pamphlet; in March he published another, and in July a third. He would not have busied himself thus without remuneration. "For my ordinary drudgery," he once asserted, "I shall be paid my ordinary price."[8]

It would be quite wrong, however, to suppose that Combe's successful career as a political writer came about merely through a convenient "deal" worked out by three or four men for their mutual profit. The arrangement which launched Combe on his new career would have been quite impossible had not public events produced a parliamentary situation unique in British history.[9] The fall of Lord

North's Government in 1782 had precipitated a power struggle among the various factions which had for a time found a deceptive unity in opposing Lord North and the whole conduct of the American war. After three cabinets had fallen in rapid succession, the King made William Pitt First Lord of the Treasury in December 1783, and the general elections of 1784 confirmed him unmistakably in power. The Opposition, meanwhile, had become hopelessly split. Although Charles James Fox, aided by the Duchess of Devonshire and a bevy of Whig beauties, had won his own fiercely contested Westminster election, he seems increasingly to have discredited himself with the nation at large. Pitt, meanwhile, was looking more and more safe, more and more conservative, and the electors liked the image. Only twenty-four when he assumed office, he maintained his position as head of the Government for over seventeen years, and then after a three-year interval he again took office and died as Prime Minister in 1806. He achieved this remarkable record in years of crisis only because he recognized from the first the realities of the political situation and adjusted—or perhaps "trimmed"—his policies accordingly.

The right of the King to choose his own ministers was not then seriously questioned; Pitt held his office because he was acceptable to the King, not because he was the recognized leader of a majority in the Commons. He was compelled to follow a course which would be at least minimally acceptable both to Parliament and to the Crown. There was as yet no party organization to support him in this difficult position. Parliament was simply not structured on party lines; the terms Whig and Tory, in fact, are of little help in understanding the divisions either in Parliament or in the country at large. There was, to be sure, one substantial group in Parliament which could normally be counted on to support policies favoured by the Crown, for it consisted of men who either held or wished to hold various lucrative positions in government offices. It is estimated that more than a fourth of the Members of Parliament were such servants of the King, or placemen. So long as Pitt's policies were acceptable to the King, he could count on the votes of this large group, but he had no comparable "party" of his own. A relatively small group would normally vote either for or against Pitt according to their alignment with the Government or with the Opposition, but these men were motivated more by personal loyalties than by party philosophy. On any issue coming before Parliament, therefore, both the Government and the Opposition had to seek actively for support from members who were in actual fact independent voters. These men regarded themselves as above party or—as they preferred to call it—faction; they listened attentively to the arguments pro and con, and they felt that they made up their minds solely on the merits of the issues debated. It was a situation to call forth the best efforts of parliamentary debaters, and not surprisingly it produced the most brilliant array of forensic talent ever to sit at one time in the Commons: Fox, Sheridan, Burke (not always an effective speaker, but one who commanded high esteem), Wilberforce, Pitt himself, and others. Undeniably, it was the Age of Eloquent Reason.

Outside Parliament there was the same need to appeal to independent judgements, and both Government and Opposition were prompted to publish scores of pamphlets, often closely reasoned and extremely well written, on the great issues of the hour. This is by no means to say that political controversy was always conducted on a high philosophical plane; one need only examine some of the more outrageous satires (*not* by Combe) or the savage caricatures of Gillray, Woodward, or the young Rowlandson to see that this period was also—like some others—an Age of Violent Unreason. But at another level there was a large body of thoughtful men who were bound neither by party nor by personal loyalties in their political sympathies, men who regarded themselves as patriotic independents and who wished at least the illusion of being free to make up their minds on public questions. Both Government and Opposition undertook to reach this large public through a subsidized press and subsidized pamphleteers. Combe was not the only pamphleteer of the time who was paid to act as what we would call a publicist or a public relations officer. Nor was John Walter alone in accepting a pension from the Government; all publishers of newspapers sought such subvention from one source or another, and those whose enterprises survived almost certainly obtained it. The remarkable thing is not that writers and publishers were subsidized, but that so many excellent pamphlets were written and published. Just as the late eighteenth century was the great age for political oratory, it was also, and for much the same reason, the age of great pamphleteers—Edmund Burke, Tom Paine, Dr Richard Price, Thomas Erskine, and many of lesser fame including, though anonymously, William Combe.

It is unlikely that Combe's emergence as a pamphleteer was accidental. For ten years he had shown a keen awareness of shifting
trends in popular writings and had readily adapted himself to them.
The general elections in the spring of 1784 and the parliamentary
session which followed made it abundantly clear that William Pitt
was for the time being firmly established in power. It seemed the
right moment for Combe to speak out when in May 1785, just five
months before going to prison, he published his first political pamphlet, the verse satire mentioned in the last chapter and called *The Royal
Dream: or the P[rince] in a Panic. An Eclogue, with Annotations*
(Fores). It put Combe firmly on the side of the King and Pitt as
opposed to the Prince of Wales and Fox. There was some risk even
in this seemingly safe position. The Prince, like other Hanoverian
heirs, had become a rallying-point for the Opposition, and there was
no doubt that if he came to power through the death or incapacity of
the King he would at once discharge Pitt and install his own favourite
as Prime Minister. Nevertheless, Combe's satire advises the heir
apparent to busy himself with "the gay delights" of youth (advice
which the Prince notoriously did not require) and to stay out of
politics.

> 'Tis wiser far to pass your present hours
> In courtly palaces and ladies' bowers,
> In Cupid's lists to urge love's warm debate,
> Than aid a factious uproar in the state.
>
> (Page 15)

The author professes to encourage the Prince in all kinds of dissipation as a mean of acquiring knowledge of man's ways and learning to
rule his people. Prince Hal had followed such a course and "'mid
thieves and villains learned to grace a throne", but the Prince is
warned that his own Falstaff (i.e. Fox) is not content merely with
whim and revelry. Although above petty crimes, he intends to rob the
treasury.

> Trust not his words; what tho', in accents loud,
> He roars of freedom to a gaping crowd,
> In his base heart the secret wishes crave
> To soil the crown and make the prince a slave.
>
> (Page 30)

The lines are witty and sharp, and the "annotations" (prose introduction and footnotes) contain scandalous references to people and

events which would amuse contemporary readers—especially if their sympathies were on the side of the Government. But whatever its merit as a topical satire, *The Royal Dream* made little stir at the time, possibly because Combe was unable to keep the pot boiling from his new quarters in the King's Bench Prison. It may well have accomplished his real purpose, however, for it announced unmistakably his availability as a pro-Ministerial writer. And whoever it was who later proposed that Combe should be employed by the Treasury, whether John Palmer or another, he very probably did so with a copy of *The Royal Dream* in his hand.

* * *

The Regency Crisis, which led as we have seen to Combe's employment as propagandist for the Ministry, began in November 1788 with the insanity of the King and the entirely justified doubt that he would ever be able to resume his public duties. The Opposition at once demanded that the Prince of Wales be made Regent, but Pitt not unnaturally postponed decisive action as long as possible, since the Prince was certain to ask Fox to form a new government. In anticipation of that eventuality, in fact, the Prince hastily called Fox back from the Continent, where he was travelling with his mistress, Mrs Armistead, later his wife. Pitt himself made preparations for returning to private life, but continued to find excuses for avoiding a Regency. Constitutional issues were raised, the King's health was closely watched for signs of improvement, and finally a Bill was prepared which attached limitations of power to the office of Regent. Meanwhile, the Prince was openly conspiring with the Opposition—with Sheridan and Fox in particular—and together they made their plans for assuming power. Then, to the relief of the nation and the confusion of the Foxites, George III suddenly regained his sanity and Pitt was again secure. The crisis had lasted from November to February, and when it was resolved both Pitt and the King found their positions greatly strengthened, the one in power, the other in the nation's affections.

The threat to Pitt's ministry prompted Combe to write three vigorous pamphlets, all published by Walter at the Logographic Press. The first of these was the highly successful *Letter from a Country Gentleman to a Member of Parliament on the Present State of Public Affairs*, published January 31, just prior to the King's recovery.

The pamphlet is in a sense another of Combe's supposititious works, for it purports to be written by a disinterested, patriotic, right-minded "Country Gentleman" long removed from active political life. The writer, in fact, assumes a posture of lofty superiority not unlike that maintained by William Pitt in all his public dealings. From this aloof point of view he writes at the request of his Member of Parliament an account of the passing scene "in the present very singular and important crisis". It is a vigorous pamphlet, quite without Combe's former posturing—some of the best prose, in fact, which he ever produced. Disinterested or not, the views he expresses are precisely those of orthodox Pitt supporters.

If there is a subject of these kingdoms more unconnected than another with the leading persons in either of the contending parties—it is myself. Mr. *Fox* I have never seen since he was a boy, and Mr. *Pitt* I have never seen at all. I have personally no political hopes or fears whatever. Not all the power of Ministers, nor all the wealth of the Treasury, would tempt or bribe me to quit the shade of those woods where I was born, whither I have retired to pass the remainder of my days, and where I hope to die. You will, therefore, receive the sincere, and perhaps the curious effusions of an honest, an unbiassed, and tranquil spirit, upon the business that agitates the national mind on the lamentable incapacity of the sovereign of the empire.

The first observation which occurs to me is this:—that, at the moment, when the heavy affliction of his M A J E S T Y 's illness interrupted the government of his country, public affairs were conducted with great apparent wisdom:—the nation was recovering very fast from the distress of a most unfortunate and expensive war;—commerce was extending its limits—the revenues were increasing their income—and, though loaded with a most burthensome and unparalelled [*sic*] weight of taxes, the nation was satisfied. Wise alliances had been formed, and others were forming. The energies of our government had been made known to the world, and the British character raised to its former importance in the eye of mankind, without the imposition of any new burthen on the people, or any infringement on those funds which had been already appropriated by Parliament, to the regular diminution of the national debt. Such, I think, was our situation; and a better, could hardly be expected, when the nation was called to contemplate the most affecting object a prosperous people could behold, and to provide such means as were necessary to supply the unprecedented exigencies of the very alarming juncture.

The first wish my mind urged me to express was in common with the whole kingdom, that his M A J E S T Y might be shortly restored to his capacity of transacting the public business of the nation. The second desire of my heart was, that the administration of Government might proceed without any change in the persons who composed it.

(Pages 4–5)

[152]

He little thought that the King's illness would be taken by the Opposition as "the signal to make an attempt to seize the helm", much less that they would be encouraged in such an effort by "a great personage". But such was the case. He considers the various possible reasons for the Prince's behaviour, none of which seems convincing. "It would be insulting his understanding to imagine that he does not know how to distinguish between men qualified to amuse his convivial hours at *Carlton House*, or the *Marine Pavilion* [at Brighton], and such as are bound to assist in the solemn councils of the State." He writes at some length of the Prince's "mysterious connection" (he never says "marriage") with Mrs Fitzherbert, always alluded to as "Mrs. F——", but he rejects the idea that the relationship has political implications. The only plausible explanation, indeed, is that the Opposition leaders have succeeded in misleading the Prince's "young and amiable mind". With this, he proceeds to comment on each of the Opposition leaders by turn: the Duke of Portland, Lord North, Burke, Sheridan, and various others, all of them unqualified, we are told, for political leadership. In summary, the Prince has thrown his influence behind a party which "consists on the one hand, of great property, some virtue and no talents; and on the other, of great talents, without any property or virtue at all".

He then gives a tabloid history of the Opposition since the King's illness:

No sooner was the awful visitation of Heaven on our *Sovereign* communicated by the Royal Physicians to the *Prince of Wales*, and the Administration, than the scattered Members of the party began to hold up their heads, and enjoy the enlivening expectation of a better and more honourable dependence than the *Faro Table*, which had so long been the principal support of so many of them. Mr. *Sheridan* was ordered to remain in waiting by a great personage, to receive his communications, and to perform such little agencies for him as the critical juncture might be thought to require. Nothing, however, could be done but to disseminate reports, to scatter opinions, and propagate doctrines, in order to prepare the people for their designs, as soon as Mr. *Fox* could be brought from the continent, to give them form and put them in motion. That gentleman was, at this time, conducting such a woman as Mrs. *Armistead* through *France* and *Italy*, and was called from that honourable duty to head his party, and govern an Empire.

(Pages 44–45)

On Fox's return, the writer continues, the Prince became openly a supporter of the Opposition and demanded that he should be called immediately to act as Regent for his father. The Foxites insisted that Parliament must yield to this demand as royal prerogative, but fortunately a "wise spirit of precaution" prevailed, and Parliament determined that it had the constitutional right to exercise its best judgement in the matter. At this, the supporters of the Prince raised a great commotion and began at once

to shape paragraphs, frame hand-bills, and propagate falsehoods; in short, to do their utmost, by any and every means, to inflame the people against the *King's* friends, and to influence the public mind in favour of their own masters. . . . Inflammatory hand-bills seem to have been blown through the air, to our market towns, in order, (as one of my farmers expressed himself) to make the people as glad as the writers of them, that the *King* was out of his mind.

(Page 48)

Combe speaks of the Bill now before Parliament to appoint a Regent with limited powers—in particular, forbidding the appointment of new ministers—and gives the arguments for and against such limitation as advanced by the two parties. Far from disapproving the Bill, he argues, the King on his recovery will be grateful to the ministers who have protected the nation against rapacious men and, if they have been displaced, will at once call them back to office. He then praises Pitt in almost the same words as those of the Dedication of the *History of Commerce*. Finally, he addresses the Prince directly, gratuitously supplying His Royal Highness with a dozen pages of "disinterested" advice.

The *Letter from a Country Gentleman* was Combe's most successful political venture. In February both reviews praised the work and its author: "masterly", said the *Monthly*; "a discriminating hand", exclaimed the *Critical*. Combe produced "additions" for the fourth edition (February 18)—actually only four paragraphs, but they justified mention on the new title-page. By that time another bookseller had a pamphlet on the market with a title so similar to Combe's that Walter published an advertisement in *The Times* warning the public to beware of this deception.[10] And by April Combe's pamphlet was doing so well that Kearsly felt justified in publishing *An Answer to the Country Gentleman's Letter*, actually a clever parody which follows Combe's topics in virtually the same order, but with reverse argument. As a professional, Combe would by no means regret this publication which necessarily advertised his own, and on May 19 the eighth edition of his *Letter* was announced. Years afterward, men still recalled the title when the Regency Crisis was mentioned.

* * *

The success of this pamphlet prompted Combe and his bookseller to publish another on March 20 and to identify it as "By the Author of a *Letter from a Country Gentleman to a Member of Parliament*". This was *The Royal Interview: A Fragment* (Logographic Press), an imaginary dialogue between the King, now fully recovered, and his erring son, the Prince of Wales. The King questions his son closely on his behaviour in the recent crisis: Why had he chosen Sheridan of all people as his advisor? Why had he acted contrary to the wishes of the people? What measures did his proposed ministers intend to take if they were raised to power? They discuss the various Whig leaders individually and, except for the Duke of Portland, the King condemns their motives and their intelligence. Finally, the King tells his son what he should have done to meet the emergency and advises him to redeem himself henceforth by more suitable behaviour.

Let me exhort you to turn your back on *Circe* and her crew and join the votaries of virtue. . . . Check the ardour, and change the nature of your pleasures. Encourage art, be the patron of science, and beckon virtue to your protection. Let every part of your conduct compose an assured omen of all that is great and good in the character of a Monarch: so that the rising generation may exult in the hopes that they shall enjoy the glories of your reign, and the aged patriot express his sole regret that he shall not live to behold them.—In short, so conform *your* life to honour, that I may end *mine* in peace.

(Pages 60–61)

The modern reader may find all this somewhat tedious, for Combe felt compelled to inflate his style in keeping with the royal character. A contemporary might be more sympathetic, however, for the pamphlet dealt with events and issues which were of vast importance at the time, and in the general rejoicing over the King's recovery most Englishmen shared the political views expressed in the pamphlet. To be sure, the *Monthly Review* (April) pointed out that "It happens in this, as in most argumentative dialogues on paper, the victory is predetermined: a man of straw is set up, merely to be run through at pleasure", but the same reviewer praises the author who "has, in this performance, as in his *Letter from a Country Gentleman*, proved himself an able politician, and a good writer". The public also approved the work, though with somewhat reduced enthusiasm; four editions were called for in seven months.

* * *

During the summer the Logographic Press published one more work on the Regency Crisis by the same industrious writer. This was *An History of the Late Important Period*, a routine piece of hackwork running to 543 pages. It is a compilation of the reports of the King's medical examiners, the debates in Parliament, lists of those voting for and against various measures, and the full text of the Regency Act. The book concludes with fifteen pages of "Observations on the Conduct of the Contending Parties", the only original part of the work and a direct echo, sometimes not even paraphrased, of the *Letter from a Country Gentleman*. The title was advertised on February 3 as in the press and due to appear "in a few days"; on May 19 a second advertisement announced that it would be published "shortly". It actually made its appearance on July 7. There was good reason for the delay. In June the Duke of York and the Prince of Wales had brought suit against Walter for publishing libellous statements concerning their behaviour during the Crisis. Everyone knew that they had become deeply involved in the political manoeuvres of the winter, but *The Times* had published stories about them on February 21 and 26 which were actionable. Walter was brought to trial on July 11, was found guilty, and was sentenced to serve two years in prison.[11] The offending paragraphs had been inserted at the express request of the Government, but when Walter was prosecuted no one in authority came to his aid. Manifestly there were perils in acting as a paid agent for William Pitt.

As finally published, the *History of the Late Important Period* is entirely safe if not utterly innocuous; neither Combe nor Walter could be indicted for anything it contained. It is of interest only as an example of the routine work which Combe was always ready to undertake for a price. The title merely appeared on the bookstalls for a brief period, then dropped out of sight without going into a second edition.

By this time Combe had firmly established himself in his career as political pamphleteer. He had completed his large task of editing the *History of Commerce*, making it a great vindication of Pitt's economic programme. He had written his *Letter from A Country Gentleman* and the *Royal Interview*, and both pamphlets were selling well. After some adversity and delay, his compiled *History of the Late Important Period* was finally in the bookstalls. He had also made a substantial start on those "two thousand columns in newspapers" which he was later to claim, and though much of this work was non-political, many of the paragraphs and longer pieces in support of Pitt which appeared in the *Daily Universal Register* and *The Times* must have been his. As will be abundantly evident in the next chapter, political writing had by no means monopolized his attention during these busy months, but he was clearly earning his pay as a propagandist for the Ministry and as a supporter of the Logographic Press.

In a letter to Lord Mulgrave nearly twenty years later Combe described the "terms on which I had been engaged by Mr. Pitt's former administration. These were, to obey such instructions as were given me, and when I had no instruction to act from myself and my own judgment, as occasion offered; £200 was the stipulated salary. By Mr. L[ong]'s obliging and friendly behaviour personally to my-self, and the letters which he sometimes wrote to me, I have the best reasons to believe that he was satisfied with my conduct.[12] How much of his writing during the first half of 1789 was on instructions, how much on his own initiative, one can only guess. But there can be little room for doubt that Mr Long would be satisfied with Combe's output during these productive months.

* * *

After precariously surviving the Regency Crisis, Pitt seemed to have complete hold on the electorate, and the time was ripe to confirm his popularity by dissolving Parliament and holding national elections. Under the Septennial Act they could in no case be postponed beyond 1791, but early in 1790 they began to be much talked of as imminent. Combe accordingly began preparing a campaign pamphlet which— given its name—be barely completed in time. On June 10 *The Times* announced his *Considerations on the Approaching Dissolution of Parliament* (Logographic Press); the same issue revealed that Parliament was that day to be dissolved. Subsequent issues of the pamphlet quietly suppressed the word *Approaching* from the title. A second edition with the shortened title appeared July 7.

The *Considerations* purport to be from the pen of the same "Country Gentleman" who had written the *Letter* a year earlier, and the suppositious manner is maintained as before, the anonymous author standing aloof from the partisan struggle, disinterested, unemotional, and concerned only for his country's welfare. Taking his cue from Pitt himself, Combe writes somewhat condescendingly to the electors: "From the circumstances of my life and situation, I, perhaps, may be better qualified to judge of those principles which should govern your conduct at the important period that approaches, than the greater part of you." He defines his position as that which subsequent generations have called "realistic"; he is in favour of virtue in the abstract, but he finds it not altogether practical in this imperfect world. He will not hold out deceptive promises of a perfect society; he acknowledges at once that there is corruption in government. He does not favour it, but "in the present state and fashion of the higher orders of the people, no minister would be able to carry on the public business without it".

Since both the King and Pitt now opposed reform of Parliament, the "Country Gentleman" takes the same position; sensible men, he assures us, cannot regard the present moment as the time for correcting the inequities of representation. He believes that certain reforms may ultimately be necessary to preserve the Constitution, but he takes the position now becoming popular with conservatives: reform of Parliament, however desirable in theory, must wait until peace has been restored and the national burdens have been reduced. This was now Pitt's attitude, and, in fact, it remained his attitude. After 1785 he never again urged reform. The times were adverse. "Who would repair their house in a hurricane?" demanded William Windham, and the nation echoed the query.

Except for this passing allusion to Parliamentary reform, Combe altogether ignores the real issues. There is no mention of repealing the Test and Corporation Acts to give dissenters full political rights. Wilberforce and his opposition to the slave trade are never alluded to. Combe charges the electors with but one duty—to choose between the Ministerial and the Opposition parties and to support that choice without regard to personal feelings about either men or issues. He then discusses the Opposition at length and unfavourably, the Ministry briefly and favourably. He rehearses the familiar details of the Regency Crisis, describes the well-known shortcomings of the Prince and his friends, and specifies the faults of Fox, Burke, and the others. Sheridan, who has already been dismissed as merely "a political adventurer", is not at this point even mentioned. Nor is the Duke of Portland named; Pitt was still courting support from his followers among the conservative Whigs.

Coming finally to a discussion of the Ministerial party, Combe declares that it is unnecessary to praise Pitt. He devotes a few complimentary lines to his character and accomplishments, pauses only to defend the recent imposition of new and much-resented taxes, and concludes that the electors must decide for themselves whether or not the nation's peace and prosperity are due to Pitt's statesmanship. At this point he breaks off, leaving the choice—if by this time there is one—to the wisdom of the electors.

Combe's management of his argument cannot have displeased Pitt's supporters, though its manner as well as its substance must have been a source of irritation to the Opposition. It is all written with an air of open-minded, disinterested patriotism. There is no eloquence: Combe was incapable of that, and in any event eloquence was the stock-in-trade of Fox and Sheridan. Without mentioning them he warns his readers not to be deceived by their rhetoric. "Eloquence is among the first of human talents: it commands some,—it dazzles many,—it delights all;—but it possesses, at least, an equal power of doing evil as of doing good; and, perhaps, there is no art more pernicious to mankind than that of making the worse appear the better reason" (pages 17–18). Combe's avoidance of all argument over the pressing issues of the day followed a pattern set by Pitt himself, who was biding his time while those very issues were splitting the Opposition. It was safe only to discuss the Regency Crisis, for the Foxites had lost prestige in the outcome of that affair and there was political advantage in keeping it alive as an issue. Anyway, Pitt wanted a quiet election, and he got one very much on the terms defined by Combe. The Parliament which convened in November was little changed from that which had been dissolved in June.

Combe seems to have written this pamphlet cautiously, as well he might with Walter still in Newgate for publishing things he had not even undertaken on his own initiative. Whatever his instructions for the *Considerations* had been, he was treading softly. He had avoided libel suits so far, but prudence was clearly indicated. For the two years which followed Combe was even more cautious; so far as can be ascertained, he published no political writings whatever.

* * *

Combe's reticence concerning reform in his *Considerations,* though inconsistent with the mood of the country in 1790, was a faithful reflection of Ministerial policy. Pitt's moderate Bill for the reform of Parliament had failed to pass in 1785—chiefly, so Pitt and others believed, because the country at large was not then sufficiently interested in reform. But no one could complain of any such lack of interest in England five years later. Reform was very much in the minds of Englishmen by that time, partly because they had just celebrated the centennial of their own Revolution of 1689 and were advocating new reforms to bring that revolution up to date, and partly because the stirring events in France had heightened interest in liberty and made reform the topic of the hour. Most historians believe that Pitt could then have pushed his Bill through Parliament, but he made no effort to do so, and reform was deferred for forty-two years. Pitt's apologists have been at some pains to explain his silence on the subject, particularly during the months following the elections of 1790. He seems to have continued to think of himself as a reformer, but he, too, easily rationalized failure to act on the ground that the time was not propitious: the reform movement might get out of hand, as it had in France. After the September (1792) Massacres in Paris, there might have been some force to this argument, but few would have found the reason cogent in 1790 or 1791. One tends, however reluctantly, to attribute Pitt's silence to a less theoretical consideration. The King opposed reform, and Pitt wished to remain Prime Minister.

Pitt's silence regarding the early course of the French Revolution is easier to understand. He contented himself with essentially noncommittal statements and left discussion of the real issues to the Opposition—which eventually was torn asunder by violent disagreement. Charles James Fox, for example, had no hesitation in speaking out. He hailed the meeting of the States General in May 1789 as signalling the end of despotism, and a few weeks later he was calling the Fall of the Bastille the greatest and best event in human history. His ablest friend, Edmund Burke, took the opposite position and argued that the revolution in France was repudiating the past, destroying human rights, and laying the foundations for war and tyranny. Until late in 1792 Pitt was able to remain aloof, and by that time Fox's supporters were one by one abandoning their leader and going over to Pitt's side. Burke publicly renounced his friendship with Fox in May 1791, and finally only a handful of former colleagues remained in the Opposition camp. Had Pitt declared his position, or had Combe declared it for him, whatever that position might have been, the Foxites could have attacked it. As it was, they could only attack each other.

Fortunately for Pitt, a conservative Englishman had no need to speak out against the French Revolution during the first three years of its course. The reforms proclaimed by the National Assembly during those years were not unlike those which the English had won a hundred years earlier, and, of course, no one could anticipate the more drastic actions and the appalling bloodshed still to come. Each new event in France seemed to come as a surprise to the English, who believed again and again that the revolution had run its course. On July 13, 1789, for example, *The Times* unluckily announced that Paris was calm and that "The revolution in the change of government appears to be complete". Seven days later it was compelled to report the events of July 14, and surprise as well as consternation is evident in the three columns headed "Rebellion and Civil War in France". A single sentence describing the fall of the Bastille is buried deep in the article; the significant news is the sudden eruption of mob violence, which could only remind the English of their own recent Gordon Riots.

Pitt voiced conventional regret that such mob scenes had occurred, but he was not yet moved to express opposition to the Revolution itself. Indeed, Englishmen of all classes were for three years disposed to be sympathetic. Certainly, the embarrassments of the French Government aroused little sympathy in Whitehall, where officials had been trying for years to outwit their rivals in the European power struggle. In the City, conservative businessmen also managed to view events across the Channel with equanimity if not positive enthusiasm, for the long-standing commercial rivalry between the two countries predisposed London merchants to regard the upheaval as a not unwelcome trade advantage. No doubt they—like the King himself— were encouraged in this attitude by memories of their losses in the

American War and of French intervention in that disastrous struggle. As *The Times* pointed out in reporting the fall of the Bastille,

> The French soldier on his return from that emancipated continent, told a glorious tale to his countrymen —"That the arms of France had given freedom to thirteen United States, and planted the Standard of Liberty on the battlements of New York and Philadelphia." The idea of such a noble deed became a general object of admiration, the sweets of a similar state were eagerly longed for by all ranks of people, and the *vox populi* had this force of argument—"If France gave freedom to America, why should she not unchain the arbitrary fetters which bind her own people."

English complacency in this ironic turn of events was not to last long, however, for within two years it became apparent that just as France had found an example in America, England might now find one in France. As early as October 1790, Burke made this point in his impassioned *Reflections on the Revolution in France*, but English opinion had not yet turned against the Revolution. The immediate effect of Burke's pamphlet was not what he had anticipated; many of his friends were alienated—Fox in particular—and his influence was diminished. Some thirty-eight books and pamphlets were published in reply to Burke, including those by Mary Wollstonecraft, James Mackintosh, and Joseph Priestley, but the most memorable was Tom Paine's *Rights of Man*, the first part of which appeared in March 1791. For the moment it must have seemed to most Englishmen that the defenders of the French Revolution and of reform had the better of the argument. Then violence broke out—not on behalf of reform, as many had anticipated, but against the reformers! The Constitutional Society of Birmingham had arranged a dinner on July 14 to celebrate the second anniversary of the fall of the Bastille, and for several days an angry mob had expressed its indignation by running riot in the streets shouting "Down with Dissenters" and "No false Rights of Man", destroying homes of prominent Nonconformists, and otherwise demonstrating their loyalty to Church and State. Birmingham's most prominent reformer was the dissenting minister and chemist Joseph Priestley, and though he had had little to do with the dinner, his Unitarian chapel was destroyed, his house demolished, and his laboratory burned. To many Englishmen (though not to the

King), the would-be reformers seemed by contrast a sober, conservative group of men who held commemorative dinners and organized societies instead of destroying property.

Then early in 1792 agitation for reform was intensified. In January, Thomas Hardy, a Westminster bootmaker, was instrumental in organizing the London Corresponding Society for the Reform of Parliamentary Representation. Formed on the model of the Jacobin Club in Paris, this organization began actively promoting those very reforms which Pitt had once favoured, but which he was now resolutely opposing. In February the second part of Paine's *Rights of Man* appeared; far more inflammatory than Part One, this pamphlet attacked Pitt rather than Burke and openly advocated revolution. The Government took steps to suppress the work, but could not prevent its being widely circulated. In April a group of Foxite Whigs organized a reform society known as the Friends of the People, and on April 30 one of its members, Charles Grey (the man who was ultimately responsible for the Reform Bill of 1832), gave Parliament notice that he would propose reform legislation during the next session. It was finally time for Pitt to speak out. He had been silent during the debate on the Birmingham disorders, but he now vigorously opposed Grey's proposal. By midsummer Combe felt authorized to enter the controversy, and in August or early September he published his *Word in Season to the Traders and Manufacturers of Great Britain* (Stockdale), a firmly conservative appeal to businessmen, urging that they of all people should resist the subversive arguments of Tom Paine and the reform societies.

The anonymous author identifies himself as a member in good standing of the class he is addressing. "I was born to competence, which I owe to the successful industry of my father." His early admiration for the British Constitution has been confirmed and strengthened by a life of reading, reflection, and disinterested observation of public events. He is astonished that anyone should think it possible for successful businessmen to doubt the virtues of the English system. Who are these agitators, he asks, who are sowing seeds of discontent among us? And his answer is the inevitable *ad hominem*: "The persons who compose the societies, and who have established them, as they announce the matter, for constitutional reformation, are men, I am not afraid to say, of weak heads, of bad hearts, or desperate fortunes." They seek to achieve their ends in two ways, by advocating a revolution like that which has occurred in France and, more insidiously, by destroying men's belief in the very basis of our social structure—subordination. They are, in other words, revolutionaries and levellers.

Although Combe pretends to maintain his usual disinterested-observer manner in this pamphlet, he cannot but reflect the mounting tensions of that last summer of peace before the long war. Writing just before the August and September Massacres in Paris, he could still hope, as Pitt and the nation hoped, that war might be avoided. But already events in France and fears of similar events in England had stirred men's passions to the fever pitch. If Combe's logic now seems rather less than perfect, one should remember that he was writing at a time of great national and international crisis—never a moment conducive to cool reasoning. The *Word in Season* expressed those passions strongly and is, in fact, a good index to the state of popular opinion during the summer of 1792. The emotional atmosphere of that crucial period comes through vividly as Combe heightens his rhetoric to compare conditions in France and England:

> As for the blessings which the people of England would derive from following the example of France, let us for a moment consider, by way of recommendation, the actual blessings which the French themselves enjoy, in consequence of their boasted Revolution.
> Their King is himself a captive—in what is called a land of liberty. Their National Assembly is a mob.
> Their arrêts, their decrees, and their laws, are changed every hour, as the caprice of the moment or the violence of the populace directs. . . .
> Their ancient nobility is degraded—their clergy pillaged—their commerce almost annihilated—and their colonies in a rapid progress to ruin.
> Property, personal security, liberty, and life, are equally endangered; and neither their laws nor their magistrates have sufficient strength or power, to punish theft, robbery, or murder.
>
> (Pages 8–9)

The inventory of evils continues: "convulsed and torn to pieces by contending factions", "riots, insurrections, and massacres", "altars pillaged", and "Religion . . . subdued". And the blessings derived from these circumstances?

> It is said that . . . the subjects of France are a free people.
> Yes,—the gentleman of landed property may call himself free,— but, at the very moment he is boasting of his freedom, his castle may

be seized by the banditti of his neighbourhood, and the walls of it stained with his blood.

The merchant may boast of the fulness of liberty, but his warehouses are empty, his correspondents are silent, his capital is lost, and his credit is gone.

The tradesman may sit in his shop, and delight himself with the idea that he is a free man—but he sells nothing.

The artist may exclaim—liberty is the friend of genius, the encourager of the arts—but, alas! it has not left him a single patron.

The manufacturer may be elated that his country is blessed with freedom;—but the fire blazes no more on his forge, and the useless loom is occupied by the spider's Web. . . .

Such are the comforts of a revolution, which Mr. Paine and his adherents recommend to your imitation.—A Revolution, which, while it has plunged France into every distress that can befal a nation, gives a few uncertain, ruinous, and short lived privileges, to a small band of the most worthless people in it.—These are the consequences of a Revolution brought on by mad, tumultuous, unreflecting, popular insurrections, excited and fomented by factious clubs and societies; and who, alone, of twenty-five millions of people, are in any degree the gainers, if gainers they can, with truth, be called, by this general calamity.

(Pages 10–13)

To contrast with this account of conditions in France, Combe presents a glowing picture of general well-being in England. In doing so, he indirectly answers Tom Paine's criticisms of Pitt's financial policies and, though without naming them explicitly, suggests that the two reforms most insisted upon—parliamentary representation and religious toleration—are, in fact, quite unnecessary. Who could justly complain of Pitt's taxes or his budget when the nation is so prosperous? Combe even justifies the Test and Corporation Acts (which deprived Catholics and dissenting Protestants of certain civil rights) in one sentence: "Consider the state of the established Church, and you will find it to be maintained and supported on principles of moderation: power and trust are confined, as they must necessarily be, to those who join in the national religion; but at the same time, a free toleration is granted to every different sect of Christians, and the rights of private opinion and liberty of conscience are held as sacred and inviolate" (page 16).

His answer to the parliamentary reformers may have struck them as disingenuous, but its air of reason and goodwill must have seemed plausible to many readers:

It may be true that, according to strict, arithmetical calculation, the nation at large is not represented in a fixed, accurate proportion between the numbers in different districts; but, in effect, has any part of the country, whether immediately represented or not, any cause to complain of a want of parliamentary service;—and though Manchester, Birmingham, and other considerable towns, have no actual representatives in Parliament, is there a Member of the House of Commons who would not be proud to transact their parliamentary business? I must, indeed, repeat my opinion, that our representation, in its present state, is perfectly adequate to all the purposes for which a representation of the people can be desired: at all events, any change in it should proceed from the most mature and temperate deliberation; and while notions are agitated, subversive of all government, it is not a season in which those temperate reforms, which might, perhaps, at other times be practicable, could safely or prudently be attempted.

(Pages 29–30)

The first part of this argument doubtless seemed reasonable to readers whose towns and cities were represented in Parliament. It would in any event have a familiar ring in 1792, for Englishmen were well acquainted with the doctrine that Members of Parliament represented the whole country rather than merely the constituency which elected them, but Combe is reversing an accepted idea when he argues that cities without their own elected representatives in Parliament could easily find members "to transact their parliamentary business". The businessmen of Manchester and Birmingham would understandably be more attracted by the second part of his argument: reform may be theoretically desirable, but it would be dangerous to undertake it at this time. That was now Pitt's position, and it was to prevail until 1832.

Although Combe implies that the reform societies are the revolutionaries whom he is addressing, his arguments really apply only to Tom Paine, whom many of the reformers had by this time repudiated. The reform societies did not advocate violent overthrow of the Government. If revolutionary at all, they were so only in the English sense of seeking by constitutional means to correct the blatant inequities inherent in a long-out-of-date system of electing Members of Parliament. But Tom Paine, in Part Two of the *Rights of Man* (February 1792), had come very close to sedition; indeed, the Royal Proclamation against seditious writings which was issued on May 21 was an *ex post facto* condemnation of Paine's pamphlet. By identifying the reform associations with Paine's doctrines, Combe—and the

Government itself—sought less to prevent a violent revolution (which, in fact, they thought unlikely)[13] than to discredit the whole reform movement.

Combe's pamphlet addressed itself to levellers as well as to revolutionaries, and here again he is in reality attacking the reform societies, identifying them with Paine's doctrines and giving their democratic theories the opprobrious name "levelling". Stoutly defending the class system, he insists that "We cannot all be masters or all servants; wealth will be the lot of some, and labour and poverty of others. If equality in these matters be one of the Rights of Man, the English do not have it." But "there is no right which a reasonable man would wish to enjoy, that you do not possess under the existing government of your country,—You have every right, but the right of doing wrong."

Since he is addressing traders and manufacturers, he concludes by stressing the importance of the class system in an industrial society. Suppose the workers of Manchester or Birmingham said to their masters, "You shall now toil for us." What would happen? Ruin for all, rich and poor alike. "Indeed, it appears to me, that, in places particularly devoted to trade, manufactures, and commerce, there can be no evil so much to be dreaded as popular commotions." This line of argument may ignore a good many important issues, but to many of Combe's readers it seemed an entirely satisfactory view of the matter. In any event, the propagandist is not addressing posterity, and the *Word in Season* was highly regarded by contemporary readers. Stockdale issued seven editions in rapid succession, and several other editions were published and given wide distribution by the counter-revolutionary societies.

Reviewers differed, needless to say, according to their political bias. The *Critical Review* (June 1792) summed up its verdict in two sentences: "Some plain truths in favour of the constitution, and of contentment with our situation. We are glad to see one instance of real patriotism, and can faithfully commend the design and the execution."

The *Monthly* (September 1792), however, took a rather less sympathetic position: "The writer greatly exaggerates the troubles, and much misrepresents the affairs, of France, in order to discredit the Revolution. On the contrary, he draws such a flattering picture of the state of our own country, that we sincerely wish it were literally true;

and yet, strange to tell, he seems to dread a general insurrection of the people! How can these things be?"

Within five months England was at war with France, but at the moment Combe was once again in the centre of the controversy, and once again he was voicing the opinions held by Pitt while the latter maintained his aloof silence above the squabbles of politicians and pamphleteers. There is more than a suggestion here of the ventriloquist-puppet relationship, and the puppet continued to draw his pay from the Treasury. A few days after the appearance of *A Word in Season*, Combe wrote and signed the following receipt, now preserved at the Public Record Office: "Reced Septr 21 1792 of Charles Long Esq the Sum of One hundred pounds. Wm Combe."[14] It was his semi-annual stipend from his employer.

* * *

By 1795 the affairs of the Prince of Wales were claiming renewed attention in Parliament, and Combe once more felt called upon to expostulate. The Prince had been an embarrassment to the nation since his expensive affair at the age of eighteen with the actress, Mrs Mary ("Perdita") Robinson. His amorous adventures may at first have been looked upon with indulgence by a society notoriously lax in such matters, but his extravagance was no mere peccadillo. When he came of age in 1783 his debts were already phenomenal; Parliament at that time granted him an income of £50,000 from the Civil List and gave him outright £60,000 to satisfy his creditors and set up his establishment at Carlton House. The following year he fell in love with Mrs Fitzherbert, an attractive widow and a Roman Catholic. Because of her religion she was disqualified from becoming the wife of the heir apparent, and to the evident surprise and dismay of the Prince she was unwilling to become his mistress. Finally, in a melodramatic scene which took place in the presence of the Duchess of Devonshire (who was herself—at the very least—his intimate friend), the Prince and Mrs Fitzherbert plighted their troth, using for the purpose a ring borrowed from the Duchess. Rumours got abroad that they intended to marry, and Charles James Fox wrote to the Prince urging him not to do so. The Prince replied denying the engagement, and four days later (December 15, 1785) the ceremony took place. The marriage was kept a close secret, however, and when in 1787 Parliament was again asked to vote a large sum of money to pay the Prince's debts, Fox rose in the Commons and solemnly assured the House that the gossip concerning the marriage was false. Perhaps he thought he was telling the truth; in any event, Parliament was satisfied and voted to grant the Prince the sum of £221,000.

This generous concession was by no means a final solution to the problem. The marriage with Mrs Fitzherbert should by law have disqualified the Prince from succeeding to the throne, but it was tacitly regarded as morganatic (a relationship not recognized by English law), and the two lived together more or less happily until 1794, when the Prince—though only temporarily—broke off with his wife. This action was taken partly at the insistence of his then mistress, Lady Jersey, and partly in order to facilitate legal marriage to a suitably Protestant German princess, a cousin whom he despised, Princess Caroline of Brunswick. By contracting a marriage which might provide an heir to the throne, he hoped to persuade Parliament once again to pay his debts, now greater than ever. On December 8, 1794, the marriage took place by proxy in Germany, and in April the Princess arrived in England to join her husband, almost a total stranger. Lady Jersey was installed at once as her lady-in-waiting.

Although the Prince had agreed in 1787 never again to ask Parliament for help in paying his debts, his royal father now acted for him and once more laid the matter before the House of Commons. By this time the Prince's debts ran to £630,000. It seemed a heavy burden to impose on a highly promising marriage, and Parliament dutifully, but with understandable reluctance, voted to relieve the bride and groom of this embarrassment.

Combe's new pamphlet appeared three months after the arrival of Princess Caroline in London. During those months the bookstalls had been loaded with a succession of anonymous publications discussing the affairs of the Prince. Characteristically the writers gave little attention to his amatory adventures; what really aroused public concern was his wildly irresponsible dissipation of public funds. The titles of these pamphlets give a good indication of the mood of the times: *A Poetical Epistle from a Little Insolvent Debtor to a Great Insolvent Debtor*; *A Letter to the Prince of Wales on a Second Application to Parliament to Discharge Debts Wantonly Contracted since May 1787*; *A Loyal but Solemn Expostulation Addressed in a Moment of General Distress, Dismay, and Apprehension, to a Thoughtless and Imprudent*

Young Man; and, more simply, *Thoughts on the Prince's Debts*. By contrast with these titles, Combe's is indeed restrained: *Two Words of Counsel, and One of Comfort. Addressed to His Royal Highness the Prince of Wales* (T. Mason). It appeared in July 1795.

There is no denying that in this pamphlet Combe again rejoices rather too obviously in the role of moral counsellor; his admonishments to the Prince to quit party politics and give up lavish dissipations (the two words of counsel) are in a style which strikes the modern reader as tedious and offensive. His assurance that the Prince may yet regain "the enthusiastic affection" of his people (the word of comfort) now seems piously unconvincing. It is only fair to remind ourselves, however, that Combe was not dealing with some half-legendary wastrel of the distant past, but with an immediate and inescapable fact of contemporary society, a very real threat to a monarchy already endangered by events on the Continent.

> If, therefore, a vicious court, and a profligate nobility, have been, in a great measure, the combined cause of the French revolution, and if a virtuous court, and the national stock of British virtue, have preserved to this country its government, laws, and constitution; how much, Sir, it behoves [*sic*] your Royal Highness in the principles of self-interest and policy, as well as duty, to maintain, support, and encourage, by your conduct and example, the national character; and, by a decorous as well as dignified demeanour, to deprive the enemies of our country and government of any hope, that your succession to the crown will produce that relaxation of national virtue, which leads to national depravity, and ends in national ruin.
>
> (Pages 33–34)

The point seems valid, and indeed the whole pamphlet is a rather touching reminder of the pathetic hope then widely felt in England that the Prince's marriage might, in fact, bring about a change in his character, that a dissolute Prince might now, in Combe's words, "become stationary in the temple of Hymen", and settle down to accept adult responsibilities. The hope was, of course, wildly unjustified; the Prince had no intention of settling down to any regularized existence. The marriage was a disaster from the first; after the birth of their only child, Princess Charlotte, the two formally separated. The subsequent history of the Prince was no more edifying than that which has been related, but Combe was never prompted to offer him further advice.

* * *

By 1797 the war with France had dragged on for four years and had for the most part gone badly. Fear lest Britain be infected by the revolutionary spirit had led to legislation limiting basic freedoms; the Habeas Corpus Act had been suspended, and the Seditious Meetings Act and the Treasonable Practices Act had been passed to discourage agitation for reform. Constantly mounting taxes, a decline in foreign trade, and generally depressed business conditions at home had rendered the war more and more unpopular, and Pitt was attempting to seek an honourable peace, though his second peace mission had failed in December 1796. In February 1797 the Bank of England was forced to suspend gold payments, and business prospects seemed more gloomy than ever. Ireland was on the point of open rebellion; French troops, had, in fact, landed on that island in December, but the move had proved abortive. And in mid–April British seamen mutinied at Spithead. It was a gloomy spring.

Not the least of Pitt's troubles during these months was the appearance of a closely reasoned and well–documented attack on his war policies by Thomas Erskine, *A View of the Causes and Consequences of the Present War with France*. The topic was timely, and the author was a popular hero who had won acquittals for three celebrated clients in the sensational treason trials of 1794. Within a few months his 138-page pamphlet had gone into thirty-seven editions. Clearly it was time for Combe to reassure the public concerning the wisdom of Pitt's policies. It must have been the most difficult of his political assignments.

Primarily to answer Erskine, but at the same time to justify the restrictions recently imposed on civil liberties and to defend the suspension of specie payments, Combe produced in June his *Plain Thoughts of a Plain Man, Addressed to the Common Sense of the People of Great Britain: with a Few Words, en passant, to the Uncommon Sense of Mr. Erskine* (J. Bell). In order to maintain some semblance of disinterested candour and patriotism, Combe composed the body of this pamphlet without any direct mention of Erskine. Although his review of the war touches on most of the topics discussed in Erskine's pamphlet, the "Plain Man" at first pretends to ignore that publication altogether. After an eloquent and reassuring appeal to "the courage, wisdom and magnanimity of the British Nation", he proceeds to analyse the causes of the present disorder and reviews the general conduct of the war, defending Pitt's decisions and his wartime policies throughout—as, of course, he was bound to do. Once more he gives the orthodox ministerial interpretation of events without introducing worrisome complications. Though entitled *Plain Thoughts of a Plain Man*, the pamphlet consists in reality of very cleverly contrived thoughts of a man highly skilled in manipulating public opinion. They may be addressed to plain men, but they are by no means a plain man's thoughts. Combe was a skilful propagandist with a shrewd knowledge of ordinary people and of the workings of their minds. He never tried to make his readers understand complicated ideas. Instead, he gave them uncomplicated ideas in impressive language, stirring emotions by arguing the non-committal with urgency and conviction:

> If it should be asked what we have gained by the war, an answer has been furnished me by a distinguished Member of the House of Commons—We have gained "all that we should have lost if we had not engaged in it:"—Our Constitution, our Religion, our Liberty, our Property—in short, our existence as a people.
>
> (Page 13)

> The original object of revolutionary France was universal revolution; that is, the general destruction of established governments and religions. The object of England was to check and subdue that destructive spirit.
>
> (Pages 28–29)

> It may be considered as a strong measure to suspend the Habeas Corpus: but the occasion demanded it; and I will boldly ask, what faithful subject or good citizen has suffered from that suspension?
>
> (Pages 40–41)

> If, in civil affairs, a man enjoys the right to do every thing which is not particularly injurious to his neighbors, or generally detrimental to society, he possesses as much liberty as he can reasonably wish to use. . . . And such is the liberty . . . which is possessed by every subject of Great Britain.
>
> (Pages 49–50)

> I cannot but congratulate my country on possessing a Minister, whose courage can look public calamity in the face, whose sagacity can follow it through it remotest consequences, and whose wisdom will apply the remedy.
>
> (Page 64)

Having reviewed the circumstances which led to the outbreak of war, the reasons for continuing the war, and the justification for now seeking peace with the new French Government, Combe is apparently beginning his peroration ("Let us then bear the pressure of the present extraordinary crisis with the magnanimity of English-men . . .") when he tells his readers that he has just learned of the suspension of specie payments by the Bank of England. The device is none too convincing, for Combe's pamphlet did not appear until some four months after that event, but it enables him to complete his discussion of the war before turning to this new topic. He now says, in sum, that the suspension will save the national credit. "It can be . . . of little consequence whether guineas appear in metallic form, and jingle in a purse, or whether they are made of paper, and lie in a pocket-book—if they are equally guaranteed by Government in their nominal value for current traffic." He praises Pitt for his wise handling of the financial crisis, asserts that the Bank is perfectly sound, and concludes that "the present period of difficulty and danger will, by your characteristic patriotism and courage, increase the honours of the British name, and secure the prosperity of the British people". This reassuring sentiment is followed by the signature "A PLAIN MAN".

As though it were a matter of quite secondary importance, the section addressed to Erskine is added as a postscript, and for forty-five pages he abandons his aloof, disinterested manner and directly attacks this critic of Pitt's régime. Combe's oblique approach to what was presumably the main point of the pamphlet seems well devised; the reader who has followed Combe's line of thought to this point is un-likely to quarrel with him now as he defends government policies against partisan attack. He accuses Erskine of writing with ulterior motive—namely, of promoting the cause of the Foxites. He accuses him of distorting the truth and, even worse, of giving aid and comfort to the enemy. It is a hard-hitting, rousing attack, just the sort of thing common readers enjoy in public controversy. Though it may strike one today as more than slightly disingenuous, it shows Combe as a polemicist well able to defend himself and his party with bared knuckles.

Combe was not alone in attacking Erskine at this time; both William Gifford and John Bowles wrote answers to his pamphlet. But the *Plain Thoughts of a Plain Man* could not be ignored either, and on July 8 Erskine's publisher, John Debrett, announced a reply: *A Short Statement of Facts . . . Occasioned by a Pamphlet Entitled "The*

Plain Thoughts of a Plain Man." *By a Real Plain Man.* As propagandist, Combe might not welcome refutation, but as hackwriter he could only be gratified by recognition and free advertising.

For the next six years Combe neither produced political pamphlets nor engaged in public controversy of any kind. As we shall presently see, he was busily engaged in other matters, and indeed his pay from the Treasury may have stopped. In May 1796 John Boydell believed that Combe's annuity had been discontinued and that his remuneration, if any, depended upon what he produced.[15] If true, this new arrangement could explain his sudden production of the *Plain Thoughts* after two years of silence on political topics. By the end of 1797, however, Combe's income was so visibly reduced that his friends thought he was no longer working for the Government at all. Although he was working for the publisher of the pro-Ministry *Anti-Jacobin*, he had no connection with it.[16] Nor is there any evidence that he was writing for *The Times*; his connection with that newspaper and with John Walter had terminated with the abandonment of logographic printing in January 1792. Except for one pamphlet which he published in 1801, he produced no more political arguments after the *Plain Thoughts* until 1803, when he returned to *The Times* and resumed his career as journalist.

CHAPTER VI

HISTORIAN

You've too much honest pride to be
A scribbler to the Treasury,
Where you must wait the lagging hour,
And cringe to images of power. . . .
This will not do, my learned friend,
You must to better things attend;
All thoughts of Downing Street forgo,
And stick to Paternoster Row.
                              —Doctor Syntax

ON APRIL 5, 1790, *The Times* published a sensational story about an unnamed lord and his mistress, attributing it to a collection of such anecdotes which had recently appeared in four volumes entitled *The Devil upon Two Sticks in England*, "a kind of continuation of the celebrated Spanish Novel of the same title, though written if possible in a superior stile". Though Spanish only in setting and inspiration, *Le Diable Boiteux* by Le Sage had been translated as *The Devil upon Two Sticks* and had been enormously popular. This new "continuation" of that novel is praised by *The Times* as one of the best publications of recent years. "The author is not known," the paper continues, "though the stile of writing, and the nature of the anecdotes, fix it on some gentleman of first rate abilities, as well as knowledge of high life." The gentleman in question was no other than William Combe, Esq., who must also be suspected of having written this flattering notice.

In the French original a crippled demon named Asmodeus conducts the worldly education of Don Cleofas by using supernatural powers to reveal in scene after scene the secret realities of Madrid society; Combe merely transported the two characters to London and permitted the action to continue much as before. The simple structure was precisely what he always preferred; it required no detailed planning and was capable of being continued almost indefinitely. In the Preface to this work, as in that of the R[oya]l Register, Combe advertised his willingness to extend the publication on demand: "If the public should condescend to be pleased with these volumes, there are three or four more at their service." The public was in fact pleased, and Combe resumed the narrative at once. The first four volumes appeared on March 1, 1790; a second edition was advertised on July 6, and a third "with considerable alterations and corrections" on January 1, 1791. On the following day, volumes five and six were published. (Twenty years later, as we shall see, he enlarged it still further.)

The Devil upon Two Sticks in England is a work which deserves more attention than it has received from literary and social historians. Unlike Combe's sentimental novels, this satirical narrative was not written in a hurry; the first chapters, as we have seen, appeared in John Walter's newspaper three years before publication in book form. Moreover, the novel is unlike anything else ever written by Combe. It is a carefully ordered narrative, comprehensive in scope, portraying the vanities and vices of a whole society rather than those of a few individuals or a single social class. From first to last it is a dark and bitter work suggesting disillusionment of a kind which the author reveals nowhere else. It was written, to be sure, in a time of demoralizing anxiety while the English, themselves endangered by popular discontents, watched the collapse of the old régime in France.

The bitterness of the novel explains why Combe felt compelled to write his reassuring political pamphlets from a supposititious point of view, that of "a man who has long been retired from what is called the bustle of life". A *Letter from a Country Gentleman* might well take the long view, its author serenely unaware of ugly contemporary realities. *The Devil upon Two Sticks in England* brings those harsh realities immediately before the reader and gives him no escape from them. When it lapses, as it occasionally does, into sentimental mood, the blend of cynicism and sentiment only darkens the picture.

Unlike the R[oya]l Register, of which it is a kind of narrative equivalent, the novel does not invite the reader to play the game of identifications. A few individuals are mentioned more or less explicitly, but by and large the portraits are not particularized. The novel is panoramic, and the author justly calls it a representation of "the manners of the present times". Although "every character and circumstance delineated or described in it, is taken from the persons and events of the present period", Combe makes it clear that he is drawing composite portraits; the details are all true, but they have been drawn from various individuals and events, recombined to serve his purpose. He was clearly proceeding with caution, as well he might, since much of the novel was written during the months when the proprietor of the Logographic Press was being prosecuted for libel; by the time it was published John Walter was in Newgate Prison. Combe's circumspect avoidance of personalities, though perhaps disappointing to his contemporary readers, makes the novel far more readable today than the particularized R[oya]l Register with its veiled references to long-forgotten scandals.

The narrative begins with the arrival of Asmodeus and Don Cleofas from Spain, taking first a position at the top of the Monument. The Demon proposes to show his willing pupil "the genius of a great people", beginning with the City because "the glory of this nation is supported and encreased by its commerce". They quickly move to more interesting quarters of the town, however, obtaining a quick view of characters and situations in St James's Park, the Green Park, Devonshire House, the gaming-clubs, St James's Palace, the Horse Guards, Whitehall, and finally the Drury Lane Theatre. At this point two identifiable personalities make their appearance. Asmodeus is inclined to think that "there never was a period when the English stage was at a lower ebb than at the present moment. It cannot boast one tragic actor of superior merit; and a single actress . . . alone supports the dignity and pathos of the tragic scene." The Demon says she is well paid for her acting, but he adds that she loves money better than her reputation. Unfortunately, she is too much under the influence of her brother, who has no ability whatever, yet considers himself a great actor and theatrical authority (I, 101–7). John Philip Kemble had just become manager of the Drury Lane; his sister, Mrs Sarah Kemble Siddons, acted in his company.

Asmodeus and Don Cleofas walk along the Strand to Temple Bar, where a chance remark shows that Combe had not forgotten the gruesome sight of the heads of traitors exposed there when he was a boy in the neighbourhood. The last heads mounted there had been those of the Scottish lords who had taken part in the uprising of

'Forty-Five; one of them had remained until 1772, when it disappeared in a high wind. The two observers recall that horror, then
wander about the City and back to the West End, commenting on the
human viciousness to be found in all ranks of society. They see a
young woman who is dejected because she "had been for some time
afflicted with a dropsy, which is daily increasing upon her. But . . .
a few weeks retirement in the country, and a skilful midwife, will rid
her of her disorder." They watch three ladies of fashion being taught
the precautions to take in card-playing "to secure them from having
their pockets picked, when they may be obliged to engage in it". A
beautiful girl is declining all offers of marriage until she receives one
carrying with it a coronet; Asmodeus reveals her destiny—to die an
old maid. There is a pathetic young woman who regards herself as a
widow because her fiancé had died just before their wedding day.
Another has just been jilted by her fiancé who has seen her being rude
to her father, sufficient evidence to him that she will make a scolding
wife. Another melancholy figure is "Mira of the Dale", whose story
Combe had first told in the columns of the *Daily Universal Register* for
January 31, 1787. "Having lost an husband whom she adored, . . .
she nourishes her affection for his memory with an enthusiasm that
fills her friends with the most painful apprehensions that her reason is
affected" (III, 142–8).

These sentimental episodes seldom pall on the reader as they do in
Combe's other novels. They are usually short, often very short indeed,
and they always serve to heighten the irony of the narrative, either by
contrast with frankly cynical passages or more commonly by containing within themselves some element of human baseness. Thus, the
story of Mad Susan is a mixture of pathos and disillusionment.
Susan's dearest friend marries a Mr Freeman and goes to the Continent with him for three years. On their return, Mr Freeman's
"libertine attentions" turn to Susan herself. She resists, but unavailingly. "Poor Susan is now a wretched maniac, and will remain so to
the end of her days. In her more tranquil intervals, she knows her
friends, is sensible of her situation, and calls herself Mad Susan. She
loves to dress her hair with flowers, as you now behold her, and
amuses her shattered imagination by singing melancholy ditties."
The passage may be conventionally reminiscent of Ophelia, but the
reader will also be reminded of Combe's unfortunate wife, Maria,
still confined in a madhouse. Combe makes a point of telling us that

it costs Susan's father £300 a year "to place her under the best care, and to provide every comfort which her lamentable situation is capable of receiving" (III, 160–8).

Presently the mood of the narrative changes as Don Cleofas observes three physicians engaged in lively discussion. With his usual innocence, he assumes that they are debating the proper treatment of their patient, but Asmodeus assures him that he is mistaken. "Their professional business was dispatched in a very few minutes, and they are now engaged in a violent dispute on politics:—but to complete the scene—their political altercation will be interrupted and cut short, by the information that their patient has breathed his last. Thus it is that medical men habitually trifle with death, till he knocks at their own doors" (III, 187). It is, in short, the familiar dance of death which recurs throughout Combe's writings.

Asmodeus and Don Cleofas then visit a number of scenes, each of which presents a whole collection of characters. First they go again to the Drury Lane Theatre and see a well-dressed young man (actually a tailor who has made his own clothes), a pickpocket, a pharmacist's assistant, a young surgeon ("offering his services to cure them of a disorder, of which he has not hitherto been able to cure himself"), a German baron employed as a pimp, a drunkard, a number of soldiers, some gamblers, a grocer, a reviewer of plays for the newspaper (who has missed the play, but is busily gathering information from the crowd), a wealthy merchant in distress (he has just seen his mistress in a box with another man), and finally various prostitutes soliciting passers-by.

Another scene presenting its own collection of subjects is Westminster Abbey, where every tomb suggests an ironic story to Asmodeus, who finds the ostentatious display of marble and epitaph incongruous with the true characters of the deceased. Presently the ghosts themselves begin to appear, one of them that of Samuel Johnson. "That huge spectre, whose air and gait mark no common discomposure, was a colossus of human literature, whose talents and writings have ranked him among the first names of his country. But he had just been informed, that a lady, at whose house he was for many years a frequent guest, has, from a most unpardonable vanity, written and published memoirs of her friend; in which she describes him as a *monster of absurdity*, in order to prove that he was, according to her own expression, *the first of perishable beings*" (IV, 37). Mrs

Thrale's *Anecdotes of Johnson* had been published in 1786, just a year before Combe had begun writing this novel.

Asmodeus and Don Cleofas then make the rounds of fashionable morning scenes. They walk again through St James's Park, they see the ageing Jack Wilkes, they observe various dukes and lords. At one point they find a nobleman and his son arranging the calendar of their calls on the same woman. They stroll down Pall Mall. And they finally come to the great mansion of Lord and Lady Villiers on Grafton Street, where Mr Christie is auctioning all their possessions. Combe had told the whole story in a verse satire of 1777, of which this passage is partly paraphrase, partly amplification. On reprinting the novel in 1811, Combe inserted at this point the entire satire, first published as *The Auction*.

Eventually the Devil and his protégé arrive at Sir Joshua Reynolds's gallery of portraits. The artist is praised as one whose future reputation would be secure except that "he obstinately continues to make use of such transient colours, that many of his best works have decayed before their master". Again Combe is remembering one of his verse satires. Inevitably, the portraits suggest to Asmodeus a fine set of ironies. The two observers come to the portrait of Mrs Siddons as the Tragic Muse. The painting is called "a very striking likeness of the favourite tragic actress", but Asmodeus remarks that "here is another instance of fortuitous elevation,—for this actress, but a few years ago, was the heroine of a barn,—performing in tragedies, comedies, farces, and pantomimes" (IV, 110). It was perfectly true, as who would know better than the author? Combe had himself been backstage in that same barn twenty-eight years earlier.

By the end of the fourth volume Asmodeus is promising Don Cleofas, and incidentally Combe is promising his readers, that "To-morrow we will renew our progress,—for much remains to be discovered to you.—In due course I shall introduce you to the Court of the Sovereign, and the two Houses of Parliament; the Gaols, and Bedlam;—the Courts of law, and the infernal regions" (IV, 256). Although a writer in the *Monthly Review* (August 1790) felt compelled to observe that "the London air seems to have cramped the wit of the strange devil from France", Combe had again anticipated popular interest in his subject. Within six months three editions of the work had been called for and two additional volumes had been published. In 1811 he published yet another edition, still in six volumes, but by that time much larger ones. "Having been induced to believe, that a new edition of this work would be acceptable to the public," he then wrote, "I have carefully corrected the former one, and made such copious additions to it, as, with the necessary increase of letter-press, will be found to amount to near two volumes of the work in its original form." And then, optimistic to the last, "I shall only add, that, if the public should not appear tired of the work, I have three or four additional volumes at its service." But no more volumes, nor even another edition, appeared. By that time Doctor Syntax was making his first tour, and Combe was beginning a new career writing tetrameter couplets for an audience no longer interested in prose satire.

* * *

The Devil upon Two Sticks in England ended Combe's years with John Walter on a genuinely original and literary note, confirming the new reputation which he had been achieving. The reviewer for the *Monthly* (August 1790), though somewhat reluctant to praise this work, gave it four pages of space and paid tribute to the author, whom he recognized but tactfully refrained from naming. "Abilities, indeed, and those of a high rate, the author of this work, if we are not mistaken in the person, certainly possesses; and we are persuaded that to his pen the public are indebted for a variety of agreeable entertainment, and useful instruction, both in prose and verse." Despite his anonymity in public, Combe was by this time well known by professionals in the book trade, who were also remembering his earlier success with the *Diaboliad* series. By 1796 he was being referred to in print as "Mr. Combe, the eccentric author of the Diaboliad", and his writing was called "the work of an able hand".[1] Even the general reading public was beginning to know his name.

By 1791 success had brought Combe a new conception of his role as a professional writer. He had demonstrated to himself and to others that he might aspire to higher dignities as a practising man of letters than any he had hitherto attained. He would, in fact, be a historian. The R[oya]l Register had tended more and more to become a history of the times, and when that project was finally broken off Combe was already talking about writing a *History of the Present Reign*. We are told that he actually issued proposals for such a work and by 1795 hoped to publish within two years. He "spoke with

great confidence about it" as "something congenial to his mind".[2]
But business conditions in England were worsening rapidly in 1796,
and by the following year the nation was suffering acute financial
distress. It was no time for booksellers to undertake large speculative
projects. Nevertheless, Combe continued to talk of his *History* and
perhaps to write it. As late as 1818 he told Major Cockburn, "If I live
long enough to correct, I shall leave behind me the history of my
own times,—which will be six volumes, at least, in heavy quarto."[3]
The work, he said, was by that time written down to 1801, but he
wished the manuscript to be destroyed unless he lived to give it final
revision. Several of his acquaintances later reported that Combe
himself burned his papers shortly before he died. If he did so, one
can only regret the act, for the intended masterpiece would have been
a fascinating document, however puzzling it might have proved to
subsequent historians.

While hoping to produce this major work, Combe was busily
engaged in writing or editing a whole series of "histories" of one
kind or another, beginning with his edition of Anderson's *History of
Commerce* and its 700-page volume of economic history which he had
himself researched and written. That volume had been completed in
1789, the same year in which he had published his *History of the Late
Important Period*—hackwork, perhaps, but clearly "historical".
Between that publication and the beginning of his career as newspaper
editor in 1803, Combe was to edit, translate, or ghost-write ten
substantial historical documents, including such important volumes as
Meares's *Voyages*, Anderson's *Embassy to China*, Grant's *History of
Mauritius*, and Mackenzie's famous *Voyages from Montreal*. To the
end of his life, Combe was to use the word *history* in his titles whenever possible and often incongruously, publishing "histories" of
Westminster Abbey (1812), Oxford (1814), Cambridge (1815),
the public schools (1816), Madeira (1821), and finally, at the age
of eighty, *The History of Johnny Quae Genus* (1822), the anticlimax
to the Doctor Syntax series. Some of these works are still cited with
respect, but the anonymous historian has gone unrecognized.

It was history, in a sense, which provided Combe with his chief
writing assignment after the demise of the Logographic Press. His
last publication for John Walter, the two-volume continuation of *The
Devil upon Two Sticks in England*, was advertised in *The Times* on
January 2, 1792. The first announcement of his next big undertaking

appeared the following day, when John and Josiah Boydell invited subscriptions to an ambitious work entitled *The Picturesque Views and Scenery of the Thames and the Severn, the Forth and the Clyd* [*sic*], *from Their Sources to the Sea*. These "views" were to be engraved from drawings by Joseph Farington, R.A., and were to be accompanied by a prose account significantly mentioned as "an original History of those Rivers". The historian is not named, but the reader is assured of his competence: "The literary part the Proprietors have every reason to expect will contribute its full share towards the completion of their object." The first two volumes are promised, overoptimistically to be sure, for delivery the following year; all five are to be ready by the spring of 1794. Indeed, Messrs Boydell blandly assert that "the materials for the whole work are almost entirely completed". They were trying to forestall a similar publication which was soon forthcoming from the pen and pencil of Samuel Ireland, but it seems unlikely that they would make these rash promises if they had not even engaged their writer. In any event, Combe clearly lost little time in finding new employment when Walter decided to discontinue logographic printing.

The new arrangement, whenever it was made, was a fortunate one for Combe. He did not work on it continuously, for he undertook various other editorial tasks at the same time. But when he was occupied with "the Rivers" he was paid by the week—a circumstance which Farington thought responsible for the slow progress of the work. Re-titled *An History of the Principal Rivers of Great Britain*, the project seemed likely to occupy Combe for a decade; the first two volumes, subtitled *An History of the Thames*, appeared respectively in 1794 and 1796, leaving three more in prospect. Those later volumes were finally cancelled, as we shall see, but meanwhile these five years were the most prosperous of Combe's professional life. Farington recorded in his diary the amounts Combe received for the *Thames*: £364 for the first volume, £200 for the second (a time limit having been imposed on the historian before the second volume was undertaken). At the same time, Combe was profitably engaged in a variety of routine projects. He edited or wrote two pamphlets for Humphrey Repton, the famous *Letter to Uvedale Price* (1794) and the *Sketches and Hints on Landscape Gardening* (1795). What he received for the work is not known, but Debrett paid him £100 for writing Æneas Anderson's *British Embassy to China* (1795) and probably the same

amount for his anonymous *Letter to a Retired Officer* (1796).[4]
Another task which interfered to some extent with his work on the
Thames was the editing of a two-volume novel, *Alf von Deulmen; or,
The History of the Emperor Philip, and His Daughters* (J. Bell, 1794),
translated from the German of C. B. E. Naubert by "Miss A. E.
Booth". Neither the extent of Combe's duties nor the amount of his
pay is known; he could not read German himself, but he could now
command substantial remuneration merely for revising a manuscript
and preparing it for press. He was, of course, drawing his £200
pension throughout these years and producing an occasional political
pamphlet. His highly successful *Word in Season* appeared in 1792 and
must have netted him substantial profit. His income from all sources
can scarcely have been less than £500 a year. It may have been somewhat more.

Combe's contract with the Boydells was fortunate also in that it
put him in touch with the most prominent artists of the time and with
their wealthy patrons, a circle which he found highly gratifying and in
which he assumed a respected place. Since 1786 John Boydell and his
nephew Josiah had been commissioning paintings illustrative of
Shakespeare from all leading English artists. By 1791 their shop, the
Shakespeare Gallery, had sixty-five of these paintings on display, and
more were being added every year. The two Boydells were themselves artists and engravers as well as dealers, and John was prominent
in the City, having just ended his year as Lord Mayor of London. No
wonder their shop in Pall Mall was a fashionable gathering-place for
artists, connoisseurs, and men-about-town. Combe must have known
the place well even before the proprietors engaged his services; he had,
in fact, mentioned it in his *Devil upon Two Sticks in England*. After
January 1792 he was seen there regularly.

The *History of the Rivers* was undertaken primarily as a means of
employing the artist and the engraver profitably. The Boydells were
genuinely interested in promoting English art, and their great Shakespeare project had demonstrated the willingness of the public to
subscribe for expensive books containing engravings, whereas few
people would ever buy that many separate prints. It was necessary,
however, to have letterpress to fill the volume; Shakespeare's plays
would serve the purpose admirably, to be sure, but prints on other
subjects required the preparation of an appropriate text. Farington
had agreed to make a series of drawings for the *History of the Rivers*,

and in order to attract subscribers he would portray the country houses and estates of such wealthy families as might be expected to purchase copies. The work was planned in large part as a vanity publication, and Combe was a good choice for a writer to supply the requisite compliments. He was perfectly willing to do so, and indeed he went beyond the expectations of publisher and artist in some of his flattery. His old aptitude for cultivating aristocratic acquaintances now stood him in good stead.

There is far more to the *History of the Thames*, however, than fatuous compliments to subscribers; Combe was, in fact, taking his historical responsibilities seriously. It is evident that he made an extensive study of source materials before writing this work, for the pages are filled with antiquarian lore culled from an impressive number of authorities. He quotes from Bishop Asser's ninth-century chronicle of King Alfred's reign, from Stow, Leland, Dugdale, and most often from Camden. He had consulted more recent works also, works such as Bishop Corbet's *History of the Military Government of Gloucester*, William Stukeley's *Itineraria Curiosa*, Bishop Tanner's *Notitia Monastica*, and, of course, Pennant's *Journey from Chester to London*. He cites local authorities on the places he visits, recording stray bits of archeological information and noting historical monuments. His use of this material, largely by paraphrase and quotation, fills many pages, but it will impress few readers today. There is no real assimilation of this learning, but the writer has made it clear that he has gone to his sources. The narrative brightens when Combe undertakes to tell what he sees. It reads, perhaps, more like a guide-book than like systematic history, but this is the result of a plan which compels him to follow the course of a river rather than the course of time.

There is no room to doubt that he made a painstaking effort to gather all available information concerning his subject. Indeed, this may be the explanation for the delays in submitting copy for the first volume; the second manifests no comparable research and was completed more quickly. Combe must have spent weeks in reading and taking notes, though where he found the books can only be conjectured. He had borrowed Camden's *Britannia* from Mr Burbidge of the Shakespeare Gallery, and a letter preserved at the Bodleian Library indicates that he did not return it until 1797.[5] But the other books which he quotes would for the most part be found only in the greatest libraries. The British Museum would have had them, but it no longer has a complete record of the readers admitted in the eighteenth century. There is no mention of Combe's name in such records as survive.[6]

*   *   *

"We visited" the source of the Thames "in the month of June", Combe wrote, beginning his account of the scenes along that river, "where nature has worked with so soft a pencil". The *we* is editorial; Farington did not undertake his sketching trip until Combe had planned the work and selected the places to be portrayed. He spent several weeks making a leisurely trip down the river, and his account of the experience suggests that it was one of the happiest times of his life. The weather was fine, the scenery beautiful, and his entertainment at various great houses along the way gratifying to his self-esteem. It is the only time that he ever left an explicit record of his experiences over a period of days and weeks. Even here one finds no intimate revelations, but the descriptive character of the book imposes a personal point of view which cannot be fully detached, even when Combe is writing in the third person.

The Thames valley is especially beautiful in summer, and Combe describes it with vivid if sometimes sentimental appreciation. His style is often overelaborate, but scene after scene along the river comes through as actually observed. One even senses the shock of surprise with which Combe caught unexpected glimpses from his boat.

> As the river winds, Bagley appears in different points of view, but always rising in the horizon. In a short turn of the stream, where a reedy bank excluded every other object, a very singular, though transient, effect was produced by the breeze, which, as it passed over the reeds, bowed their heads, and let in a momentary view of Oxford. This pleasing and unexpected circumstance, which at first surprised, continued at intervals to delight us, till we approached Kenington, a village at a small distance from the river, which gave a picturesque effect to the verdant slope that it adorns; and as the stream winds beyond it, an old farm house, with hanging orchards, enlivens the landscape.
>
> (I, 177–8)

The orchards at that time of the year would be in bloom, and the scene was undoubtedly memorable. Here and elsewhere one has the feeling that Combe was taking notes on the spot, heightening his vocabulary as his emotions were stirred, but nevertheless recording what he actually saw. That he does tell us what these scenes looked like in 1792 is evident from his description of Blenheim, which remains unchanged today. Then as now, a visitor entering the gate could not but feel the strong impact of Vanbrugh's architecture and "Capability" Brown's landscape.

> On entering the park . . . there is the finest burst of magnificent prospect that art has ever produced. It is not a transition from nothing to something, but from nothing to everything. The castle in the opposite distance, the intervening lawn skirted by stately groves; the beautiful extent of water, with the superb bridge that stretches across, and the wood that rises beyond it; the lofty column, and vast expanse of verdure, finely varied with plantations, and enlivened with flocks of sheep and herds of deer, are the principal features of a scene, where art, under the influence of munificent taste, has clothed rural nature in a sumptuous but appropriate apparel, which no other place can boast.
>
> (I, 87)

As his boat is leaving Oxford, he notes students rowing their boats or strolling about Christ Church Meadows, and presently "The eye glances to the left over a wide extent of corn fields to the lofty summit of Shotover-hill; and to the right, a long range of meadows is bounded by the shaggy top of Bagley-wood; while a fine silvery length of river is terminated by the swelling bank of Ifley, thick with trees, and the ancient tower of the church rising above them." He then glances back and says that "Oxford, on a retrospective view, is a beautiful and affecting object, which, discovering only the towers and domes of its colleges and public buildings, appears in the pure solemnity of its academic character" (I, 176–7). His description of Oxford seems perfunctory and is without the slightest suggestion that he had ever been a student there—in itself strong evidence that he had not been. By contrast, when he later comes to Eton, he acknowledges "the emotions of a grateful mind" and explicitly identifies himself as "her matured offspring", quoting a stanza from Gray on the playing fields "where once my careless childhood stray'd".

The high point of his expedition was his visit to Nuneham Park, the seat of George Simon, second Earl Harcourt. At various times he was later to speak of his acquaintance with the Harcourts, though any connection he had with them must have been tenuous. On this occasion he had asked his friend Edward Jerningham to write to the Earl

requesting permission for him to visit Nuneham. The Earl had replied
as follows:

Dear Mr. Jerningham,

In consequence of your letter I gave orders that, if Mr. Combe came to
this place, I should be informed of his arrival, meaning to show him all the
attention due to a man of his literary eminence, and to a person recommended
to me by you. Since which, I have received from him one of the most obliging
and best-written letters I ever saw, to which I have returned a not less civil,
though an extremely stupid and ill-written reply. . . .

H.[7]

Combe arrived in July during the celebration of the annual Spinning
Feast, originally given the villagers by Lord and Lady Harcourt "to
encourage industry among the women of their parish, by giving
annual prizes to a certain number of the best spinners of thread".
The scope of the festival had now been enlarged to include recognition of meritorious behaviour on the part of the men. Prizes of merit
were distributed by the rector in a morning church service, where
individuals were singled out for honourable mention and their
virtuous conduct publicly described. Individuals thus recognized were
permitted to paint a star and a large M over their Meritorious doors.
After the service in the church, a picnic dinner was served in the park,
followed by a spinning contest, various sports in the afternoon, and
a dance in the evening. "The Nuneham Spinning Feast is formed to
be a school of virtue and industry", Combe writes approvingly. On
the occasion of Combe's visit, the Bishop of Durham, Shute Barring-
ton, was present, "and we cannot refrain from observing that it was
graced by his manners, encouraged by his words, and dignified by
his presence". Combe always paid his respects to a lord, whether
temporal or spiritual.

Oddly enough, there is no mention of another guest who was
present at the Spinning Feast, though he alluded to the meeting nine
years later. According to a note in Farington's diary, Mrs Siddons
told of meeting Combe there and of his behaving oddly, at first paying no attention to her, then suddenly becoming most attentive.
Farington conjectured that Combe may have been self-conscious
because of his recent attack on the actress in the *Devil upon Two
Sticks in England*. Mrs Siddons knew of this attack and said that she
could not understand why he had called her miserly. "She should not
have been surprised if from a shyness of manner she had been called

proud; but knew no ground on which the other accusation could be founded. She was by education and necessity made careful, but that had never led her to meanness."[8]

Combe's pleasure in being entertained by Lord and Lady Harcourt led him to make this section disproportionately detailed and extravagantly complimentary. Even Henry Fuseli, who at Farington's request wrote a long and favourable account of Volume One for the *Analytical Review* (June 1794), condemned the Nuneham description severely. The beauties of the park, he says, "have betrayed [the author] . . . into a minuteness of detail which more than borders on partiality, for the account of the flower-garden alone occupies six pages". He adds that the "language, in general elegant and animated, becomes in that wilderness of delight . . . confused and obscure from the aggregation of ornaments". Combe devoted altogether twenty-seven pages to Nuneham, four times as much as to Windsor Castle and Park, and Fuseli was not the only reader to raise objections.

Jerningham also prepared the way for Combe to visit other families on his itinerary. In an undated letter now at the Huntington Library, Combe acknowledges this assistance and tells something of his activities during the summer. Addressed to Jerningham, it reads as follows:

I thank you again & again for your obliging communication of Mr. Blounts kind attentions of which I scarce know how to express myself as I ought.—

I shall leave Town on Wednesday or Thursday next for Mr. Loveden's at Buscot Park near Farringdon,—and after having re-examined the upper part of the Thames, I shall proceed to Oxford, & from thence by Water to Maple Durham.—All this will occupy abt. a Week.—So that I shall probably, about Wednesday or Thursday se'nnight, be in a situation to avail myself of Mr. Blount's very great politeness, for which I must beg you to express my acknowledgements à la Jerningham.

If Mr. Blount would add to his kindness by favouring me with two Lines as a Passport to Maple Durham,—I should land upon its banks with a more perfect satisfaction.—

Permit me to thank you for your kind interposition in my favour, & believe me to be

Yr very affecte &c
Wm Combe

Cravin Hill Friday Evening.——[9]

Volume One of the *Thames* does indeed contain a print of Buscot Park, "the seat of Mr. Loveden, finely situated on an eminence on the

Berkshire side of the river". It speaks also of Maple Durham, "a small village which contains a seat of the ancient and respectable family of the Blounts". That Combe obtained access to the house is evident from his description of two portraits which it contained "of Mrs. Martha Blount, the distinguished friend and favourite of Mr. Pope, and one of that poet, in which he appears with a more social and lively air than any representation of him we have ever seen; as if he were in the circle of his friends, rather than in converse with his muse" (I, 235).

Combe's reception was not always so generous; Horace Walpole, by this time the fourth Earl of Orford, declined to admit him to Strawberry Hill. Writing to Daniel Lysons on August 9, 1792, he begged to be excused from receiving "the gentleman who is to write the account of Mr. Farringdon's [sic] 'Views of the Thames'". He receives many such requests, and the recent death of his nephew, the third Earl, has involved him in perplexing business affairs. "And when you recollect that I am seventy-five, and consequently may have few hours to amuse the little leisure I have, I cannot part with any more of them, to contribute my insignificant information to works of which I am not likely to see the completion."[10] It is a reasonable letter which gives no suggestion that Walpole had recognized Farington's writer as the man whom he had once called "the infamous Coombes". But Combe did not relish what might be interpreted as a snub, and accordingly he devoted only one page to Strawberry Hill, saying merely that the house is "full of elegant rarity and curious prettiness". Its works of art and its "happy adoption of Gothic taste", he says, are too well known to require detailed description (II, 2).

Walpole did live to see the completed work, however, and to tell Daniel Lysons that the style of the descriptions was "too flowery".[11] He evidently said as much and more to the artist himself later, for on May 5, 1796, after calling on Walpole, Farington had a talk with Combe at the Shakespeare Gallery. "I told him", he noted in his diary, "that I was very sorry he had introduced the word *prettiness* into his account of Strawberry Hill. He asked why I did not object to it before; I said because when I saw it, it was too late, the sheet being printed."[12] We are not told Combe's comment; perhaps he made none at the moment, but the criticism rankled in his memory. He was not inclined to accept with indifference any suggestion that he was lacking in professional competence. Fifteen years later, when he was writing topographical descriptions for another artist, he was again called upon to deal with Strawberry Hill, by that time the home of Mrs Damer. He began his second account of the place by resolutely asserting that "the house, with its scenery, presents a very pleasing object to the river, and may be considered as a cabinet of curious prettiness".[13]

* * *

Combe's association with Farington had one incidental result of which he had no knowledge. The artist was keeping a diary, naming names and setting forth details. Although he was no great diarist in any literary sense, he kept a factual record of his daily activities from July 1793 to the very day of his death in 1821, and Combe is mentioned in over seventy entries, mostly between 1793 and 1799. No comparable record survives for any other period of his life.

Farington's first mention of Combe occurs in the entry for July 15, 1793: "Went to the Shakespeare Gallery, where I met Mr. Bulmer, the printer, who informed me he had recommenced printing the first volume of the *Thames* after a very long cessation, and that it will now go on uninterruptedly as Mr. Combe has promised to supply him with manuscript as wanted" (page 6).[14] The artist was not yet very intimate with Combe, and all the early references to him are impersonal, concerned entirely with professional matters. They are of special interest, however, in indicating how much Combe was entrusted with responsibility for the publication. It was he who apportioned the space, selected many of the subjects for Farington's sketches, prepared the manuscript (which was often seen by no one else until it was in print), read the proof, and in general managed the entire project. The Boydells (especially Josiah, who seems to have been the more active partner in dealing with this publication) and Farington had the final decision regarding business matters, but they left most literary and editorial decisions to Combe. The three principals were in constant communication, but each was trusted in his own province.

That Combe was by no means inclined to neglect the practicalities of the work is fully apparent from Farington's entry for November 1, 1793: "At Mr. Davenport's, I found a letter from Mr. Combe, who recommends me to make a view of Culham [about two miles below Henley], as it may induce a certain set of subscribers. Culham is now the property of Mr. West, a brother of Lord Delawarr, who married a co-heiress. The other sister married the young Mr. Powis of Hardwick, who sold Mr. West his share of Culham. The Marquis of Blandford has rented the place. At present Mr. Law, one of the sons of the late Bishop of Carlisle, and who made a fortune in India, rents it. Mr. Law married a daughter of the Archbishop of York, Dr. Markham" (pages 32–33). This impressive list of prospective subscribers was decisive; Culham was included. Evidently not all of Combe's research was historical.

Whenever Combe was not gathering his materials he worked at the Gallery. Farington regularly saw him there with his "old crony",[15] George Steevens. "Shakespeare Steevens", as he was called, had been at Eton with Combe and had probably helped rescue him from the Army. He had revised Johnson's edition of Shakespeare and was now preparing that of the Boydells. Though occupied on different projects, the two men were closely associated and consulted with each other. Thus, Farington proposed to refer one of Combe's suggestions regarding the *Thames* to Steevens, "a friend to the work". Should "a botanical account of the plants which grew on the sides of the Thames" be included? Steevens thought it inadvisable, and the idea was discarded.[16]

Farington mentions many tasks, however, which Combe performed independently. He speaks of Combe's decision to end the first volume at Teddington, of his preparing a tentative title-page for the artist's approval, of his correcting proof sheets, and of his plans for future volumes of the *Rivers* series. On September 17, 1794, Combe "told me he had not the least occasion to go on the River Medway with me, that he had been from Tonbridge to Rochester and had received from a friend a sufficient account of the country below Chatham to Sheerness, that it would be increasing the expense for no purpose, that he must treat the Medway in a more slight manner than he originally intended. . . . I delivered to him a list of my intended subjects, which he approved of highly. . . . He said the work would not wait for him and that he should have been ready in June" (pages 220–1). Two weeks later the two men again met at the Gallery. "I . . . told him it would be necessary to make an opening for a view of Penshurst and that Maidstone, contrary to his expectation, made an excellent subject. . . . He approved much of the introduction of Penshurst" (pages 223–4). These notes and others like them reveal a practical and efficient side of Combe's character which without the diary might not be suspected.

In addition to describing Combe's methods of work, Farington tells a good deal about the man himself and about his social activities during the 1790s One entry, for example, describes a dinner given by the artist for Josiah Boydell and Combe on November 14, 1793. It was then just a month after the execution of Marie Antoinette in Paris, and Combe as usual on such occasions was prepared to supply appropriate anecdotes.

> [He] informed us of many particulars of the condition and behaviour of the Queen of France after her condemnation. When she was carried back from the tribunal where she had received sentence of death, she requested that she might see her children, which was refused. From this moment she appeared to have lost her senses, and continued in a state of insanity till her death. In the cart in which she was carried to execution, she took the executioner for the Dauphin and spoke to him as such. She recognized the Tuileries, and wondered she did not see her children at the windows. . . . Combe says the Dauphin, or rather infant King of France, is now under the management of a man who was formerly a shoemaker, who is directed to instruct him in everything vicious and immoral.
>
> (Pages 47–48)

Combe's conversational talents made him a welcome guest at dinner parties and other social gatherings. Farington describes a New Year's Eve dinner (December 31, 1793) at the Freemason's Tavern with Combe, Josiah Boydell, Benjamin West, and William Peters. On February 10, 1794, Combe had dinner with Richard Cosway and his talented wife, Maria. He was often a guest in that household, for Cosway was one of his oldest friends. On November 29, 1794, Combe was one of a distinguished company attending the Chaplain's dinner at St. James's. He is frequently mentioned in the diary as taking part in other social activities, attending lectures with his friends, discussing the politics of the Royal Academy before and after the annual elections, talking about the war with men who dropped in for a casual call at the Shakespeare Gallery. Various of his friends before and after this time commented on Combe's social graces; Farington specifies occasions and took notes on the conversations.

One learns that on December 7, 1793, "a heavy morning and wet day", Farington met both Steevens and Combe at George Dance's studio, where Dance made "very like" drawings of the two writers

(Plate 10). Several years later, on February 15, 1798, Farington discovered Combe sitting for his portrait in Northcote's studio; the painting was finished and became the property of Major Charles "Jacobin" James.[17] On his death in 1821 the portrait was sold, and its present whereabouts are unknown. Northcote had also painted a portrait of the writer in 1795; this he sold to Ackermann for £10 in 1812, but what became of it is unknown.[18] Lonsdale's portrait had a similar fate: Combe borrowed it and failed to return it. It, too, has disappeared.[19]

The tribute to Combe's abilities which must have been most gratifying to his self-esteem was that recorded by Farington on May 6, 1794. Combe could not have read the diary, but he would hear of the episode. "Boydell called. Had been with the King this morning an hour and a half while the family were at breakfast and . . . presented the first volume of the River Thames. The King placed it on his knee and turned over *every* leaf. He expressed his approbation of the work. He asked Boydell who wrote the historical part. B. said Mr. Combe, who was the author of the *Letter from a Country Gentleman*, etc. The King enquired further about his publications till B. told His Majesty that C. wrote the *Diaboliad*. The King said he was a clever man" (page 160).

* * *

Combe, meanwhile, was rising in the world. We have seen that his letter to Jerningham was dated from Craven Hill, a street in Paddington just north of Kensington Gardens. On December 16, 1794, Josiah Boydell told Farington that Combe now had a servant and was keeping a horse given him by Robert Mackreth. Combe, we know, had performed a service for Mackreth, who as proprietor of White's gambling-club had been involved in embarrassing and costly litigation. In 1786 he had been found guilty of taking undue advantage of one Fox Lane, a young aristocrat, and had been required to refund £20,000 to him. Fox Lane had been represented in court by Sir John Scott, later Lord Eldon, whom Mackreth had eventually challenged to a duel. Sir John ignored the challenge and in 1793 brought a legal action against him for assault. He won the case, and Mackreth was sentenced to six weeks in the King's Bench Prison.[20] Combe then wrote a defence of Mackreth, putting his whole case in the best light possible. It must have been an assignment which put

10. *William Combe, drawn by George Dance, 1793. National Portrait Gallery*

Combe's somewhat scanty legal training to the test. The document was never published, but it served its purpose if it helped Mackreth save face. At any rate, Combe collected his fee, in this instance a horse. He had not had one since as "Count Combe" he had made such an impression at the Bristol Hot Wells in 1768.

Then on February 3, 1795, Farington received startling news. Nathaniel Marchant, a minor artist and member of the Royal Academy, told him of having been at the Cosways the night before and learning that Combe had eloped with Charlotte Hadfield, Maria Cosway's sister. They had been married the previous Wednesday (January 28). Charlotte had been in the country for a month—just where is not stated—and had written the Cosways a letter informing them of her marriage. It was the first hint they had received of any attachment between the two. No record of the marriage has been found in any parish register; conceivably it never occurred, since Maria Combe was still alive at Stephen Casey's madhouse and another marriage would have been bigamous. But thereafter Combe and Charlotte lived together for a time, then for many years they lived apart, as man and wife.

The union, whatever its nature, brought little happiness to either party. Combe was fifty-three, Charlotte probably in her early thirties.[21] Both needed a home of their own; Combe had been living precariously and without his wife for most of the nineteen years since his marriage to Maria, and Charlotte had been making her home with her married sister, an awkward situation at best. There was ample reason for her to be attracted to Combe, a tall, handsome man, well dressed, with fine manners and a genuinely distinguished appearance. They shared a love of music; both of them sang and played the harpsichord. He was the same age as her sister's husband, and he was certainly better looking. He was intimate (as he would be sure to mention) with lords and statesmen, artists and writers. He had an endless supply of entertaining anecdotes about the great and the near great. More discriminating individuals than Charlotte found his conversation amusing, his company welcome. Richard Cosway had been his friend since boyhood; Maria Cosway continued to be his friend and correspondent after the death of her husband. Farington, the Boydells, the men on *The Times* (then and later), Edward Jerningham, Samuel Rogers, Lord and Lady Harcourt, George Steevens, various men in the Pitt ministry—if not, indeed, the Prime Minister himself—all respected Combe and found him socially acceptable. Why should not Charlotte marry him? She would not know about Maria Combe, hidden away in a private madhouse out in Plaistow, Essex. At her age she would feel competent to make her own decision. And even the King had called Combe a clever man!

Combe, for his part, needed a wife and a home, and Charlotte was, according to one writer who knew her, "a most amiable woman".[22] And so they joined forces, and Combe bought her a harpsichord. They lived for a time in Knightsbridge, then in June 1795 they moved their possessions to a place near Harrow where Combe had leased a house and garden for £40 a year.[23]

How long the two lived together and how they managed their affairs after Combe's fortunes took a turn for the worse in 1797, we have no way of knowing. A letter written by Combe on November 26, 1802, speaks of something which had been sent to his home as having been "received by Mrs. C——".[24] The incident could scarcely have occurred before 1798; more probably it was in 1799. But these domestic arrangements were necessarily terminated by Combe's imprisonment for debt on May 4, 1799. Soon thereafter we hear that Charlotte has gone to live with one "Mrs. Curtis of King's County, Ireland". She corresponded with Combe, however, and returned at least once—in August 1821 after Cosway's death—to visit her sister and see her husband. When Combe died in 1823, Charlotte wrote to ask for his watch and ring. "*To me*," she wrote, underlining the words, "they possess a greater value than a stranger could feel."[25] Disappointing as their union had evidently proved, she had remained in communication with her husband, and even after years of separation she cherished some tenderness for him.

* * *

Combe's prosperity lasted only through the first year and a half of his marriage to Charlotte. During these eighteen months he completed the second volume of the *Thames* and put it through the press, while at the same time editing or writing Humphrey Repton's two pamphlets, Æneas Anderson's *Embassy to China* (a 300-page book), and a vigorously argued *Letter to a Retired Officer* (Debrett, 1796), an attempt to save Colonel John Fenton Cawthorne from being expelled from the House of Commons. Cawthorne had been court-martialled for mishandling the funds of the Middlesex Militia, though his friends insisted he was guilty only of bad judgement. For a price— £100—Combe prepared an able defence.[26] A reviewer for the *Monthly* (June 1796), knowing that Cawthorne had been expelled on May 2, called the pamphlet "an apology . . . for his particular acquaintance, to enable him to retain a place in their society". The task must have been difficult, he added, but the author "has executed it in a manner which will probably give satisfaction to Mr. Cawthorne's friends". Once again Combe was making literary use of his legal training.

The ever-mounting expense of the *History of the Thames* was of great concern to the Boydells, and by the time the second volume was ready for distribution they realized that the *Rivers* series could not go on unless expenses were drastically reduced. Early in March 1796 Josiah Boydell discussed this matter with Combe, insisting particularly on reducing his expense account. Combe said he could not possibly describe the River Clyde and the Firth of Forth without visiting them, but he thought a three-week trip to Scotland might serve his purpose (page 559). Two months later he agreed to combine the two descriptions in a single volume, but there is no evidence that the work was actually undertaken. Business conditions were worsening, the war was going badly on the Continent, and there were runs on country banks which caused them to make large withdrawals from the Bank of England. In February 1797 Pitt's Government authorized the Bank to suspend gold payments, and everyone expected banknotes to be depreciated. Stocks fell to lower levels than any they had reached during the American war, and national morale was under serious strain, especially when mutinies occurred in the Royal Fleet in April and May. At the Shakespeare Gallery it was agreed that the country was proceeding to ruin and that the Opposition would rather defeat Pitt than France. The Boydells, who had their capital invested in a huge collection of paintings and engravings pending publication of their edition of Shakespeare (1802), were in desperate straits. By October they had abandoned all thought of continuing with the *Rivers* series and were offering to refund the money received from subscribers, very few of whom objected in 1797 to receiving cash from any source.

Combe often figures in the conversations recorded by Farington during these months, for his anecdotes were amusing and he himself was, as always, something of a mystery. Farington made a point of noting details of Combe's history as they came to light, and eventually he gathered a good deal of information. On November 27, 1795, he wrote, "Combe says he is 52 years old and Cosway many years older [he was actually 53, and Cosway was the same age]. Combe when a boy learnt accounts at a school in Windmill Street, where Cosway occasionally came, and at that time drew heads for five shillings each" (page 433). One evening a year later Farington and several of his friends talked about Combe, each one contributing what he knew of the man's mysterious past. For the first time Farington heard the story of Combe's inheritance (though the amount of it was exaggerated and Alderman Alexander was said to be Combe's uncle). He heard, too, of Combe's misfortunes after wasting his legacy, including the story that he had been "a soldier in Spain and in England". The Reverend Richard Penneck told of his having been discovered as a waiter at an inn, and someone else described his marriage to "a mistress of Lord Beauchamp (the present Marquis of Hertford) from whom she had an annuity". The wife's subsequent insanity was mentioned, and her confinement in a madhouse (page 823). On still another occasion, Farington learned correctly the date of that unfortunate first marriage, 1776 (page 215). Eventually, he managed to piece together a good deal of the story.

These reports of Combe's affairs begin to reflect a sharp decline in his prosperity after the appearance of the Cawthorne defence. In 1797 Boydell believed that he had not been receiving his pension for a year, but instead was being paid for whatever he published. If this was the case (and it may not have been), Combe should have been well rewarded for his *Plain Thoughts of a Plain Man*, for it was highly successful. But whatever he made by it was inadequate to his needs. By autumn his affairs were becoming desperate. In October he was going to the Westalls' several times a week, asking for pen and ink to do his writing, staying to dinner and tea, and in general making a nuisance of himself (page 1106). On at least one occasion he arrived at Farington's in time for breakfast, though the diary records the fact without any implied annoyance. The *Anti-Jacobin* began appearing on November 20th, published by J. Wright, for whom Combe had often worked; its pro-government policies would seem to offer Combe an opportunity for employment, but Farington was told that he had nothing to do with it or with the Government but was reduced to soliciting booksellers for miscellaneous hackwork (page 1184). And at Hoppner's it was reported that "the staple employ of Combe is writing sermons" (page 1186), probably the "seventy-three sermons" which he later mentioned. Farington soon reports (pages 1234–5) Combe expressing critical opinions on homiletics—for he would need to display his competence to those who knew of his clerical ghost-writing.

* * *

In the spring of 1798 Combe's creditors became insistent. His bill at the tailor's was long overdue, and he had not paid for the household furnishings purchased during his short period of prosperity. On May 17 he was required to sign a note for £77. 17s. 6d., acknowledging his indebtedness to Matthew and William Stodart, harpsichord makers. Meanwhile, he had obtained some money from another source, as evidenced by a still-uncancelled note preserved at the Pierpont Morgan Library:

April 2 1798

I promise to pay G. Romney Esqr or his Order, on Demand, the Sum of One Hundred Pounds, for value received.

Wm Combe

£100.0.0

George Romney was one of the artists employed by the Boydells on their grandiose Shakespeare project; Combe could have met him at the Gallery or could have been introduced by one of the many artists he knew at this time. Regrettably it must be added that Romney's mind was failing by 1798; his son later wrote that various unnamed people found it easy to take advantage of the old man in his last years.[27] Combe would not be conscious of an intent to defraud the artist, but he had an unlimited capacity for self-deception where money matters were concerned. He sturdily maintained his jaunty posture through these trials, and seven months after borrowing this money he was able to write Romney a reassuring letter:

Monday Novr. 12 1798

My dear Sir,

I have called several times in Cavendish Square, & you were always at your Villa.—I have frequently designed to see you there in your rustic glory, but my engagements & the shortness of the days have prevented my enjoying that pleasure.—It will not, however, be long, before I shall take an opportunity to wait upon you, and to repay the obligation You were so very good as to confer upon

Your faithful & obliged hble serv—
Wm Combe

[Addressed on the outside :]
G. Romney Esqr
 Hampstead[28]

The letter is more than a little disingenuous, for on November 1 he had had another accounting with Messrs Stodart's solicitor and had signed a new note, this time for £160. The amount covered the unpaid note of May 17 as well as other charges for "work and labour, care, trouble, journies [*sic*] and attendances before that time done, performed, taken, and bestowed by the said Matthew and William Stodart by themselves and their servants with their horses, carts, and carriages for the said William Combe at his special instance and request and also for divers materials and necessary things before that time found and provided".[29] During these same months he was also signing notes and making promises to Robert Douglas and Robert Lambert, who were pressing him for a debt of £80. The full details of their efforts to collect are unknown, for the Plea Roll setting forth their charges has not come to light. But an entry in the King's Bench Commitment Book, presently to be cited, proves that they, too, were following the usual procedures and preparing to take legal action.

Despite these rude distractions, Combe continued to press his claims as historian. On November 5 Farington went to the Academy and discussed the forthcoming elections there with various members. Northcote had two suggestions; he urged the election of Prince Hoare as Secretary for Foreign Correspondence to succeed James Boswell, and he mentioned Combe as a candidate for election as Professor of History. He said that Combe had talked to him about the post and had promised actually to deliver lectures if he were elected. "I replied", Farington wrote in his diary, "that it must be considered *who had filled that situation*." He underscored the words as he recalled the historian whom Combe would be succeeding, Edward Gibbon. "The Academy could hardly elect a person for what he might do." And he added, with manifest relief, "Northcote seemed to feel it as I did" (page 1345). Both men knew Combe well; they respected his ability as writer, enjoyed his company, and tolerated his eccentricities, but neither could conceive of him as William Combe, R.A. No one else seemed a suitable candidate, however, and the position remained vacant for several years.

The frustrated historian continued to find a few hackwriting assignments during the winter. In particular, he was employed by James Colnett to assist with his *Voyage to the South Atlantic and Round Cape Horn into the Pacific Ocean*, privately published in 1799, though dated 1798. The extent of his responsibility for that book is unknown; in listing the title among his works Combe wrote, "Translation [*sic*] of Colnett's Voyage to South America", obviously an error since Colnett was English. A long note on Thomas Falkner and his account of Patagonia suggests Combe's hand, for the *Description of Patagonia* had been his initiation to editorial work in 1774. The Dedication and Introduction are in Combe's most florid style; the rest of the book is straightforward narrative, probably only edited by Combe. Of his other hackwriting tasks at this time, nothing is known. Possibly he was still writing an occasional sermon.

It must have been at this juncture that Combe wrote an undated letter to Jerningham which shows the attitude he was able to assume when faced with imminent imprisonment for his debts. "It is impossible for me to attend you to Harcourt House", he wrote; "I am under the Necessity, at least my heart tells me so, of going to an Hotel of a very different kind, and whose Porters are of a very different temper;—who make no difficulty of letting you in, but are rather scrupulous ab^t letting you out.—In short I must be at the King's Bench; It is an unpleasant Errand, but I console myself with the hope of that reward, which is promised to those who visit the Prisoner."[30]

The long-anticipated bailiff arrived on May 4, 1799, and for want of bail Combe was taken into custody. On "Monday next after the Morrow of the Ascension", which is to say on May 13, he was brought to trial before the King's Bench on the charges of Robert Douglas and Robert Lambert, who sued for £40. 11s. 6d. plus large damages and costs. Combe, who had no attorney, could say "nothing in bar or foreclusion of the said action", and the court found for the prosecution. The sheriff was directed to determine the amount of damages suffered by the creditors, and Combe was returned to prison.[31]

A week later, on May 20, the painful process was repeated in behalf of Matthew and William Stoddart, demanding £102. 10s. 0d. plus the usual costs and damages.[32] Subsequently, on a date not revealed by such records as have come to light, Thomas and Philip Griffith made their demands: £15. 12s. 9d.,[33] and finally Stephen Casey asked for £193. 10s. 0d. Without costs and damages, which sometimes exceeded the original debt, these sums come to £352. 4s. 3d. Only the first two cases, however, were recorded in the King's Bench Commitment Book, where a summary was entered for each prisoner when first committed. In the margin, where one looks for the date of the prisoner's discharge, appear only the words, "Died 19th June 1823."[34] Although Combe would be granted a great deal of limited freedom, he was to remain under the jurisdiction of the King's Bench for the rest of his life.

CHAPTER VII

JOURNALIST

What human nature's known to feel,
These pages must with care reveal;
What human nature's doom'd to do,
These pages hold in public view:
Of all things that we daily see,
That give the passing history,
The Journalists are bound to tell,
When things go ill, when things go well.
—Doctor Syntax

SINCE THE rest of Combe's life was to be spent either within the walls of the King's Bench Prison or in their shadow, it is necessary to give some account of that grim feature of Georgian life. Though now only vaguely remembered, it was once all too familiar to Londoners, a dark and constant reminder of authority. As such, it was understandably a primary target of the Gordon Rioters, who in 1780 made a point of destroying it. The prison was promptly rebuilt, however, and when Combe entered it the structure was relatively new. Located in Southwark, three-quarters of a mile south-west of London Bridge and about the same distance east of Westminster Bridge, it was equally accessible and menacing to the City and the West End. All classes of society were well aware of its existence.

Several of Combe's contemporaries, themselves prisoners or former prisoners, wrote descriptions of the place and the conditions of daily life which prevailed there, matter-of-fact handbooks for the guidance of other unlucky debtors. The picture which they unconsciously set forth, however astounding to modern readers, was to be the background and for several years the foreground of Combe's daily life as journalist and later as comic poet.[1]

The Bench, as it was called, stood on the north side of Borough Road just west of what is now the Borough High Street. A huge place, it consisted of one very large building, two or three smaller ones, and a prison yard, or "parade", the whole being surrounded by a twenty-five-foot brick wall with bristling iron spikes at the top. It was not a thing of beauty from the street; it was intended to look threatening, and it did so. As one entered the gate—and the guards admitted anyone during the day-time—the chief feature to be seen was the main building, which extended nearly the full length of the west wall and had a wing at each end. It contained 176 rooms for which the Marshal charged the occupants one shilling per week; ordinarily two prisoners were "chummed" in each room. On the back of this building, the "common side", were twenty-four rooms crowded with prisoners who were unable to pay anything. Even the common-side prisoners had to pay for their mattress and bedding if they were to have any—sixpence for the first night, three halfpence for every succeeding night (or a penny each if two prisoners shared the bed). On the "Master's side", the charge was twice this amount: threepence a night or twopence each if shared. The eight most exalted prisoners occupied the eight commodious rooms in the State House, a building extending into the yard from the south wall; for these quarters the prisoners paid two shillings and sixpence a week. Beyond the State House was an area reserved for the game of rackets, which was played against the east wall. There was a public cookhouse at the north end of the Parade, and near it was the market. The rest was open space, a large area though by no means excessive for the five or six hundred prisoners, not to mention their daytime visitors.

No meals were provided; everyone was expected to make do as best he could. Common-side prisoners were entitled to fourpence, later sixpence, a day from their creditors, and also they were allowed to stand at the gate with a begging-box, the money being divided equally among them. There were shops in the yard where food and supplies could be bought, all run as private businesses by prisoners, and hucksters daily pushed their carts through the gate to sell their wares in the open market. The rooms contained fireplaces where one might do minimal cooking if he could afford fuel, and there was a public kitchen where food could be prepared. There were also several private kitchens "at which the better sort pay for having their dinners dressed". Water was free.

The average cost of living was estimated at twelve shillings a week, but some prisoners hired servants, of which there was a ready supply, and maintained establishments thought to cost at least ten guineas. If one had the money, he could obtain virtually anything he wanted within the walls, and oddly enough even credit was available there. "Of the prisoners, some have a property, or an income, to subsist upon; some a regular allowance from their friends; some are obliged to feed like moths upon their clothes [i.e. sell or exchange them for food], and some have to depend wholly on chance, or accident, to lengthen out a miserable existence; while others, and those of the greatest number, carry on some trade or business, as regularly as if they had been born and bred within the walls." Most of the prisoners, it is no surprise to learn, "live extremely hard, and seldom know what it is to have a good dinner; nor are instances wanting of persons having actually perished, from a total deprivation of the common necessaries of life".

Several of the public amenities were famous in their day and are often mentioned in contemporary accounts. A public house stood just inside the entrance, one of the best outlets controlled by the Barclay, Perkins Brewery. It sold porter at threepence halfpenny a pot, "and as there is always a quick draught for it, near five hundred butts being used in the course of the year [roughly 1,200 pints a day], it is much better, perhaps, than can be had out of doors". At night, prisoners unable to rent rooms or find free space on the common side were allowed to sleep on the floors and benches of this pub. There was also a second tap, slightly higher class, called the Brace, having once been kept by two brothers named Partridge. Other features of the Bench included a coffee-room which served meals, a wine-room catering only to the best element, and a nondescript "place where porter is allowed to be drank". None of these establishments sold whisky, gin, or brandy, for by a rule of court the use of spirits within the walls was prohibited, "unless medicinally". There were, however, places in the yard well known to the prisoners where one could obtain a stronger drink merely by whistling—thus avoiding the necessity of requesting anything illegal. These were called Whistling Shops. It is reassuring to learn that there was also a prison chapel where divine services were held every Sunday, but there was no infirmary, no medical supervision or care, no provision for supplying the indigent, with food or blankets.

When the gates were opened in the morning visitors of all kinds crowded into the yard—relatives, friends, business associates, pick-pockets, hawkers, casuals of every description. Boys came in to play rackets, skittles, or bowls, using the place as a public playground. No questions were asked of these visitors, and prostitutes entered freely to ply their trade in this community of enforced idleness. The prisoners, we are told, were "of the most miscellaneous nature; and it would be strange indeed, if amongst such a promiscuous group, there were not some entirely lost to all sense of shame, and wholly abandoned to every species of vice and infamy". George Hanger, the eccentric who was discharged from the prison just before Combe's entry, went even further in his autobiography (edited by Combe and published in 1801). According to his account, "Unless a man be of a certain age, of a bold and firm mind, and of undaunted resolution . . . he soon sinks into drunkenness and dissipation; and, what is worse, loses every sense of honour and dignity of sentiment—every moral principle and virtuous disposition, with which he may enter these walls—from the immoral contagion that is to be found in them." Of women prisoners, Hanger wrote, "Those who are good become bad, and those who are bad become worse."[2]

Although prison, like death, was said to be a great leveller, the class system was respected at the King's Bench. It was necessary to make a proper entry, and Combe would know this from his previous experience. In any event, it was second nature for him to maintain appearances under trying situations. Here as elsewhere he would insist on being treated as a gentleman, and there is good evidence that he succeeded; one document explicitly names him as Gentleman, while a prison record listing the names of eighty-nine debtors adds Esq. only to Combe's.[3] And even at this moment of embarrassment his financial position would set him apart from the others. He had his business connections with the booksellers and probably entered prison with the understanding that he was to do hackwork there for both John Debrett and John Wright. Certainly he turned out a massive amount of translating during his imprisonment, and he may well have requested some advance payment in order to procure suitable quarters when he entered. If he found himself "chummed" with another prisoner, he would only need to pay him three shillings and sixpence a week to vacate the room in order to have it to himself. However the matter was arranged, Combe managed to establish himself in reasonably satisfactory quarters and straightway went to work.

Knowledge of Combe's new address did not immediately reach his friends, but Farington in his usual manner gradually pieced the story together. "Fuseli told me Combe is confined in King's Bench", he wrote on July 1, 1799, two months after his arrest. At the Shakespeare Gallery, on October 4, he heard that Combe was still confined for debts of £70 to the tailor and £50 for a harpsichord, adding that Combe was very well contented with an arrangement which permitted him to work without any temptation to waste time. And then on February 8, 1800, Farington learned that Combe, now out of prison, had called on Westall. No more exact information concerning the time of Combe's release has come to light, but at most he had spent only ten months within prison walls before being granted the privilege of living outside. The time may have been somewhat shorter.

"I rejoice to hear of Combe's escape from his cell", wrote Samuel Rogers on March 28. "He will now see more of his friends. If you should visit him again, pray remember me very particularly to him. His name stands very high in this country."[4]

* * *

Combe's work in the King's Bench Prison during this period of confinement consisted chiefly in translating five large books dealing with recent military, diplomatic, and antiquarian activities on the Continent and in Egypt.[5] All of them were published by either Debrett or Wright in 1799 and 1800, and together they total over 2,400 pages— a very substantial output. It is the kind of literary work which would be least interrupted by the general confusion and uproar of the prison, and the concentration which it required would provide Combe with an escape from the harsh facts of his existence during those weeks and months.

In addition to these translations, however, he published some original work at this time which, if it was written in prison, shows a greater degree of resolution. Debrett was beginning the publication of a new annual, the *Asiatic Annual Register*, which attempted to do for India and the Far East what the *Annual Register* had been doing for England. It provided a chronicle of events in Asia, a list of civil and military appointments, a compilation of state papers, speeches in Parliament, "characters" of men in the news, tracts, poetry, and reviews of relevant books. Combe contributed several articles to the first two volumes, those for 1799 and 1800 (published in 1800 and 1801), but he mentions only one of them by name, "An Account of the Life of the Late Governor Holwell", which appears in the first volume.[6]

Governor John Zephaniah Holwell was long celebrated as one of the twenty-three survivors of the Black Hole of Calcutta, the accepted version of that shocking affair being the one he himself published in 1758.[7] Combe repeats the story in his careful summary of Holwell's career, and his *Asiatic Annual Register* account was long regarded as a useful source of information concerning both the Governor and his miraculous escape with twenty-two others from the fate of their 123 companions. Historical accounts for over a century perpetuated the legend just as Combe, and before him Holwell, told it. Recent historians, to be sure, have raised serious questions about this famous story, some believing it at best a fantastic exaggeration. Whatever the truth may be, Combe was only incidentally involved; he merely put in order the account available to him.

Combe's "escape from his cell", whenever it occurred, was no more than permission to live outside the walls but within "the Rules", a carefully defined area surrounding the prison. He rented quarters from a Mrs Ryves at 12 Lambeth Road, which remained his address, though not always his residence, for the rest of his life. Neither he nor the other sixty or seventy prisoners living in the Rules felt compelled to abide strictly by the restriction, but they usually made their forays into London by night. Combe was far from the Rules when he paid his call, presumably at a late hour, on Richard Westall in Upper Charlotte Street. The authorities were very lax in supervising their charges, but it was prudent not to flout the regulations too obviously. The privilege was granted by the Marshal at his own option and could be withdrawn at any time if he thought it advisable. Prisoners eligible for the Rules need only find someone willing to be their security and to pay "seven guineas and a half if the debt is £50, and ten guineas if £100, and five guineas, perhaps, for every other £100". The amount was based not on the total indebtedness but only on that part of it creditors were, in fact, likely to demand —a somewhat imprecise system. Combe would have to pay about twenty-five guineas, not a trifling sum, to be sure, especially in terms of its present-day equivalent, but one that Combe could easily manage if his hackwork was producing its usual remuneration. The book-sellers who had a stake in his forthcoming productions would prob-ably be willing to go his surety.

Early in 1801 he undertook to edit and in part to ghost-write Alexander Mackenzie's important account of his explorations in western Canada, *Voyages from Montreal, on the River St. Laurance, Through the Continent of North America, to the Frozen and Pacific Oceans*. A letter addressed to the publishers, Messrs Cadell and Davies, and postmarked April 1, 1801, dates the actual beginning of his work:

Wednesday 12 o'clock

Gentlemen,

I have not received the Account of Mr. Hearne's Travels, which are so necessary to assist me in my progress, but particularly at the Commence-ment of it. I really wait for it.—Mr. Mackenzie who has just called upon me, —informs me that it is sent,—but I have not received it.—Will you be so obliging as to rectify the mistake if there be any—

I am
Your obed^t hble Svt—
Wm Combe[8]

The Hearne referred to was another early explorer who is, in fact, mentioned "at the commencement" (page 2) of the published narra-tive. Mackenzie's book contains over 400 quarto pages and has come to be regarded as a classic of early Canadian exploration. Combe completed it from Mackenzie's journals and notebooks, but internal evidence, as well as this letter requesting source material, suggests that he did a good deal of research in gathering information of his own. An introductory survey of the fur trade in the Candian North-west has every appearance of being his work, though it was doubtless written under Mackenzie's direction. It runs to 132 pages and is written in Combe's workmanlike manner. In the Preface signed by Mackenzie the explorer states his reason for delaying publication, the voyages having taken place in 1789 and 1793; he has been too busy and has not felt qualified to write the book, "being much better cal-culated to perform the voyages, arduous as they might be, than to write an account of them". The sentence is as nearly an acknowledge-ment of ghost-writing assistance as convention permitted. The Preface is dated London, November 30, 1801. The title-page is also dated 1801, but the work did not appear until May 5, 1802.

Although Combe was working on Mackenzie's book throughout

1801, he managed in the same year to publish three other works. One of them was a political pamphlet, *Brief Observations on a Late Letter Addressed to the Right Hon. W. Pitt, by W. Boyd, Esq. on the Stoppage of Issues in Specie by the Bank of England* (Debrett). Pitt undeniably needed public support at the time, but the defence came too late. The Government fell in February, just as the pamphlet appeared. Meanwhile, Combe was also turning out a long, rambling work in two volumes, written, or at least substantially revised, from the manuscript notes of George Hanger. This odd collection of observations on various subjects, moral and immoral, features an engraving of the putative author hanging by his neck from a gibbet and bears a title of over 150 words—in brief, *The Life, Adventures, and Opinions of Col. George Hanger* (Debrett). It reflects little of Combe's mind or craftsmanship, and may be passed over without further comment. In this same year, however, he did some more original work in assembling *The History of Mauritius* (printed by Bulmer for the author) from the papers of the late Charles Grant, Viscount de Vaux, at the instigation and in the pay of the author's son. This book, dated 1801, actually appeared on January 6, 1802. It had been a busy year, but as Combe later remarked, "Those who are familiar with the conduct of my life, well know that I am not in the habit of sparing myself."[9]

Something went amiss, however, in 1802, and he produced only one book. Just what happened is unknown, but a letter addressed to his friend John Taylor and postmarked November 26, 1802, shows his indignation at being, as he thought, defrauded by a mysterious and somewhat unsavoury David Scott & Company.

Thursday Evening

My dear Sir,

It can do no harm, in case you should have another opportunity of speaking upon my business with Mr. Hartwell, or any other person who is in habit of communicating with that Gentleman, to put you in possession of the grounds on which I found the Opinion that the House of David Scott & Co. is to be considered as having employed me; and on whom I, consequently, have a claim for some further remuneration.—

Soon after the original Instructions were communicated to me by Mr. Cochrane, he brought me a Draft for an hundred Guineas signed David Scott & Co. and payable to Wm. Combes, Esqr. or Bearer, for charges; Which Draft was received by Mrs. C—— [and] received at Down, Free & Co. Bankers in Bartholomew Lane, on whom it was drawn.—

The Question therefore is very short & very simple. If that House did not employ me, for what purpose, or in what relation, was the draft, already mentioned, issued from it in my favour? — Besides, it was paid in advance, & Mr. Cochrane informed me that I was to consider it as a retaining Fee, to be completed by an enhanced remuneration, when the work was completed.—

I accordingly considered Mr. Cochrane as the Agent of Mr. Scott's House, & it was on that ground alone that I proceeded in fulfilling the Commission. — I had no reason to suppose that Mr. Cochrane was in a situation to reward me; & though I had every disposition to oblige him; the circumstances in which I was involved at that time, would not allow me, to give my time to anyone, without an adequate consideration.

At all events I have the means in my power of repaying myself, and as I am neither treated with Justice or common civility,—I am not bound by any principle of Honour, or sentiment of Delicacy, to refrain from employing them.—And I will employ them.—

Yours faithfully,
W. Combe.[10]

London directories of the period identify David Scott & Co. as merchants with offices at 9 Broad Street Buildings and George Hartwell as a navy agent at the same address. In 1798 the firm was accused of engaging in illicit trade with the enemy, France, by transporting Indian goods in a Danish ship from a Dutch port, Batavia (now Jakarta), to a mysterious destination in Europe. The scheme became known through the capture of correspondence by the British, though identities were concealed under pseudonymns. (Or were they real names?) It was all very mysterious, and no doubt it was highly profitable to someone. To make the affair even more sensational, David Scott, Sr, now retired from the firm, was a trusted Director of the East India Company and a member of its Secret Committee. In 1798 he was charged with complicity in the operations of the firm, supposed to be entirely under the management of his son, David Scott, Jr. After a debate at East India House on March 5, 1799, the father was exonerated, but a reviewer in the *Anti-Jacobin* (April 1800) very reasonably thought his innocence was still open to question.[11]

At some time during this controversy, probably in 1799, David Scott & Co. engaged Combe's services, presumably to write a legalistic defence of the accused parties, as he had for Robert Mackreth in 1794 and again for Colonel Cawthorne in 1795. What went wrong with the arrangement this time is not known, but Combe's angry letter reveals a side of his personality not seen elsewhere. Despite the time wasted over this unlucky affair, Combe managed to produce one piece of routine editing for John Debrett in 1802. This was Æneas Anderson's account of the campaign in Egypt, a 560-page book which fell stillborn from the press on November 29. It was his last effort of this kind until 1809. For the next six years he devoted himself entirely to journalism.

*　*　*

Combe's first employment as newspaper editor—though the word *editor* in that sense was not yet in common use—was in 1803, but the circumstances which launched him on this new career had been developing since 1801. They formed, indeed, the topic of a London season, filling the newspapers with a storm of controversy, innuendo, slander, and outrageous paragraphs. Though now long since forgotten, the affair of the Dilettante Theatre in Tottenham Street (now Tottenham Court Road) has its small place in the history of the London stage and, more particularly in so far as Combe was concerned, in the rise of disinterested dramatic criticism in the newspapers.

The episode began with a private "theatrical fête" arranged in February 1801 by a man well known in London society, Colonel Henry Francis Greville. He invited a "select circle" of his friends to an evening of informal entertainment provided by themselves—music, dramatic readings, and a "picnic", or rather what would now be called a potluck supper: every guest was to provide a share of food and wine. The party turned out to be a great success; the guests were from the same social circle, the food was good if highly miscellaneous, and the amateur entertainment was much enjoyed. "Every person present acknowledged the satisfaction of passing an evening of such rational amusement, and divested of the monotony of a rout."[12] There was general agreement that more parties like this should be arranged, and soon a formal organization, the Pic Nic Society, was being formed to hold a series of such evenings during the following winter. The details of this scheme were all left in the hands of Colonel Greville and a committee of gentlemen managers.

We are assured that the plans for the Society were unexceptionable. It was restricted to "persons of the first rank and distinction", each of whom was asked to pay a subscription of six guineas and to contribute six bottles of wine to the cellar. Ten women of rank and social standing consented to act as lady patronesses and to form a membership committee in order "that persons in the habit of living together might belong to their books, and, at the same time, the eligibility of the subscribers be secured". The Duchess of Devonshire led the list of patronesses. The Society proposed to meet once a fortnight "to enjoy the amusements of acting, music, and dancing, and to conclude with a supper, and catches and glees". It all seemed, or was made to seem, an innocent and amusing idea.

Colonel Greville evidently promoted the Pic Nic Society vigorously. An organization was perfected, two hundred and thirty members paid their subscriptions, and "a little theatre" (Combe calls it that) was devised in Hyde's Concert Rooms, Tottenham Street, which had been rented for the purpose. A group of men, all members of the Society, formed an amateur orchestra; others were expected to take roles in dramatic productions. It was not deemed suitable for the ladies to perform as amateurs either in the orchestra pit or on the stage; professionals would be hired to take feminine roles in any plays which might be produced. Cards and dice were explicitly prohibited in the rooms. The whole arrangement, Combe assures us, was discreet to the last degree.

Perhaps the emphasis on play production was greater than Combe would have us believe; in any event, the managers of the two Theatres Royal, particularly Richard Brinsley Sheridan, manager of the Drury Lane, took steps to prevent what seemed an invasion of their monopoly. Sheridan kept himself informed of developments through his son, Thomas, a member of the Pic Nic Society and, indeed, one of the managers. Early in 1802, and not long before the season of twelve evenings was to open, Thomas Sheridan warned Greville that "his father considered the institution injurious to the property of the Drury Lane Theatre". He added that the proposed amusements, concerts, dialogues, "proverbs", whatever they might be called, would be in violation of the Royal Patent held by the established theatres. Colonel Greville insisted that he had no intention of infringing on private property and said he had competent advice assuring him that he was well within the law. However that might be, Sheridan replied, his father had authorized him to inform the Pic Nic Society that every possible means would be employed to prevent it from proceeding with the plan. This assertion was confirmed by a letter which R. B. Sheridan addressed to Greville on February 17: "I feel myself bound by every just consideration, to oppose, by all legal and fair exertions, a scheme which, though certainly not so intended, leads in my opinion to the utter destruction of the property of the established theatres."[13]

Meanwhile, a newspaper attack, led by the *Morning Post* and promptly joined by the *Morning Herald* and other papers, was launched against the Society and all its members. Combe says that the *"Corps Paragraphique"* was acting under instructions from Sheridan and that "for its indecency, scurrility, and falsehood, this attack surpassed anything ever seen in the London papers". Although asked to do so, the *Morning Post* refused to publish Colonel Greville's statement of the aims of the Pic Nic Society and the nature of the organization; instead, a "succession of malevolent paragraphs, and wilful misrepresentation, respecting the club, continued to appear". The *Oracle* took the same position, refusing to publish Greville's denial that gambling was permitted and printing instead the following note: "The public, perhaps, are not aware, that *deep play* and *private rooms* form a conspicuous part of the rules of the new club in Tottenham-street."[14] Seventy of the members forthwith resigned.[15]

In replying to Sheridan's letter of February 17, Greville requested a personal interview in order to discuss the matter. The two men were able to reach a settlement reasonably satisfactory to each, and on March 17 *The Times* published a letter in which Sheridan set forth the conditions under which the proprietors of the Theatres Royal were willing to withdraw their objections to the scheme. There should be no more than ten performances, the actors should all be amateur, and each printed announcement or programme should state that the play was given with the consent of the established theatres. The first performance, which had been postponed pending these negotiations, was reviewed in the same issue of *The Times*. It had consisted chiefly of a dialogue written by Colonel Greville recounting the trials of the Society. The reviewer could find nothing to justify the recent scandalous charges. "The Entertainment closed at a rational hour; the Supper was at a quarter past eleven, instead of half past twelve; there was no dancing, and no gambling was introduced or thought of. The dialogue was chaste, and the audience consisted of many of the most respected families." This reassurance had little effect upon the paragraphers, however; the topic was too rich in scandalous possibilities for them to abandon it, and their running comment on high life in Tottenham Street continued throughout the spring.

The caricaturists inevitably joined the hue and cry, Gillray in particular producing several outrageous comments on the subject. One of the best of his caricatures is that entitled "Blowing Up the Pic Nics" (Plate 11), showing the amateurs (identified as Lady Buckinghamshire, Lady Salisbury, Lord Cholmondeley, Colonel Greville, and Lord Mount Edgcumbe) on the stage rehearsing Fielding's *Tom Thumb* while Sheridan leads the embattled professionals (Kemble as Hamlet, Mrs Billington, and Mrs Siddons as Lady Macbeth) and the ghost of Garrick rises from the underworld. Sheridan, accused of writing anonymous squibs for the newspapers, is shown wearing a mask and waving his pen through the names of several papers. The leading personalities on both sides evidently seemed equally ridiculous to Gillray.

In his frustration at being unable to reach the public, Colonel Greville resorted to a printed handbill which was distributed to the crowds in front of the Drury Lane and the Covent Garden, but he found it had little effect. Eventually, he resolved to start a weekly newspaper of his own, calling it the *Pic Nic*. Combe was employed at two guineas a week to "conduct" the paper, i.e. to edit it, and the first issue appeared on January 8, 1803. The Pic Nic Society went out of existence two months later, after only eight of its permitted entertainments, but Greville continued the war against the theatre monopoly for six months, first in the *Pic Nic*, then in its successor, prudently renamed the *Cabinet*. Later in the year the fourteen numbers of the *Pic Nic* were republished in two volumes, Combe supplying an introduction giving the official version of the affair from first to last. Since a second edition appeared in 1806, Greville finally succeeded in getting his story told to a good many readers, though too late to save his theatre club.

* * *

Not many issues of the *Pic Nic* survived original publication, but Charles Burney the Younger, an indefatigable collector of newspapers and himself a member of the Pic Nic Society, saved every copy. Together with all his priceless collection of newspapers, these came into the hands of the British Museum, bound with a number of the printed announcements which he received from the Society. They still make entertaining reading. Each issue was printed on a single sheet of good paper folded quarto, eight pages of material almost as miscellaneous as the original picnic supper: articles on the tense

11. *Blowing Up the Pic Nics, by Gillray, 1802. British Museum*

international situation and the troubles of the Addington ministry, original essays by "The Man in the Moon", a few of Combe's sentimental "fragments", a series entitled "View of French Literature", sketches, poems, and, most important, reviews of plays and articles on the theatre. The paper was well edited and well printed, and although Combe was the only writer who was paid for his services, the *Pic Nic* must have cost Colonel Greville a good deal of money.

Horace Smith tells how the proprietor assembled his remarkable staff of volunteers, including James and Horace Smith, Richard Cumberland, Sir James Bland Burgess, John Wilson Croker, J. C. Herries, and one or two others unnamed. "Mr. Combe, the voluminous and well-known writer, being the editor", he says, writing in 1840, when the word *editor* had come to be used in this sense. "To accommodate the latter gentleman, who had resided for many years in the rules of the King's Bench, the weekly meetings at Hatchard's did not commence until it was night, an arrangement which afforded the indispensable protection of darkness to the worthy editor." Horace Smith knew Combe well, admired his talents, and observed with amusement his odd ways. "He passed all the latter portion of his life within the Rules, to which suburban retreat the present writer was occasionally invited, and never left him without admiring his various acquirements, and the philosophical equanimity with which he endured his reverses."[16]

Editing a newspaper without a paid staff inevitably had its problems, and Combe often found himself without enough copy to fill all the columns. Smith tells of one expedient which the hard-pressed editor sometimes adopted, and his account of it throws light on an ambiguous side of Combe's career. "If a column or two of the newspaper remained unsupplied at the last moment, an occurrence by no means unusual, Mr. Combe would sit down in the publisher's back room, and extemporize a letter from Sterne at Coxwould, a forgery so well executed that it never excited suspicion."[17] This information has relieved the minds of Sterne scholars who have been well aware of the three letters in the issues for February 19, March 5, and March 26. Combe's imitations of Sterne are very good indeed, but he tended to repeat himself, as he does in these three *Pic Nic* letters, and thus often gives himself away. By this time he had been imitating Sterne for thirty years and could do it passably without difficulty.

Apart from the Sterne items, we have little information concerning

the authorship of individual pieces in the *Pic Nic*, though the reader
will often suspect Combe's hand. Did he write the political articles
which began each number? They are consistent in manner and substance with his earlier political pamphlets. The rather fulsome
tribute to Pitt in the first issue strongly suggests his handiwork,
though Pitt was at the moment out of office. These rhetorical exercises are interesting today only as reflecting the mood of England
during that year of uneasy peace with France, 1802–3. They are, as
Horace Smith later wrote, "strongly imbued with the Buonaparte-
phobia of the period". Combe almost certainly wrote many of them;
before the year was out, as we shall see, he was writing pieces for
The Times in precisely the same manner.

Other things by Combe are scattered through the pages, for the
most part unidentifiable. One poem of curious interest seems to be
his; originally signed "Z" in the newspaper, it was reprinted in book
form with the signature quietly changed to "C", as nearly an acknowledgement of authorship as Combe would permit himself.

> Samuel Johnson.
> Herculean strength, and a Stentorian voice,
> Of wit a fund, of words a countless choice:
> In learning rather various than profound,
> In truth intrepid, in religion sound:
> A trembling frame, and a distorted sight,
> But firm in judgment, and in genius bright;
> In controversy rarely known to spare,
> But humble as the publican in pray'r:
> To more than merited his kindness, kind,
> And tho' in manners harsh, of friendly mind:
> Deep-ting'd with melancholy's blackest shade,
> And, tho' prepar'd to die, of death afraid—
> Such JOHNSON was—of him with justice vain,
> When will this nation see his like again?
>
> C.[18]

Whatever its literary merits, and they are not very notable, the poem
summarizes the conventional view of Johnson in 1803.

A similar change in signature occurs with another fourteen-line
poem, this one explicitly called "Sonnet". It is addressed "To ———,
with a Profile in Paper". The silhouette may or may not be the one
reproduced in this book (Plate 1), but the author sends it, wishing,
he says,

to give
Th'unreal features of a real friend:
Amid the storms of fortune doom'd to live,
To Hymen's joys he looks not to ascend:
But since, depriv'd of Fortune's gen'rous aid,
He cannot give himself, he gives his shade.

C.19

It is the paper's revolutionary handling of theatrical matters, however, which gives the *Pic Nic* its chief significance today. Colonel Greville had found to his intense annoyance that the newspapers were completely subservient to the established theatres, perhaps their most important source of revenue. The detailed announcements of current and future productions and, perhaps even more importantly, the "puffs" which appeared in the news columns were highly profitable, and needless to say the reviews were discreet. Plays and actors might be cautiously criticized, but never the managers. The theatre monopoly was in firm control, and nothing approaching candid criticism was tolerated. This was the situation which had led the newspapers to attack the Dilettante Theatre so viciously, and Greville and his collaborators were resolved to expose it. They announced their intention with a firmly written manifesto in the first issue.

> Refusing all play-house bribes, their criticisms on the Drama and all that appertains to its departments shall be unchecked by any mean or slavish controul. They will feel no more delicacy in appreciating the merits of a Proprietor, than those of an Author or Performer—all are equally the servants of the Public, open to remark and amenable to reproof. Candour will teach them to raise and foster depressed and unassuming merit, while justice, and every manly principle will concur in chastising arrogance, repressing presumption, and throwing from their stilts those whom the ready and constant plaudits of venal adulators have raised to an undue eminence.

The attack on the monopoly began then and there. Since only the Drury Lane and the Covent Garden were permitted to produce plays (except during the summer, when they were closed and the Haymarket could do so), they had comfortably adapted themselves to being without competition. The demand for seats was so great that the new Drury Lane Theatre which opened in 1794 could seat 3,611 spectators. Since the Covent Garden was only half as large, it was the Drury Lane which the *Pic Nic* chiefly criticized in complaining about the difficulty of hearing and seeing plays in vast structures. One

12. *Drury Lane Audience as seen from the Stage. From a print dated August 11, 1804. By permission of Sir John Summerson*

writer, evidently Combe himself, objects to the size of stage required by such a large theatre. "Alpine nature may be represented, and stupendous art may be imitated, but the scenery of domestic action, or intellectual life, must fail in the display. . . . The drawing-rooms are temples, and the temples are cathedrals, while the actors are puppets . . . and the drama reduced to the dumb show of a ballet." Recalling great actors of the past, he says, "In a theatre of such dimensions, Garrick must have roared; Mrs. Pritchard must have ranted; and Mrs. Cibber must have screamed, in order to have been heard, while all the delicacy of acting, and the nice touches of their art must have been lost in distortion and declamation." In confirmation of this opinion, he cites one whom he regards as the best living authority. "I have heard Mrs. Siddons, whom I once met in the country, lament, that she has been frequently checked, in the finer parts of her characters, from the unconscious appearance of the audience, which told her, in the inarticulate language of vacant stare, that she was not heard". The engraving reproduced on page 221 (Plate 12) shows the Drury Lane audience as seen from the stage and visibly supports this complaint. The reference to seeing Mrs Siddons in the country is a characteristic Combe touch; he had indeed seen her, as we know, ten years earlier at Lord Harcourt's country estate. And another change in the signature marks the article as by Combe: "X" in the newspaper, "C" in the book.

What London needs, the *Pic Nic* insists, is more theatres to share the patronage of these huge audiences. In the second issue of the paper a writer makes a telling point by contrasting London and its two theatres with Paris and its seventeen. The latter are listed by name, together with a brief description of the activities of each, showing the enormous variety thus made possible. Subsequent articles seem modest indeed when they ask merely for one more licensed theatre in London.

The *Pic Nic* reviews are candid, but they are thoughtfully written, temperate, and fair. One of the best of them appears in the second number (January 15), a discussion of *She Stoops to Conquer* at the Drury Lane, with Bannister as Tony Lumpkin. The writer compares it with the original production of 1773, in the old—and much smaller —Drury Lane. Combe himself could not have seen that production, for it took place while he was making a bare living with Roger Kemble's company of actors in the Midlands. But he had probably seen the original Tony Lumpkin when John Quick repeated the role in Bristol on August 23, 1775; it was Quick's greatest role and one of the triumphs of the century. (And Quick, it may be added, had performed in Combe's own play that summer.) Inevitably, the *Pic Nic* reviewer found the present performance of Tony Lumpkin greatly inferior to Quick's. Indeed, the entire production now at Drury Lane is inferior; Bannister is called an excellent comedian, but miscast in this role, which should have been assigned to Collins, another actor in Sheridan's company. The brunt of the criticism must thus be borne by the management, not the actors.

Criticism of the managers was indeed a novelty in the London press. Of this same Drury Lane performance, for example, the *Morning Post* (January 7) prudently remarked, "Considerable praise is due to the managers for the style in which the piece was brought forward, and the discrimination displayed in arranging the cast of characters." And of Bannister as Tony Lumpkin, the reviewer said, "We never knew him greater, nor perhaps anybody else so great." A month later (February 7) a paragrapher in the same paper was asking "what crimes the Pic Nics have committed that they are obliged to do penance once a week in a dirty sheet".

Subsequent issues of the *Pic Nic* and the *Cabinet* discuss Arthur Murphy's *The Way to Keep Him* (comparing a current revival with the original production of 1760 and praising Murphy's skill as a writer of comedies), Colman's *John Bull, or the Englishman's Fireside*, "Holcroft's lively though vulgar comedy of the *Road to Ruin*", and a few others more briefly treated. These reviews are in the same style as the first and set a new standard for newspaper critics of the theatre. At the same time, the *Pic Nic* carried general articles on the theatre, discussing such matters as the opening of the summer season at the Haymarket, the architecture of the Covent Garden and the Drury Lane, the relative merits of the productions at these playhouses, and the dangers implicit in government control of the stage. One issue contains an amusing dialogue in the manner of Dryden, in which three classically named speakers discuss theatrical matters, particularly the size of the London theatres. This article was contributed, we now know, by James Smith.[20] All the writers, however, reveal a knowledge of the subject far beyond that of the then usual newspaper reviewer; they know critical theory, stage history, and French as well as English theatrical practice. Although the *Pic Nic* was violently anti-Gallic in politics, the Pic Nic Society had been much interested in the Paris theatre, had produced plays in the French language, and had been accused, among other things, of trying to start a French theatre in London. This more cosmopolitan point of view brought a new (and in those times suspicious) breadth of outlook to the *Pic Nic*, adding force to the reiterated themes of the paper: the need for more and smaller theatres and for disinterested theatrical news and criticism.

As might have been expected, the *Pic Nic* inherited the abuse which had been heaped upon the Society. It seemed advisable in the second issue to say that there was no connection between the two, an assertion which slightly stretched the truth. In the eighth issue (February 26) a brief note announced that "the Pic Nic Society is at an end". But the name proved too strong a burden for the struggling paper, and after fourteen issues it was abandoned. The *Morning Post* (April 12) celebrated its passing with a verse elegy called, somewhat loosely, an imitation of Gray. But the following Saturday the same paper reappeared, now called the *Cabinet*. Some unspecified changes in the management had occurred, but the paper was to have the same contributors. Although Combe continued as editor, the official sponsor was now John Hatchard, from whose Piccadilly bookshop the *Cabinet* was published. Hatchard had had some vague connection with the *Pic Nic*; the editorial meetings, as we have seen, had been held after hours in his bookshop. But he now seems to have taken a financial interest in the publication. After twelve issues, however, the sponsors gave up the struggle. "Combe conducted the newspaper called the Cabinet, for which he had two guineas a week, but it is dropped", Farington duly noted in his diary.[21]

Even before the demise of the *Cabinet*, Combe had characteristically begun negotiating for new employment, and by July 1803 he had assumed new duties as "virtual editor"[22] of *The Times*. He was to hold this post for five years, and it was to prove the most responsible, most orderly, and most anonymous of his many careers.

* * *

When John Walter II became proprietor of *The Times* in January 1803 he found it on the verge of collapse. Circulation had dropped alarmingly, and profits were virtually non-existent. William Walter, his brother, who had taken the paper over from their father, had proved to be totally incompetent as proprietor, and there now seemed little chance that it would survive. Fortunately, the situation was so desperate that the younger John Walter was given a completely free hand, both in business management and in editorial policy. He had ideas about journalism which were then unheard of in newspaper offices. He wanted a well-written, efficiently managed paper, free to publish the news and express opinion without deferring to special interests or private parties. To achieve this end, he immediately set about reforming policies and gathering a new staff of writers. He could not, however, manage everything himself; in particular, he needed an experienced hand to supervise the writing staff and edit the paper. Within six months he brought "Old Combe" back to Printing House Square.

Combe was a logical choice for the position. He had been a highly productive writer and editor for the first John Walter from 1786 to the end of 1791, and although chiefly concerned with the affairs of the Logographic Press, he had written a good deal for *The Times* and had learned the routine of newspaper practice. Since that time he had come to be increasingly known and respected by printers and book-sellers in London. He was now conducting a weekly paper much interested in politics and the theatre and revealing in both respects attitudes very similar to Walter's. Men in the business would know that the *Cabinet* could not last much longer, and anyone seeking editorial assistance would think at once of the man who was conducting that expiring weekly. In any event, and even before the last issue of the *Cabinet* appeared, Combe began contributing to *The Times*. On June 8 the first of a series of letters appeared, all except the first signed "Valerius". They were stoutly written political articles similar to those which had regularly appeared in the *Pic Nic* and *Cabinet*. Given prominent position in *The Times*, often as leading articles, they seemed essentially the official voice of the newspaper.

Some years later Combe told Henry Crabb Robinson how he had agreed, at first reluctantly, to work for *The Times*. The two men were having dinner with Walter on November 16, 1812, when their host was suddenly called away by news of his father's death. The guests remained for a time, talking of the old man. Combe was the only one present who had actually known him, and he gave the others a colour-ful but essentially accurate account of the first John Walter's business methods. He told how contradiction and suppression fees were extracted from individuals about whom unflattering news had been printed or was about to be printed, the common practice of newspapers in that era. When the younger John Walter first approached him, Combe said, he had no reason to suppose that he was any different from his father and refused to enter into any permanent arrangement with him. Then an incident occurred which showed that the policies of the paper had indeed changed. An article had been published about a man named Travers, who had sent a contradiction together with £20 to get it published. Walter handed the letter to Combe and asked what should be done about it. "I suppose the £20 is a sufficient answer to the question," Combe cynically replied. But to his surprise, Walter thought it should be published and the money sent back. Combe in astonishment exclaimed, "Who got you?" Then he added, "Until you can get someone more useful to you than myself, I will stay with you. So have no more anxiety on that head."[23]

The story, like so many others told by Combe, does not quite check with the facts. Travers made a very indiscreet speech at the Guildhall on June 29, 1803. According to *The Times* of the following day, he had strongly opposed the income tax, saying, "If no other tax can be found less unjust, the Country ought to perish rather than owe its salvation to it." On July 1 a paragraph appeared saying that this was the sort of remark which might be expected in such a place as Cobbett's *Register*—condemnation indeed. Valerius referred to the matter on July 4. No letter from Travers is printed, though one appeared in the *Morning Chronicle*. On July 6 *The Times* did print a brief summary of the explanation which Travers had given in the *Chronicle* letter, but only to refute it. That ended the episode. But Combe's reference to Travers provides an acceptable date for the beginning of his work on *The Times*. The first Valerius letter appeared on June 8, the last issue of the *Cabinet* on July 2, the comments on Travers from June 30 to July 6. The force of these converging circumstances is not weakened by a chance reference to Sterne in the leading article for July 5. One may safely conclude that Combe took up his duties at *The Times* during the first week of July.

Combe's duties on *The Times* were largely supervisory, though he always did a certain amount of writing. He seems to have produced leading articles on occasion; perhaps he wrote them regularly, as his successor, John Stoddart, did. One may reasonably suspect that he wrote some of the dramatic criticism; a review (September 28, 1803) of a performance by Mrs Siddons, his one-time pupil in elocution, looks like his work and contains a telltale reference to Sterne. He wrote the obituary of his "old friend" Lord Harcourt which appeared on May 1, 1809. But it is useless to search for his contributions in *The Times*, which then spoke, as it continued to speak until 1967, with "disembodied voice". All contributions were anonymous, the earlier practice of occasionally appending initials having been abandoned. The only surviving account of Combe's work on the paper is that written by Henry Crabb Robinson, a colleague who joined the staff in 1807. The two men were often dinner companions at John Walter's table, and Robinson left a good many notes on their conversations in his diary. Toward the end of his life, when writing of this period in his *Reminiscences*, he recalled his association with the older man.

> There is another character who belongs to this period properly. And who as a character is more worth writing about than any individual connected with Walter. Indeed I have known few to compare with him.
>
> It was on my first acquaintance with Walter that I used to notice in his parlour a remarkably fine old Gentleman. He was tall with a stately figure and handsome face. Already advanced in life, he did not appear to work much with the pen but was chiefly the consulting not the operating man. When Walter travelled he used to be more at the office and to decide in the *dernier resort*.[24]

Having written so far, Robinson added, "His name was George Combe." Nowhere does he call him William; if he had ever heard Combe's first name, he was unable to remember it. No one seems to have been on a first-name basis with Combe; he was always addressed as Mr Combe, and in Robinson's time he was commonly referred to as Old Combe. There was both affection and a touch of amused toleration in the name.

Not only did John Walter II put a stop to contradiction and suppression fees; he went so far as to refuse puffs for current theatrical attractions, hitherto an important source of revenue. The historian of *The Times* says that this unheard-of policy so shocked the elder Walter that he partially disinherited his son.[25] But the new proprietor was firmly determined to free the paper from domination by the theatres, and his editor was prepared to give him strong support in achieving this end. That the two men were in complete agreement on this point is evident from a letter which Walter wrote in 1807 during his quarrel with Kemble over advertizing rates. Speaking in the third person, he wrote, "For his part [Mr Walter] thinks it would be for the interest of the papers in general to render themselves entirely independent of the theatres, and to do their duty to the Public by ceasing to make favourable misrepresentations of their performances."[26] The *Pic Nic* had expressed the same opinion repeatedly. Perhaps it had been unnecessary for Combe to suggest this position of independence or to urge Walter to adopt it, but we may be sure that the two men were in complete agreement on the policy. They were a good working team, and their friendship, which continued long after Combe left *The Times*, is evidence that they enjoyed the relationship.

One of their best decisions with respect to theatrical criticism was to bring Barron Field to *The Times*. This friend and correspondent of Charles Lamb's began writing play reviews during the 1805–6 season, and the quality of the *Times* criticism shows an immediate improvement. Something of the same thing was happening in other London papers; Leigh Hunt began writing for the *News* in May 1805, later transferring to the *Examiner*. On various occasions when Field was unable to write his reviews for *The Times*, Hunt substituted for him. It was, in fact, the beginning of modern dramatic criticism in the newspapers.[27] Perhaps the *Pic Nic* had not been alone in seeking this reform; perhaps *The Times* and its editor had the support of other newspapers as well as that of such critics as Hunt and Field, but their achievement of independent and competently written criticism of the theatre must have gratified the author of Colonel Greville's manifesto published in the first issue of the *Pic Nic*.

*   *   *

Combe's life as editor of *The Times* was not an easy one. He lived at 12 Lambeth Road, a good two-mile walk from Printing House Square, and he made his trips back and forth by foot unless, as was sometimes the case, he caught a coach for part of the way. The nature of his work on a morning newspaper, as well as the rather casual vigilance of the tipstaff, made it necessary for him to take these trips out of the Rules by night. He seems to have managed on less sleep than most people require, getting home from the office at from three to five o'clock in the morning and sleeping until ten or at the latest noon. Once he mentions not getting to bed at all. His afternoons were devoted to personal matters, writing letters, paying and receiving calls, reading, and trying as usual to keep one step ahead of his creditors.

One afternoon in the spring of 1804 he wrote the following somewhat mysterious letter:

Wednesday afternoon

Sir,

    You have every reason to complain of me, & I equally acknowledge the liberality of your particular conduct, in this disagreable [sic] business. I have only to observe that I am exerting every nerve to put an end to it, & prevent the unpleasant consequences of legal process. Nor am I without the most sanguine hope that this will still be in my power. — I am

Your most obed^t hble Servt

Lambeth Road Wm Combe

On the outside the letter is addressed, "Mr. Reardon, Attorney at Law, Corbet Court, Grace-Church Street." It is postmarked April 27, 1804.[28]

Daniel Reardon was attorney for Stephen Casey, whose long-postponed action against Combe was now resumed. Casey, as we have seen, owned the madhouse in which Maria was confined, a place duly licensed by the Royal College of Physicians. It was located on the west side of Greengate Street, just off Barking Road, Plaistow, Essex, some twelve miles east of St Paul's.[29] When the case finally came before the King's Bench in the spring of 1805 Combe was formally charged with a debt which now amounted to £400 "for meat, drink, washing, lodging, cloaths, and other necessaries by the said Stephen before that time found and provided for Maria, the wife of the said William at the special instance and request of the said William".[30] The tedious process dragged on until November 27, when Combe, though already in nominal custody, was again committed until such time as he should pay the stated debt, together with costs and damages of £193. 10s.—in all, nearly £600. This new judgement against Combe did not necessitate his return to prison, but it would call for additional security, which John Walter would be expected to provide, and also for an additional fee, perhaps thirty-five guineas, payable to the Marshall for the privilege of continuing to live within the Rules. And so, for a time, Combe's life might continue as before.

Another source of concern during these years was his interrupted employment as propagandist for the Government. Pitt's first administration ended in February 1801, just when Combe's political *Brief Observations* appeared. He immediately applied to Addington for a renewal of the arrangement, but his services were declined in a courteous letter enclosing an additional half-year's pay, £100, "that the suddenness of my dismission might not prove an inconvenience to me". Pitt resumed office in 1804, however, and Combe was reappointed, serving until that Minister died in January 1806. Then, to Combe's intense annoyance, he was unable to collect the last £100 due him, even after Lord Mulgrave had interceded in his behalf. He wrote Mulgrave a long and eloquent letter setting forth these and other such details as he wished to disclose and arguing the justice of his claim.[31] Acknowledging that he had not been very active recently on behalf of the Government, he wrote, "The latter months did not admit of my venturing my own unauthorized opinions; but I never hesitated when I saw my way clear before me. I wanted instruction and I did not receive it." Except for the pamphlet which he had published in 1801, his political writing in recent years had taken the form of strongly pro-Government articles in the *Pic Nic* and *Cabinet*, the Valerius letters first published in *The Times* and then reprinted in book form, and the leading articles which he had written or supervised for *The Times*.

Mulgrave replied to this letter on March 13, 1806, expressing regret at Combe's disappointment, but saying that it was now beyond his power to change the situation.[32] This response struck Combe as by no means doing justice to his mistreatment, and he did not readily forget slights. A year or so later, when Mulgrave had become First Lord of the Admiralty in the Portland Administration, he passed Combe sitting on a bench in St James's Park and stopped to greet him. Farington recorded the story as told him by John Taylor. "Combe, without rising, answered him carelessly and without any respect, and after a slight conversation Lord M. left him, feeling himself rather rejected than encouraged and comparing, he said to Taylor, the profound attention paid to him at the Admiralty with the repulsive manner of Combe."[33]

* * *

Combe's needs were not fully satisfied by the recognition which he received as a man of letters and as one long accustomed to associate with important people. That was his public image, and his ego was gratified by it, but privately he was a lonely man deprived of the warmth and affection which others find in the family circle. Whether he could respond fully to warmth and affection may be doubted, but he was always searching for intimate companionship. He was admitted to various family groups at one time or another, but only as an outsider, a family friend, a welcome caller—sometimes, alas, a bit tedious. He was befriended by the Cosways in the 1790s, and though he eloped with Maria Cosway's sister the family accepted the relationship and he remained a close friend and confidant, particularly of Mrs Cosway. After living with him for perhaps four years, Charlotte went off to Ireland and he was again left alone. Evidently he and Charlotte at some time adopted a daughter, though she remains a shadowy figure whom he only once alludes to, and then as a disappointment.[34] According to Henry Crabb Robinson, recalling Combe in later years, "He used to be attended by a young man who was a sort of half servant, half companion, and who Walter said was his natural son."[35] Another writer, one rather closer to Combe's personal affairs than either Robinson or Walter, identifies the youth as an adopted son whom Combe educated and later, after some disagreement, repudiated.[36] All of Combe's attempts to establish intimate personal relationships seem, indeed, to have ended in disappointment.

During his years in Lambeth Road he occasionally called on "the ladies in Edgware Road", the home of Mrs Stevens, and it was there that he met Marianne Brooke, a young woman who was sometimes employed as a seamstress. Marianne was kind to him and, it must be inferred, exploited the relationship. As the acquaintance grew into a sentimental attachment Combe lavished Marianne and her family with gifts and, according to one angry acquaintance, changed the whole tenor of their lives, supplying most of the furnishings of a house they took in Camberwell. After Combe's death, his letters to Marianne were published in a small volume "by William Combe, Esq." It was edited by a man named Birch who had taken a room with the Brookes and to whom Marianne had transferred her affections. The publication gave great offence to Combe's friends, one of whom—evidently Anthony Ryves, the son of his landlady—copiously annotated a copy of the book which is now in the British Museum.[37] The annotations together with the forty-three letters supply a running comment on Combe's life between December 29, 1806, and the spring of 1809.

Were it not for the absurdity of the relationship, the *Letters to Marianne* would have a certain faded charm, fatuous as some of them undeniably are. Combe was once more playing his role as Man of Feeling, which he had learned forty years earlier under the tutelage of Laurence Sterne, but Marianne was ignorant of that outworn convention. Twice Combe sent her books in the sentimental vein, but she failed to understand the message. The friendship was well established by the end of 1806, when Combe invited Marianne to spend New Year's Eve with him, hearing Madame Catalani at the Opera and then on the following evening to go with him to the theatre. "It will give me an opportunity of closing this year, and beginning the new one with *you*." Two weeks later he wrote, "Your whole acquaintance with me has been one continued scene of affectionate offices, kind expressions, and graceful attentions: it occupies, as yet, but a few months; nevertheless, you have crowded as much goodness into that short space, as would, in the ordinary course of things, be sufficient for as many years." Clearly Marianne was playing her hand adroitly, for the annotator here remarks, "Mr. Combe used to present her with most handsome presents." After another six weeks, Combe invited her to attend a performance of Handel's *Messiah*, and on another occasion he suggested that they go to the Covent Garden to see Mrs Siddons as Lady Macbeth.

The letters often contain references to his trips to and from the office, and these supply personal details otherwise entirely missing from the chronicle of his life. Once he writes, "I repassed the bridge this morning as St. Paul's struck three; and in all my pilgrimages over those arches, I never experienced such an inhospitable passage—rain, storm, and cold!—The very lamps were generally extinguished, and I had no light either from heaven or earth." One morning he arrived home at four "after two miles walk through fog and frost"; another time he reported, "I encountered a storm which made a perfect water-butt of me." These trips inevitably took their toll, and on occasion Combe was forced to stay in bed to nurse a cold. Marianne evidently made solicitous inquiries about his health, and he often gave her a report. In one letter he speaks of being summoned to the office in mid-morning and not returning home until 2 a.m. the following day. "The want of rest, for I had not time to lay down as I proposed, and the great exertions I was obliged to make throughout the day, brought on a giddiness in my head, so that I reeled about like a drunken man, and was obliged sometimes to rest against the rails of the houses to recover myself." It cannot have been the life a man of sixty-five would choose, but Combe never spoke of it with self-pity.

One letter—and only one—deserves quotation in full:

Monday, March 9, 1807

My Dear Marianne,

As it is the modern practice of all *great men*, when they are sick, to publish a daily account of their situation, it becomes me to adopt the custom. Yesterday I arose, after a night of interrupted sleep, in a state of depression, which I never before experienced. I was, for the first time in my life, afflicted with a morbid melancholy: I could not read, I could not write; the sun appeared to shine bright to every eye but mine, so I darkened my room, and sat in a moping mood till near three o'clock, when a gush of involuntary tears convinced me that I must resist the wretched and increasing propensity; and, having received an invitation to dinner, from a medical acquaintance, a very experienced man, and who is ever ready to manifest kind dispositions to me, I roused myself, and went to him. He was at table with his family when I arrived, and when I had taken my seat, he proposed to me to take off my great-coat, so loosely did my common-coat hang about me. In short, I appeared so different from what he had always seen me, that he insisted on my taking a glass of wine,—if he had proposed hemlock, I should have been very indifferent about it, so I tasted Madeira for the first time in my life; but I drank your health in it, and down it went. It neither did me good nor harm; and I returned home with a prescription in my pocket, which I have not read, to dream of dragons and griffins, and other monsters of a sickly imagination.

This morning my head is a great deal better; but the depression of spirits still distresses me: I have not laughed for two days; and I purpose, at present, to go and dine with one of the cleverest men in Europe. We shall be alone, and he is always kind and indulgent to me; so I shall see what his highly illuminated mind can do for me. To-morrow I shall go to Mr. Lonsdale, for I must get the picture done, while any thing of a good look remains, or he will get no credit from it.—I shall call in my way, to ask you how you do; though I cannot flatter myself with the hope that you can fulfil your intention of accompanying me thither. At all events, you will, perhaps have the goodness to write me a line or two by my Mercury, to let me have the very great pleasure of knowing that your cold and its accompaniments have been alleviated.

I remain your ever affectionate friend,
W. Combe[38]

The editor supplies a footnote to the wine-drinking episode, explaining that Combe drank nothing but water, an eccentricity already mentioned in the present work. The annotator has pencilled two comments in the margin. The "medical acquaintance" is identified as Jesse Foot of Dean Street, Soho. (Combe was later to compile his *Life of Arthur Murphy*.) And Lonsdale is revealed as a relative of the Brooke family. That Lonsdale actually finished the picture we know, since he exhibited it at the Royal Academy that same spring. Nearly twenty years later he wrote to someone who had known Combe, "I shall be much obliged if you will have the goodness to cause my picture of the late Mr. Combe to be sent to me, Mr. C. borrowed this picture of me to show to some friend, and kept it till his death."[39] The painting is now lost or unidentified.

Many references to Charlotte Combe in Ireland occur among these letters to Marianne. On February 11, 1807, he speaks of receiving a long letter from Mrs C——. "She tells me, I have not sent her any thing since the new year," he writes, and asks Marianne to find some material and make a little present which he may send his wife in Marianne's name. The commentator dourly adds, "For which Mr. Combe paid her. Before Mr. Combe became acquainted with them, they got their bread by satin stitch!" A month later he was sending Marianne a gift (two pairs of Limerick gloves) from his wife, and with it a part of her accompanying letter, "to let you see how she expresses herself to me respecting your kindness to her. . . . She thanks me again and again for my interesting account, as she calls it, of the B——'s family." Here the annotator has written, "Mr. Combe in the hight [*sic*] of his infatuation represented the whole of the B family in a most interesting point of view. So much so that Mrs. C. felt it a bounden duty to pay them every attention possible in return." Some time later (Combe seldom dated his letters) he wrote, "I have this moment received a letter from Ireland of twelve pages, written at different times, so that Mrs. C—— I am sure is not well, though she writes in apparently very good spirits. . . . She wishes for a variety of things to be sent." In March 1809 she has written "to request that I would send her some silk-worms' eggs in a letter". Whatever else Charlotte's letters contained, they seem always to have included requests.

* * *

Combe's nightly violation of the Rules of the King's Bench could not but finally come to the attention of the authorities, and in June 1808 they took action. "It will, I very much fear, be some time before I shall have the pleasure of seeing you again", Combe wrote to Marianne. "The unpleasant circumstance which you know has been for a considerable period hanging over me, has, and without the least immediate intimation, at length overtaken me." The pencilled annotation explains, "Mr. Jones and Mr. Brooshoof met Mr. C. under the Asylum Wall and insisted upon his going within the Walls of K.B." William Jones was the Marshal, B. E. Brooshoof one of his assistants. The Asylum, or House of Refuge, founded by Sir John Fielding for the protection of orphaned girls, stood in Mead Place, just outside the Rules and on Combe's way to and from Marianne's house in Camberwell.

It was, of course, necessary for Combe to let John Walter know what had happened, and he wrote as follows:

King's Bench, Wednesday morn.

My dear Sir

It will astonish you for I am sure it has astonished myself that I am at this moment an Inhabitant of this place and that instead of the pleasure of attending you last night, I had the very great displeasure of being conducted here. I was liable to it, but having escaped for five years I thought myself safe from any inconvenience. Nor can I well devise the malice wh[h] has operated on the occasion for malice it must have been.—But so it is—I need not add that it will be necessary for us to meet. It was a most fortunate circumstance however that I had obtained some knowledge of Colonel Dennis or I should not have had a place to lay my head upon; and at his Apartment in the *State House* of this building I am at present to be found— God bless us all I say—that it should happen at the present moment is abominably vexatious. But who can controul his fate——

Your most obliged and humble Serv[t]
W. C.[40]

These letters had both been written on a Wednesday morning, and surviving records of the King's Bench show that Combe availed himself of the Day Rules to leave the prison on Wednesday, June 29, and again on Saturday and Monday, July 2 and 4.[41] In less than a week, that is, he used the three privileges he would be allowed until the next term of court beginning in October. These privileges were intended to permit prisoners to come to some arrangement with their creditors, but Combe presumably used them to wind up his affairs at *The Times* office. The urgency of unfinished business evidently compelled him to take his Day Rule privilege the morning after his arrest. But on the third of his expeditions outside the walls he also had a social engagement.

It is Farington again who tells of the dinner party given on July 4, 1808, by William Smith, a politician and patron of the arts. In addition to Farington and Combe, the guests were mostly artists with whom both had long been intimate: Thomas Lawrence, Martin Shee, William Beechey, Robert Smirke, George Nicoll, Henry Thomson, Joseph Nollekens, and Thomas Rickman. Several members of the host's family were also at the table, including his adopted daughter, Sarah Williamson Smith, the talented young actress then beginning her career at the Covent Garden Theatre. Perhaps Combe met her for the first time that evening; in any event, as we shall see, they soon became good friends. It was the kind of gathering which Combe most enjoyed and in which he displayed his conversational talents to advantage. He was seated to the left of his host, and after the latter proposed a toast, "Success to the Spaniards", Combe talked knowledgeably about that country, at the moment engaged in a struggle with Napoleon. There is no evidence that anyone present was aware that Combe was due back at the Bench before the gates closed. Farington would have been sure to mention it had he known.[42]

For his first night in prison Combe was a guest in the State House, but he was soon established there in one of the choicest rooms, Number 2 on the top floor,[43] with its view out over the prison wall to the distant hills of Kent and Surrey. (In the engraving reproduced here, Plate 13, the State House may be seen in the left background.) He made himself comfortable, seldom left his room, received callers, and systematically went about his writing. He managed to convey the impression of a man quite at ease with his lot, philosophically accepting confinement as an opportunity to work without distraction.

But there were distractions. "Some time ago," he wrote in his private notebook, "in the State House Stair-case, there was an outrage committed which woke me out of my sleep . . . and continued for at least two hours, with an alarming violence as was proved by not only pulling down the door of a room, but the very frame and brickwork to which it was attached." He had complained to the authorities of the fifty or sixty boys who used the yard as their public playground until the gate closed at night. "My complaint", he wrote, "is that such a noise is made by them, who have no right to be in the

13. *King's Bench Prison, 1809. From the Microcosm of London, by Pugin and Rowlandson*

place, to the disturbance of those who are compelled to be there. . . .
This evening I was saluted with the title of the Bloody old Thief, who`
wanted to turn out the boys."[44] The indignity was even more painful
than the uproar.

It was no longer possible for him to call on the Brookes with
presents for the family or to take Marianne to the theatre, and the
monotonous days provided little he could suitably write letters about.
The correspondence continued, though with visibly declining interest
on both sides. On April 26, 1809, Combe wrote, "My old friend,
Lord Harcourt, is dead. I am told he has left me fifty pounds to purchase anything I please, as a memorial of him." And he promptly
composed a long, effusive tribute to Lord Harcourt which was printed
in *The Times* on May 1. But Combe was not mentioned in Lord Harcourt's will,[45] and the family, to Combe's disappointment, took no
notice of the article. Only one more letter to Marianne is published;
though others may have been written, the correspondence soon
lapsed. According to the annotator, Combe was heartily sick of it
before it ended. He was never so entangled again; though he subsequently enjoyed the friendship of various young ladies, his relationship with them involved no such awkward situation as had arisen with
the predatory Miss Brooke.

On New Year's Day 1811, Combe wrote a long letter to his friend,
Edward Jerningham, in reply to one received more or less by accident
at the Bench. There was no delivery of letters from the prison post
office, and he did not care to crowd in with the other prisoners inquir-
ing there for mail. He expected to be addressed at 12 Lambeth Road,
where someone would deliver his letters by hand. Combe tells Jerningham of his life in the State House, omitting the more unpleasant
details:

I am in excellent health and admirable spirits, & in the full enjoyment
of Mr. Pope's trio of human comforts, Food, Cloaths, and Fire.—Nay more,
I am in the uncontrouled and uninterrupted possession of my own thoughts.—
In this populous spot, I know not a single person; and out of my apartment
which is spacious, airy and commanding no common prospects, both metro-
politan and provincial, I have never been but four times in two years, but
for a few necessary minutes in the Evening.—I took two country walks in
June,[46] one of which was sixteen miles and the other eighteen; and in the
beginning of the last month, My peregrinations were not less than twelve
miles, with a little variation into Town to look at the outside of Covent
Garden Theatre, which has not a trace of Taste or science,—nor did I

return to my den with any other sensation of fatigue than just made my chair pleasant to me. . . .

The fact is I live with my own thoughts; and you will readily believe that I have time enough to indulge them when I tell you, that I never rise later than nine, and that I never retire to my Hammock before two.[47]

Jerningham replied, telling Combe that he would mention to Lady Harcourt the *Times* memorial, "which in my opinion should have induced her to express her thanks in writing", and sent a copy of his "little poem", *The Old Bard's Farewell*, inscribed "To William Combe, Esq., with Mr. Jerningham's respectful compliments".[48]

Combe was to remain in his "den" until mid-1812,[49] four years in all, much the longest of his three terms of imprisonment. His career as journalist was necessarily terminated, for Walter was forced to employ someone else to take his place (John Stoddart, Hazlitt's brother-in-law). But during these years Combe was busily initiating a new career as comic poet, writing *The Schoolmaster's Tour* for serial publication, retitled when published in book form *The Tour of Doctor Syntax in Search of the Picturesque*. Nothing which he had ever written could have suggested that he was capable of producing a comic poem, but this work which he completed at the age of seventy was to prove enormously popular and give him an anonymous reputation for over a century.

CHAPTER VIII

COMIC POET

I'll make a tour,—and then I'll write it.
You well know what my pen can do,
And I'll employ my pencil too:—
I'll ride and write, and sketch and print,
And thus create a real mint;
I'll prose it here, I'll verse it there,
And picturesque it ev'ry where.
                              —Doctor Syntax

COMBE BEGAN his four-year prison term shortly after his sixty-sixth birthday, and in the remaining fifteen years of his life he produced a continuous stream of prose and verse amounting finally to more than thirty volumes. In sheer bulk, this output has probably not been equalled by any other writer at a comparable time of life. Much of it, to be sure, can only be called competent hackwork, but a good deal of it remains curiously interesting today. A number of the works which he produced at this time have been reprinted in the twentieth century.

This phase of Combe's career came at a time when the hand-coloured aquatint was at the height of its popularity, and much of his work consisted in producing commentary to accompany plates and so to justify their publication in book form. The aquatints were and are charming, but the printed matter was ordinarily regarded as of secondary importance. The names of the artist and engraver were given prominence; the author of the letterpress was seldom mentioned. The first publishers to make extensive use of the aquatint process were John and Josiah Boydell, and their most successful venture was the two-volume *History of the Thames*. Combe, as we have seen, wrote the letterpress.

Even while the Boydells were publishing the *Thames* at their Shakespeare Gallery in Pall Mall, Rudolph Ackermann opened a rival shop, the Repository of Arts, at 101 Strand, the site today of the Savoy Hotel. Ackermann was a good businessman and a friend of artists and the arts. Dealing in prints, artists' supplies, and books relating to the arts, he established a thriving business which remained in the hands of the family until World War II. In 1808, just when Combe was taking up residence in the Bench, Ackermann was beginning to publish one of the most successful of all aquatint-letterpress works, the *Microcosm of London*. Ultimately the three volumes contained 104 plates, the joint work of the elder Pugin and Thomas Rowlandson; Pugin engraved the architectural details, Rowlandson the figures. The first two volumes appeared in monthly parts through 1808 and into 1809, the letterpress being supplied by W. H. Pyne; the third volume, which began to appear in April 1809, was written by Combe.

For the rest of his life Combe was to be engaged in this kind of journeyman work, writing prose and verse to accompany aquatints, chiefly those turned out by Ackermann's staff of engravers and colourists. The books produced by this collaboration include many items highly prized by collectors today: *History of Westminster Abbey* (1812), *Antiquities of York* (1813), *Poetical Sketches of Scarborough* (1813), the histories of *Oxford* (1814), *Cambridge* (1815), the *Colleges* (1816), *Maderia* (1821), and most important of all his work with Rowlandson, the three *Tours of Doctor Syntax* (1812, 1820, 1821), the *Dance of Death* (1815, 1816), the *Dance of Life* (1817), and *Johnny Quae Genus* (1822). During these years he also produced similar books for other publishers, including *The Thames, or Graphic Illustrations* (1811), *Picturesque Views on the Southern Coast* (1826), and *Pompeii* (1827).

To call this massive accomplishment hackwork is by no means to suggest that it is negligible. Much of it was routine work written to order, but something of interest may be found in nearly every volume of what the author called his "ordinary drudgery". Nor can all of this writing be called routine. The compilation of seven hundred pages on Westminster Abbey, for example, required a diligent search for information, and many volumes of antiquarian lore must have been brought to his quarters while he was performing this assignment. There was certainly no library in the Bench, yet Combe manages to cite learned authorities and even gives the impression of carefully sifting his evidence. The work is, in fact, a considerable piece of scholarship which goes far to substantiate his claim to the title of historian. Inevitably he occasionally falls into his "empty" style, a kind of non-committal automatic writing which with many flourishes says virtually nothing. But what was there to say about one monument after another? It was necessary to fill the pages between the prints, and fill them he did. The list of nearly seven hundred subscribers ranges from Her Majesty the Queen and His Royal Highness the Prince Regent to William Combe, Esq. It is unlikely that any subscriber felt compelled to read the two elephant quarto volumes straight through, but anyone idly turning the pages would be impressed by the astonishing variety of sources quoted by the author.

The same kind of painstaking compilation is present to some extent in most of these volumes. The little-known *History of Maderia*, written when Combe was nearly eighty, is an interesting example. After the usual introductory history with its factual information, this book contains a series of coloured prints "by a resident of the island". They have a naïveté which evidently appealed to Combe as, indeed, they appeal still. He described each in simple prose followed by a set of tetrameter couplets. These verses are trifles and they pretend to be no more, but they add a certain charm to the last book of this kind which he wrote.

One work from this period, and one only, deserves attention purely on the score of Combe's letterpress, and this it has received to an astonishing degree from a certain class of readers and even, though grudgingly, from literary historians. Before Combe had been in prison a year the first numbers of his comic poem, *The Schoolmaster's Tour*, began appearing in Ackermann's *Poetical Magazine*, accompanied by Rowlandson's most famous series of prints. When it had run its course, it was carefully revised, enlarged, and published in book form as *The Tour of Doctor Syntax in Search of the Picturesque* (1812). For over a century it was to be a household favourite in many countries, and not merely for the celebrated aquatints which it was written to illustrate. The story of this curious "poem" is one of the oddest in the annals of literary history, but the work is not merely an oddity. The character of the absurd but somehow winning clergyman could not have caught the fancy of so many readers, however unsophisticated, had it not been conceived with imagination and portrayed in the verses as well as in the prints with verve and originality. Doctor Syntax is the last of a notable line descending remotely from

Don Quixote and more immediately from Parsons Adams and Primrose. He merits his place among those eccentrics.

* * *

Three men collaborated in creating the estimable Doctor Syntax,
though a fourth is said to have suggested the character and a fifth to
some extent provided a model. Thomas Rowlandson (1756–1827),
the gifted artist and caricaturist, had found a friend and patron in the
enterprising art dealer, Rudolph Ackermann (1764–1834), who was,
however, hard pressed to find an ample market for the energetic and
even more hard-pressed artist. By midwinter 1808–9, the great
Microcosm of London was going well, though Ackermann by that time
was looking for someone to write the letterpress for the third volume.
If a de luxe publication could be successful, as this one was, perhaps a
popular series in a light vein would appeal to a larger audience,
especially if production costs could be reduced and the price set somewhat lower. But what subject would best serve this purpose? In
addition to having an appeal for the general reader, it must suit the
comic genius of the artist and be capable of indefinite continuation as
long as the public remained willing to buy copies. It was a problem
which only Rowlandson could finally resolve.

One evening early in 1809 the artist talked the matter over with
John Bannister, the actor. He was planning, he said, "to sketch a
series, where the object may be made ridiculous without much thinking". He had recently been travelling in Devonshire and Cornwall
making sketches along the coast, and his travelling companion on that
trip had suggested himself as a sufficiently absurd hero of such a
series. Another artist might have found him a suitable subject: he
weighed rather more than three hundred pounds. Although Rowlandson may have been tempted—he spoke of him as a "walking turtle"—
he decided against using a fat man as hero. "I want one of a totally
different description," he said, and mentioned William Gilpin as a
possible model. Gilpin had long been famous as a sketching traveller
and as author of "picturesque tours". Although he had died in 1804,
the republication of his tours in 1808 had again brought his name
before the public. The thought of portraying an itinerant sketching
parson and schoolmaster was thus already forming in Rowlandson's
mind when Bannister took up the idea.

"I have it!" exclaimed the actor, and proceeded to describe a subject closely resembling Doctor Syntax. "You must fancy a skin-and-bone hero, a pedantic old prig, in a shovel-hat, with a pony, sketching tools, and rattletraps, and place him in such scrapes as travellers frequently meet with,—hedge ale-houses, second and third-rate inns, thieves, gibbets, mad bulls, and the like", adding a few other unspecified suggestions. This enthusiasm and possibly some of these ideas helped crystallize the artist's plan, but there is no occasion to give Bannister full credit for conceiving the work. His biographer, however, who tells this story, had no doubt about it. "Bannister gave his ideas, Rowlandson adopted them, Coombes explained them by a well-written poem; and to this conversation, and to the lively invention of Bannister, the public is indebted for a highly favoured publication, 'The Tour of Dr. Syntax.' "[1] However this may be, one is justified in believing that the conversation took place and that Rowlandson was encouraged by his friend.

The artist began turning out drawings of Doctor Syntax and his adventures at once, working with his usual rapidity and producing more sketches than were ever used in the published work.[2] It only remained for Ackermann to find his writer. Fortunately, he learned at this time that the very man who had produced the admirable prose descriptions for the *History of the River Thames* was still doing journeyman work for the booksellers and was at the moment confined in the King's Bench Prison. A walk across the bridge would bring Ackermann to Combe's door, Number 2 in the State House of the Bench, and there was no possibility of finding him not at home. The two men conferred, and quickly reached an understanding which was to continue without interruption until Combe's death fourteen years and many books later.

It was a gentleman's agreement rather than a formal contract. Combe undertook to supply Ackermann with letterpress for his various publications. He would write the third volume of the *Microcosm of London*, would contribute a monthly feature for Ackermann's magazine, the *Repository of Arts*, and would produce other miscellaneous hackwork as needed. And he would write comic verses to accompany Rowlandson's caricatures. No explicit fee or salary was stipulated; instead, Combe was given a drawing account. Years later Ackermann was to remark that Combe never ceased to draw until he ceased to breathe.[3] Had a fixed amount been guaranteed, it would

[244]

14–21 (opposite): *the title-page of the Tour of Doctor Syntax, by Rowlandson, followed by seven of the plates, actual size. The originals are hand-coloured aquatints.*

THE TOUR

of

DOCTOR SYNTAX,

In Search of the

A Poem.

Ut Pictura, Poesis erit; quæ, si propius stes,
Te capiat magis: et quædam, si longius abstes.
Hæc amat obscurum; volet hæc sub luce videri;
Judicis argutum quæ non formidat acumen:
Hæc placuit semel, hæc decies repetita placebit.

Horat. Ars. Poet.

Plate 1.

London. Pub. 1st May 1812, at R. Ackermann's Repository of Arts 101.Strand.

DOCTOR SYNTAX.

SETTING OUT ON HIS TOUR TO THE LAKES.

Designed & Etched by. Rowlandson.

Plate 11.

London. Published May 1.1812. at R. Ackermann's Repository of Arts 101 Strand.

Design'd & Etch'd by Rowlandson.

DOCTOR SYNTAX TUMBLING INTO THE WATER.

Plate 17.

London, Pub. May 1812, at R.Ackermann's Repository of Arts, 101, Strand.

Design'd & Etch'd by Rowlandson.

DOCTOR SYNTAX DRAWING AFTER NATURE.

Plate 20.

London. Published 1 May 1812, at R. Ackermann's Repository of Arts 101. Strand.

DOCTOR SYNTAX. RURAL SPORT.

Designd & Etchd by Rowlandson.

Plate 33

London. Publish'd May 1 1812 at Ackermann's Repository of Arts, 101, Strand.

Design'd & Etch'd by Rowlandson.

DOCTOR SYNTAX READING HIS TOUR.

Plate 25.

London. Pub.¹ May 1.ª 1812, at R.Ackermann's Repository of Arts, 101, Strand.

Designd & Etchd by Rowlandson.

DOCTOR SYNTAX & BOOKSELLER.

Plate 29.

London, Publish'd May 1, 1812 at R. Ackermann's Repository of Arts 101 Strand.

Design'd & Etch'd by Rowlandson.

DOCTOR SYNTAX Taking Possession of his Living.

have rendered Combe vulnerable to his creditors and their lawyers, whom he had no intention of paying. John Timbs, who later came to know Combe and various people associated with him, was confident that Ackermann paid the writer "a sum sufficient to support him respectably".[4] He thought that Combe must have received not less than £400 a year, and in view of the continuous flow of copy from the writer's pen during those years, the amount does not seem excessive. Nor did it seem so to Ackermann, whose son was later to say that Combe "was supplied liberally, his works were profitable, and the publisher was satisfied".[5]

Combe went to work without delay. The first part of his *Microcosm* volume appeared in April 1809, as did his first contribution to the *Repository of Arts*, where he began a sentimental series of monthly items called "Amelia's Letters". Ackermann's new monthly, the *Poetical Magazine*, made its appearance on May 1, carrying the first instalment of *The Schoolmaster's Tour* with one of the best prints Rowlandson prepared for this series. Some attempt was made to create a magazine as absurd as the poem; it was to consist entirely of verse, even including advertisements and death notices—though the magazine contained few of either. According to the Prospectus (published in the April *Repository*), it offered itself as "a receptable of inoffensive poetic compositions of every kind". In addition to *The Schoolmaster's Tour*, which forms the leading feature of each issue, the magazine contained poems by a large number of contributors, many of them visibly amateurs. Two coloured aquatint plates appeared in each issue, one and sometimes both relating to Doctor Syntax. The magazine was edited by Ackermann's trusty hack, Frederic Schoberl, who also edited the *Repository* and various other publications. Combe evidently wrote much of the secondary material, including most of the descriptions accompanying topographical prints. Many of the shorter pieces are signed "W. C**e", "C", "Comicus", and "Lambeth Road". But the success of the magazine—for it *was* successful—derived from the immediate popularity of *The Schoolmaster's Tour*. It ran for two years, then when publication ceased the twenty-four monthly numbers and four supplements were bound into four volumes. Of the supplements, only the last contains any part of the *Tour*, and it gives some evidence of haste in rounding out the story, rather as though the decision to terminate the magazine had been made on short notice.

The Syntax narrative was unique in more ways than one. Combe himself knew that it was a strange performance and described it in the Advertisement to the printed volume:

> The following Poem, if it may be allowed to deserve the name, was written under circumstances, whose peculiarity may be thought to justify a communication of them.——I undertook to give metrical Illustrations of the Prints with which Mr. Ackermann decorated the *Poetical Magazine.* . . . [He explains that he wrote the copy which accompanied most of the miscellaneous prints as well as those concerned with Dr. Syntax.] Those designs alone to which this volume is so greatly indebted, I was informed would follow in a series, and it was proposed to me to shape a story from them.—An Etching or a Drawing was accordingly sent to me every month, and I composed a certain proportion of pages in verse, in which, of course, the subject of the design was included: the rest depended upon what my imagination could furnish.—When the first print was sent to me, I did not know what would be the subject of the second; and in this manner, in a great measure, the Artist continued designing, and I continued writing, every month for two years, 'till a work, containing near ten thousand Lines was produced: the Artist and the Writer having no personal communication with, or knowledge of each other.

Although Combe and Rowlandson did not meet while this joint work was going forward, we need not suppose that there was no communication between them. At first, certainly, Combe took his hints from the drawings which were sent him, though much that is most characteristic of the early cantos is entirely his own. As the work progresses, Rowlandson gives evidence of picking up hints from the verses. Nor was the scheme of the book entirely left to chance; as early as Canto XII, Combe is setting in motion the action that will eventually conclude the book, and in the final cantos the prints provide a suitable background for the intended conclusion. Combe and Rowlandson may not have conferred, but they understood each other's intentions. The most likely intermediary is Rudolph Ackermann, the active third party to the collaboration.

* * *

A year elapsed between the final issue of the *Poetical Magazine* and the separate publication of *The Tour of Doctor Syntax in Search of the Picturesque*. During the interval Rowlandson prepared a frontispiece portrait of Doctor Syntax and an absurd title-page in which the word

Picturesque is spelled out partly in tumbling ruins, partly with letters engraved on a stone (Plate 14)—preliminary notice of the satire in store for the reader. Combe meanwhile carefully revised the entire text, substantially improving it. (A few further improvements and corrections were introduced in the second edition, the text quoted in this book.)[6] A new canto also appears in the separate publication, "The Battle of the Books", but whether the verses and the plate were prepared at this time or had been prepared earlier and omitted when the *Poetical Magazine* was hastening to its end is not known. The canto has the appearance of an afterthought, which is what Combe called it in his Advertisement. It bears no structural relationship to the rest of the poem, but merely forms a commentary on the anachronistic ways of Doctor Syntax in a hostile world.

Ackermann announced the new book for May 1, 1812, priced one guinea with the plates, ten shillings sixpence without them.[7] No copy of the separately published verses has come to light, but the advertisement of such a volume shows that popular interest did not centre exclusively in the plates. In the century that followed several editions appeared without them, and others with altogether different illustrations. But Rowlandson's talents and Combe's so perfectly complement each other that separate publication would now be inconceivable.

The opening lines establish at once the tone of the tour and the character of the good Doctor. Rowlandson's aquatint shows Syntax issuing from his door to mount a nag which is being held by an unkempt ostler. As he draws on his gloves, the departing traveller blandly ignores the admonishments of his wife, who stands at the door visibly imparting her instructions (Plate 15). Combe need only be shown this sketch and told that subsequent plates would show the good man "in such scrapes as travellers frequently meet with" to enter at once into the spirit of the project. So, now, could any reader of Goldsmith, Fielding, and Smollett. Even the hero's name would not be far to seek: Doctor Syntax, obviously, proverbial name for a clerical pedant.

Combe immediately sets the scene with gusto and establishes the mood of relaxed good humour:

> The School was done, the bus'ness o'er,
> When, tir'd of Greek and Latin lore,
> Old Syntax sought his easy chair,
> And sat in calm composure there.

His wife was to a neighbour gone,
To hear the chit-chat of the town;
And left him the infrequent pow'r
Of brooding thro' a quiet hour.
Thus, while he sat, a busy train
Of images beseiged his brain.
Of Church-preferment he had none,
Nay, all his hope of that was gone.
He felt that he content must be
With drudging in a Curacy.
Indeed, on ev'ry Sabbath-day,
Thro' eight long miles he took his way,
To preach, to grumble, and to pray;
To cheer the good, to warn the sinner,
And, if he got it, eat a dinner.
To bury these, to christen those,
And marry such fond folks as chose
To change the tenor of their life,
And risk the matrimonial strife.
Thus were his weekly journeys made,
'Neath summer suns and wintry shade;
And all his gains, it did appear,
Were only thirty pounds a year.

Taxes were growing higher every year; food was so expensive and his school-boys were "so prone to eat" that he could barely meet his expenses.

E'en birch, the pedant master's boast,
Was so increas'd in worth and cost,
That oft, prudentially beguil'd,
To save the rod, he spar'd the child.

While brooding thus, the Doctor is suddenly interrupted by the arrival of his wife, whom Combe portrays very much in the manner suggested by Rowlandson's print. The character is stereotyped, but the lines are amusing:

Good Mrs. Syntax was a lady
Ten years or more beyond her hey-day;
But tho' the blooming charms had flown
That grac'd her youth, it still was known
The love of power she never lost,
As Syntax found it to his cost:
For as her words were used to flow,

He but replied or, YES, or NO.—
When e'er enraged by some disaster,
She'd shake the boys and cuff the master:
Nay, to avenge the slightest wrong,
She could employ both arms and tongue;
And, if we list to country tales,
She sometimes would enforce her nails.
Her face was red, her form was fat,
A round-about, and rather squat;
And, when in angry humour stalking,
Was like a dumpling set a-walking.
'Twas not the custom of this spouse
To suffer long a quiet house:
She was among those busy wives
Who hurry-scurry through their lives;
And make amends for loss of beauty
By telling husbands of their duty.

When Syntax is able to interrupt the flow of his wife's observations, he tells her of his plan to make a sketching trip and publish it. He will "ride and write and sketch and print" and make as much money as "Doctor Pompous" has gained by doing the same thing. The contemporary reader would immediately think of William Gilpin and his tours. He might already have caught an allusion to Gilpin in the economy which Syntax practised with the birch; Gilpin was opposed to indiscriminate corporal punishment and seldom resorted to it in his school. But there is otherwise almost no personal satire in the poem. Gilpin's theory of the picturesque is satirized, but not the man.

The ensuing cantos describe the adventures of Doctor Syntax as he journeys about the country on his long-suffering nag, Grizzle. His route takes him by way of Oxford to York, where he is entertained by Squire Hearty, then on to Castle Howard in Yorkshire, where he visits Lord Carlisle. (Frederick Howard, fifth Earl of Carlisle, had been Combe's contemporary at Eton. Two months before the first issue of the *Poetical Magazine,* he had been unmercifully satirized by his former ward, Lord Byron, in *English Bards and Scotch Reviewers.*) Lord Carlisle offers his patronage of the projected book and invites Syntax to visit him in London. The Doctor then pursues his way to Keswick, where he meets Squire Worthy and his engaging family. After a day or two there, he goes on to Liverpool and thence, by a devious route, to London, where he stays for two weeks in Lord Carlisle's town house, completing his book and arranging for its publication. He then returns home—somewhere, perhaps, in Wiltshire. The tour has taken about eight weeks.

As he makes this journey, he meets with all the predictable roadside adventures. He loses his way; he is attacked by highwaymen who steal his purse and tie him to a tree (but Mrs. Syntax has sewn his banknotes in his clothing); he is rescued by two passing damsels; he loses Grizzle and finds her; he is overcharged at an inn and disputes with the landlady; he bestows chaste kisses upon the chambermaid and various other females; he is attacked by a bull; he mistakes a gentleman's house for an inn; he is forced to share a room with a man who tries (unsuccessfully) to rob him; in one bucolic scene he plays his fiddle for rural dancers; he reads from his manuscript until his audience falls asleep; he enters a church and preaches a sermon; he has various amusing adventures in London. Then, after his return home, he receives a letter from Squire Worthy offering him a living with £400 a year. His troubles are ended.

Adventures of this kind already seemed old-fashioned when the poem was coming out, but as narrated by the equally old-fashioned Doctor Syntax they had a kind of innocent quaintness. The poem seemed as unpretentious as the good Doctor himself, a reminder of simpler times and an amusing contrast to such poetic narratives as *The Lady of the Lake* which appeared in 1810. Moreover, it offered an escape from the tensions and anxieties of the continuing war with France which had been going on for twenty years. The *Critical Review* (May 1813) acknowledged as much in commenting on the book. "Dr. Syntax may be classed amongst those good-humoured poets, who beguile a weary hour, chase away an uneasy thought, or suspend the operation of the cares and mortifications of the day, by the perusal of a pleasant or a laughable tale."

It was the character of Doctor Syntax himself, however, which won the affections of several generations. The *Monthly Review* (January 1813) called him "a new and well-drawn character" and "a Parson Adams of a peculiar school". The reviewer found himself compelled to respect Syntax, notwithstanding the ludicrous situations into which he was continually falling. "As we attend the Rev. Divine in his rambles in search of the picturesque, he grows in our good opinion, and the ridiculous traits in his figure and character do not hide the excellence of his heart; so that, when we are constrained to laugh, we are forced to esteem." The writer was forced, in fact, to esteem the work as a whole. "We do not recollect any modern book which has afforded us equal amusement with this Tour; and if we are warm in our commendations, it is because the perusal of it has left a pleasing impression on our minds." There was some justification for this praise, and the critic was by no means alone in his warm response to the book.

* * *

The criticism of picturesque theory in the poem is laughable, but it is also informed and serious. Rowlandson's prints treat the subject comically, showing the solemn sketcher tumbling over backward into a lake (Plate 16) or turning his back on graceful figures in order to draw a set of grotesque beasts. Combe's verses reflect the artist's fun, but they make a specific point regarding the theories advanced by Gilpin and allude to particular passages in his books. For Combe had long been interested in the picturesque, had known and quarrelled with Uvedale Price, and had assisted Humphrey Repton with two of his works on the subject. Even while he was writing *The School-master's Tour* he was engaged in producing letterpress for W. B. Cooke's engravings of picturesque scenery along the Thames. Describing "Old Houses, near Eton College", he had quoted and paraphrased Gilpin and Price, defining the picturesque as "a quality, *in some objects*, which renders them fit and proper to be imitated in painting. Its vital principle is to be found in that spontaneous and seemingly fantastical variety, which nature never fails to produce when left to herself; she is its fostering parent, and art its mortal foe. Ruggedness, roughness, and abruptness, are to the picturesque, what softness, smoothness, and undulating lines are to beauty."[8]

Gilpin, on the other hand, by no means regarded art as the mortal foe of picturesque beauty. "We must ever recollect", he wrote, "that nature is most defective in composition; and *must* be a little assisted." He never painted literal transcripts from nature, and readers had complained that they could not find the actual places represented in his tours. "I hold myself at perfect liberty," he insisted, ". . . to dispose the *foreground* as I please; restrained only by the analogy of the country. I take up a tree here, and plant it there. I pare a knoll, or make an addition to it. I remove a piece of paling—a cottage—a wall —or any removable object, which I dislike." The resulting sketch, he argued, "preserves more the *character* of the landscape than the *real* one".⁹ These solemn pronouncements cry out for the satire which Rowlandson and Combe provide in Canto II. Doctor Syntax has lost his way on the moor and comes upon a weather-beaten signpost from which all the lettering has faded. He sits down to rest a few minutes and decides to make a drawing of the post.

> Tho' your flimsy tastes may flout it,
> There's something *picturesque* about it:
> 'Tis rude and rough, without a gloss,
> And is well cov'red o'er with moss;
> And I've a right—(who dares deny it?)
> To place you group of asses by it.
> Aye! this will do: and now I'm thinking,
> The self-same pond where Grizzle's drinking,
> If hither brought 'twould better seem,
> And faith I'll turn it to a stream;
> I'll make this flat a shaggy ridge,
> And o'er the water throw a bridge:
> I'll do as other sketchers do—
> Put anything into the view;
> And any object recollect,
> To add a grace, and give effect.
> Thus, tho' from truth I haply err,
> *The scene preserves its character.*

The serious satire on the picturesque is not renewed until Canto XIII, where Syntax declines an invitation to go hunting with Lord Carlisle.

> Your sport, my Lord, I cannot take,
> For I must go and hunt a lake;
> And while you chase the flying deer,
> I must fly off to Windermere,
> Instead of hallowing to a fox,
> I must catch echoes from the rocks.
> With curious eye and active scent,
> I on the *picturesque* am bent.
> This is my game; I must pursue it,
> And make it where I cannot view it,
> Though in good truth, but do not flout me,
> I bear that self-same thing about me.
> If in man's form you wish to see
> The *picturesque*, pray look at me.
> I am myself, without a flaw,
> The very *picturesque* I draw.

As Gilpin himself had remarked, "The pleasures of the chace are universal. . . . Shall we suppose it a greater pleasure to the sportsman to pursue a trivial animal, than it is to the man of taste to pursue the beauties of nature?" In his *Tour to the Lakes* he devoted ten pages and six plates to a discussion of picturesque qualities to be found in animals. He acknowledges that the horse is a nobler and more elegant animal than the cow, but insists that "in a picturesque light the cow has undoubtedly the advantage, and is every way better suited to receive the graces of the pencil". The lines of the horse are too smooth and round, "whereas the bones of the cow are high, and vary the line, here and there, by a squareness, which is very picturesque". He speaks of picturesque grouping of cows and sheep, adding that "human figures also combine very agreeably with animals."[10] The idea provides both Rowlandson and Combe with humorous material. The verses just quoted continue as follows:

> A Rector, on whose face so sleek
> In vain you for a wrinkle seek:
> In whose fair form, so fat and round,
> No obtuse angle's to be found.
> On such a shape no man of taste
> Would his fine tints or canvas waste:
> But take a Curate, who's so thin,
> His bones seem peeping thro' his skin;
> Make him to stand, or walk, or sit,
> In any posture you think fit;
> And, with all these fine points about him,
> No well-taught painter e'er would scout him;
> For with his air, and look, and mien,
> He'd give effect to any scene.
> In my poor beast, as well as me,
> A fine example you may see;
> She's so abrupt in all her parts:
> O what fine subjects for the arts!

Combe continues this theme in the following canto, where Syntax first encounters Squire Worthy and his family. "I want some living thing," he says, "to show how far the picturesque will go." Someone calls his attention to the birds flying overhead, and he expresses his old-fashioned delight in the sheer plenitude of nature, evidence to him of the Creator's artistry.

> As a philosopher I scan
> Whate'er kind Heav'n has made for man;

> I feel it a religious duty
> To bless its use and praise its beauty.

All nature is beautiful, he says, but not all of it suits his purpose as a sketcher of the picturesque. The pigeon is a fine subject for a poet, but Syntax prefers him in a pie. The birds enchant the eye and ear, but they defy the artist's attempt to group them.

> But tho', indeed, I may admire
> The greyhound's form, and snake's attire,
> They neither will my object suit
> Like a good shaggy, ragged brute.
> I will acknowledge that a goose
> Is a fine fowl, of sov'reign use:
> But for a picture she's not fitted—
> The bird was made but to be spitted.

As for the quadrupeds, he acknowledges that they may all be attractive to the artist, but many of them have no place in a picturesque scene. His own Grizzle is a better subject for his sketches than any fine race-horse, and he mentions the most famous one of all.

> To a fine steed you sportsmen bow,
> But *picturesque* prefers a cow:
> On her high hips and horned head
> How true the light and shade are shed. . . .
> The unshorn sheep, the shaggy goat,
> The ass with rugged, ragged coat,
> Would, to a taste-inspir'd mind,
> Leave the far-famed *Eclipse* behind:
> In a grand stable he might please,
> But ne'er should graze beneath my trees.

The print which accompanies this canto shows Syntax blandly sketching a group of farm animals, all with their mouths open and evidently producing a barnyard symphony of inharmonious sounds. To heighten the absurdity, Rowlandson has placed the Squire and two ladies behind Syntax—attractive figures in face and dress, obvious interlopers in this otherwise grotesque scene (Plate 17). When one of the young ladies asks Syntax to sketch her portrait, he tells her that he is unable to do so.

> In vain, fair maid, my art would trace
> Those winning smiles, that native grace.

The beams of beauty I disclaim;—
The *picturesque's* my only aim:
My pencil's skill is mostly shown
In drawing faces like my own,
Where Time, alas, and anxious Care,
Have plac'd so many wrinkles there.

The satire on the absurdities of picturesque theory virtually ends here, though in Canto XIX Combe returns to the theme briefly and states his conclusions. He loves all the rich variety of nature, he says; he dislikes the drafting-board regularity of Palladian art, but he is unwilling to reject beauty of any kind. His preferences run to the picturesque, but he finds absurdity in some of the extreme notions of the theorists. He proceeds to describe a charming scene, moderately picturesque, and sketches it without adding unnecessary roughness. Some men, he tells us, would insist on bringing in pigs to wallow in the foreground, but he will do nothing of the kind.

For I most solemnly aver,
That he from genuine taste must err,
Who flouts at grace or character;
And there's as much in my old wig
As can be found about a pig.
For, to say truth, I don't inherit
This self-same *picturesquish* spirit
That looks to nought but what is rough,
And ne'er thinks Nature coarse enough.

He dislikes art which is overtrim, but he vows never to deviate from nature which must always give delight. This is his last word on the subject.

English writers continued to discuss the picturesque, but after the first *Tour of Doctor Syntax* enthusiasts tended to be more cautious. Jane Austen mentions it in several of her novels, but she was well aware of Rowlandson's and Combe's laughter. In a letter of March 2, 1814, she writes, "I have seen nobody in London yet with such a long chin as Dr. Syntax."[11] Thomas Love Peacock and others satirized the movement, and Ruskin dealt contemptuously with it in *Modern Painters*. But only the absurdities of the movement were touched by this criticism; its central concepts were gradually assimilated into English thought, and the term itself continues to have its uses in the discussion of art. But since Doctor Syntax created his landscape from a post and expounded the picturesque attributes of livestock, writers have been wary of the more extreme theories once solemnly propounded by William Gilpin.

*   *   *

The narrative takes a somewhat different course once Combe and Rowlandson have dropped the picturesque, and for a time there appears to be some indecision concerning the action. To some extent, artist and writer seem at cross-purposes. Rowlandson's plate for Canto XVI shows Syntax selling Grizzle; evidently the artist had grown tired of the poor beast. Combe circumvents him by having the buyer give the horse back to Syntax, but she does not appear in the next nine plates. Soon Doctor Syntax himself abandons her, leaving her to be cared for by a former owner while he takes a stage-coach to London. Meanwhile the action moves through several unrelated episodes; Syntax fiddles for country dancers in a charming print, but uninspired lines (Plate 18); he sympathizes with a weeping milkmaid in a mock-sentimental scene interrupted by the girl's irate mother; he visits Liverpool, giving Rowlandson an excuse to produce a print of the new Exchange in that city; he preaches a dreary sermon in a badly drawn church. The best episode in this series, accompanied by perhaps the best print in the book, occurs when Doctor Syntax is seated in a country inn and is prevailed upon to read from his manuscript. He does so with much pride of authorship—and straightway puts his audience to sleep. Only two lovers in the background, who are otherwise engaged, remain awake (Plate 19). Combe's lines closely follow the print:

> Syntax now felt a strong desire
> To smoke his pipe by kitchen fire,
> Where many a country neighbour sat;
> Nor did he fail to join the chat:
> When, having supp'd and drank his ale,
> And silence seeming to prevail,
> He slowly from his pocket took
> His trav'lling memorandum book;
> And, as he turn'd the pages o'er,
> Revolving on their curious lore,
> Th' exciseman, a right village sage,
> (For he could cast accounts and gauge,)

Spoke for the rest—who would be proud
To hear his Rev'rence read aloud.

Syntax readily consents and begins reading a long passage about
the beauties of nature, tapping his foot to mark the rhythm. The
effect, unfortunately, is soporific:

Each hearer as th' infection crept
O'er the numbed sense, unconscious slept!
One dropp'd his pipe—another snor'd—
His bed of down an oaken board;—
The cobbler yawn'd, then sunk to rest,
His chin reclining on his breast.
All slept at length but *Tom* and *Sue*,
For they had something else to do.
Syntax heard nought; th' enraptured elf
Saw and heard nothing but himself:
But, when a swineherd's bugle sounded,
The Doctor then, amaz'd—confounded—
Beheld the death-like scene about him;
And, thinking it was form'd to flout him,
He frown'd distain—then struck his head—
Caught up a light, and rush'd to bed.

Canto XXI shows neither artist nor writer to advantage. The plate
reveals Syntax preaching in a country church and again putting his
auditors to sleep, but Rowlandson's perspective is faulty and his
invention too markedly Hogarthian. The sermon which Combe devises
for Doctor Syntax is perhaps intended to remind the reader of Parson
Yorick, but it is not one of the author's better efforts. Man is born to
misery, the good doctor says, citing Job 5:7 as his text, and he
proceeds to set forth all the familiar evidence with overtones of
Gray's Eton ode and Shakespeare's Seven Ages of Man. For the
nonce comedy is suspended.

At this point the action takes a new direction and moves rapidly
toward conclusion. The scene changes to London, permitting Combe
to deal with matters he had long been concerned with: booksellers and
authors, theatres and critics, men of learning and men of business.
As the guest of Lord Carlisle, who has now arrived in town, Syntax
busies himself with completing his book and arranging for its
publication. Canto XXII describes an interview between Syntax and
Vellum, an ignorant, hard-headed bookseller of Paternoster Row

(Plate 20). No one knew the race of booksellers better than Combe, whose first success as hackwriter had occurred thirty-five years earlier while he was producing books and pamphlets for John Bew, also of Paternoster Row. The portrait of Vellum is generalized, but his arrogant treatment of Syntax and his abrupt change of manner on seeing Lord Carlisle's letter of recommendation would not fail to call up memories.

The reminiscent mood is evident throughout the London episodes. In Canto XXII Syntax is asked by his host to recount the history of his life. The narrative which follows carefully avoids all particulars, but it contains unmistakable allusions to various phases of Combe's checkered career. Most of the quotations printed as epigraphs to the chapters of the present work are drawn from this canto.

For Canto XXIII Rowlandson provided a timely view of the new Covent Garden Theatre which had opened in September 1809, a year and a half before the print appeared in the magazine. It shows Doctor Syntax seated in the back row of the stalls watching Falstaff on the stage. After the performance Syntax has a conversation with a newspaper critic who is to review the play. The ignorance of the critic makes the dialogue a new version of Tom Jones and Partridge at the theatre and enables Combe once more to express his views concerning the ever-increasing size of theatres (this one seated 3,000), the decay of acting since the great days of Garrick and Quin, and the irresponsibility of newspaper critics.

"The Battle of the Books", Canto XXV, which was introduced at this point in the separately published *Tour*, is Combe's somewhat ambiguous conclusion to this nostalgic section of the work. In a dream Syntax sees classical learning going forth to attack the massed forces of mercantilism and, in fact, driving them off the field. It is an indecisive battle, however, for after routing the enemy the classics merely return to gather dust on their undisturbed shelves. However the conflict may ultimately go, Syntax congratulates himself on his classical education, persuaded that learning gives "an unmixed pleasure/Which gold can't buy, and trade can't measure."

The tale is hurriedly brought to a conclusion in Canto XXVI. Doctor Syntax leaves London, and after four days of travel (managed in twenty-one lines) he arrives home, having retrieved Grizzle on his way. At first he keeps Dolly in suspense, smoking his pipe and drinking his ale while she rebukes him for failing to write his book and make a fortune. At length he slyly produces a twenty-pound note and offers to show her half a dozen others, whereupon she smothers him with affection. While she prepares his dinner, Syntax soliloquizes for some three hundred lines on the theme of Bear and Forbear, evidently the leading principle of his life and in Combe's opinion the moral tendency of the book. Then in a few days comes the letter from Squire Worthy offering Syntax the living of Sommerdon with an income of £400 a year. Doctor Syntax and his wife set out for their new home in a chaise drawn by the faithful Grizzle, who now makes a final appearance in Rowlandson's plate. On their arrival they are welcomed by the townspeople (Plate 21), and thereafter, the reader is assured, "the good parson, horse, and wife / Led a most comfortable life".

* * *

The reviews paid little attention to the *Tour of Doctor Syntax*; Ackermann's publications were thought of as collections of prints rather than as "books". The *British Critic* (July 1812) gave it a perfunctory notice, and the *Critical Review* (May 1813), a full year after it had appeared in book form, gave it two sentences. Only the *Monthly Review* (January 1813) gave it generous consideration in a review which has already been quoted. The author of that review was evidently motivated in part by personal considerations, having discovered Combe to be the author. Readers will be surprised, he says, by the anonymous author's statement that he is a man of advanced years. "Their wonder, however, will be abated, and the justice of our praise be less liable to question, when we add that we understand these verses to be the composition of Mr. Combe, the well-known author of the *Diaboliad*, which so much amused the town by its poignant satire, five-and-thirty years ago." Others, too, penetrated the anonymity at this time and gave his name wider currency than it had had before, though without distinguishing him sharply from his famous cleric. He was referred to as "Doctor Syntax", "Dr. Combe", "the author of Doctor Syntax", and at least once as "Mr. Combe (Dr. Syntax)". Once, to be sure, a friend who remembered Combe's insistence upon being designated "Esq." called him "Squire Combe," but most people beyond his immediate circle understandably confused the man with his fictional character.

The popularity of the character is beyond question. We are told that Syntax hats, walking-sticks, and snuff boxes made their appearance in the shops,[12] and pieces of Syntax china carrying Rowlandson's pictures of the good Doctor may still occasionally be found in the antique shops. At the present writing china bearing the familiar Syntax designs is again being manufactured. The Syntax vogue was most in evidence between 1812 and 1825, but Doctor Syntax and his tours remained popular for many years. In particular, the demand for new editions of the *Tour* continued throughout the century and into the next. Ackermann published his ninth edition on June 2, 1819, then brought out two continuations, *The Second Tour of Doctor Syntax, in Search of Consolation* (1820) and *The Third Tour of Doctor Syntax, in Search of a Wife* (1821). In 1823 he issued a cheap, pocket-size edition comprising all three tours; how many times this Miniature Edition was reprinted is unknown, but an edition dated 1828 has been seen. In 1838 Ackermann and Tegg published the first tour with new illustrations by Alfred Crowquill (Alfred Henry Forrester); copies dated 1844 and 1865 have been noted. Other publishers issued *The Three Tours of Doctor Syntax* as follows: C. Daly (*c.* 1848), Nattali and Bond (1855), Chatto and Windus (1868 and often reprinted), Alexander Murray and Son (1869), Frederick Warne and Co. (The Chandos Classics, n.d.), and Methuen (1903). Many of these editions appeared also in America, where in the 1880s the poem was even printed for free distribution by Warner's Proprietary Medicine Company in Chicago.[13] The first *Tour* appeared also on the Continent, translated into Danish (Copenhagen, 1820), French (Paris, 1821), and German (Berlin, 1822). John Timbs had good reason to call Doctor Syntax "a large prize in the lottery of publication".[14]

The popularity of Doctor Syntax himself and the success of this scheme for publishing prints accompanied by Hudibrastic verses did not pass unnoted by other booksellers. At least twelve imitations appeared between 1815 and 1828, several of them professing to be "by Doctor Syntax". All of them have at various times been ascribed to Combe, though he had nothing to do with them and sought by every means at his disposal to disavow them. In the *Second Tour*, after Syntax expresses his indignation at these spurious works, Mrs Worthy urges him to write another one of his own to "drive the braggarts from the field". The world, she says, will welcome a new book by the genuine Syntax.

For where's the city, where's the town,
Which is not full of your renown?
Nay, such is your establish'd name,
So universal is your fame,
That Dunces, though to dullness doom'd,
Have with a Dunce's art presum'd,
To pass their silly tales and tours,
And other idle trash, for Yours.

At the end of the *Second Tour* he speaks again of these imitations by "a spurious Syntax". He calls them "downright dishonest dealing" and appends a footnote in which he begs leave "to state in honest prose" the works he has written. He names the first *Tour*, the *Dance of Death*, the *Dance of Life*, and the present (second) *Tour* as "the only works in the same style by the same author". By the time he had written the *Third Tour* and came to write the Preface he could view the phenomenal success of his work more complacently. "It may, perhaps, be considered as presumptious in me, and at my age, to sport even with my own Dowdy Muse, but, from the extensive patronage which *Doctor Syntax* has received, it may be presumed that, more or less, he has continued to amuse: And I, surely, have no reason to be dissatisfied, when Time points at my eightieth Year, that I can afford some pleasure to those who are disposed to be pleased."

* * *

Combe himself had much of Doctor Syntax's good humour in the race of adversity, his ability to maintain his poise even under trying circumstances. His resolute good spirits are abundantly evident in a letter which he wrote in 1810 from the King's Bench Prison. He had availed himself of the Day Rule on March 27 in order to pay a visit to his friend, Major James Pattison Cockburn, in Woolwich. Among other things, he needed to discuss the letterpress which he was to write for a series of Alpine sketches by Cockburn. His business had been concluded by mid-afternoon, and Combe had gone to the Shakespeare Tavern in Woolwich to await the return coach. When it became evident that no coach was coming, he set out on foot and, catching a ride for part of the distance, he barely reached the prison before the gates were closed for the night. The next day he wrote the following letter:

Wednesday Afternoon

Mon Cher Major.

I am, without any mental reservation, a tough old Stick. The people at the Shakespeare ought to have sent word, as they had but just entered the house, that they were not furnished for the reception of Company, which was actually the case. For after waiting an hour in a dirty room, I was shewn to a Chamber very deficient in the Apparatus of such an Apartment. In short, under all circumstances, and being rather disposed to an incipient Rheum, of threatening sensations, I took a plug of Spanish Liquorice, and laid down upon the bed Hat and all, for no Night-cap was to be obtained, just as I left the Arsenal. In this Array, however[,] I contrived to sleep till ½ past six: when I arose, and without girding my Loins, for they had never been un-girded, I took my Umbrella and walked, philosophically and contemplatively to one mile beyond Deptford, when a Coach conveyed me to the Bricklayers Arms; when I had another mile, *pour comble de bonheur*, to walk, before I reached home.—However at a quarter before ten, I was in close contact wi[th] my best friend, my arm-chair.—Feeling a little queer, but tolerably cheerf[ul], and not disqualified for obeying your commands which I enclose. —Now, I recommend you to follow my example, and always make the best of the worst, but not to do, as I sometimes have done, been contented with the worst, when I might have got the best.—But that I fear, is the nature of the *beast*, as the man said when he heard a magpie chatter.—So Adieu, & remember me most kindly to the Ladies of your household, and believe me,

Yours very truely &c. &c. &c. &c. &c. &c. &c. &c. &c.

Over the Alps & the Tyroll
Upon my honour & my Soul
Wherever you go, wherever you're found,
On Mountain top, or under ground,

W C —15

Like Doctor Syntax, Combe was a man of many friendships. Those of his youth have disappeared without a trace, except for such record as survives of his intimacy with Laurence Sterne and, vaguely, Richard Cosway. We are told in general of his social talents as a young man, but more personal information is altogether lacking until in his old age he cultivated friends much younger than he, men who survived him and wrote about him after his death. Combe was seventy years old when he was finally released from prison, but he resumed his social life with the old vigour, dining out with cultivated men and women and entertaining them at his quarters in Lambeth Road.

One unnamed contemporary speaks of Combe's passing his last years "in literary ease in the purlieus of the King's Bench", adding

[262]

that his quarters were suited to the needs of a literary man. "There
. . . he enjoys much excellent society; and in the midst of an
extensive library, his time is constantly exercised for his own profit
and the gratification of the world."[16] That Combe had an extensive
library is evident from the record which still survives of its sale by
Saunders, an auctioneer in Fleet Street, long since succeeded by
Hodgson & Co. (now Sotheby's "Hodgson's Rooms").[17] The sale
took place March 2–12, 1824, but since Combe's books were
catalogued with those of other collectors, there is no definite evidence
of the extent of his library. It is amusing to note that Saunders's
auction room was also the place where Doctor Syntax (*Second Tour*,
Canto XXXIII) saw his own *First Tour* put up for sale. He nodded
with pleasure as the bidding continued, only to find that his nods had
been taken as bids and that he was himself the purchaser. He auto-
graphed the book, however, put it up again for sale, and made a nice
profit. The story is still told at Hodgson's, now moved around the
corner from the site described by Combe. It is a bookman's story, and
Combe was—among other things—a bookman, a great accumulator
of books and papers if not exactly a collector.

Those friends who called on him in Lambeth Road or who entertained him in their homes were often men of some distinction in the
publishing world: John Taylor, editor of *The Sun*; John Walter II,
proprietor of *The Times*, Peter Frazer and Crabb Robinson, members
of *The Times* inner circle; men of letters such as Samuel Rogers, Sir
Egerton Brydges, James and Horace Smith. Major Cockburn and his
family obviously liked him and took pleasure in his company. Combe's
concluding words of greeting to the ladies in his letter to Cockburn
are both graceful and characteristic, for he enjoyed his friendships with
young women much as Doctor Syntax did, and they in turn held him
in affectionate regard.

One young woman who called on Combe in Lambeth Road, or who
intended to do so, was the charming young actress, Sarah Smith,
later Mrs G. W. Bartley. Combe had met her, as we have seen, as early
as 1808. She had made her début at the Covent Garden with Mrs
Siddons in 1807, then had risen rapidly in popularity until she
became a formidable rival of that veteran actress. When the new Drury
Lane company was formed in 1812, Miss Smith was employed as
leading lady, making her début with that company on December 1 as
Isabella in Southern's *First Marriage*, one of Mrs Siddons's great

roles. On the day following that performance, Combe wrote her a letter of congratulation:

Wednesday Evening

My dear Miss S——

I wrote to a Gentleman long versed in Dramatic Matters to request his attendance on you last night. He did so. And his words to me are,—"It was an admirable performance.["] This is no common praise, when coming from a person of his Judgement and experience.—I do not know whether you feel yourself affected by the Newspapers.—I hope not, as it is long since they have by their ignorance or the partialities undeceived the public as to the rectitude of their opinions. You may take their advice, if at any time you feel it to be just; but be not mortified by their blame. Remember Nature, and you cannot err. The Criticism in the Times did not altogether please me. The writer is a man, as I am told, for I know him not, of some talents, and has acquired a flashy, imposing manner of hashing up old opinions and giving them new currency. But I have reason to think that, if I had not happened to have interposed, you would have been brought on Scene by Scene, in a Comparison with Mrs. Siddons, and have fared little better than if she had held the pen.—His devotion to that Actress is perfectly outrageous; and last Year he was so extravagant in his praises, as to receive an intimation, to curb his dramatic passion for that venerable piece of perfection.

Another Gentleman has just informed me, that the theatre was agonized by you; and a more decided, & heartfelt Applause was never witnessed on any occasion.— I have mentioned these matters to satisfy you if you possibly want satisfaction; and to confirm it, if your heart, as I trust is the case, is overflowing with it.

This is a dirty sloppy, cold catching part of the world, so I will excuse your projected visit to it, till the first Frost.—

Your very affectionate and faithful friend

W. C——[18]

On the outside, the letter is addressed to Miss Smith, 23 Leicester Square, and postmarked December 3, 1812. Combe had mentioned the actress in Canto XXIV of the *Tour of Doctor Syntax*, first published in the *Poetical Magazine* for April 1810. There he notes that Shakespeare's art still lives on the printed page,

> But when the Actor sinks to rest,
> And the turf lies upon his breast,
> A poor traditionary fame
> Is all that's left to grace his name.
> The Drama's children strut and play,
> In borrow'd parts, their lives away;
> And then they share the oblivious lot;
> Smith will, like Cibber, be forgot!

[264]

Cibber with fascinating art,
Could wake the pulses of the heart;
But hers is an expiring name,
And darling Smith will be the same.

A footnote in the *Poetical Magazine* (suppressed in the final version) regrets that the theatrical managers have permitted "that admirable actress and excellent young woman, Miss Smith" to leave London and seek fame in Ireland. "We have now no actress, in her principal line of performance, on the London stage, who is worth looking at." The remark would be read not only as a compliment to Miss Smith but also as an implied slap at her rival, the great Mrs Siddons, whom Combe had known for forty years. His feelings about the woman who unluckily remembered his own humiliating struggles as a young man were understandably ambivalent. On occasion he could speak of her in glowing terms, but she always remained a living reminder of days he preferred to forget.

There is good evidence of Combe's friendship with various other young ladies during the last decade of his life. On February 14, 1813, he sent a versified valentine to Miss Anna Gouldsmith, evidently to patch up a minor disagreement, since he asks her to frown on him no more.[19] It is rather better than most of his sentimental verses, though scarcely deserving quotation. Two weeks later Combe wrote to Miss Harriet Gouldsmith, possibly Anna's sister, advising her in matters of religion. He cautions her against believing "the horrible doctrine" of election and reprobation. "It is fatalism of the most horrid, because most blasphemous kind, as it represents the God of Justice and of mercy, as sending creatures into this world, on purpose as it were to be condemned to eternal misery in another." On the subject of faith he remarks, "We may believe anything which is not inconsistent with the Justice, the Mercy, and the Goodness of God.—If we study the Sermon on the Mount and abide by its Doctrines,—if we do unto others as we would they should do unto us,—We need not fear our final allotment. Notwithstanding all our imperfections, we may rely with confidence on the Justice of a Creator who made us." And he signs himself "with great regard" her "sincere friend & faithful humble servant."[20] It is a letter which cautions against enthusiasm, bigotry, and fanaticism, and it sets forth the middle-of-the-road Church of England position. Doctor Syntax had said much the same thing in Hudibrastics.

There is no identifying the "Miss Chaters" to whom Combe inscribed a copy of the *Dance of Life* on December 15, 1817,[21] but several of his letters to Miss Angelica Ackermann survive as evidence of the terms on which he was received by the ladies of his employer's family. One of them, undated, playfully accepts an invitation to dinner:

My dear & Charming Angel - i - ca,
I will obey your celestial
Commands, by taking mortal food
with you on Monday.
With all humility
Your sincere friend
and
Earth-born Admirer,
W[m] Combe[22]

Meanwhile, far removed from these young ladies and their friendly attentions to Combe, long out of sight and so far as possible out of mind, Maria Foster Combe had lived out her life under the care, good or bad, of Stephen Casey. And now, after some thirty-five years of confinement as hopelessly insane, Maria finally died and was given suitable though very quiet burial. The only details which have come to light are those contained in a macabre bill for funeral expenses submitted by one John Tullah, the undertaker who, as his bill states, had made the necessary arrangements at the instance of Stephen Casey. Maria had now become "Mary", and the parish register, if it were to be found, would probably so record the name. The churchyard is not specified in the bill, but "Church dues" of seventeen shillings are included. Addressed to "Mr. Coombes", the statement is dated January 14, 1814, possibly the date of the funeral, possibly a subsequent date to allow a decent interval between the death of this forlorn woman and the inevitable accounting of expenses. Those curious in such matters will find the charges set forth in the document preserved in the Berg Collection of the New York Public Library. The fourteen items, including coffin, hearse, and one coach with attendants wearing rented gloves and hatbands of mourning, amount finally to £14. 14s. 6d., a sum which Combe paid on March 3, a few days before his seventy-second birthday. It was one bill which Combe paid promptly, saving the receipt, which survives with the bill.

* * *

Combe seems never to have been a more congenial dinner companion than during these last years. "Although a mere water drinker," wrote his friend John Taylor, "his spirit at the social board kept pace with that of the company."[23] That he was often present at the table of John Walter II we know from the diary of Henry Crabb Robinson, who repeatedly met him there. One evening when Combe was absent, being detained at the King's Bench Prison, Walter and his friends talked of him. Thomas Amyot told one often-repeated tale of the old man's well-known "comic infirmity". Horace Walpole had told the same story, but Amyot gave a version which he had heard from Dr Samuel Parr. Robinson's manuscript diary gives the following account:

Parr was formerly acquainted with old Combe and mentioned his infirmity of lying— He was once in company with him when he gave an account of a very beautiful cottage either in the lakes or some celebrated spot which he described with the greatest minuteness & with it's name and at the same time spoke of it as his own. Unluckily the proprietor himself was present; and was so provoked at Coombes impudence; that he declared himself the Owner very bluntly. C. however was not in the least confounded and in the most easy way possible said, I am happy Sir that you do justice to my powers of description & my correctness in describing And if you are the proprietor, as I dare say you are I wish you health & long life to enjoy it— Your good health Sir!

Parr spoke otherwise civilly of C. & desired to be remembered to him as an old acquaintance.[24]

This was written on September 6, 1812. Two months later Combe was again at large and dining with his friends. Robinson duly recorded the fact in his diary for November 16: "Dined with Walter. Met old Coombe there. He appeared to be unaltered from his long residence in the King's Bench and was very amusing & in his manners gentlemanly. He did not lye so much as usual." At a similar dinner on February 1, 1814, "Old C. was as he generally is, entertaining. He spoke of the lawyers of his youth. He says he was called to the bar and I suppose this may be true. . . . He says the great men of that time were quite unlike those of the present." The theme was a favourite of Combe's, and Doctor Syntax had lamented the same deterioration.

> Heaven bless me! Where has Learning fled?
> Where has she hid her sacred head?
> O how degraded is she grown,
> To spawn such boobies on the town!

Again on May 16 the men dined with Walter, and Robinson reported "An amusing conversation with the old man. As usual we talked abo^t great men. And with every man we spoke abo^t he had been intimately connected. viz the Harvey family, by whom he had been nearly bro^t into parliament for Bury. He had met the King of France (Louis 18) in Westm^r Abbey & had had a long convers^n with him, finding him a highly cultivated & well informed man." There was always some basis of truth in Combe's anecdotes; Monsieur le Prince had, in fact, just returned to France after five years in England, and Bury was a pocket-borough of the Herveys. "This is quite a comic infirmity," said Robinson on June 18, 1816, "carried as it is to such an excess that it can deceive no one."

On February 4, 1817, Combe was again "very entertaining".

He was well acquainted with Churchill the Satirist—used to dine with him—but declined his acquaintance—it being descreditable for a young man rising in the world to be much with him—He used to ask his landlady who kept a tavern, to dine with the party. She was a respectable woman & Churchill used to frighten her as he expressed it by his blasphemies—Come now—he used to say when Lamb was on the table—I will cut up the Lamb of God—He wrote rapidly & one day at dinner [word came from] the printer saying it wanted 12 lines to complete a poem—[space left for the title] C. rose, stood at the side table, composed & wrote down instantly the last lines of [space] which are very excellent.

It must have been Robinson who failed to supply the name of the poem. Had it slipped Combe's mind, he would have improvised.

* * *

In May 1820 Combe lived for a time with a family in Thavies Inn, Holborn. Neither the occasion of his visit nor its duration is now known, but it was here that young Dr George Lefevre encountered him and formed the vivid impressions subsequently recorded in his *Life of a Travelling Physician*.

"You must write a book," said the old gentleman to me, just as he awoke from his nap in the back parlour. "I want to see you write a book. Where are the young ladies?" And he took a pinch of snuff, and yawned again in his chair. "You may make it extremely interesting, and any of your friends will give it a dash of science for you. The mineral springs in Germany are good for a physician, and they are of as much service to him at home as abroad." . . . I replied, however, modestly, that my peregrinations had extended only to one foreign country, and I could not well write upon the German springs unless I had really visited them. "No necessity in the world," he replied, "for leaving the city; you will find every thing that you want without going a mile from your own door." He then gave me such instructions upon the subject as almost made me believe I had been on the spot, which he told me how to describe."

(I, 78–79)

There follows the episode, already recounted in the present work, of his asking "the young ladies" for more of the gooseberry pie and then consuming as much of it as eleven custards could cover. After telling this story, Dr Lefevre describes Combe as he appeared to a young man of twenty-two:

It was only in his later years that I knew him, and then even it was impossible to suppose that he ever could have been younger. Replete with anecdote, and polished in his manners, he won the affections of all who knew him; and notwithstanding the mystery attached to his history, you forgot all that conjecture could suggest, in the fund of entertainment which his conversation afforded. . . .

It was the author of "Dr. Syntax," who visited in the family where I then resided. I know not what was his chief attraction in this quarter, unless it were the gooseberry pies and custards, which he certainly demolished with a peculiar gusto. His anecdotes, which seemed to spring fresh from the bottom of an inexhaustible well, paid amply for the cost of the mountains of pastry which he consumed. . . . There were a few things in the old man's habits which were not very agreeable. He uniformly fell asleep before the cloth was wholly removed from the dinner table, and he was rather negligent in his person. His conversation, however, was always most polished, and the outer was forgotten in the inner man.

(I, 82–83)

Combe was at that time writing the final cantos of the *Second Tour of Doctor Syntax* and often read aloud from his manuscript, just as his own itinerant clergyman had done—though not, one hopes, with the same soporific effect. Several passages in the *Tour* were evidently written with this audience in mind. When Doctor Syntax arrives in London this second time he was fortunate in finding a quiet place to stay.

> For free from the street's rattling din,
> He found repose in THAVIES INN,
> Where from the town's unceasing riot,
> He could enjoy his time in quiet. . . .

This place appear'd a calm retreat
For learning, or the Muses' seat,
Such as he thought could scarce be found
Within the City's ample bound.

At the end of his stay in London, Doctor Syntax returns to this theme, praising Thavies Inn, the "goodness" dwelling there (his hosts), "smiling beauty" (the young ladies), and the "pleasing neighbour" (Lefevre). The passage concludes with lines reminiscent of Shenstone's often-quoted stanzas "Written at an Inn at Henley":

The few days Syntax pass'd in town
He seldom was an hour alone.
He had a pleasing neighbour found,
Indeed, he might have look'd around,
And made a long, enquiring pother,
Before he found out such another.
Here he the social evening felt,
Where beauty smil'd, and goodness dwelt.
Here he met all things to his mind,
With constant kindness over-kind.
—Wherever he is doom'd to go,
In this meand'ring scene below,
In the world's busy to and fro,
He never will, in all its din,
Forget the good of Thavies Inn.

It was both compliment and advertisement for the quiet inn located on a secluded courtyard off what is now Holborn Circus. A block of offices on the site bears the name today.

By May 1, 1821, Combe had finished the *Third Tour* and could write, with manifest relief, "This prolonged work is, at length, brought to a close." The death and burial of Doctor Syntax in the last canto was, he mistakenly thought, insurance against yet another sequel to his adventures. A work of a different kind, however, was already in hand and by June 5 was approaching completion. On that day Combe wrote to Angelica Ackermann postponing a dinner engagement until June 12, when he would be able to bring the completed manuscript of the *History of Madeira* to "pappa".[25] That book was published later in the summer, and before the year's end— for there was no stopping his pen—Ackermann had also published the first five parts of the *History of Johnny Quae Genus, the Little Foundling of the Late Doctor Syntax*. Meanwhile, Combe continued to produce his monthly piece for the *Repository of Arts*, having missed only five issues since April 1809. The last series, known as "The Female Tatler", ran until April 1822, when his long writing career ended. It had been maintained at almost this pace for forty-nine years.

* * *

On July 4, 1821, Combe's oldest friend, Richard Cosway, went out for a ride in Regent's Park, suffered a stroke, and died in the carriage before it reached home. The following month Charlotte returned from Ireland to help her sister, Maria Cosway, settle family affairs, and presently Combe was writing to assure her Irish friends of her safe arrival. Her relationship with these friends is never entirely clear, but she evidently stayed with a Mrs Curtis of King's County and visited frequently with a Mrs Swinney, Kildare Street, Dublin. On August 20 Combe wrote a polite letter to Mrs Swinney. "I have very great pleasure in acquainting you, according to your very obliging request, that Mrs. C—— arrived after a very pleasant voyage of twenty hours, during which she had not a moment's sickness, at Liverpool. Her Journey to London was equally agreeable." He thanks her for the hospitality which she has extended to Charlotte in Dublin and sends "her love and grateful thanks". The letter is dated from Lambeth Road.[26]

Combe gave the two sisters what help he could in settling their affairs. The house in Edgware Road had to be vacated, Cosway's effects disposed of,[27] and his papers put in order for a memoir which Combe agreed to write. Maria wanted to return to Italy as soon as possible and hoped that her sister would go with her, but Charlotte was bent on going back to her friends in Ireland. By the time Maria reached Italy she was certain that everything had gone wrong and poured out her worries to Combe in a letter written from Lodi on January 24, 1822. She had expected Charlotte to sort out the family papers, give Combe what he needed for the memoir, and put aside for future publication Maria's own journals and letters. "I told Charlotte to return me my letters and those which regarded only myself and were not of use to you, as I had a particular objection to her taking them to Ireland." But her sister has written only twice in six months, and now Maria is convinced that nothing has been done as she intended. "I wished much to see you before I set out, I told her so, but the uncertainty of your being able to come—not knowing how to contrive it and the many things I had to do in those last days, made me lose this satisfaction." She thinks Charlotte's friends have imposed on her good nature and are taking advantage of her. "Feelings of blood and friendship in me go for nothing. I said and did all I could to induce her to come with me, but could go no farther when I found more attraction on the other side."[28] Maria's genuine distress and the total confusion of her affairs are fully evident in this letter. And running through it is the touching—and of course futile—expectation that Combe will somehow set things right.

One would like to know more about Charlotte's visit to London in 1821, as one would about so many other matters bearing upon Combe's private thoughts, but to the very end he kept his personal life to himself. We know only that he continued to live at 12 Lambeth Road, that he was frequently a guest at Ackermann's table, and that he spent his days industriously writing on at undiminished pace. The young John Timbs visited Combe in 1822, and though he was later to mention the visit several times he gives only one detail of the interview: "We remember to have visited him in the Rules, near the New Bethlem Hospital, where we learnt that he had written a memoir of his chequered life." The call was probably a short one, for a footnote informs us that Timbs had approached the old man with a request for information about his personal history, precisely the subject Combe always avoided. "The object of our call was to obtain some few biographical particulars of Mr. Combe; but he churlishly refused our application, adding that he should write his own life, and leave it to the world. We are not aware that he did so."[29] Combe's projected autobiography became a legend with the anecdotalists after his death. He certainly talked of it to others besides Timbs. Various writers mention his destruction of private papers before his death and suggest a conventional explanation for the holocaust: he had quarrelled with someone—possibly Anthony Ryves—and did not wish him to profit by their publication. However this may be, we may rest assured that any autobiography which Combe might write would only tighten the curtains which he had drawn about his essential privacy.

He began but did not complete the promised memoir of Cosway. To be sure, Charlotte may not have sent him the necessary materials, but the fragmentary manuscript gives pathetic evidence of Combe's inability to write about the friend whom he had known since boyhood. One can only conclude that he found himself too personally involved in his memories of Cosway: the schooldays so long ago, the marriage to Maria Foster which Cosway had witnessed, the elopement with Charlotte, the times of hardship in 1799, and doubtless other matters which we know not of. The manuscript of *Johnny Quae Genus*, which was written at this time, shows the old readiness in composition and runs on line after line with scarcely a correction, but the memoirs of Cosway are filled with corrections, revisions, false starts, and broken thoughts.[30] It finally ends in the middle of a sentence without having yielded a single personal detail in all its two thousand words. The manuscript tells us nothing about Cosway, but indirectly it reveals a good deal about Combe.

By contrast with this halting manuscript, a letter written as he was approaching his eighty-first birthday displays remarkable firmness of hand and mind (Plate 22):

November 24, 1822.

My dear Miss A——
    I thank you for your charming present, and, while my Memory holds its place, the command it conveys shall not be disobeyed. At the beginning of next week, I will do myself the pleasure of waiting upon you, of which I will give you due notice.—You will do me the favour to present my thanks to Mr Ackermann, and believe me

Your very old and faithful friend
Wm Combe

Lambeth Road,
12   Surrey.[31]

Although he feels "very old" and knows that memory sometimes fails, he maintains his old-fashioned courtliness and a dignity belying his years.

These were his last words for the record. Nothing further is heard from or about him until the afternoon of June 19, 1823, when *The Sun*, a paper edited by Combe's friend John Taylor, carried a leading article announcing his death "this morning at his apartments, Lambeth-road, in the eighty-second year of his age". The following day, *The Times*, the paper with which Combe had long been associated, spoke of him with respect and affection. One hears overtones of Old Combe's many dinner-table conversations at the home of John Walter in the *Times* article. "He was a gentleman who, in the course of this protracted life, had suffered many fortunes, and had become known

. . . to so many people in every rank of society, that it hardly seems necessary to draw his character. . . .There was hardly a person of any note in his time, with whose history he was not in some degree acquainted." Both of these obituaries, as well as the others which appeared in the newspapers and magazines of the time, speak of his many writings and mention a few of them by name, suggesting that his career had included much that the world would never know. The *Sun* writer put this most explicitly: "The Life of Mr. Coombe, if impartially written, would be pregnant with amusement and instruction; but those whose literary contributions might have provided interesting materials, are probably most of them with him in the grave; and he will hereafter be chiefly remembered as the Author of Doctor Syntax." Combe had long outlived any who might have betrayed him.

Combe's burial on June 22, 1823, is recorded in the Church of St George-the-Martyr which stands opposite the site of the King's Bench Prison. The entry, signed by the Reverend W. G. Plees, Minister, gratuitously includes the information that Combe died "With the Rules"—in other words, an undischarged debtor.

As might have been expected, his affairs were found to be in extremely bad order. He left more than the usual current debts, including £90 due Mrs Ryves for back rent, and there was, of course, no money for the funeral. Nor was the promised legacy, a manuscript account of his life and times, to be found among his papers. Rudolph Ackermann, aided perhaps by one or two others, paid for the funeral and straightened things out as well as possible. No tablet was erected either in church or graveyard, though Combe had thoughtfully provided a suitable Latin epitaph.[32] The sale of his library eight months later at Saunders's auction-rooms took care of some part of the debts, but no exact figures are available. The chief complaint, however, came from Charlotte, who wrote the following letter to Ackermann two weeks after the funeral:

July 7th 1823

Dear Sir

I yesterday reciev'd by a letter from Anthony Ryves, the Afflicting confirmation of the very distressed Circumstances of Mr Combe— That he should have been So *Improvident* as to have left an accumulation of Debts, is to My Mind most *painful* as well as *Incomprehensible* —— To *you*, I shall not attempt to express the grateful feelings of my heart for your Unremitting Kind Attentions to My Unfortunate Husband. I can only assure you that I am

November 26 1822.

My dear Miss A —

    I thank you for your charming present, and, while my Memory holds its place, the command it conveys, shall not be disobeyed. In the beginning of next week, I will do myself the pleasure of waiting upon you; of which I will give you due notice. — You will do me the favour to present my thanks to Mr Ackermann, and believe me

    your very old and faithful friend

Lambeth Road,
   Surrey.
12

22. *Letter written by Combe in 1822. From the Berg Collection, New York Public Library*

indeed sensible of the full Extent of your friendly assistance and Lament that it never can be in my power to offer you a grateful remembrance, unless the M.S. Papers which you Kindly Collected and which are in Mrs Ryves's hands should prove deserving your acceptance.—Anthony mentions that you thought some were of Value. I have [not] the smallest Idea what they contain, and therefore you are the best judge if they are worth more than the £90— due to M^rs R— I can only say that I should be most happy could I present them to you *unincombered* by so havey a Debt; but it is totaly Impossible for Me to discharge M^rs R— Claims, and My sincere wishes are that they might prove of Value to you, far beyond the debt that must be discharged— I sh^d have been gratified to have had the Ring that M^r C— constantly wore and his watch, for *to me* they posses a greater Value than a Stranger could feel, but as M^rs R— demand is so enormous I cannot venture to express my wishes on the Subject.

I Remain with Sincere Regards
Your Obliged
Charlotte Combe

Mrs Curtis requests me to mention that she has been expecting an answer to a letter she had written to you————[33]

Charlotte shows to advantage in this letter, which is certainly a more orderly piece of writing, despite its spelling, than the distraught communication which Maria had sent to Combe a year and a half earlier. She must have been a woman in her sixties at the time of her husband's death. The two had been going their separate ways for twenty-five years, but they had continued to correspond, and the present letter seems a mixture of wifely annoyance and affection. J. T. Smith calls Charlotte "a most amiable woman" who "was invited into the agreeable society of her steady friend, Mrs. Curtis . . . a lady remarkable for her benevolence, literary attainments, and most elegant manners; with whom she still [1828] resides, and is treated with all the kindness of a sister".[34] Maria remembered her sister in her will: "I give and bequeath to my beloved sister Charlotte Hadfield widow of William Coombe, gentleman, now in Ireland, the sum of £1,000 for her sole and separate use."[35] It was the last appearance of Combe's name in a legal instrument. Maria died January 5, 1838; the date of Charlotte's death is unknown.

* * *

Without ignoring his many shortcomings as a man—indeed, with full acknowledgement of them—one concludes that William Combe was a remarkable and in many ways an admirable person. He lived a long life, suffered many reverses—by no means all his own making, accepted them with dignity and without discernible self-pity, and maintained his poise and self-respect (some might say his vanity) to the end. He had a gift for friendships, was a good if not entirely credible conversationalist, was held in affectionate regard by many discriminating men and women. He did not pay his debts, to be sure, and his Cheapside forebears would have been painfully embarrassed by his financial irresponsibility. But his forebears embarrassed him, too, and he tried to put them out of his life.

The present writer has a liking for Old Combe, even after searching out and recording all the available details of his inglorious life. Many of the details, most of them, are lost beyond recovery, and perhaps that is just as well. But he remains a singular person, sometimes absurd, sometimes pathetic, talented and posturing, sympathetic and lonely, courageous, gifted, and long-suffering. One sees him most vividly, perhaps, in his King's Bench quarters, steadily writing on and on, pausing occasionally to discuss business with a caller or to toss off a debonair note to a charming young lady. He was undeniably a man of parts, a gentleman, and a curiously interesting enigma; that was his posture, and he maintained it.

Much of Combe's voluminous output is simply journeyman work without the slightest claim to literary merit. This fact is by no means to his discredit. He was making a precarious living by the only means available to him, and he came to be highly regarded by the public and by his booksellers. He was a competent editor and ghost-writer, a tireless producer of letterpress for expensive art books, a dealer in literary merchandise. Had he been no more than this, his career would still be of interest to literary historians. But he was indeed more than this. Not a few of his works have a lasting if secondary literary interest. Had he signed them, even by a pen name, he would be known today as a diligent minor writer, a journalist, and an editor. Since he chose anonymity, he is either unknown or is dismissed as a hackwriter, a forger, and a perennial inhabitant of debtors' prison.

Perhaps no one else will ever undertake to examine the man's huge product, but students of literature would be well advised to consider his better things. These would include his first little book of stylized sentiment, *The Philosopher in Bristol*; the best of his satires, notably *The Diaboliad*, *The First of April*, and the *Dialogue in the Shades*; the novel in imitation of Le Sage, *The Devil upon Two Sticks in England*; and for good-natured fun, *The Tour of Doctor Syntax in Search of the Picturesque*. Specialists should study from their various points of view such other works as *The R[oya]l Register*, the *Letters of the Late Lord Lyttelton*, the *Original Letters of the Late Reverend Mr. Laurence Sterne*, the political pamphlets, the *History of the Thames*, and the theatrical reviews in the *Pic Nic*, the *Cabinet*, and *The Times*. Above all, readers should know the name of the man responsible for these writings. His name was William Combe, Esq.

NOTES

CHAPTER I

1. Henry Crabb Robinson's diary and reminiscences are quoted by permission from the manuscripts in Dr Williams's Library, London. Page references are to the typescript of the diary, in this instance to II, 301, and V, 190. References to the reminiscences are to Edith J. Morley's printed version in *Henry Crabb Robinson on Books and Their Writers* (London, 1938), in this instance to I, 11–13.

2. [Sir George Lefevre,] *Life of a Travelling Physician* (London, 1843), I, 78–84.

3. Laurence Sterne, *Letters*, ed. Lewis P. Curtis (Oxford, 1935), p. 294.

4. Will of Robert Combes, Jr., P.C.C. 269 Glazier.

5. Ms. vol., Guildhall Library.

6. "Digested Copy of the Registers of Burials of the Quarterly Meeting of London and Middlesex, 1700 to 1749," Friends' House Library.

7. Will of Humphrey Hill, P.C.C. 146 Browne.

8. Tallow Chandlers Company, "Register of Apprentice Bindings, 1685–1740": "Wm. Alexander son of Richard Alexander formerly of the Parish of St. Peter in the County of Wilts, Maltster defunct, apprenticed to Isobel Archer, living widow of Joseph Archer citizen and tallow chandler of London, is apprenticed for seven years from the first of this month [December 1704]" (IV, 173). Guildhall Library.

9. Tallow Chandlers "Stamp Book," under date of Oct. 1, 1716. Guildhall Library.

10. *The Intelligencer: or, Merchants Assistant* (London, 1738) lists "Alexander William, and Com. Wood-street." The firm is so listed in all directories until it appears as "Alexander and Combs, Wood street" in the

The page numbers in the right margin, from top to bottom: 2, 3, 4, 5, 6, 6, 7, 7, 7, 7.

Complete Guide to All Persons Who Have Any Trade or Concern with the City of London (1749).

7   11. Tallow Chandlers "Court Book, 1747 July 8 – 1779 Oct. 5": "At a Court of Assistants holden for this company on Friday the thirteenth day of July, 1750 . . . The names of severall persons being presented to this Court Out of which to choose a Master and four Wardens and this Court proceeding to a choice Doth unanimously choose for Master . . . for the year ensuing . . . William Alexander Esqr. One of the Sherriffs of London Master, being the second time of his being Chosen Master of this Company" (pp. 50–51). He took office September 4, 1750 (p. 52). Guildhall Library.

7   12. Alfred B. Beaven, *The Aldermen of the City of London* (London, 1906), II, 131.

7   13. Obituary, *Gentleman's Magazine*, Sept. 1762, p. 448.

7   14. St. Alban's Wood Street, "General Register, 1662–1786," Christenings: "Sarah D^{tr} of Wm Alexander & Mary Gibbons was born Nov. 22. bapt. 26. [1749] Mr. Smith, Lecturer." Guildhall Library.

8   15. Combe is called godson by Alexander in his will.

8   16. St. Alban's Wood Street, "General Register, 1662–1786."

10   17. A. H. Cox, *Harmondsworth Heritage* (West Drayton, Middlesex, 1955).

12   18. *History of the Principal Rivers of Great Britain*, I, *The Thames* (1794), p. 296.

12   19. *Philosopher in Bristol* (Bristol, 1775), I, 60.

12   20. R. A. Austen-Leigh, *Eton College Register, 1753–1790* (Eton, 1921). Combe's name appears in the school list for 1753, the first available when Austen-Leigh compiled the *Register*. After the publication of that work, however, a list dated Oct. 13, 1752, came to light and was published in *Etoniana*, No. 48 (Oct. 31, 1930), pp. 763–64. It does not contain Combe's name. Austen-Leigh does not indicate the time of year at which the list for 1753 was taken; ordinarily, he says, these lists were taken in the spring.

13   21. Two large manuscript volumes entirely in Combe's hand, owned by Mr. John F. Fleming of New York, hereafter referred to as the Fleming Papers. By permission of the owner, they are frequently quoted or cited in the present work.

NOTES

22. *Letters of the Late Lord Lyttelton*, II (1782), 31.   13

23. *History of the Rivers*, I, 292–93.   13

24. *History of the Colleges* (1816), "Eton," p. 61.   14

25. Will of Robert Combes, Jr., see note 4. Much information about the   15
family is also found in the will of Robert Combes, Sr., P.C.C. Glazier No.
6 folio.

26. Joseph Farington, *Diary*, Windsor Typescript, p. 433. (The MS. of   16
the Farington *Diary* at the Royal Library, Windsor Castle, has been generously made available to scholars in an indexed typescript deposited in the
Print Room of the British Museum. All references to the *Diary* in the present
work utilize the pagination of this typescript.)

27. The death of William Alexander is noted in the *Gentleman's Maga-*   17
zine, Sept. 1762, XXXII, 448. The Saint Alban's Wood Street Register
records his burial on Sept. 30, 1762. His will is P.C.C. 408 St. Eloy, p.
281.

28. The basic facts of Combe's membership in the Inner Temple are set   17
forth in R. A. Roberts, *A Calendar of the Inner Temple Records* (London,
1896, etc.), V, 123, 129, 169. The details are to be found in the manuscript
records preserved by the Sub-Treasurer of the Society. The best description
of legal education at the time is that of Sir William Holdsworth, *A History*
of English Law (London, 1903, etc.), XII, 15–40.

29. Thomas Campbell, *Life of Mrs. Siddons* (London, 1834), I, 39–40   19
and note.

30. Letter to Hall-Stevenson, May 19, 1764 (*Letters*, pp. 213–14).   20

31. Harlan W. Hamilton, "William Combe and the *Original Letters of the*   20
Late Reverend Mr. Laurence Sterne (1788)," *PMLA*, LXXXII (Oct.
1967), pp. 420–9.

32. Sterne, *Letters*, p. 216 n.   20

33. *Original Letters of the Late Reverend Mr. Laurence Sterne* (London,   21
1788), pp. [1]–2.

34. Letter to Hall-Stevenson, Nov. 13, 1764 (*Letters*, pp. 232–3).   21

35. Letter to Garrick, Mar. 1765 (*Letters*, p. 235).   22

page   CHAPTER I *continued*

22   36. Horace Walpole, *Last Journals*, ed. John Doran (London, 1910), II, 95 n.

22   37. *Repository of Arts*, Aug. 1, 1823, p. 87.

22   38. John Camden Hotten, ed., *Doctor Syntax's Three Tours* (London, 1868), p. viii. Hotten cites certain unspecified "Court Guides of the time."

22   39. Combe's account of how he came to write the *Letters of the Late Lord Lyttelton*. His manuscript, now at the Huntington Library, is quoted in Chapter IV.

22   40. Letter to Hall-Stevenson, July 15, 1766 (*Letters*, p. 281 and n. 9).

22   41. *Original Letters*, p. 183.

23   42. Letter to Becket, Aug. 30, 1766 (*Letters*, p. 288).

23   43. Letter to Combe, dated by L. P. Curtis: "? 7–9 Jan. 1767" (*Letters*, pp. 293–94).

24   44. *Original Letters*, pp. 78–79.

24   45. Catalogue Number 126, Scribner Book Store (1942), offered these volumes as Item 188 and reproduced the inscriptions.

24   46. *Letters*, p. 295 n. 4.

24   47. Henry Crabb Robinson's diary, May 16, 1814 (Typescript, IV, Part I, 132, reference to a seat in Parliament which fell vacant in 1768) and June 18, 1816 (Typescript, V, 190, reference to being with Hervey in Bath when preparations were going forward for his divorce in the ecclesiastical court, or just prior to Feb. 11, 1769). Both stories are "lies of ostentation and vanity", but they are probably derived from some association between the two men in Bath during 1768 or Jan. 1769. Various other references make it probable that the two men were acquainted.

25   48. Quoted from "one of Horace Walpole's notebooks" by Mrs. Paget Toynbee, ed., *Supplement to the Letters of Horace Walpole* (Oxford, 1918), II, 153.

25   49. Quoted by Thomas Moore, *Memoirs, Journal, and Correspondence*, ed. Lord John Russell (London, 1853–56), II, 201.

26   50. Reginald Blunt, *Thomas Lord Lyttelton* (London, 1936), pp. 72–73.

CHAPTER II

1. All references to Thomas Campbell in this chapter pertain to his account of Combe, *Life of Mrs. Siddons* (London, 1834), I, 39–46.   27

2. Alexander Dyce, *Recollections of the Table-Talk of Samuel Rogers* (London, 1856), p. 113. Fitzpatrick and Fox were in France during the winter of 1771–72. In his unpublished dissertation on Combe (University of Minnesota, 1938), Franz Montgomery shows that another man, one William Coombes, was a student at Douai in these years. The surviving records of Douai College mention neither name, but in any event Fitzpatrick had reason to know the man himself, not merely the name. The two were probably acquainted before Combe dropped out of fashionable society; certainly they had friends in common and moved in much the same circle. By the time Fitzpatrick told Rogers the story, he had himself been satirized by Combe in the *Diaboliad*.   28

3. Letter to Mason, April 18, 1777, *Horace Walpole's Correspondence*, ed. W. S. Lewis, XXVIII, 303.   28

4. James Smith, *Memoirs, Letters, and Comic Miscellanies*, ed. Horace Smith (London, 1840), I, 19 n.   28

5. *Notes on the Suppression of Memoirs* (Paris, 1825), p. 17.   29

6. Dyce, *Recollections*, p. 115.   29

7. Campbell says the incident occurred when Sarah was "about fifteen", but that would be in 1770, two years before Combe could possibly have joined the Kembles. Sarah left the company some months before her marriage, Nov. 25, 1773, but the episode could have occurred during the winter of 1772–73.   29

8. Joseph Farington, *Diary*, Nov. 8, 1796 (Windsor Typescript, p. 823).   30

9. John Camden Hotten, "The Author of 'Doctor Syntax'", *Doctor Syntax's Three Tours* (London, 1868), p. xi. Hotten's account of Combe is undocumented and full of palpable errors, but it is based on manuscripts which have since disappeared and on oral traditions. He had talked with John Timbs and perhaps others who had known Combe in person, possibly a doubtful advantage since Combe was so prone to improvise legends about himself.   30

10. *Of the Patagonians* (Darlington, 1788), p. [1].   30

11. Advertisements of performances at the theatre in High Street appear   30

in *The British Chronicle, or Pugh's Hereford Journal* from April 8 (*Comus*, with Dr. Arne's music) to May 20 (*Theodosius, or the Force of Love*).

31   12. Advertisement in the *London Evening Post*, Jan. 25–28, 1777, quoted in Chapter III.

31   13. A manuscript note in a contemporary hand, written on the flyleaf of Vol. I, *British Chronicle, or Pugh's Hereford Journal*, Hereford Public Library.

32   14. Mrs. Paget Toynbee, ed., *Supplement to the Letters of Horace Walpole* (Oxford, 1918), II, 153.

33   15. Dyce, *Recollections*, pp. 113–14.

34   16. R. A. Austen-Leigh, *Eton College Register, 1753–1790* (Eton, 1920), s.v. Palmer.

34   17. Information about Bristol is derived from the contemporary newspapers and from the following works: John Latimer, *Annals of Bristol in the Eighteenth Century* (Bristol, 1893); Stanley Hutton, *Bath & Bristol* (London, 1915); Arthur L. Salmon, *Bristol: City, Suburbs & Countryside* (London and Bristol, 1922).

35   18. As a Man of Feeling, Combe in 1775 might exploit the pathos implicit in the phthisical patients at the Hotwells, for their disease was the conventional favourite with sentimental writers. By 1784, however, he had come to a more realistic position: "That the generality of public water-drinking and bathing places should be scenes of amusement and pleasure, is very natural, and may be very proper; but I really think the Bristol Hot Wells should be an eternal exception. The disease, for whose cure application is made to these waters, is of such a nature as to render every species of public recreation, in the highest degree, unsalutary and obnoxious; nevertheless here are balls, public breakfasts, and all the train of amusements which are suitable only to health and spirits. There is also a master of the ceremonies to regulate the whole, who is very obliging and attentive to the duties of an office which does not belong to such a place as this. Phthisical patients have no business at a ball or a public breakfast; a cotillion was not formed for them: the fatigue of dress, the hurry of pleasure, hot rooms, and night air, to persons so afflicted, are so many secret arrows from the quiver of fate: yet, on an accidental visit to the rooms on one of their gay mornings, I saw a number of gasping shadows dancing away, without meaning a pun, as if they had not an hour to live, and coughing in time to the music that inspired them" (*Original Love Letters between a Lady of Quality and a Person of Inferior Station*, Letter XXVI, quoted from the Dublin edition, pp. 199–201).

NOTES

19. Published by permission from the original in the Henry W. and   36
Albert A. Berg Collection of The New York Public Library, Astor, Lenox
and Tilden Foundations.

20. George Symes Catcott, *Descriptive Account of a Descent Made into*   38
Penpark-Hole in the Year 1775 (Bristol, 1792), pp. 31–38. The incident is
mentioned in many books about Bristol, and references to it still occasionally occur in the local newspapers.

21. The visitor may possibly have been Thomas, Lord Lyttelton. The   39
thirtieth of the *Letters of the Late Lord Lyttelton* (Vol. I, 1780), presumably
written by Combe, describes a scene at the Hotwells closely similar to this
episode in the *Philosopher in Bristol*, though purporting to be described by
the unfeeling Lyttelton. "I exhibited myself . . . at a public breakfast at
the Hot Wells, and sat down at a long table with a number of animated
cadavers, who devoured their meal as if they had not an hour to live; and,
indeed, many of them seemed to be in that doleful predicament. But this was
not all. I saw three or four groups of hectic spectres engage in cotillions: it
brought instantly to my mind Holbein's Dance of Death; and methought I
saw the raw-boned scare-crow piping and Tabouring to his victims.—So I
proceeded to the fountain; but, instead of rosy, blooming health, diseases of
every colour and complexion guarded the springs. As I approached to taste
them, I was fanned by the foetid breath of gasping consumptions, stunned
with expiring coughs, and suffocated with the effluvia of ulcerated lungs."

22. A copy of the *Philosopher in Bristol* in the author's possession con-   41
tains annotations in a contemporary hand identifying Amanda as "Miss
Clara Stonehouse, dr of Dr Stonehouse." The father would be the Dr (later
Sir) James Stonhouse mentioned in the D.N.B. The annotator of the volume
has written his own name on the title page, "W. Speare" and under the
title, the author's: "Mr Coombes." He also identifies the victim of the Pen
Park Hole tragedy: "Mr Newman [*sic*], of Bristol, & of Wadham Coll with
me. Who fell into Pen-Park Hole, a Cavern, near Bristol." According to
Alumni Oxoniensis, William Speare entered Wadham College, March 3,
1770, aet. 18. He took his first degree in 1774, entered the church, and
became a prebendary of Exeter in 1810. He died in 1812. The same source
names Thomas Newnham as a student of New College. Catcott spells the
name Newnam.

23. "Preface of the Editor," *Letters Supposed to Have Been Written by*   47
Yorick and Eliza (London, 1779), I, ii–iii.

24. Ibid., I, vii.   48

25. *Felix Farley's Bristol Journal*, Sept. 9, 1775, p. 3.   48

50   26. Robert Cole, "William Combe and His Works," *Gentleman's Magazine*, May 1852, pp. 467–72.

50   27. John Doran, *Annals of the English Stage*, ed. Robert W. Lowe, (London, 1888), III, 152.

52   28. Quoted in obituary of Combe, *Bristol Observer*, July 16, 1823. The narrator thought the second young lady was Miss Galton, an impossibility, as Franz Montgomery has shown (*William Combe*, University of Minnesota, 1933, p. 46). She may well have been Clara Stonhouse, Combe's Amanda and Hannah More's friend and neighbour.

52   29. James Sketchley, *Bristol Directory* (1775), gives these addresses. Mary Alden Hopkins, *Hannah More and Her Circle* (New York, 1947), p. 25, says the two houses stood side by side on Park Street but gives slightly different numbers.

52   30. See above, n. 21.

53   31. *Daily Universal Register*, Oct. 3, 1786, "Sketch for a Chapter on Widows" (*Philosopher in Bristol*, II, 135–41), and Oct. 13, 1786, "The Generous Sailor" (Ibid., I, 28–30).

CHAPTER III

55   1. The book was briefly noticed by the *Critical Review* (March 1776) and by the *Monthly Review* (July 1776). So few copies were sold that the work is virtually non-existent in the libraries.

57   2. Iris Gower, *The Face without a Frown* (London, 1944), pp. 30–31, 85–87, 128ff.

58   3. *Morning Post*, Feb. 25, March 31, 1777.

58   4. "They say Mrs. Rudd has been at the play in Lord Lyttelton's chariot. If the Duchess [of Kingston] is acquitted, I suppose he will take her into keeping too, to show he is convinced of *her* virtue also" (Horace Walpole to Lady Ossory, Dec. 20, 1775, *Horace Walpole's Correspondence*, ed. W. S. Lewis, XXXII, 286).

59   5. By finding her guilty of bigamy, the Peers asserted that she was still legally the wife of Augustus John Hervey, now third Earl of Bristol. She was thus Countess of Bristol and entitled to plead benefit of clergy. As late as Feb. 5, 1787, more than eight years after her death and twenty-one years

after her trial, the *Daily Universal Register* published a squib about her, possibly by Combe. The best account of Elizabeth Chudleigh is Elizabeth Mavor, *The Virgin Mistress: The Life of the Duchess of Kingston* (London, 1964).

6. The facts are summarized by Lewis Bettany, *Edward Jerningham and His Friends* (New York, n.d. [1919]), pp. 166–67.   59

7. The definition is attributed to Berkeley Craven by Harriette Wilson, herself something of an authority on the behaviour of gentlemen. *Memoirs* (London, 1929), p. 187.   60

8. *Horace Walpole's Correspondence*, ed. W. S. Lewis, XXVIII, 303–4 and n. 21.   62

9. Thomas Campbell, *Life of Mrs. Siddons* (London, 1834), I, 42 n.   63

10. Sir Egerton Brydges mentions Combe's "coarseness of accent" in his *Note on the Suppression of Memoirs* (Paris, 1825), p. 18. Combe was an old man when Brydges knew him, but the criticism of Combe's rhymes in the 1770s may indicate a faulty accent. A writer in the *Critical Review* (Dec. 1777, p. 474) complains, somewhat hypercritically, of these rhymes: boast-lost, soothe-truth, care-ear, hear-prayer, tomb-come, survive-to live, dare-star, ton-Wimbledon, trod-abode, toil-smile, fear-there, ear-prayer, song-tongue, these-blaze, dare-war, woe-too, bear-fear, wear-star, son-own.   63

11. Thomas Campbell's version of the story, *Life of Mrs. Siddons*, I, 43 n.   65

12. The satirical scheme of having various candidates compete for office was becoming slightly worn. Writing his *Life of Cowley* during the *Diaboliad* epidemic, Samuel Johnson called the device "a mode of satire, by which, since it was first introduced by Suckling, perhaps every generation of poets has been teazed" (*Lives of the English Poets*, ed. G. B. Hill, Oxford, 1905, I, 15).   65

13. *Morning Post*, Dec. 19, 1776.   66

14. Viscount Irvine's will, P.C.C., 290 Hay.   68

15. Reginald Blunt, *Thomas Lord Lyttelton* (London, 1936), p. 160.   69

16. *Note on the Suppression of Memoirs*, p. 17.   72

17. Farington, *Diary*, May 6, 1794 (Windsor Typescript, p. 160).   72

page   CHAPTER III *continued*

72   18. Horace Walpole, *Last Journals*, ed. John Doran (London, 1910), II, 95–96.

72   19. Walpole's copy of the *Diaboliad* with annotations in his hand is preserved at the Harvard College Library. "John a' Coombe" is a pun on John-a-nokes, a conventional appellation for an unnamed party to a legal action.

72   20. *Horace Walpole's Correspondence*, ed. W. S. Lewis, XXVIII, 304 n. 21, 470.

73   21. Historical Manuscripts Commission, Fifteenth Report, Appendix, Part VI, *The Manuscripts of the Earl of Carlisle, preserved at Castle Howard*, p. 320.

74   22. The best lines in the poem are those devoted to Macpherson:
        One, with a rage for Language smitten,
          Stores up all Babel in his head,
        Translating tongues that ne'er were written,
          In such as never will be read!

78   23. Letter to Mary Berry, quoted by Lewis Melville, *The Berry Papers* (London, 1914), p. 44.

78   24. *Last Journals*, II, 95.

82   25. *Letters of the First Earl of Malmesbury* (London, 1870), I, 61.

82   26. J. T. Smith, *Nollekins and His Times* (London, 1829), I, 61.

82   27. Iris Gower, op. cit., p. 36.

85   28. Ibid., p. 24.

85   29. John Doran, *A Lady of the Last Century* (London, 1873), p. 215.

86   30. *Morning Post*, March 31, 1777.

89   31. A copy has recently been acquired by the British Museum.

94   32. The *Macaroni Magazine* had published an absurd engraving of Lord Villiers in 1772, showing him as "The Nosegay Macaroni", a fop dressed in the extreme of fashion.

96   33. Reviewing *The Refutation*, a writer says, "We entirely agree with

this antagonist of Mr. C——'s" An asterisk points to a footnote identifying Mr. C—— as the author of the *Diaboliad*. *Monthly Review*, March 1778, pp. 235–6.

34. *An Interesting Letter to the Duchess of Devonshire* (J. Bew, 1778);   98
An Heroic Epistle to Sir James Wright (J. Bew, 1779); *The World as It Goes, a Poem. By the Author of the Diaboliad* (J. Bew, 1780); *The Traitor. A Poetical Rhapsody* (J. Bew, 1781, a satire against Franklin, no known surviving copy); *A Letter to Her Grace the Duchess of Devonshire* (Sewell, 1784, concerning the Westminster elections and attributed to the author of the earlier letters to the Duchess—i.e., Combe—by the *Monthly Review*, May 1784, no known surviving copy); *The Royal Dream; or the P[rince] in a Panic. An Eclogue, with Annotations* (S. W. Fores, 1785).

CHAPTER IV

1. Review of *Original Love Letters between a Lady of Quality and a Person*   102
of Inferior Station, Critical Review, LVIII, 319.

2. Margaret R. B. Shaw, ed., *Second Journal to Eliza* (London, 1929),   102
p. xxxi.

3. Anon., "Junius", *Quarterly Review*, Dec. 1851, p. 111.   102

4. Charles Whibley, Foreword to *Second Journal to Eliza*, p. [v].   102

5. D. A. Winstanley, *The University of Cambridge in the Eighteenth*   106
Century (Cambridge, 1922), pp. 55–138. Thomas Gray's poem "The Candidate" is a comment on this election.

6. G. E. C[ockayne], *The Complete Peerage*, ed. Vicary Gibbs, III (London,   107
1913), 573–4; *Town and Country Magazine*, July 1770, pp. 363–8: "Account of the Trial of his R.H. the Duke of C. for criminal conversation with Lady Harriet G——r."

7. Combe's account of contemporary eloquence in Volume VII utilizes   108
the materials already assembled for Letter LV, *Letters of the Late Lord Lyttelton*, II, published earlier in the same year.

8. *Letters between Two Lovers and Their Friends* (Dublin edition, 3 vols.   112
in 1) p. 194.

9. "Combe assured me that it was with him, not Sterne, that 'Eliza' was   113
in love; that he used to meet her often beside a windmill near Brighton; that he was once surprised in her bed-chamber, and fled through the window,

page C H A P T E R I V *continued*

leaving one of his shoes behind him; that, some days after, he encountered her as she was walking with a party on what is now the Steyne, and that, as she passed him, she displayed from her muff the toe of his shoe!" Alexander Dyce, *Recollections of the Table-Talk of Samuel Rogers* (London, 1856), pp. 114–15.

113   10. Lewis P. Curtis, "Forged Letters of Laurence Sterne", *PMLA*, L, (Dec. 1935), p. 1084.

114   11. Shaw, *Second Journal*, p. xxxviii.

114   12. Curtis, "Forged Letters", pp. 1076–1106.

114   13. Wilbur L. Cross, "Not Sterne but Combe", *Saturday Review of Literature*, Dec. 21, 1929, VI, 587. See also Henri Fluchère, "Laurence Sterne et William Combe", *Revue anglo-américaine*, VIII (1931), 313–28.

115   14. This first section of the work, eighty-seven pages in the original edition, is the part which is most closely imitative of Sterne. It makes use of topics suggested by the *Letters from Yorick to Eliza* and duplicates topics and even phrases from the *Philosopher in Bristol*. Such references as that to plaster casts of Nollekins' bust of Sterne, first advertised in 1775, suggest that the work was in hand by that date.

116   15. Curtis, "Forged Letters", p. 1087.

116   16. Laurence Sterne, *Letters*, ed. Lewis P. Curtis (Oxford, 1935), p. 321.

117   17. If Combe did in fact write the first part of the *Letters Supposed* in 1775, the version of this story which appeared in the *Philosopher in Bristol* could conceivably have been drawn from his manuscript of the as yet un-published work.

120   18. James Boswell, *Life of Johnson*, ed. Hill-Powell, IV (Oxford, 1934), pp. 298–99.

120   19. *Horace Walpole's Correspondence*, ed. W. S. Lewis, XXVIII, 487.

122   20. "We must fairly acknowledge that we have some doubts whether they are the genuine productions of lord Lyttelton, or the work of some ingenious imposter; in that case we can only say, that the paste approaches so near in its lustre to the real diamond, that they cannot easily be dis-tinguished from each other; and we are inclined to think, that if my lord

NOTES

CHAPTER IV *continued*   *page*

were now alive, he would not wish to disown them." *Critical Review*, March 1870, p. 214.

21. Thomas Frost, *Life of Thomas Lord Lyttelton* (London, 1876): "I   123
incline to the view that the letters were the genuine epistles of Thomas Lord Lyttelton, and I am strengthened in my belief by the strong similarity of their tone and style to those of the autograph letters of that nobleman with which I have been favoured" (pp. xix–xx). Reginald Blunt, *Thomas Lord Lyttelton* (London, 1936) justifies his use of the letters on sounder grounds: "Whether the letters were all written by Combe or whether they were genuine letters padded out with extraneous material in order to make the book a best seller must ever remain a moot point; but there can be no reason to doubt the authenticity of Combe's recollections of his friend. Tom's conversation, like his acknowledged letters, was, it may be confidently assumed, apt to turn upon himself, and Combe, it may be, wrote down what he was told simply from memory. In these more exacting days he would have compiled a volume of reminiscences, peppered with quotation marks, showing where Tom began and he ended; and as that kind of book, only lacking these guides in truth, it seems reasonable to treat this correspondence" (p. 22).

22. The account of Lord Lyttelton's marriage in Letters XXXIII and   123
XXXIV is inconsistent with that given in manuscript letters of undoubted authenticity. Lord Lyttelton would have known that George D[uran]t of Letter XXXVIII was the son, not the brother, of the clergyman at Hagley. Lord Lyttelton had himself designated George Ayscough as the man to edit his father's works, though Letter XXV says that Ayscough had been appointed editor by the father's will.

23. Quoted by Frost, p. xiii.   126

24. Habeas Corpus was restored in 1801.   128

25. Huntington Library, MS. HM 3166. Published by permission.   128

26. H. C. Robinson, *Diary*, Feb. 4, 1817 (Typescript, V, 357).   128

27. Ilchester, *Home of the Hollands* (London, 1937), p. 96; Jesse, *George*   130
Selwyn and His Contemporaries (London, 1882), IV, 141.

28. *Devil upon Two Sticks in England* (1790), III, 166.   137

29. P.R.O., K.B. 122/518. No. 1291.   139

30. P.R.O., K.B. Commitment Book No. 10.   139

CHAPTER V

141   1. [Stanley Morison], *History of "The Times"*, I (London, 1935), 1–74.

141   2. Walter had reason to complain of his first editors. In 1783 he had published *An Introduction to Logography* by the inventor of that process, Henry Johnson. The title page unluckily claimed the patronage of "His Najesty".

142   3. *Daily Universal Register*, Aug. 25, 1786.

142   4. Unsigned pieces in Combe's manner begin with "The Forgery" on Aug. 30 and 31. This is followed by "An Affecting Story", Sept. 7; "Conscience. A Fragment", and "On the Pleasure of Reflection", Sept. 9; and "Grief", Sept. 14.

143   5. These letters and Combe's connection with them are discussed in Harlan W. Hamilton, "William Combe and the *Original Letters of the Late Reverend Mr. Laurence Sterne*", *PMLA*, LXXXII (Oct. 1967), pp. 420–29.

145   6. P.R.O., Pris. 7/7. Discharges.

147   7. *History of "The Times"*, I, 51.

147   8. From a draft of a letter to an unknown correspondent, Fleming Papers.

147   9. This account of the political situation during Pitt's Ministry is based primarily on the following works: Donald Grove Barnes, *George III and William Pitt, 1783–1806* (Stanford, 1939); Betty Kemp, *King and Commons* (London, 1957); Sir Lewis Namier, "Monarchy and the Party System", *Crossroads of Power: Essays on Eighteenth Century England* (London, 1962); J. Holland Rose, *William Pitt and the Great War* (London, 1914). For more general historical background: J. Stephen Watson, *The Reign of George III, 1760–1815* (Oxford, 1960).

154   10. "Mr. Walter begs leave to inform the public, that three impressions of the above-mentioned and popular pamphlet [*Letter from a Country Gentleman*] has [*sic*] been sold in little more than a fortnight, and that a fourth edition, with additions, is this day ready, to supply the eager demand of the town. At the same time, it is his duty to mention that a publication is advertised by J. Stockdale, with a title so similar to that of this *popular* pamphlet, as to justify the opinion, that it is adopted for the insidious purpose of foisting off his own publications for those of the Logographic Press" (*The Times*, Feb. 18, 1789).

CHAPTER V *continued* *page*

11. Walter was imprisoned in Newgate from Nov. 23, 1789, to March 7,   156
1791 (*History of "The Times"*, I, 52–61).

12. Robert Cole, "William Combe and His Works", *Gentleman's*   157
Magazine (May 1852), p. 469. Charles Long was Pitt's Secretary of State
for Home Affairs. It may be inferred from the letter here quoted that Combe
worked under his direction.

13. Two entries in Farington's *Diary* show that Combe's personal   167
opinions were sometimes more moderate than those expressed in his
pamphlets. "Coombes does not think anything is to be apprehended from
the State of the popular mind. He thinks the great majority is not affected
by bad principles, but that a certain active set of men who are seen every-
where make a deceptious appearance" (Nov. 27, 1795, Windsor Typescript, p. 433). "Coombes has no notion of invasion, but thinks the Ministry
act politickly by working on the peoples apprehensions—it supports government, and presents a high state of preparation" (April 17, 1798, Windsor
Typescript, p. 1235). Cf. Erich Eyck, *Pitt versus Fox* (London, 1950),
pp. 318–19.

14. P.R.O. 30/8/229, Fol. 152.   168

15. Farington, *Diary*, May 11, 1796 (Windsor Typescript, pp. 614–15).   174

16. Ibid., Dec. 28, 1797 (p. 1184).   174

CHAPTER VI

1. Jeremiah Whitaker Newman, *The Lounger's Common-Place Book*   181
(London, 1796), s.v. Lyttelton.

2. Farington, *Diary*, May 12, and Nov. 27, 1795 (Windsor Typescript   182
pp. 343, 433).

3. Letter to Cockburn, printed in Chapter IV.   182

4. Farington, *Diary*, Apr. 25, 1796, and Aug. 24, 1797 (Windsor   184
Typescript, pp. 593, 1085).

5. Letter to Burbidge, Mar. 22, 1797, Bodleian Library, Ms. Montagu   185
d.6. (f, 457).

6. Letter to the present writer from P. B. C. Bridgewater, Esq., Secretary   186
of the British Museum: "The earliest Register of Readers which we possess

is from 1820, but there is no trace of a William Combe's name in it for the period 1820–1823. . . . We also checked our earlier records but . . . these also have failed to produce a reference to William Combe."

188   7. Lewis Bettany, *Edward Jerningham and His Friends* (London, 1919), p. 93.

189   8. Farington, *Diary*, Dec. 1, 1793 (Windsor Typescript, p. 61). The passage refers to "July last", making it uncertain whether Combe's visit to Nuneham occurred in 1792 or 1793. The present writer concludes that the episode occured in 1792, but in view of conflicting evidence in this diary and elsewhere the possibility of a second visit in 1793 is not entirely excluded.

189   9. Huntington Library, MS. JE 243. Published by permission.

190   10. *Horace Walpole's Correspondence*, ed. W. S. Lewis, XV, 217–18.

190   11. Farington, *Diary*, May 10, 1794 (Windsor Typescript, p. 162).

190   12. Ibid., May 5, 1796 (p. 606).

191   13. *The Thames: or Graphic Illustrations* (London, 1811), s.v. Strawberry Hill.

191   14. Page references to Farington's *Diary*, when inserted in the text, are based upon the Windsor Typescript of the original manuscript.

192   15. Sir Egerton Brydges, *A Note on the Suppression of Memoirs* (Paris, 1825), p. 17: "At length he was discovered in the ranks of a regiment of the line at an inn, at Derby, by George Steevens, an old crony."

192   16. Dec. 16, 1795 (Windsor Transcript, p. 475).

194   17. John Taylor, *Records of My Life* (London, 1832), II, 301–2.

194   18. James Northcote, *Commonplace Book* (ms. in National Portrait Gallery), "Pictures Painted in the Year 1795", includes "Mr. Comb half length sold to Mr. Ackerman for Ten pounds June 4/-/1812."

194   19. Combe, *Letters to Marianne* (London, 1823), p. 23.

194   20. *Annual Register*, 1793, "Chronicle", p. 22.

196   21. Maria Cosway was 35; Charlotte seems to have been younger, but her birthdate is unknown.

NOTES

22. John Thomas Smith, *Nollekens and His Times* (London, 1828), II,   197
394.

23. Farington, *Diary*, June 23, 1795: "Coombes, I met at the Shakespeare   197
Gallery. He is this day removing his goods from Knightsbridge to a House
He has taken near Harrow. Bulmer told me He is to give £40 a year for it
and some land" (p. 362).

24. Letter to John Taylor, quoted in Chapter VII.   197

25. Letter to Rudolph Ackermann, quoted in Chapter VIII.   197

26. *Letter to a Retired Officer, on the opinions and sentence of a general court*   198
martial . . . for the trial of Col. John Fenton Cawthorne (London: Debrett,
1796).

27. John Romney, *Memoirs of the Life and Works of George Romney*   200
(London, 1830), pp. 251–53.

28. Both letter and note are published by permission of The Pierpont   201
Morgan Library.

29. Plea Roll, P.R.O., K.B. 122/177 (No. 1753).   201

30. The Huntington Library, San Marino, California, MS. JE 245.   202
Published by permission.

31. King's Bench Commitment Book, Number 16, s.v. Combe.   202

32. Plea Roll, see above, n. 29.   203

33. Plea Roll, P.R.O., K.B., 122/723 (No. 1064).   203

34. King's Bench Commitment Book, Number 16, s.v. Combe.   203

CHAPTER VII

1. Most of the information concerning the prison and, unless otherwise   204
identified, all quotations are from *The Debtor and Creditor's Assistant; or, A
Key to the King's Bench and Fleet Prisons; Calculated for the Information and
Benefit of the Injured Creditor, as Well as the Unfortunate Debtor* (London,
1793). Also useful is the later *Description of the King's Bench Prison; Being
a Brief Review of Its Constitution; the Prison Itself; the Rules Thereof; the Day
Rules; the Orders and Regulations of the Court; and Containing All Such Other*

page   CHAPTER VII *continued*

Matter as is Material to be Known to All Persons in Custody of the Marshal (London, n.d. [1824]). Cf. Giorgione di Castel Chiuso [Peter Bailey], *Sketches from St. George's Fields* (London, 1820; Second Series, 1821). This versified account of the King's Bench Prison notes that "More than one Syntax, elbowed on a desk,/Has studied only here the Picturesque" (Second Series, p. 51).

207   2. *The Life, Adventures, and Opinions of Col. George Hanger* (London, 1801), II, 282–84. The fourth chapter of Vol. II, from which this is quoted, is entirely concerned with conditions in the King's Bench Prison.

207   3. "William Combe, late of Paddington in the County of Middlesex, Gentleman", Plea Roll in the case of Matthew and William Stodart v. Combe, P.R.O., K.B. 122/717. The eighty-nine names are those beginning with C in the *King's Bench Commitments Abstract Book*, Vol. I (P.R.O., Pris. 5/1).

208   4. Letter to Richard Sharp, Mar. 28, 1800, quoted by P. W. Clayden, *Early Life of Samuel Rogers* (London, 1887), p. 407.

208   5. Friedrich Anthing, *History of the Campaigns of Count Alexander Suworow Rymnikski* (Wright, 1799); Jean-Baptiste Jourdan, *Memoir of the Operations of the Army of the Danube* (Debrett, 1799); C. N. S. Sonnini de Manoncourt, *Travels in Upper and Lower Egypt* (Debrett, 1800); Congress of Rastadt, *Official Correspondence* (Wright, 1800); Louis-Medeleine Ripault, *Report of the Commission of Arts . . . on the Antiquities of Upper Egypt* (Debrett, 1800).

209   6. *Asiatic Annual Register for 1799* (London, 1800), Part III, "Characters", pp. 25–31.

209   7. *A Genuine Narrative of the Deplorable Deaths of the English Gentlemen, and Others, Who Were Suffocated in the Black-Hole in Fort William, at Calcutta. . . . In a Letter to a Friend* (London, 1758).

210   8. Letter in the author's collection.

211   9. Letter to Lord Mulgrave, *Gentleman's Magazine*, May 1852, pp. 469–70.

212   10. The Huntington Library, San Marino, California, MS. HM 7260. Published by permission.

212   11. The debate is reported in the *Asiatic Annual Register for 1799* (London, 1800), State Papers: "Proceedings at the East India House",

page

pp. 148–218. See "Illicit Trade", pp. 164–83. The *Anti-Jacobin* (Apr. 1800, p. 396) discusses the case in a review of the *Asiatic Annual Register*.

12. The most complete account of the Pic Nic Society is that written by   213
Combe in the Preface to *The Pic Nic* (London, 1803), republication in book form of the newspaper by the same name. Unless otherwise attributed, all quotations relating to the Society are from this source. There is also an account of the Pic Nics in the *Reminiscences of Henry Angelo* (London, 1828).

13. The entire letter is printed in Combe's Preface to *The Pic Nic*, pp.   215
x–xii. The text printed in *The Letters of Richard Brinsley Sheridan*, ed. Cecil Price (Oxford, 1966), II, 170–71, has minor omissions owing to some mutilation of the original letter in Sheridan's hand; otherwise it is essentially as quoted by Combe.

14. Original publication not seen. Note is quoted from Combe.   215

15. Horace Smith, ed., *Memoirs, Letters, and Comic Miscellanies in Prose*   215
and Verse of the Late James Smith, Esq. (London, 1840), p. 18. Horace Smith devotes several pages to the Pic Nic controversy which corroborate Combe's account.

16. Ibid., p. 19 and n.   218

17. Ibid., p. 20 n.   218

18. January 15, 1803.   219

19. February 5, 1803.   220

20. Identified by Horace Smith, p. 21.   223

21. Aug. 7, 1803; Windsor Typescript, p. 2350.   224

22. [Stanley Morison], *History of "The Times"*, I (London, 1935), p. 80,   224
speaks of Combe as "virtually the Editor of *The Times*." Elsewhere (p. 133) he says, "Combe was, in fact, the acting editor."

23. Henry Crabb Robinson's *Diary*, Typescript II, 363–64.   226

24. Quoted from the ms., which is somewhat longer than the version   227
printed in *Henry Crabb Robinson on Books and Their Authors*, ed. Edith J. Morley, I, 11.

227   25. *History of "The Times"*, I, 48–49.

228   26. Ibid., p. 94.

228   27. William Archer calls Leigh Hunt "the first English dramatic critic, in our present acceptation of that curiously inaccurate term", but he acknowledges that it would take much "wading through old newspaper-files" to ascertain precisely who first "brought real talent and sincerity to the task of theatrical chronicling" (Leigh Hunt, *Dramatic Essays*, ed. Archer and Lowe, London, 1894, p. vii). He quotes extensively from Hunt's *Autobiography*, Ch. VII, describing earlier newspaper practice in dealing with the theatre.

229   28. MS. in the Harrey Elkins Widener Collection, Harvard College Library. Published by permission.

229   29. I am indebted to L. M. Payne, Esq., Librarian of the Royal College of Physicians, for searching the extant records of the licensed madhouses to discover the location of the one which Stephen Casey operated at numbers 5 and 6, Greengate Street, Plaistow.

229   30. Plea Roll in the case of Reardon vs. Combe, P.R.O., K.B., 122/790, No. 1057.

230   31. *Gentleman's Magazine*, May 1852, pp. 469–70.

230   32. Ibid., p. 470.

230   33. Farington, *Diary*, Jan. 21, 1820 (Windsor Typescript, p. 7713). The incident must have occurred between March 1807, when the Portland Administration was formed, and June 1808, when Combe was returned to prison.

231   34. *Letters to Marianne*, p. 13: "I will tell you what I said of you.— 'That you had filled up the vacancy which I had found in my heart, ever since my own wayward girl had left me,—to my real delight and comfort:—that I had a warm paternal affection for you;—that Mrs. C—— would share it with me, on her return to England.' " A footnote supplied by the editor explains "wayward girl" as "his adopted daughter".

231   35. Quoted from the ms., "Reminiscences, 1809". The sentence is omitted by both Sadler and Morley in their editions.

231   36. Letter signed "M. L. B.", *Mirror of Literature, Amusement, and Instruction*, Jan. 3, 1835, p. 3. John Timbs, edited the *Mirror*. The youth in question seems to have been Anthony Ryves, the son of Combe's landlady.

37. Two copies of the *Letters to Marianne* in the British Museum contain   231
the same pencilled annotations, one copied from the other. The original
appears to be that bearing the number C. 61. b. 5. This copy once belonged
to W. J. Thoms, to whom it had been given by Edward Dalton in response
to Thoms' inquiry published in *Notes & Queries*. It seems then to have passed
into the hands of Dr. Doran, a later editor of *Notes & Queries*. A slip pasted
into the book contains the following handwritten statement: "I believe the
notes in pencil in this book were written by Mrs. Rives [*sic*]." The handwriting, however, closely resembles that of her son Anthony Ryves, whose
inscription in a copy of *Tristram Shandy* is shown in an illustration of Item
188, Catalog 126, Scribner Book Store. Also in the book is a letter from
Wyatt Papworth to Thoms conjecturing that it had belonged to Anthony
Ryves. Papworth was the author of various letters signed "W. P." which
appeared in *Notes & Queries* concerning Combe.

38. *Letters to Marianne*, pp. 21–23.   233

39. *Notes & Queries*, June 12, 1852, pp. 558–59.   234

40. *History of "The Times"*, I, 133–34. Quoted by permission of Times   235
Newspapers Limited.

41. The *Day Rule Book of the K. B. Prison* (1808–1809) (P.R.O., Pris.   235
10/201) shows that Combe took advantage of the Day Rule on June 29,
July 2, July 4, Nov. 23, and Nov. 24, 1808.

42. Windsor Transcript, p. 4105.   236

43. "At No. 2, in the State House, was written the famous Doctor   236
Syntax, and several other noted literary publications", *Description of the
King's Bench Prison*, p. 6.

44. Fleming Papers.   238

45. P.C.C., Loveday 371.   238

46. Combe was mistaken in the month; the *Day Rule Book of the K. B.*   238
Prison (1810) shows that he took the Day Rule on July 10 and 11, 1810.

47. The Huntington Library, San Marino, California, ms. JE 243.   239
Published by permission.

48. Bodleian Library.   239

49. Someone mistakenly told Farington on June 26, 1809 (Windsor   239
Transcript, p. 4401) that Combe was then living in the Rules, but letters
written from the Bench and quoted in this chapter prove the contrary.

CHAPTER VIII

page

244   1. John Adolphus, *Memoirs of John Bannister* (London, 1839), I, 290–91.

244   2. Unused sketches survive in the library of the Victoria and Albert Museum, the New York Public Library, and the Harvard Library.

244   3. Quoted by John Camden Hotten, ed., *Doctor Syntax's Three Tours* (London, 1868), p. xxviii.

245   4. John Timbs, *Lives of Wits and Humourists* (London, 1862), II, 354, and *English Eccentrics and Eccentricities* (London, 1866), II, 205.

245   5. Hotten, op. cit., p. xxviii. Combe, too, expressed his satisfaction with the arrangement in his Advertisement to the *First Tour*, "Mr. Ackermann was satisfied with my Service and I was satisfied with his remuneration of it."

247   6. In quoting from the second edition, I have corrected obvious typographical errors and to some extent normalized the punctuation, which often seems erratic and was perhaps the typesetter's responsibility.

247   7. Announced for publication May 1 in *Repository of Arts*, Apr. 1812. Advertised in *The Times* (May 12) as having been published on the announced date.

251   8. *The Thames, or Graphic Illustrations* (London, 1811), I, unpaged.

252   9. *Three Essays* (London, 1808), pp. 67, 68, 164.

253   10. *Observations, Relative Chiefly to Picturesque Beauty, Made in the Year 1772 . . .* , commonly called *Tour of the Lakes* (London, 1788), Section XXXI, pp. 251–61. The running head of the *First Tour of Doctor Syntax* is "Doctor Syntax's Tour to the Lakes".

255   11. Jane Austen, *Letters*, ed. R. W. Chapman (Oxford, 1932), II, 92.

260   12. Hotten, op. cit., p. xxvii.

260   13. The only known surviving copy is that at the Princeton University Library.

260   14. *English Eccentrics and Eccentricities* (London, 1866), II, 203.

262   15. Ms. in the author's collection.

16. *Public Characters of All Nations* (London, 1823), p. 408.   263

17. A copy of the sale catalogue is retained in the auction rooms: *A*   263
Catalogue of a Miscellaneous Assemblage of Books in General Literature
including the library of William Combe, Esq. deceased, "Author of Dr.
Syntax's Tours", &c. &c. . . . which will be sold at auction, by Mr.
Saunders, at his Great Room, "The Poets' Gallery", No. 39, Fleet Street, on
Tuesday, March 2d, 1824, and 12 following days (Sundays excepted) at
Half-Past Twelve o'clock precisely. To be viewed, and catalogues had, price
1s. each. The catalogue lists 3774 items but does not indicate which are from
Combe's library. Many of his own works are included, however, as well as
those of all his favourite authors.

18. Ms. in the author's collection.   264

19. Ms. in the Berg Collection, New York Public Library.   265

20. Ms. in the author's collection. The letter is dated Tuesday, Mar. 2,   265
which would place it in 1813.

21. Copy in the Case Western Reserve University Library.   266

22. Bound with copy of *Letters to Marianne*, British Museum 10920.   266
Published by permission.

23. Obituary in *The Sun*, June 19, 1823.   267

24. Typescript, II, 301.   267

25. Ms. in Harvard Library.   270

26. Ms. in British Museum. This letter was enclosed in one addressed   271
to Mr. Swinney, "as the Office", Combe explains in a postscript, "very
ungallantly, does not frank Letters addressed to Ladies". Published by
permission.

27. John Taylor, close friend of both Combe and the Cosways, evidently   271
gave some assistance at this time. On June 6, 1821, a month before Richard
Cosway's death, he wrote a letter to R. W. Elliston, Manager of the Drury
Lane, offering on behalf of the Cosways to sell him certain of Richard's
court costumes. "Mrs. Cosway, late of Stratford Place, has been disposing
of all the valuable Pictures and rarities which her husband had been many
years collecting.—Delicacy prevented her putting into the general sale
many Court Dresses which her husband had worn on State occasions.—She
thinks you might find them useful for the theatre and has requested that I

will apply to you on the subject.—I have no doubt that you would find them very useful for the theatre, and obtain them on reasonable terms.—Mrs. Cosway now lives at N°. 31 Edgware Road.—At all events be so good as to let me know if the offer is acceptable to you, or favo[ur] her with a call" (ms. in the author's collection).

272   28. The original letter is at the library of the Victoria and Albert Museum. It is printed in George C. Williamson, *Richard Cosway, R.A.* (London, 1905), pp. 92–94.

272   29. Review of Thomas Campbell's *Life of Mrs. Siddons*, in *The Mirror of Literature, Amusement, and Instruction*, Aug. 9, 1834, p. 106. The review appeared anonymously, but John Timbs, who was editor of the magazine at that time, told the same anecdote in several signed books.

273   30. Fleming Papers, II, unpaged.

273   31. Published by permission from the ms. in the Henry W. and Albert A. Berg Collection of The New York Public Library, Astor, Lenox and Tilden Foundations.

274   32. "Whether there will be any desire, or rather means, of suspending a piece of marble over my grave, I have my doubts". This note, found among Combe's papers after his death, is followed by the epitaph:

> Vir fuit nec sine doctrina,
> Nec sine sermonum ac morum suavitate;
> Vixit nec sine pietate erga deum,
> Nec sine honesta de numine ejus opinione:
> Nec vero sine peccatis multis,
> Nec tamen sine spe salutis
> A domino clementissimo impetrandæ.

("He was a man not without learning, not without gentleness of speech and manner; he lived not without devotion towards God and not without many sins, but not without hope of obtaining salvation from a most merciful Lord". Translation by Andrew Hutchinson, Esq.) Combe's ms. is bound in the British Museum copy of *Letters to Marianne*, 10922.aaa.21. Published by permission.

276   33. Ms. bound in the same copy of *Letters to Marianne*. Published by permission.

276   34. John Thomas Smith, *Nollekens and His Times* (London, 1828), II, 394.

276   35. G. C. Williamson, *Richard Cosway, R.A.* (London, 1905), pp. 87–88.

BIBLIOGRAPHY

ANY ATTEMPT to compile Combe's bibliography must begin with his own lists as published after his death in the *Gentleman's Magazine* in 1824 (XCIV, Part II, 643–44) and 1852 (NS. XXXVII, 467–72). The second of these is the more comprehensive, but the first gives a few of the titles more exactly. According to Robert Cole, who published the 1852 list, Rudolph Ackermann wrote to Combe on June 8, 1823, asking for "a list of all the works you have wrote or sent to press". This was only eleven days before Combe's death, but there is every reason to believe that Combe had been working on the compilation for some time. In addition to seventy-five titles, he set down dates of publication and details of format with an accuracy which suggests a painstaking search through his accumulation of books and papers. Unfortunately he made no attempt to distinguish between the works he had written and those he had merely edited, but there is no reason to doubt that he had some responsibility, great or small, for every title he mentioned. Furthermore, he seems not to have forgotten many titles; a few items have been added to the list, but he mentioned virtually everything of importance which will be found in the present bibliography.

Most of Combe's papers have disappeared, including many of those which Robert Cole described in the *Gentleman's Magazine*, but two large volumes of original manuscripts, now in the hands of John Fleming of New York, constitute an invaluable source of information regarding Combe's writings during the last decade of his life. These volumes, here referred to as the Fleming Papers, are frequently cited in the present study.

A great deal of information concerning Combe and his writings survives in the letters and memoirs of contemporary men of letters. Horace Walpole, Samuel Rogers, Henry Crabb Robinson, Thomas Campbell, James and Horace Smith, Sir Egerton Brydges, and the anonymous authors of Combe's obituaries all mention with varying degrees of accuracy books which Combe wrote or edited. But the most useful information of this kind, particularly for the decade of the 1790's, is that supplied by Joseph Farington's *Diary*. The eight volumes published by James Greig (1922–1928) comprise only a portion of the manuscript now in the possession of the Royal Library, Windsor Castle. A typed copy of the full manuscript, together with a detailed index, has been deposited in the Print Room of the British Museum and generously made available to scholars. References to the *Diary* in the present work are to this "Windsor Typescript".

Each title has been checked against the three Combe bibliographies which have been independently produced in recent years. The first of these is the present writer's doctoral dissertation (Cornell, 1934), here referred to as HWH. The second is the doctoral dissertation by Franz Montgomery (Minnesota, 1938), referred to as FM. The third is the Catalogue of the British Museum, revised for publication in 1947 and under continuous revision since that date. Books owned by the Museum and catalogued as by Combe are identified by the initials BMC.

The notes appended to the various titles provide information in the following order: (1) Date of first publication as indicated by the newspaper announcement and by the month in which the work is first mentioned by the *Critical Review* (*CR*), *Monthly Review* (*MR*), *Gentleman's Magazine* (*GM*), *London Magazine* (*LM*), or other periodical. The year in which these announcements occur is not stated unless it differs from that of the title page. (2) Combe's mention of the title in the 1852 list. When useful, the 1824 list is also quoted. (3) Other evidence of Combe's authorship. (4) Bibliographies listing the title (i.e., HWH, FM, BMC). Finally, translations of the various titles are mentioned when they come to light, but no systematic search for them has been undertaken.

The titles are classified as follows: I. Works Wholly or Primarily Written by Combe. II. Works Edited, Translated, or Containing Contributions by Combe. III. Newspapers and Periodicals with Contributions by Combe. IV. Unpublished Manuscripts by Combe.

1. WORKS WHOLLY OR PRIMARILY WRITTEN BY COMBE

Additions to the Diaboliad. See *The Diaboliad*.   *page*

Antiquities of York. [With 41 coloured plates.] Drawn and etched by 241
H[enry] Cave. pp. iv, [23]. London: R. Ackermann, 1813. 4to.

Combe: "Description of Antiquities in the City of York. 4to."

HWH, FM.

The Auction: a town eclogue. By the Honourable Mr.———. pp. iv, 12. 93–5
London: J. Bew, 1778. 4to.

Jan. 17 *Morning Post*, Jan. *CR.*

Combe: "The Auction; a Town Eclogue. 1780".

The entire poem was reprinted in the 1811 edition of the *Devil upon
Two Sticks in England*, III, 244–50.

HWM, FM, BMC.

Brief Observations on a Late Letter Addressed to the Right Hon. W. Pitt, 211
by W. Boyd, Esq. &c. on the stoppage of issues in specie by the Bank
of England, &c. &c. pp. 35. London: J. Debrett, 1801. 8vo.

Feb. *MR*

Combe: "Brief Observations, &c. on the Stoppage of Issues in Specie,
&c. 1801".

HWH, FM.

Clifton, a poem. In imitation of Spenser. pp. x, 16. Bristol: Printed [for the 35, 45–6
author] by G. Routh, 1775. 4to. [2nd ed., Bristol: Rouths & Nelson,
and London: G. Robinson, 1776.]

1st ed., June 12, 1775, *Sarah Farley's Bristol Journal*; 2nd ed., June 1,
1776, *Gazetteer*, June *GM, LM.*

Combe: "Clifton; a poem, in Spenser versification, published at
Bristol".

George Routh's bill for printing this poem, addressed to Combe, is
now in the Berg Collection, New York Public Library.

HWH, FM, BMC.

Considerations on the Approaching Dissolution of Parliament. Addressed 157–9
to the elective body of the people. With some account of the existing

page

parties, &c. By the author of the Letter to [sic] a Country Gentleman, Royal Interview, &c. &c. pp. 76. London: Logographic Press, 1790. 8vo.

June 10 *The Times*. The 2nd edition, announced on July 7, dropped the word *approaching* from the title, Parliament having been disolved. June *MR*.

Combe: "Considerations on the approaching Dissolution of Parliament. 1790".

HWH, FM, BMC.

241 The Dance of Life, a poem, by the author of "Doctor Syntax"; illustrated with [26] coloured engravings, by Thomas Rowlandson. pp. [ii], ii, 285. London: R. Ackermann, 1817. 8vo. [First published in 8 monthly numbers.]

Engraved t. p. is dated Dec. 1, 1817; a presentation copy of the work bears the date Dec. 15 in Combe's hand. (Case Western Reserve University Library.)

Combe: "The Dance of Life. 1 vol. carried on in the same manner as the *English Dance of Death*, but the type being larger the lines in each monthly number were less."

HWH, FM, BMC.

Descriptions to the Plates of Thames Scenery. Engraved by W. B. Cooke & G. Cooke, from original drawings by eminent artists. [Unpaged, plates in separate volume having no t.p. but bearing binder's title, *Thames Scenery*.] London: John Murray and W. B. Cooke, 1818 [sic for 1822, date of engraved t.p.].

A variation of *Views on the Thames*, p. 319.

175–81 The Devil upon Two Sticks in England: being a continuation of Le Diable Boiteux of Le Sage. 6 vols., pp. vii, 228; 243; 234; 256; [iv], 271; [iv], 239. London: Logographic Press, vols. 1–4, 1790, vols. 5–6, 1791. 12mo. 4th [enlarged] edition, 6 vols., pp. viii, 285; [iv], 292; [iv], 286; [iv], 291; [iv], 285; [iv], 295. London: Sherwood, Neely, and Jones, 1811.

Six introductory sections first published in the *Daily Universal Register*, June 20, 29, July 4, Aug. 1, 15, Sept. 8, 1787. 1st ed., 4 vols., Mar. 1, 1790; 2nd ed., July 6; 3rd ed., Jan. 1, 1791; vols. v and vi, Jan. 2: *The Times. Repository of Arts*, Sept. 1810: "A new edition of the *Devil upon two Sticks in England*, by Mr. Combe, is in press; enlarged with a great variety of new characters, down to the present year" (p. 170).

page

Combe: "The Devil upon Two Sticks in England. The last edition, with considerable additions, in 6 vols."

HWH, FM, BMC.

The Diaboliad, a poem. Dedicated to the worst man in His Majesty's 64–75
dominions. pp. iv, 24. London: G. Kearsly, 1677 [1777]. 4to.

Additions to the Diaboliad, a poem. Dedicated to the worst man in H[is] 73–4
Majesty's dominions. By the same author. pp. 13. London: G. Kearsly,
1677 [1777]. 4to.

The Diaboliad, a poem. Dedicated to the worst man in His Majesty's 73–4
dominions. A new edition, with large additions. pp. iv, 34. London:
G. Kearsly, 1677 [1777]. 4to.

1st ed., Jan. 25 *Public Advertiser*, Jan. *CR*; *Additions* and new ed., Mar.
13, *Morning Post*, Mar. *CR*.

Combe: "The Diaboliad. In two parts. 1776–7." He should have written
1777–8; the second part appeared in 1778.

HWH, FM, BMC.

The Diaboliad, a poem. Part the Second. By the author of part the first. 96–7
Dedicated to the worst woman in His Majesty's dominions. pp. iv, 46.
London: J. Bew, 1778. 4to.

Mar. *CR*.

Combe: (see preceding entry.)

HWH, FM, BMC.

A Dialogue in the Shades between an Unfortunate Divine, and a Welch 86–9
Member of Parliament, lately deceased. pp. iv, 20. London: J. Bew,
n.d. [7777]. Fol.

July 11 *Public Advertiser*, July *CR*.

Combe: "Dialogue in the Shades, between Dr. Dodd and Chase Price."

HWH, FM, BMC.

The English Dance of Death, from the designs of Thomas Rowlandson, with 241
metrical illustrations by the author of "Doctor Syntax". 2 vols.
[engraved frontispiece, t.p., and 72 coloured plates], pp. vii, 295;
299, [v.] London: R. Ackermann, 1815, 1816. 8vo. [First published in
twenty-four parts, nine in 1814, twelve in 1815, three in 1816.]

Engraved t.p. of completed vol. dated Mar. 1, 1816. Jan. 1817 *MR*.

page

Combe: "The Dance of Death. 2 vols." Manuscript is among the Fleming Papers.

HWH, FM, BMC.

129 The Fast-Day: a Lambeth eclogue. By the author of the Auction. pp. 32. London: J. Bew, 1780. 4to.

Mar. 4 *Morning Chronicle*, Apr. *CR, GM*.

Combe: "The Fast Day; a Lambeth Eclogue. 1780".

HWH, FM, BMC.

76–84 The First of April: or, the triumphs of folly: a poem. Dedicated to a celebrated Duchess. By the author of the Diaboliad. pp. iv, 38. London: J. Bew, 1777. 4to.

Apr. 14 *Public Advertiser*, Apr. *CR, LM*.

Combe: "The First of April; a Poem. 1777".

HWH, FM, BMC.

An Heroic Epistle to Sir James Wright. pp. 22. London: J. Bew, 1779. 4to.

Jan. *CR, MR*.

Combe: "Heroic Epistle to Sir James Wright. 1779".

HWH, FM, BMC.

85 An Heroic Epistle to the Noble Author of the Duchess of Devonshire's Cow, a poem. A noble author. pp. iv, 11. London: J. Bew, 1777. 4to.

June 2 *Public Advertiser*, June *CR, LM*.

Not listed by Combe.

Advertisement in this pamphlet: "Lately published, by the same author, a Poetical Epistle to Sir Joshua Reynolds, Knt. and President of the Royal Academy". See p. 315.

HWH, FM.

241, 270 The History of Johnny Quae Genus, the little foundling of the late Doctor Syntax: a poem, by the author of the three tours. [With twenty-four coloured engravings by T. Rowlandson.] pp. iv, 268. London: R. Ackermann, 1822. 8vo. [First pub. in eight parts, five dated 1821, three dated 1822.]

Combe: "Quae Genus. 1 vol. was carried on in the same manner as Dr. Syntax". The Fleming Papers contain the manuscript in Combe's hand.

HWH, FM, BMC.

A History of Madeira. With a series of twenty-seven coloured engravings, 241–2,
illustrative of the costumes, manners, and occupations of the inhabitants 270
of that island. pp. vii, 118. London: R. Ackermann, 1821. 4to.

Combe: "The History of Madeira. 1 vol. 4to."

Combe's ms. is among the Fleming Papers. In a letter to Angelica
Ackermann dated June 5, 1821, Combe wrote, "My only reason for
preferring Friday [for dining with the Ackermanns] was that I fear I
shall not have prepared sufficient copy of Madeira to go to Press before
that day" (ms. in Harvard College Library).

HWH, FM, BMC.

The History of the Abbey Church of St. Peter's Westminster, its antiquities 241–2
and monuments. With 84 coloured engravings after Pugin, Huett, and
Mackenzie. 2 vols., pp. xviii, 335; 279. London: R. Ackermann, 1812.
[First published in 16 monthly parts.]

Combe: "The History of Westminster Abbey. 2 vols. 4to." His ms.
is among the Fleming Papers.

Included among the subscribers: "Wm. Combe, Esq., London".

HWH, FM, BMC.

The History of the Colleges of Winchester, Eton, and Westminster: with 182
the Charter-House, the schools of St. Paul's, Merchant-Taylors,
Harrow, and Rugby, and the free-school of Christ's Hospital. [With
48 coloured engravings.] pp. vii, 56, 72, 27, 32, 34, 22, 40, 34, 43.
London: R. Ackermann, 1816. 4to. [First published in 12 monthly parts,
beginning Jan. 1, 1816, paged as above and not repaged for book
publication.]

Combe: "The History of the Public Schools, except Winchester,
Harrow, and Rugby. 1 vol. 4to." His ms. is among the Fleming Papers.
Included among the subscribers: "Combe, W. esq."

HWH, FM, BMC.

An History of the Late Important Period; from the beginning of His 156
Majesty's illness, to the settlement of the executive government, in the
appointment of a Regent; to which are added, observations on the
conduct of the two contending parties, to the period of His Majesty's
reappearance in the House of Lords. pp. 543. London: Logographic
Press, 1789. 8vo.

July 7 *The Times.*

Combe: "A Review of an Important Period, involving the State
Proceedings on the late [i.e., in 1823] King's first Illness". 1824 list:
"The important period of his Majesty's Illness, 1789".

page

A new edition of this work was advertised in *The Times* (Aug. 26, 1789) as by the author of a *Letter from a Country Gentleman to a Member of Parliament*.

FM.

183–94, 198   An History of the Principal Rivers of Great Britain. Vols. I and II [No more published]: An History of the River Thames. [With 76 aquatints by J. C. Stadler after drawings by Joseph Farington.] pp. xvii, 312; viii, 294. London: J. and J. Boydell, 1794, 1796. fol.

June 1794 *Analytical Review* (by Henry Fuseli).

Combe: "The History of the Thames. 2 vols. imperial 4to. by the Boydells".

HWH, FM, BMC.

241   A History of the University of Cambridge, its colleges, halls and public buildings. [With portrait and 79 coloured aquatint plates; some copies have in addition 16 portraits of the Founders.] 2 vols., pp. viii, 302; 332. London: R. Ackermann, 1815. 4to. [First published in 20 monthly parts, the first on May 1, 1814.]

Not listed by Combe.

Ackermann's *Repository of Arts* (Aug. 1, 1823) lists the title among those written by Combe for this publisher. Combe's name appears in the list of subscribers.

HWH, FM, BMC.

241   A History of the University of Oxford, its colleges, halls, and public buildings. [With 82 plates; some copies have in addition 33 portraits of the Founders.] 2 vols., pp. xv, xxv, 281; 267. London: R. Ackermann, 1814. 4to.

Combe: "The History of the University of Oxford. 2 vols. 4to."

Ackermann's *Repository of Arts* (Aug. 1, 1823) lists the title among those written by Combe for this publisher. Combe's name appears in the list of subscribers. His ms. is among the Fleming Papers.

HWH, FM, BMC.

289 n. 34   An Interesting Letter to the Duchess of Devonshire. pp. 113. London: J. Bew, 1778. 8vo.

Feb. *CR*.

Combe: "Interesting Letter to the Duchess of Devonshire".

HWH, FM, BMC.

page

The Justification: a poem. By the author of the Diaboliad. pp. viii, 40. 90–2
London: Printed for the author and sold by J. Bew and H. Gardner,
1777. 4to.

Dec. 6 *Morning Post*, Dec. *CR, MR, GM.*

Combe: "The Justification; a Poem. 1777".

HWH, FM, BMC.

A Letter from a Country Gentleman, to a Member of Parliament, on the 151–5
present state of public affairs . . . pp. 75. London: Logographic
Press, 1789. 8vo.

Jan. 31 *The Times*, Feb. *MR.*

Combe: "Letter from a Country Gentleman to a Member of Parliament.
1789".

HWH, FM, BMC.

Letter to a Retired Officer, on the opinions and sentence of a general court 197–8
martial, held at the Horse Guards, Nov. 27, 1795, and on many
subsequent days, for the trial of Col. John Fenton Cawthorne, of the
Westminster Regiment of Middlesex militia. London: J. Debrett,
1796. 4to.

June *MR.*

Combe: "Letter of a Retired Officer, being a defence of Colonel
Cawthorne".

J. Farington, Apr. 25, 1796: "Boydell . . . has seen Col. Cawthorne
frequently, and engaged Coombes to write a defence for him under a
feigned name which Bulmer has printed. Coombes asked £100 for
writing it" (Windsor Typescript, p. 593).

HWH, FM.

Letters between Amelia in London and Her Mother in the Country: written 245
by the late William Combe, Esq. Author of the Three Tours of Dr.
Syntax, &c. &c. &c. pp. iv, 310. London: R. Ackermann, 1824. 12mo.

Originally published in Ackermann's *Repository of Arts*, q.v. The issue
for June 1, 1824, contains the following announcement: "Mr. Ackermann will publish in a few days, in a pocket volume, with an elegant
frontispiece, *Letters between Amelia in London and her Mother in the
Country*, from the pen of the late William Combe, Esq. the popular
author of the 'Three Tours of Dr. Syntax'". Oct. *MR.*

The original binder's title read, "Letters from Amelia by Dr. Combe."
(Copy in Bristol Reference Library.)

HWH, FM, BMC.

133–5 Letters between Two Lovers and Their Friends. By the author of Letters Supposed to Have Been Written by Yorick and Eliza. 3 vols., pp. vii, 95; 96–190; 191–302 (pagination of Dublin ed., 3 vols. in 1). London: J. Bew, 1781, 12mo.

July *MR*.

Not listed by Combe, but the reference in the title to the *Letters Supposed* is strong evidence of his authorship. This work is advertised in two other publications by Combe, *Letters of the Late Lord Lyttelton* and *Letters of an Italian Nun and an English Gentleman*. These cross-references normally indicate common authorship.

HWH, FM.

131–3 Letters of an Italian Nun and an English Gentleman. Translated from the French of J. J. Rousseau. pp. xiv, 190. London: J. Bew, 1781. 12mo.

June *CR*, *LM*.

Combe: "Letters of an Italian Nun and an English Gentleman. 2 vols."

HWH, FM.

118–31 Letters of the Late Lord Lyttelton. 2 vols., pp. vii, 222; [iv], 260. London: J. Bew, 1780, 1782. 8vo.

Vol. I, Feb. 24, 1780, *St. James Chronicle*; Mar. *CR*, *GM*. Vol. II, May 1782 *CR*.

Combe: "Lord Lyttelton's Letters. 2 vols. duod."

J. Farington, Jan. 14, 1807: "Westall & J. Aytoun dined with me. Coombes told them he was the Author of a publication entitled Letters from [sic] the late Lord Lyttleton [sic]" (Windsor Typescript, p. 3560). See discussion of authorship in Chapter IV.

HWH, FM, BMC: "Commonly attributed to W. Combe, who himself claimed the authorship, but sometimes considered genuine".

225–6 The Letters of Valerius, on the state of parties, the war, the volunteer system, and most of the political topics which have lately been under public discussion. Originally published in "The Times". London: Sold by J. Hatchard, 1804, 8vo.

Mar. 17 *The Times*: "This day is published . . . *Letters of Valerius* . . . Printed for J. Stockdale". (Note that the publisher's name is omitted from t.p.) May *MR*.

Not listed by Combe, who was on the editorial staff of *The Times* when these letters were printed and may have felt bound by that paper's policy of anonymity. The letters were published virtually as leading articles expressing the official views of the paper.

HWH, FM, BMC.

Letters Supposed to Have Been Written by Yorick and Eliza. 2 vols., pp. 112–8
xiv, 15–176, 180. London: J. Bew, 1779. 8vo.

July *CR.*

Combe: "Letters supposed to have passed between Sterne and Eliza. 2 vols." 1824: "Letters supposed to have been written by Yorick and Eliza, 1779, 2 vols."

Combe's authorship was not seriously questioned until the work was republished in 1929 as authentically Sterne's under the title *Second Journal to Eliza* and with an introduction by Margaret R. B. Shaw. Although that book met with little favour from scholars, it makes necessary a detailed discussion of the authorship in Chapter IV.

HWH, FM, BMC: "Stated in the preface by the editor to be spurious. Usually attributed to William Combe, who himself claimed authorship, but sometimes considered the genuine work of Sterne".

Letters to Marianne. By William Combe, Esq. pp. xiv, 85. London: 231–4,
Thomas Boys, 1823. 12mo.   238

Sept. 27 *Literary Gazette* (review by William Jerdan).

HWH, FM, BMC.

A Letter to Her Grace the Duchess of Devonshire. pp. 16. London: Fielding 84
and Walker, 1777. 4to.

Apr. 24 *Public Advertiser*, May *MR, LM*

Combe: "A Letter to the Duchess of Devonshire. 1777".

HWH, FM, BMC.

Observations on Ackermann's Patent Moveable Axles, for four-wheeled carriages, containing engraved elevations of carriages, with plans and sections, conveying accurate ideas of this superior improvement. pp. [iv], 60. [With 5 plates.] London: R. Ackermann, 1819. 4to.

Not listed by Combe, but his ms. is among the Fleming Papers.

Observations on the Present State of the Royal Academy; with characters of living artists. By an old artist. London: Logographic Press, 1790.

Mar. 9 *The Times.*

page

Combe: "On the Disputes of the Royal Academy".

Although no copy of this pamphlet has come to light, its tendency may be inferred from a discussion of the same subject in another of Combe's works published that year, the *Devil upon Two Sticks in England*, VI, 212–18.

20–1,   Original Letters of the Late Reverend Mr. Laurence Sterne; never before
142–3   published. pp. 216. London: Logographic Press, 1788. 12mo.

Of these 39 letters, the first 33 appeared in the *Daily Universal Register* and (after the paper changed its name) *The Times* at irregular intervals between Jan. 11, 1787, and Jan. 17, 1788. Mar. *MR*.

Combe: "Letters in imitation of Mr. Sterne. 1 vol." 1824 list: "Original Letters of the late Rev. Laurence Sterne, 1788".

See Harlan W. Hamilton, "William Combe and the *Original Letters of the Late Reverend Mr. Laurence Sterne* (1788)," PMLA, LXXXII (Oct. 1967), pp. 420–29.

HWH, FM, BMC: "A compilation sometimes attributed in part to W. Combe".

TRANSLATIONS:

Lettres de Sterne. Nouvellement publiées à Londres, & traduites de l'Anglois, pour servir de supplément au Voyage Sentimental & aux autres ouvrages du même auteur. A Londres, & se trouvent à Paris chez Desray. 1788.

Lettres de Sterne à ses amis, traduites sur les originaux nouvellement publiés à Londres. A la Haye. 1789. [The title is that of another collection, but the work is in fact a translation of the *Original Letters.*]

135–7   Original Love-Letters, between a lady of quality and a person of inferior station. 2 vols., pp. viii, 149; iv, 174. London: J. Bew, 1784. 12mo.

Sept. *MR*.

Combe: "Letters between a Lady of Quality and a person of Inferior Rank. 2 vols." (1824 list: "Original Love Letters, 1784, 2 vols.")

HWH, FM, BMC.

35–42   The Philosopher in Bristol. pp. 110. Bristol: printed [for the author] by G. Routh, 1775. 8vo.

35–6,   The Philosopher in Bristol. Part the Second. pp. 159. Bristol: printed [for
42–5   the author] by G. Routh, 1775. 8vo.

Published separately, the first part on June 12, the second on July 26

(*Felix Farley's Bristol Journal*). 2nd ed., "Bristol: Printed and sold by Rouths & Nelson in Bridge-street; and by G. Robinson, bookseller, in Pater-noster-row, London", June 1, 1776, *Gazetteer*; Sept. *MR*.

Combe: "The Philosopher in Bristol. 2 vol."

George Routh's bill for printing these volumes, addressed to Combe, is now in the Berg Collection, New York Public Library.

HWH, FM, BMC.

Plain Thoughts of a Plain Man, addressed to the common sense of the 171–3 people of Great Britain: with a few words, en passant, to the uncommon sense of Mr. Erskine. pp. [ii], 113. London: J. Bell, 1797. 8vo.

July *MR*.

Combe: "Plain Thoughts of a Plain Man, &c. 1797".

HWH, FM.

A Poetical Epistle to Sir Joshua Reynolds, Knt. and President of the Royal 86 Academy. pp. iv, 22. London: Fielding and Walker, 1777. 4to.

May 9 *Public Advertiser*, May *CR*.

Combe: "Heroic Epistle to Sir Joshua Reynolds. 1777".

Advertised on back page of *Heroic Epistle to the Noble Author of the Duchess of Devonshire's Cow* as "lately published by the same author".

HWH, FM, BMC.

The R—— ——l Register: with annotations by another hand. 9 vols., pp. 101–12 [iv], xvi, 150; [vi], 192; [vi], 170; [vi], 181; ix, [ii], 154; [vi], 183; [vi], 173; [vi], 166; vi, 167. London: J. Bew, 1778 [I and II], 1779 [III], 1780 [IV], 1781 [V and VI], 1782 [VII], 1783 [VIII], 1784 [IX]. 8vo.

Vol. I, Jan. 29, 1778, *Gazetteer*; Vols. I–II, Mar. *CR, GM*.

Combe: "Royal Register. 9 vols."

HWH, FM, BMC.

The Royal Dream: or the P—— in a panic. An eclogue, with annotations. 138, pp. xii, 25. London: S. W. Fores, 1785. 4to. 150–1

Oct. *MR*.

Combe: "The Royal Dream. 1785".

HWH, FM, BMC.

155–6 The Royal Interview: a fragment. By the author of a Letter from a Country Gentleman to a Member of Parliament. pp. 61. London: Logographic Press, 1789. 8vo.

Mar. 20 *The Times*, Apr. *MR*.

Combe: "The Royal Interview, &c. 1789".

HWH, FM, BMC.

84–5 A Second Letter to Her Grace the Duchess of Devonshire. pp. 15. London: Fielding and Walker, 1777. fol.

May 17 *Public Advertiser*, May *CR, MR*.

Combe: "A second ditto [i.e., Letter to the Duchess of Devonshire]. 1777".

HWH, FM, BMC.

The Second Tour of Doctor Syntax. See entry following the *Tour of Doctor Syntax*, p. 318.

Six Poems, illustrative of as many engravings made by H.R.H. the Princess Elizabeth. London: R. Ackermann, 1813. 4to.

Aug. 1813 *Repository of Arts*: "The same publisher [Ackermann] also announces . . . *Poetical Illustrations*, by Wm. Combe, Esq. of six engravings by Thielke, after the elegant designs of her Royal Highness the Princess Elizabeth: to be printed by Bulmer, at the Shakespeare press".

Combe: "Poetical Illustrations of Drawings by the Princess Elizabeth".

HWH, FM.

261–2 Swiss Scenery from Drawings by Major [James Pattison] Cockburn. [With 60 plates, engraved t.p. and tailpiece.] pp. 200. London: Rodwell & Martin, 1820.

Plates are dated from Jan. 1, 1819, to Nov. 1, 1820.

Not listed by Combe, but portions of the book in his hand are found among the Fleming Papers.

241 The Thames; or, graphic illustrations of seats, villas, public buildings, and picturesque scenery, on the banks of that noble river. . . . The engravings executed by William Bernard Cooke, from original drawings by Samuel Owen, Esq. 2 vols., pp. [163], [170]. London: Vernor, Hood, and Sharpe, and W. B. Cooke, 1811. 4to.

Combe: "Illustrations of Cooke's Graphic Sketches of the Thames".

J. Farington, Aug. 1, 1811: "Landseer mentioned a work carrying on by Engravers of the name of Cook. They have published a series of views in the vicinity of the Thames, to which Letter press descriptions are added, & these, He said, Cooke informed Him were written by Wm. Combe who had been employed by Messrs. Boydells for the same purpose, which Landseer thought an improper act of Combe" (Windsor Typescript, p. 5789).

An autograph letter from Combe to W. B. Cooke bears the following endorsement: "Note from Wm Combe who wrote Dr Syntax &c &c and my work of the Thames. W. B. Cooke". British Museum.

HWH, FM.

The Tour of Doctor Syntax, in search of the picturesque. A poem. [With 242–61
30 coloured aquatint plates and coloured vignette on t.p. by Thomas
Rowlandson.] pp. [v], 275. London: R. Ackermann, n.d. [1812]. 8vo.

May 1, 1812 (*The Times*, May 12: "R. Ackermann has the honour to inform the Nobility, Gentry, and the Public, that a Tour in Search of the Picturesque, by the Rev. Dr. Syntax, a Poem in thirty Chapters, printed with a new type, on large royal octavo vellum paper, and hot-pressed, price with thirty [sic] coloured engravings, 21s. or without engravings, 10s. 6d. was ready for delivery, at his Repository of Arts, 101, Strand, on the 1st of May instant. It may now be had of all the booksellers in the united kingdom.") July *British Critic*.

Combe: "Vol. 1 [i.e., the first *Tour*] first appeared in monthly detached pieces, in verse of about 300 lines, to illustrate *one* subject which I never saw till it was completed". The resulting *Schoolmaster's Tour* appeared in the monthly issues of the *Poetical Magazine* (see p. 332) and was then extensively revised before publication in monthly parts as the *Tour of Doctor Syntax*.

Monthly Review (Jan. 1813) names Combe as the author.

HWH, FM, BMC.

TRANSLATIONS:

Doctor Syntaxes Reise efter det Maleriske. Et Digt oversat af det Engelske ved K. L. Rahbek. Kiøbenhavn, 1820.

Le Don quichotte Romantique, ou voyage du Docteur Syntaxe, à la recherche du pittoresque et du romantique; poëme en xx chants, traduit librement de l'anglais, et orné de 26 gravures. Par M. Gandais. Paris, 1821.

Des Doktor Syntax Reise. Ein Gedicht in sechsundzwanzig Gesängen nebst dreissig kolorirten Steinstichen. Herausgegeben zum Besten der Königl. Preuss. Berlin, 1822.

IMITATIONS (not by Combe):

The Life of Napoleon, a Hudibrastic Poem in fifteen cantos, by Doctor Syntax, embellished with thirty engravings, by G. Cruikshank. London, 1815.

The Military Adventures of Johnny Newcome . . . with sketches by Rowlandson; and notes. By an officer. London, 1815.

The Grand Master, or adventures of Qui Hi in Hindostan, a Hudibrastic poem in eight cantos by Quiz. Illustrated with 28 engravings by Rowlandson. London: T. Tegg, 1815.

The Adventures of Doctor Comicus or the frolicks of fortune. A comic satirical poem for the squeamish and the queer. In twelve cantos, by a modern Syntax. London: n.d. [1815].

The Wars of Wellington, a narrative poem; in fifteen cantos. Embellished with thirty engravings, coloured from the original paintings, by Heath. By Dr. Syntax. London, 1819.

The Adventures of Johnny Newcombe in the Navy. A poem in four cantos. With notes. By John Mitford, Esq. R.N. London: Sherwood, Neely, and Jones, et al., 1819.

The Tour of Doctor Syntax through London, or the pleasures and miseries of the metropolis. A poem by Doctor Syntax. London: J. Johnson, 1820.

Doctor Syntax in Paris or a tour in search of the grotesque. A humorous and satirical poem. London, W. Wright, 1820.

The Old English 'Squire. . . . A poem, in ten cantos. By John Careless, Esq. Illustrated with plates by one of the family. London: Thomas M'Lean, 1821.

The Tour of Doctor Prosody, in search of the antique and picturesque, through Scotland, the Hebrides, the Orkney and Shetland Isles; illustrated by twenty humorous plates. London, Edinburgh, and Glasgow, 1821.

The Post Captain or adventures of a true British tar by a naval officer. With characteristic [coloured] engravings by Mr. Williams. London: J. Johnson, n.d.

Tom Raw, the Griffin: a burlesque poem, in twelve cantos. . . . [25 coloured engravings.] By a civilian and an officer of the Bengal establishment. London: R. Ackermann, 1828.

Nov. 1821 *MR.*

Combe: "Vols. 2 and 3 [the second and third Tours] were published in monthly numbers of about 1,000 lines for three subjects [engravings], without any opportunity of preparation but from the 16th of each month to the following first." The MS. is among the Fleming Papers.

HWH, FM, BMC.

The Third Tour of Doctor Syntax, in search of a wife, a poem. [With 24   260, 270 coloured aquatint plates and vignette on t.p. by Thomas Rowlandson.] pp. 279. London: R. Ackermann, n.d. [1821.] 8vo. [First published in parts.]

Preface is dated May 1, 1821. Nov. *MR.*

Combe: [See preceding entry.]

HWH, FM, BMC.

The Traitor. A poetical rhapsody. London: J. Bew, 1781. 4to.   135

Apr. *CR, MR.*

Combe: "The Traitor; a Poem. 1781."

No copy of this satire on Benjamin Franklin has come to light, but 30 lines are quoted in the *CR* notice.

HWH, FM.

Two Words of Counsel and One of Comfort. Addressed to His Royal High-   169–70 ness the Prince of Wales. pp. 60. London: T. Mason, 1795. 8vo.

July *MR.*

Combe: "Two Words of Counsel and one of Comfort. 1795."

HWH, FM.

Valerius's Address to the People of England. London: James Asperne, [1803]. Single sheet, fol. [Signed "Valerius. London, August 3d."]

Aug. 4 *The Times*. Entire "Address" published as a letter, the seventh of the series later published separately as the *Letters of Valerius*, q.v.

HWH, BMC.

Views on the Thames; Engraved by W. B. Cooke and George Cooke. [With 77 plates.] 2 vols., unpaged. London: W. B. Cooke, 1822. 4to.

A revision of *The Thames: or, Graphic Illustrations*, p. 316. The plates are new and bear engraved dates ranging from 1814 to 1822. Some subjects included in the earlier publication are omitted; others are

page

added. The letterpress accompanying repeated subjects is unchanged; that for the new subjects is much shorter and not in Combe's manner. The plates and letterpress were also published in separate volumes; see *Descriptions to the Plates of Thames Scenery*, p. 306.

163–8 A Word in Season to the traders and manufacturers of Great Britain. pp. 32. London: Stockdale, 1792. 8vo.

June *CR*.

Combe: "A Word in Season to the Traders, Manufacturers, &c. 1792."

HWH, FM, BMC.

289 n. 34 The World as It Goes, a poem. By the author of the Diaboliad. Dedicated to one of the best men in His Majesty's dominions, &c. pp. [vi], 37. London: J. Bew, 1779. 4to.

May 21 *Public Advertiser*, June *CR*.

Combe: "The World as it Goes; a Poem. 1779."

Horace Walpole: "I heard t' other day of *The World as it Goes*, a poem published last spring. . . . It is by that infamous Combe, the author of the *Diaboliad*." *Correspondence*, ed. W. S. Lewis, XXVIII, 470.

HWH, FM, BMC.

II. WORKS EDITED, TRANSLATED, OR CONTAINING CONTRIBUTIONS BY COMBE

144–7 [Anderson, Adam.] An Historical and Chronological Deduction of the Origin of Commerce, from the earliest accounts. Containing an history of the great commercial interests of the British Empire. . . . Carefully revised, corrected, and continued to the present time. 4 vols., pp. lxxxviii, 556; 647; 508, 271; 718. London: Logographic Press, 1787–1789. 4to.

First published in weekly numbers, beginning Mar. 3, 1787; complete works in 4 vols. published June 16, 1789, *The Times*. Aug. 1790 *MR*.

Combe: "Anderson's History of Commerce. 4 vols. 4to. The first 3 vols. corrected and enlarged, and the whole of the 4 vols. compiled, arranged, and written by me."

Listed among the subscribers: "Coombes, Wm. Esq. Harford-street, May-fair."

Title page of the Dublin edition (1790): "Carefully Revised, Corrected, and Continued to the Year 1789, by Mr. Coombe."

HWH, FM, BMC.

page

Anderson, Æneas. A Journal of the Forces which sailed from the Downs, in 212–3
April 1800, on a secret expedition under the command of Lieut.-Gen.
Pigot, till their arrival in Minorca . . . to the surrender of Alexandria.
By Æneas Anderson. Illustrated by engravings. pp. xxviii, 532.
London: J. Debrett, 1802. 4to.

Nov. 29 *The Sun.*

Combe: "Anderson's Account of the Campaign in Egypt."

J. Farington, Aug. 7, 1803: "He [Combe] methodized Æneas Anderson's acct. of Egypt but it did not sell" (Windsor Typescript, p. 2350).

HWH, FM, BMC.

———. A Narrative of the British Embassy to China, in the years 1792, 197
1793, and 1794; containing the various circumstances of the embassy,
with accounts of customs and manners of the Chinese; and a description
of the country, towns, cities, &c. &c. pp. xxiv, 278, [279–94]. London:
J. Debrett, 1795. 4to.

Apr. 4 *The Times* (Apr. 1), May *MR.*

Combe: "Anderson's Embassy to China. 4to."

J. Farington, June 1, 1795: "Coombes made up the book of Æneas
Andersons account of the Embassy to China. Anderson had kept a
minute daily journal in small pocket books and appears to have been
very attentive to circumstances" (Windsor Typescript, p. 349).
"[Isaac] Reed said Debrett told him He gave Coombe £100 for writing
Æneas Andersons account of Embassy."—Ibid. Aug. 24, 1797 (p.
1085).

HWH, FM, BMC.

TRANSLATIONS:
Erzählung der Reise und Gesandtschaft des Lord Macartney nach
China und von da zurück nach England in den Jahren 1792 bis 1794.
. . . Aus den Englischen, mit Anmerkungen und Zusätzen. Erlangen,
1795.

Relation de l'ambassade du Dr. Macartney à la Chine pendant les
anées 1792, 1793 et 1794 . . . traduite de l'anglais (par Lallemant)
sur la seconde édition d'Æneas Anderson. 2 tomes en 1. Paris: Denné
le jeune, an IV [1795–96].

Anthing, Friedrich. History of the Campaigns of Count Alexander Suworow 296 n. 5
Rymnikski, Field-Marshal-General in the service of His Imperial
Majesty, the Emperor of all the Russias: with a preliminary sketch of
his private life and character. Translated from the German. 2 vols.,
pp. xxxvi, 218; 366, 2, 15. London: J. Wright, 1799. 8vo.

Oct. *MR*.

Combe: "Campaigns of Count Alexander Suwarrow Rymniski. 2 vols. 1799." This title was added to Combe's list by another hand, but it occurs also in the list published in 1824.

Combe did not know German, and this translation is actually from the French: *Les campagnes du Feldmaréchal Comte Souworow Rymnikski*. Par Frédéric Anthing. Trad. de l'allemand par [Jacques Accarias] de Sérionne. 3 vols. Gotha, 1799. Combe's title page follows that of another French translation: *Histoire des campagnes du Comte Alexandre Suworow Rymnikski, Général-Feld-Maréchal au service de sa Majesté l'Empereur de toutes les Russies*. A Londres. 1799.

HWH, FM.

202 Colnett, James. Voyage to the South Atlantic and round Cape Horn into the Pacific Ocean. . . . Undertaken and performed by Captain James Colnett, of the Royal Navy, in the Ship Ratler. [With 6 maps and 4 plates.] pp. [ii], vi, xviii, 179. London: Printed for the Author, 1798. 4to.

Apr. 1799 *CR*.

Combe: "Translation [*sic*] of Colnett's Voyage to South America."

HWH, FM, BMC.

216, [Combe, William, ed.] The Pic Nic. [Reprint of the 14 numbers of the
297 n. 12 newspaper.] 2 vols., pp. xxvii, 225; 267. London: J. F. Hughes, 1803. 8vo.

Combe: "Pic Nic."

See entry for the *Pic Nic* newspaper, p. 331, for list of contributions identified as by Combe. Presumably he wrote the Preface to this reprint.

HWH, FM, BMC.

241 Donaldson, T. L. Pompeii, illustrated with picturesque views, engraved by W. B. Cooke, from the original drawings of Lieut.-Col. [James Pattison] Cockburn of the Royal Artillery, and with plans and details of the public and domestic edifices, including the recent excavations, and a descriptive letterpress to each plate, by T. L. Donaldson, Architect. 2 vols., pp. [vi], 60; vii, 36. London: W. B. Cooke, 1827. fol.

Not listed by Combe, but portions of the manuscript in his hand are among the Fleming Papers. The table of contents lists two sections as by "the late W. Combe, Esq." These are the "History of Pompeii", pp. 19–24, and the "History of Vesuvius", pp. 25–35.

BMC.

page

Falkner, Thomas. A Description of Patagonia, and the adjoining parts of 30–2
South America. . . . By Thomas Falkner, who resided near forty years
in those parts. Illustrated with a new map . . . engraved by Mr.
Kitchen. pp. iv, 144. Hereford: Printed by C. Pugh, and sold by T.
Lewis, London, 1774. 4to.

Jan. 27 *British Chronicle, or Pugh's Hereford Journal* (Jan. 13), *London
Chronicle* (Jan. 25–27), Mar. *GM.*

Combe: "Description of Patagonia, from the papers of the Jesuit James
[*sic*] Falkner. 1774."

New edition, edited with Intro. and notes by Arthur E. S. Neumann.
Chicago: Armann & Armann, 1935.

HWH, FM, BMC.

TRANSLATIONS:

Beschreibung von Patagonien und den angrezenden theilen von
Südamerika aus dem Englischen des Herrn Thomas Falkner. [Trans-
lated by S. Hermann Ewald.] Gotha, 1775.
Description des terres Magellaniques et des pays adjacens. Traduit
de l'Anglois par M. B**. [Marc. Theod. Bourrit.] Lausanne, 1787.
Descripción de Patagonia y de las partes adyacentes de la America
meridional . . . escrita in ingles por D. Tomas Falkner. Buenos-Aires,
1835.
Descripción de la Patagonia y de las partes contiguas de la América
del sur por el P. Tomas Falkner, S. J. Traduccion, anotaciones, noticia
biográfica y bibliográfica por el Dr. Samuel A. Lafone Quevedo. Buenos
Aires, 1911.

Foot, Jesse. The Life of Arthur Murphy, Esq. . . . pp. iv, 464. London: 234
J. Faulder, 1811. 4to.

July *CR.*

Combe: "Foot's Life of Murphy, from papers, suggestions, and
criticisms furnished by him."

HWH, FM, BMC.

Grant, Charles, Viscount de Vaux. The History of Mauritius . . . Com- 211
posed principally from the papers and memoirs of Baron Grant . . . by
his son, Charles Grant, Viscount de Vaux. Illustrated with [3 folding]
maps. pp. xxi, 571. London: Printed for the Author, 1801. 4to.

Dedication dated Feb. 2, 1801; Nov. *CR.*

Combe: "History of Mauritius, from materials furnished by the Viscount
Grant."

HWH, FM, BMC.

page

211 Hanger, George, Baron Coleraine. The Life, Adventures, and Opinions of Col. George Hanger. Written by himself. . . . 2 vols., pp. *339; 475.* London: J. Debrett, 1801. 8vo.

Combe: "Captain Hanger's Life. 2 vols. From his papers and suggestions."

HWH, FM, BMC.

2 Hunter, John. A Practical Treatise on the Diseases of the Teeth; intended as a supplement to the Natural History of those parts. By John Hunter, Surgeon Extraordinary to the King, and Fellow of the Royal Society. pp. [ii], iv, 128. London: J. Johnson, 1778. 4to.

Mar. *CR.*

Combe: "John Hunter was the worst writer that ever took a pen in hand. I wrote his essay on the teeth for him, and it was a hard job too; for not only could I not understand him, but he evidently did not comprehend his own meaning". [Sir George Lefevre], *The Life of a Travelling Physician* (London, 1843), I, 79. Cf. Lloyd G. Stevenson, "The Elder Spence, William Combe, and John Hunter", *Journal of the History of Medicine*, X, 2 (April 1955), 182–96, and Harlan W. Hamilton, "William Combe and John Hunter's Essay on the Teeth", *Journal of the History of Medicine*, XIV (1959), 169–78.

296 n. 5 Jourdan, Jean-Baptiste, Count. Memoir of the Operations of the Army of the Danube, under the command of General Jourdan, 1799. Taken from the mss. of that officer. Translated from the French. pp. xi, 231. London: J. Debrett, 1799. 8vo.

Combe: "Translation of General Jordan's Defence of his conduct during the French Revolution."

HWH, FM, BMC.

210 Mackenzie, Alexander. Voyages from Montreal, on the River St. Laurence, through the continent of North America, to the Frozen and Pacific Oceans; in the years 1789 and 1793. With a preliminary account of the rise, progress, and present state of the fur trade of that country. [With three folding maps and engraved frontispiece.] pp. viii, cxxxii, 412, [ii]. London: T. Cadell, Jun. and W. Davies, Cobbett and Morgan, and W. Creech, 1801 [1802]. 4to.

Feb. 16, 1802, *The Sun*; July 1802 *MR.*

Combe: "Sir Alexander Mackenzie's Journey across America."

In a letter to Messrs. Cadell & Davies, Apr. 1, 1801, Combe wrote, "I have not received the Account of Mr Hearne's Travels, which are so necessary to assist me in my progress, but particularly at the Com-

mencement of it. I really wait for it,—Mr. Mackenzie who has just
called upon me,—informs me that it is sent,—but I have not received
it" (ms. in author's possession). Hearne is mentioned on p. 2 of the
published work.

HWH, FM, BMC.

TRANSLATIONS:

Reisen von Montreal durch Nordwestamerika nach dem Eismeer
und der Süd-See in den Jahren 1789 und 1793. Nebst einer Geschichte
des Pelzhandels in Canada. Aus dem Englischen. Berlin und Hamburg,
1802.

Voyages d'Alex^dre Mackenzie dans l'intérieur de l'Amérique septen-
trionale, faits en 1789, 1792 et 1793 . . . précédés d'un tableau histori-
que et politique sur le commerce des pelleteries dans le Canada, traduits
de l'anglais par J. Castéra, avec des notes et un itinéraire tirés en partie
des papiers du vice amiral Bougainville. Paris, 1802.

Meares, John. Voyages Made in the Years 1788 and 1789, from China to   182
the north west coast of America. . . . By John Meares Esq. [With
charts and plates.] pp. xix, xcv, 372, 108. London: Logographic Press,
1790. 4to.

Mar. 9 *The Times*, Feb. 1791 *MR*.

Combe: "Voyage of Captain Neares [*sic*] to North-West Coast of
America."

HWH, FM, BMC.

TRANSLATIONS:

Voyages de la Chine à la côte nord-ouest d'Amérique. . . . Par le
capitaine J. Meares. Paris, 1793.

Des Kapitians [*sic*] John Meares und des Kapitains William Douglas
Reisen nach der Nordwest-Küste von Amerika . . . beschrieben von
John Meares. 1791.

[Miller, Lady Anna Riggs.] Poetical Amusements at a villa near Bath.
pp. viii, 131. Bath: L. Bull, 1775. 4to.

"Ode to the Elegiac Muse", pp. 139–43. Attributed to Combe by
anonymous but evidently well-informed annotator of a copy in the
Harvard Library. The style is similar to that of other poems by Combe,
and his presence in and near Bath when this book was compiled makes
the attribution plausible.

[Naubert, C. B. E.] Alf von Deulmen; or, the history of the Emperor   184
Philip, and his daughters. Translated from the German by Miss A. E.
Booth. 2 vols., pp. xx, 300, [iv], 305. London: J. Bell, 1794. 8vo.

page

Combe: "Translation of Alf. Von Deulmen." Since he knew no German, and since no French version has come to light, Combe presumably edited the translation.

The German original is as follows: Alf von Duelman: oder Geschichte Kaiser Philipps und seiner Tochter. Aus den ersten Zeiten der heimlichen Gerichte. Leipzig, 1791.

241 [Papworth, J. B., Francis Wrangham, and William Combe,] Poetical Sketches of Scarborough: illustrated by twenty-one engravings of humourous subjects, coloured from original designs, made upon the spot by J. Green, and etched by T. Rowlandson. pp. [iv], xv, 215. London: R. Ackermann, 1813. 8vo.

Not listed by Combe.

Sept. *MR* states that three of the sketches are by "Dr. Combe". These are "Sea Bathing", "The Shower-Bath", and "The Promenade". The book contains 20 sketches (not 21 as usually stated); of these Papworth wrote 13, Wrangham 4, "and the celebrated William Combe three chapters" (Wyatt Papworth, *John B. Papworth*, London, 1879, p. 19).

HWH, FM, BMC: "Including some poems sometimes attributed to W. Combe."

241 Picturesque Views on the Southern Coast of England, from drawings made principally by J. M. W. Turner, R.A. and engraved by W. B. Cooke, George Cooke, and other eminent engravers. [With many plates.] 2 vols., unpaged. London: John and Arthur Arch, *et al.* [including W. B. Cooke], 1826. 4to. [Published in 16 parts from Jan. 1814 to May 1826.]

Not listed by Combe, but portions of the ms. are among the Fleming Papers.

In a letter to W. B. Cooke dated Dec. 16, 1813, Turner requested that "Mr. Coombe deviate wholly" from the copy which he had himself submitted for the book (Ruskin, *Works*, ed. Cook and Wedderburn, XXXV, 588). Combe had written to Cooke that he was unable to make sense of Turner's prose descriptions (Walter Thornbury, *Life of Turner*, I, 405–6). These letters were first noted by Franz Montgomery in his dissertation, *William Combe* (University of Minnesota, 1938), pp. 139–41. The *Encyclopaedia Britannica*, 9th ed., s.v. Combe, identifies the *Picturesque Views of the Southern Coast* as Combe's. How much of the letterpress Combe actually wrote must remain in doubt since the later parts did not appear until after his death.

FM.

241 [Pyne, W. H., and William Combe,] Microcosm of London. [With 104 coloured aquatint plates after Pugin and Rowlandson.] 3 vols., pp. [v],

page

231; [ii], vi, 239; v, 280, vi. London: R. Ackermann, n.d. [1808–1811]. 4to. [First published in 26 monthly parts.]

July 1810 *CR.*

Combe: "The third volume of Ackermann's Microcosm of London. 1 vol. 4to."

Combe's authorship of Vol. III is attested by Ackermann's *Repository of Arts* (Aug. 1, 1823), p. 88. W. H. Pyne wrote the first two vols.

HWH, FM, BMC.

Rastadt, Congress of. Official Correspondence. . . . Containing the whole 296 n. 5 of the state papers from the commencement of the negotiation in December 1797, to April 1799, the period of its dissolution. From the original papers. With an English translation. pp. [viii], 723. London: J. Wright, 1800. 8vo.

Combe: "Official Correspondence at Rastadt. 1800."

HWH, FM, BMC.

[Repton, Humphry.] A Letter to Uvedale Price, Esq. pp. 20. London: 197 G. Nicol, 1794. 8vo.

Jan. 29, 1795, *The Oracle and Public Advertiser.*

Not listed by Combe.

J. Farington, June 1, 1795: "Combes regulated and corrected Reptons letter to Price, but the matter was entirely Reptons. Coombes has also assisted him in the work preparing for publication" (Windsor Typescript, p. 349). The "work preparing for publication" was *Sketches and Hints on Landscape Gardening.*

———. Sketches and Hints on Landscape Gardening. Collected from designs 197 and observations now in the possession of the different noblemen and gentlemen, for whose use they were originally made. The whole tending to establish fixed principles in the art of laying out ground. [With 16 coloured plates having overlay sections.] pp. xvi, 86. London: J. and J. Boydell and G. Nicol, n.d.

Not listed by Combe, but see note on preceding item.

Ripault, Louis-Medeleine. Report of the Commission of Arts to the First 296 n. 5 Consul Bonaparte, on the antiquities of Upper Egypt. . . . Translated from the French of Citizen Ripaud, Librarian to the Institute of Egypt. pp. 104. London: J. Debrett, 1800. 8vo.

Combe: "Translation of Ripaud's Egypt."

HWH, FM, BMC.

page

55 Salerno, School of. The Œconomy of Health. [A free translation of the Schola Salernitana with added passages.] pp. xviii, 56. London: Almond, Becket & De Hondt, and Newbery, n.d. [1776]. 8vo.

Mar. 1776 *CR.*

Combe: "The Schola Salerni, or Economy of Health."

FM.

[Shoberl, Frederic, ed.] Forget Me Not, a Christmas and New Year's Present for 1823. [Engraved gift page, engraved t.p., 13 plates.] London: Ackermann, n.d. [1822]. 12mo.

Not listed by Combe.

The Advertisement, p. vi, mentions "emblematical representations of the Twelve Months" which "are accompanied with poetical illustrations from the pen of an eminently popular writer." A footnote identifies this writer as "the author of the three *Tours of Dr. Syntax;* the *Dance of Death;* the *Dance of Life;* and the *History of Johnny Quae Genus".*

Cambridge Bibliography of English Literature.

296 n. 5 Sonnini de Manoncourt, C. N. S. Travels in Upper and Lower Egypt, undertaken by order of the old government of France. . . . Illustrated by engravings. . . . Translated from the French. pp. [ii], xl, 742. London: J. Debrett, 1800. 4to.

Mar. *CR.*

Combe: "Translation of Sonini's Travels in Egypt."

Advertised in this book: *Asiatic Annual Register* and Jourdan's *Memoir of the Operation of the Army of the Danube,* both published by Debrett. Combe was contributing to the one and had edited the other.

Both HWH and BMC identify another translation as Combe's, that by Henry Hunter published by Stockdale. FM correctly lists Debrett's publication which, in a Preface presumably by Combe, severely castigates Hunter's translation.

46–8 Sterne's Letters to His Friends on Various Occasions. To which is added, his history of a watch coat, with explanatory notes. pp. vi, 112, 169–76. London: G. Kearsly and J. Johnson, 1775. 8vo.

June 28 *Morning Post,* July *CR.* Letter 5 appeared in *London Magazine,* Mar. 1774. Other letters are said by Combe to have "made their first appearance in a provincial newspaper", but they have not been found.

Not listed by Combe, who disclaims responsibility for the publication but claims authorship of Letters 4, 5, 6, 7, 8, 9, and 10 (Preface of the Editor, *Letters Supposed to Have Been Written by Yorick and Eliza,* p. iii). One of these, Letter 9, survives in Sterne's handwriting (*Letter*

Book, Morgan Library) but the other six show the usual signs of Combe's imitations (Lewis P. Curtis, "Forged Letters of Laurence Sterne", *PMLA*, L, December 1935, pp. 1076–1106). The argument that Combe also wrote Letters 11 and 12 is less strongly supported. See the discussion of this work in Chapter III.

HWH, FM, BMC: "Including eight letters sometimes attributed to W. Combe."

Vaughan, Thomas. Fashionable Follies, containing the history of a Parisian family, with a peep into *the English character*. 3 vols., pp. xii, 298; [iv], 307; [iv], 351. [Vols. 1 and 2 first published in 1781; vol. 3, written by Combe, added to this edition.] London: Longman, Hurst, Rees, Orme, and Brown, 1810. 12mo.

Announced in Ackerman's *Repository of Arts* (July 1809): "Thomas Vaughan, Esq. has in the press, a third volume of the work entitled *Fashionable Follies*, the two first volumes of which were published by him in 1781. It will be embellished with a rich humorous design by Loutherbourg, and engraved by one of the first artists".

Combe: "The third volume, added to a former edition, of Fashionable Follies; a novel by Mr. Vaughan".

Combe quoted a passage from the new volume (III, 207–22) in his *Devil upon Two Sticks in England* (1811, VI, 146–59). A footnote identifies the source of the quotation, a characteristic device of Combe's for advertising his own work.

HWH, BMC, FM: "May be by Combe".

III. NEWSPAPERS AND PERIODICALS WITH CONTRIBUTIONS BY COMBE

Annual Register

"History of Europe" for the years 1791 (pp. [1]–280), 1792 (pp. [1]–226), 1793 (pp. [1]–287), 1794 (pp. [1]–284), and 1795 (pp. [1]–230).

Not listed by Combe.

The *Gentleman's Magazine* for June 1852, p. 538, contains a letter signed "W. T." supplementing Robert Cole's article on Combe published the previous month. The writer notes that "In the list of Combe's works, communicated by Mr. Cole, is omitted his contribution of the History of Europe to the Annual Register for the years from 1791 to 1795, on occasion of the proprietors determining to fetch up the arrear of eleven years which had occurred from 1791 to 1801 and which was effected in an incredibly short space of time".

FM.

page
208–9 *Asiatic Annual Register*

"An Account of the Life of the Late Governor Holwell" and other articles.

Combe: "Several Articles in two volumes of the Asiatic Register, particularly the Life and Character of Governor Holwell".

The account of Governor Holwell appears in Vol. 1 (Part III, pp. 25–31), the issue for 1799, published 1800. The other volume with articles by Combe must be Vol. II. Both were published by Debrett, for whom Combe was doing other work at the time.

The Cabinet (See *The Pic Nic*).

141–4 *Daily Universal Register*

142   (*a*) Items quoted from Combe's earlier publications:

"The Nosegay", Sept. 27, 1786. Reprinted with minor emendations from *Letters Supposed to Have Been Written by Yorick and Eliza*, II, 130–40 (1929 ed., pp. 135–39).

"Sketch for a Chapter on Widows", Oct. 3, 1786. Reprinted from the *Philosopher in Bristol*, II, 135–41.

"The Generous Sailor", Oct. 13, 1786. Reprinted from the *Philosopher in Bristol*, I, 28–33. The same story had been quoted with minor emendations in *Letters Supposed*, I, 65–68 (1929 ed., pp. 24–26).

142   (*b*) Items signed "C".

"Sketch for a Chapter on Widows", Oct. 3, 1786, already mentioned as reprinted from the *Philosopher in Bristol*, is the first of eight items signed "C". Since it is definitely Combe's, the others bearing this signature may also be attributed to him.

"The Woman of the Town", Nov. 6, 1786.

"Thoughts on Marriage", Dec. 5, 1786.

"An Observation Relating to the Commercial Treaty with France", Dec. 8, 1786.

"A Sentimental Fragment", Dec. 28, 1786.

"Flirtilla. A Living Character", Jan. 3, 1787.

"A Rhapsody to Eliza", Jan. 4, 1787.

"Sketch of a well-known Man of Fashion", Jan. 31, 1787.

142–3   (*c*) "Letters of the Late Mr. Sterne".

The first 33 of the 39 letters published in 1788 as *Original Letters of the Late Reverend Mr. Laurence Sterne* (q.v.) appeared in the newspaper at

page

irregular intervals throughout 1787, the last one appearing in Jan. 1788 after the *Universal Register* had been renamed *The Times*. They were published as follows: I, Jan. 11, 1787; II, Jan. 16; III, Jan. 20; IV, Jan. 25; V, Feb. 19; VI, Mar. 31; VII, Apr. 13; VIII, Apr. 24; IX, May 7; X, June 6; XI, June 14; XII, June 27; XIII, July 2; XIV, July 11; XV, July 20; XVI, Aug. 4; XVII, Aug. 10; XVIII, Aug. 18; XIX, Aug. 24; XX, Sept. 20; XXI, Sept. 28; XXII, Oct. 3; XXIII, Oct. 13; XXIV, Oct. 22; XXV, Oct. 30; XXVI, Nov. 5; XXVII, Nov. 7; XXVIII, Nov. 15; XXIX, Nov. 22; XXX, Nov. 28; XXXI, Dec. 6; XXXII, Dec. 14; XXXIII, Jan. 17, 1788.

(*d*) "The Devil Upon Two Sticks, Continued from the Celebrated 143
Novel of Le Sage".

Six items under this heading, later republished as the opening sections of Combe's *Devil upon Two Sticks in England*, q.v. The items appeared on June 20, 29, July 4, Aug. 1, 15, and Sept. 8, 1787.

(*e*) "Mira of the Dale: A Fragment".   143

Published Jan. 31, 1787, five months before the first of the "Devil upon Two Sticks" series and not identified with it in any way, this sketch was republished in the novel, III, 142–48.

European Magazine

"Letters of the Late Mr. Sterne".

Thirty of the *Original Letters of the Late Reverend Mr. Laurence Sterne* (the first 33 omitting nos. 5, 11, and 16) appeared in the *European Magazine*, reprinted from the *Daily Universal Register*, as follows: I–IV, Feb. 1787; VI–IX, May; X, XII–XIV, July; XV, XVII, XVIII, Aug.; XIX–XXII, Oct.; XXIII–XXVI, Nov.; XXVII–XXXI, Dec.; XXXII, XXXIII, Jan. 1788.

The Pic Nic [14 weekly issues, Jan. 8 to Apr. 9, 1803] continued as *The* 216–24
Cabinet [12 weekly issues, Apr. 16 to July 2, 1803], ed. by Combe.

Combe: "Pic Nic".

J. Farington, Feb. 18, 1803: "Mr. Greville [one of the organizers of the Pic Nic Society and the chief sponsor of the newspaper] has informed Hoppner that the news paper called *the Pic Nic* is now conducted by Coombe" (Windsor Typescript, p. 2185). Ibid., Aug. 7, 1803: "Coombes conducted the newspaper called the *Cabinet* . . . but it is dropped" (p. 2350).

"Original Letters of Sterne".   218

Three spurious "Sterne" letters appear in the issues for Feb. 19, Feb.

page

26, and Mar. 5. Vid. James Smith, *Memoirs, Letters and Comic Miscellanies*, ed. by Horace Smith (London, 1840), I, 17–21 and note.

219   Items signed "C" in reprinted edition:

Jan. 8. "The Theatre"; "Stanzas to Pope's Weeping Willow at Twickenham. Written in 1792".

Jan. 15. "Samuel Johnson".

Jan. 22. "The Theatre"; "A Thought for Authors".

Jan. 29. "Syllabus of a Course of Lectures in Intellectual Philosophy".

Feb. 5. "Epitaph".

Feb. 12. "Sonnet, To———, with a Profile in Paper".

Mar. 5. "Lines with a Bouquet to a Lady".

245–6   *Poetical Magazine* [24 monthly numbers and four supplements, May 1809 to May 1811].

Combe: "Assistances in verse to illustrate the principal plates, chiefly views of places, in Ackermann's *Poetical Magazine*, besides Dr. Syntax, which first appeared in that publication".

242–6   (*a*) "The Schoolmaster's Tour".

One installment in each of the monthly numbers and in the fourth supplement. Later published as the *Tour of Doctor Syntax in Search of the Picturesque*, q.v.

245   (*b*) Verse descriptions accompanying other plates, mostly topographical.

These plates appear throughout the series; some, perhaps most, of the poetic descriptions accompanying the plates are by Combe. A manuscript in his hand with a description of Denbigh Castle (printed in Number XVIII, Oct. 1810, pp. 248–49) is owned by the Harvard Library.

245   (*c*) Miscellaneous short poems. Combe's name is not attached to anything in the magazine, but 23 short poems are signed "W.C**e". They are in his characteristic manner and may be assumed to be his. Other signatures also point to Combe, notably "C" and "Comicus". A good many are unsigned but dated from Lambeth Road, where Combe maintained rooms even while in prison.

244–5   *Repository of Arts, Literature, Commerce, Manufactures, Fashions, and Politics*. London: R. Ackermann, 1802–1828.

Combe: "For several years I was a contributor to Ackermann's Literary Repository:—".

(*a*) "Amelia's Letters", Apr. 1809–Mar. 1811, omitting Feb. 1810.   245

Combe: "1st. A series of Letters from a Young Lady of Fortune on a visit in London to a sick Mother in the Country. Mr. A. did not think them lively enough for his purpose, and I did not bring them to a conclusion".

After Combe's death, Ackermann published the series as a novel, *Letters between Amelia in London and Her Mother in the Country*, q.v. It was ascribed on the title page to "the late William Combe, Esq."

(*b*) "The Modern Spectator", 56 essays (misnumbered 57), Apr. 1811–Dec. 1815, omitting May 1814.

Combe: "2nd. The *Modern Spectator*, in monthly numbers".

(*c*) "The Female Tatler", 73 essays, Jan. 1816–Apr. 1822.

Combe: "3rd. *The Female Tatler* succeeded, and was more particularly confined to female subjects. But from the intrusion of other things I fear that I took the liberty of too frequently obtaining contributions, if not occasionally stealing, from others, though on these occasions it is not improbable that I supplied my deficiency with something better than I should have myself produced."

(*d*) "Letter to Jean Jaques [*sic*] Rousseau"

Published by Ackermann in the Repository, Apr. 1824, with this note: "The following letter is extracted from the manuscript papers of the late William Combe, esq. to whose pen the Repository has been indebted for many of its pages."

The Times   224–8

Editor, 1803–1808

Combe joined *The Times* staff early in July 1803 and continued as editor until June 28, 1808, when he was arrested for repeated violations of the Rules of the King's Bench.

Letters signed "Valerian" or "Valerius", June 8, 1803–Jan. 25, 1804.   225–6

Fourteen letters published on June 8, 9, 11, 20, 22, July 4, Aug. 4, 23, Sept. 10, Oct. 21, Nov. 3, 23, Dec. 28, 1803, and Jan. 25, 1804. Only the first was signed "Valerian"; the others were signed "Valerius". The letter published on Aug. 4 appeared separately as a broadside, *Valerius's Address to the People of England*. All were subsequently published as *The Letters of Valerius*, q.v.

"Earl Harcourt", May 1, 1809.   238

Referred to in letter to Jerningham, Jan. 1, 1811 (Huntington Library).

Reprinted in Combe's description of Lord Harcourt's estate, Newnham Courtney, for Cooke's *Thames*, q.v.

IV. UNPUBLISHED MANUSCRIPTS OF WILLIAM COMBE

48–50 *The Flattering Milliner; Or, a Modern Half Hour.* Written expressly on this Occasion by a Gentleman residing near this City. [Advertised in *Felix Farley's Bristol Journal*, Sept. 9, 1775, to be performed Sept. 11.]

Not listed by Combe, but the ms. in his hand was in the possession of Robert Cole in 1852 (*Gentleman's Magazine*, May 1852, p. 469). Its present location is unknown.

On the day the farce was advertised, *Felix Farley's Bristol Journal* carried the following item: "We are informed that the piece called *The Flattering Milliner, or Modern Half-Hour*, now in rehearsal at the Theatre in King-Street, to be perform'd on Monday next, for the benefit of Mr. Henderson, is written by the ingenious Author of the *Philosopher in Bristol*".

HWH, FM.

194–6 Review of the Law Case between Mackreth and Fox Lane, *c.* 1794.

Listed by Combe as "not published".

That Combe had rendered Mackreth some service is evident from the following note in Farington's *Diary*: "Boydell told me Coombes now keeps a Horse given to him by Macreath [*sic*]". (Dec. 16, 1794, Windsor Typescript, p. 262.)

The ms. has disappeared.

272–3 Memoir of Richard Cosway, *c.* 1822.

Not listed by Combe, but the ms. in his hand survives among the Fleming Papers.

Maria Cosway to William Combe: "When we taulked of having some Memoires written on Mr Cosway and agreed no one more able than yourself I was happy to see you undertook it". Letter dated "Lodi 24 Jany, 1823", published by George C. Williamson, *Richard Cosway, R.A. and His Wife and Pupils* (London, 1897), pp. 70–71. The original letter is in the library of the Victoria and Albert Museum.

INDEX